# Introducing Linux Distros

Jose Dieguez Castro

Apress®

*Introducing Linux Distros*

Jose Dieguez Castro
A Coruña
Spain

ISBN-13 (pbk): 978-1-4842-1393-3          ISBN-13 (electronic): 978-1-4842-1392-6
DOI 10.1007/978-1-4842-1392-6

Library of Congress Control Number: 2016943372

Managing Director: Welmoed Spahr
Acquistions Editor: Louise Corrigan
Development Editor: Gary Schwartz
Technical Reviewer: Brandon Scott
Editorial Board: Steve Anglin, Pramila Balen, Louise Corrigan, James DeWolf, Jonathan Gennick,
    Robert Hutchinson, Celestin Suresh John, Nikhil Karkal,  James Markham, Susan McDermott,
    Matthew Moodie, Douglas Pundick, Ben Renow-Clarke,  Gwenan Spearing, Matt Wade
Coordinating Editor: Nancy Chen
Copy Editor: Mary Behr
Compositor: SPi Global
Indexer: SPi Global

Distributed to the book trade worldwide by Springer Science+Business Media New York, 233 Spring Street, 6th Floor, New York, NY 10013. Phone 1-800-SPRINGER, fax (201) 348-4505, e-mail orders-ny@springer-sbm.com, or visit www.springer.com. Apress Media, LLC is a California LLC and the sole member (owner) is Springer Science + Business Media Finance Inc (SSBM Finance Inc). SSBM Finance Inc is a Delaware corporation.

For information on translations, please e-mail rights@apress.com, or visit www.apress.com.

Apress and friends of ED books may be purchased in bulk for academic, corporate, or promotional use. eBook versions and licenses are also available for most titles. For more information, reference our Special Bulk Sales–eBook Licensing web page at www.apress.com/bulk-sales.

Any source code or other supplementary materials referenced by the author in this text is available to readers at www.apress.com. For detailed information about how to locate your book's source code, go to www.apress.com/source-code/.

Printed on acid-free paper

*To those who share their time, effort, and work with all of us to make the world a better place, free software is only the beginning.*

# Contents at a Glance

# Contents

# About the Author

**Jose Dieguez Castro** is a senior systems administrator currently working as a freelance consultant. Joe has worked on a wide range of projects from small to large infrastructures in both the private and public sector. When asked about his specialty, he answers, "Getting the job done." He also likes to think of himself as a developer who cares too much about free software. Photography, sports, music, and reading are the way he frees his mind from work. He can be reached at jose@jdcastro.eu.

# About the Technical Reviewer

**Brandon Scott** specializes in software engineering for desktop applications, software development kits, and distributed systems. He currently leads the development efforts for AspiraCloud Ltd., focusing on Microsoft SharePoint and Azure workstreams. Additionally, Brandon also partners with Razer Inc., aiding with the design of SDK products and open source libraries. He built his experience working for a variety of companies in different industries, such as JPMorgan Chase & Co. and Microsoft.

# Acknowledgments

First of all, my thanks go to Ken Thompson, Dennis Ritchie, Brian Kernighan, Douglas McIlroy, and Joe Ossanna for UNIX. Thanks to Richard Matthew Stallman for the GNU Project, the Free Software Foundation, Emacs, and the Free Software movement. Thanks to Linus Torvalds for the Linux kernel. And thanks to all of the corporations and community developers that for years have contributed to the development, documentation, and adoption of the Linux operating system and its distributions. These people not only helped to create the Linux ecosystem, but they also helped to make the world a better place for sure. Without all of these individuals, this book would never have been possible.

Thanks to my family and friends for their unconditional love and support.

Thanks also to the Apress team, especially Louise Corrigan, who convinced me to write this book; Nancy Chen and Jill Balzano, for their patience and hard work in coordinating this book; my editors, Gary Schwartz and James Markham, who were kind enough to deal with my broken English; and my technical reviewer, Brandon Scott, for righting my wrongs.

Most of all, my thanks go to you, the reader, for taking the trouble and using your valuable time to read this book.

# Introduction

What is a Linux distro?
Why are there so many of them?
Which one should I choose?
Which one is the best?
Why are they so hard to use?
Why are they so ugly?
Do I have to manage all of this with text commands?

If you tried to answer these questions by yourself, or sought help from others, you probably did not get a clear answer—or maybe you received several contradictory ones. The truth is that no unique answer exists for many of these questions. If you want to deal with the huge jungle of Linux distros, you need to get some things clear first. You have to learn the basic concepts and then isolate some objective facts to make an informed decision.

In this book, I show you what makes up a Linux distribution. Before that, however, I guide you through a journey in time to explore the origins of Linux itself and of free software. It's easier to understand the concepts behind a Linux distro once you know how it all began. Next, I point you to the fundamental criteria that you must consider in order to compare and choose a Linux distro. I point out which of these criteria are based on relative or absolute concepts and which are simply personal preferences. Finally, to understand why Linux has a plethora of distros instead of just a few versions like other popular operating systems, I show you the family tree of Linux distros; there are only a handful of original distros but myriad relatives.

The core of this book is the detailed analysis of ten Linux distributions, from the most popular to the most innovative. I chose them to show you a variety of distros and how they can be so similar and yet so different, from the ones suited for Linux novices to the ones tailored for Linux experts. I show you the criteria that you need to consider for each distro, and a compilation of the pros and cons of each. Even when I try to be objective, it is inevitable that here and there I introduce some personal viewpoints, but you should take into consideration only the cold facts to make your own decision; your needs and mine might be completely different.

I also show you how to install and conduct basic maintenance tasks for each Linux distro. Don't get me wrong; I do not pretend here to instruct you on how to install and administrate a Linux distro in a professional setting; that would take another book. I have two purposes here. The first one is to give you a hint of what are you going to find in each distribution and how they differ, and a book like this one is a good way to gain that knowledge. The other purpose is to debunk the rumors that Linux is very hard to install, use, and maintain; in fact, there are many friendly distros. I provide you with an introduction to how to install those distros that are commonly considered too hard and appropriate only for experts. Finally, I briefly summarize other distros that may appeal to you so that you will have a wider view of the Linux spectrum.

Linux is not only an operating system for the desktop; there are other environments where it is used. Furthermore, there are many distros that were built with only a particular task in mind. I introduce you to the other side of Linux distros: the task-oriented side.

As it is beyond the scope of this book, I also offer you a bonus chapter, available only online, where I introduce you to other operating systems that are not Linux, but that share many similarities with Linux distros.

I hope that *Introducing Linux Distros* will answer many of your questions about Linux and will help you pick the best one that is right for you. To that end, I did my best and I hope that you enjoy reading this book.

—Jose Dieguez Castro

# PART 1

■ ■ ■

# Linux Distros

In the first part of this book, you get a good perspective on Linux distros and what you must consider when comparing the various distros in order to select the right one for you. You also learn about the origins of the Linux distros and the reasons why there are so many and how they are related.

In the first chapter, you learn about the nature of a Linux distribution. In order to do that, you need to understand what Linux is, and the best way to accomplish this is to learn about its origins and a bit of its development history. Basically, I present the minimal amount of information necessary for you to put Linux and its distros in context.

The second chapter is a compilation of points you must consider in order to compare the performance and features of two or more Linux distros. Some of those points cover subjective issues, such as personal preference of one aesthetic over another, or if you like one desktop environment in particular. Nonetheless, you will have a checklist to use as starting point.

The third and final chapter in this part of the book covers the family tree of Linux distributions. This information is provided so that you know how they are related to each another (at least the more relevant distributions) and to get an idea of why there are so many of them and why one particular distro has so many derivatives.

# CHAPTER 1

■ ■ ■

# Deconstructing a Linux Distro

One of the first things that surprises new Linux users who come from other operating systems such as Windows or Mac OS is that a single entity called Linux OS does not, in fact, exist. Linux is only a kernel, not an OS, and what people generally perceive as Linux OS is actually a Linux distribution, and more precisely a GNU/Linux distribution. The Linux distribution concept is very popular, and it is commonly known as a *Linux distro*. This is the term that I use throughout the rest of the book. Don't be put off by all of these terms: I cover them in detail in this chapter.

After learning that what you thought was Linux is actually a Linux distro, here's another surprise: there is not just one unique Linux distro. Rather there are many, perhaps a few hundred, Linux distros available. Thus the task of choosing the right Linux distro for your needs can easily become an overwhelming task. Nevertheless, this first step can be critical, and there are several approaches for accomplishing this this:

---

■ **Note**   There are more than 700 Linux distros available at the time of this writing, but only about 300 are currently actively developed and supported.

---

- One way to choose a Linux distro is to follow the advice of a colleague, the recommendation of a professional, a review that you find on the Internet, a random choice, or because it is the only version you know about at the moment. If the experience is pleasant, you may wind up using that distro for a long time.

- Sometimes the experience of choosing a Linux distro is not pleasant at all. The problem could be the installation process, the desktop environment, the terminal, or the user documentation. Any of these issues might make a particular distro not right for you. From there, the process could follow one of these common paths:

  - You become angry and disappointed, so you give up on using this OS, possibly forever, or at least for a long time. You may take to the Internet to criticize the Linux distro that you tried, and you may warn your colleagues against it. Unfortunately, you might have turned into a long-term Linux user if you had only chosen the right distro at the start.

  - Let's say that you decide to try another Linux distro. After a few tests, you find the one that seems to address your expectations. You turn into a long-term, happy user of that particular distro, and you do not hesitate to test other ones.

---

**Electronic supplementary material**   The online version of this chapter (doi:10.1007/978-1-4842-1392-6_1) contains supplementary material, which is available to authorized users.

© Jose Dieguez Castro 2016
J. Dieguez Castro, *Introducing Linux Distros*, DOI 10.1007/978-1-4842-1392-6_1

- Alternatively, you try several distros, maybe even a lot of them, but you never find the one with which you feel comfortable. The problem could be that you haven't defined your needs or wants specifically enough, and so you haven't discovered which distros can cover these needs and in which manner. You may end up as a long-term, not-so-happy Linux user, or you may switch to another OS completely.

- Finally, you may be someone who thoroughly enjoys testing new Linux distros. You may use one Linux distro on a regular basis, but test new ones on a different machine or VM, or you may switch Linux distros every few months or every few years. You are probably a long-term Linux user.

As you can see, the decision-making process for choosing a Linux distro is very important. The Linux experience can be radically different from one distro to another, and finding the right one for you may be hard. This book aims to help you in process of finding the Linux distro that best fits your needs. A lot of trouble, disappointment, annoyance, and unpleasantness can be avoided if you use objective selection criteria. Obviously, previous experience, expectations, and an open mind can help with the adoption of a Linux distro. The goal of this book is to help you make your ultimate decision, or at least take your first steps in selecting a Linux distro, and then make working with Linux OS a pleasant experience.

---

■ **Note**   One of the easiest ways to choose a Linux distro is to use a service like http://distrowatch.com. The site provides rankings and a brief description of the most common distros. The differences among distros are very important. By the way, what distro do I use? I am writing this book using a virtual machine to run Windows 8 and Microsoft Word, but the underlying foundation is an Arch Linux installation managing it all.

---

# Linux Distro

What exactly is a Linux distro? A *Linux distro* is a set of components that are required to achieve a working Linux system, and the processes needed to install these components to achieve a running system. Today, a Linux distro includes the Linux kernel itself (different versions of the kernel may be integrated into the same distro for different hardware architectures, for example), the omnipresent GNU tools (more about this later), a lot of small tools that are needed to provide different services, probably a windowing system, a desktop environment, and finally a package management system with a number of software packages that can be installed by default or according to user preferences. Even when the entire installation process can be completed (more or less) through the automated distro installation process, as opposed to other operating systems, the Linux OS installation is highly customizable. A particularly unique aspect of a Linux distro is the user documentation that is provided. Even when the documentation for the numerous individual packages that comprise a distribution is delivered, many distros provide nearly complete documentation about the distribution itself, primarily relating to the installation process or how to contribute personally to the distribution.

To choose a Linux distro, you must first learn exactly why they exist and why there are so many of them. To achieve this goal, we must first dig into the origins and history of Linux itself and the circumstances surrounding its creation.

# The Origin of Linux

As is the case with many successful software projects, Linux started as a way to solve a particular problem faced by one software developer. In this case, in the early 1990s, a Finnish student at the University of Helsinki named Linus Torvalds (see Figure 1-1) wanted to be able to use at home an operating system similar to the one he used on campus. Alas, there was no option available that could satisfy his desire. He was using a version of MINIX at home, but it would not run on his PC 386 machine, so he decided to create his own OS. On August 25, 1991, he posted the following message on the `com.os.minix` newsgroup site, which would become one of the most famous quotes in computer history:

> *Linus Benedict Torvalds*
>
> *Hello everybody out there using minix -*
>
> *I'm doing a (free) operating system (just a hobby, won't be big and professional like gnu) for 386(486) AT clones. This has been brewing since april, and is starting to get ready. I'd like any feedback on things people like/dislike in minix, as my OS resembles it somewhat (same physical layout of the file-system (due to practical reasons) among other things).*
>
> *I've currently ported bash (1.08) and gcc(1.40), and things seem to work. This implies that I'll get something practical within a few months, and I'd like to know what features most people would want. Any suggestions are welcome, but I won't promise I'll implement them :-)*
>
> *Linus (`torv...@kruuna.helsinki.fi`)*
>
> *PS. Yes - it's free of any minix code, and it has a multi-threaded fs. It is NOT portable (uses 386 task switching etc), and it probably never will support anything other than AT-harddisks, as that's all I have :-(.*

***Figure 1-1.*** *Linus Torvalds, creator of Linux, at the LinuxCon Europe 2014 in Düsseldorf*

> ■ **Tip** If you are interested in a first-hand history of Linux as told by its creator, read *Just for Fun: The Story of an Accidental Revolutionary* by Linux Torvalds (HarperCollins, 2001).

This is the beginning of the history of Linux, and you can be sure that nobody at that time, not even Linus Torvalds, could imagine that someday his pet project would become one of the most ubiquitous operating systems in the world. These days you can find Linux almost everywhere. It is installed on 97% of the 500 fastest supercomputers in the world[1], on the servers that run the Internet, and on smartphones and tablets (Android OS); it is also embedded in many consumer electronics products, cars, and so on. In fact, the of two most advanced, complex, and expensive objects/projects that humanity has produced, the International Space Station and the Large Hadron Collider, are also managed by Linux. This is ironic because if you look back to the time when Linux was born, you will discover an almost identical context (absent the yet-to-be-discovered technologies), but substituting UNIX (the OS that inspired Linus) for Linux.

> ■ **Note** The first name of the Linux OS was Freax, as a combination of "free," "freak," and "x" (for Unix). Later, a maintenance technician for the FTP server at the University of Helsinki decided to name the folder where the OS was allocated as Linux (for Linus' UNIX). Torvalds, who had considered and dismissed that name (it seemed much too egotistical to him) finally consented to keep the name. Clearly, Linux is a better name than Freax.

Let's go back to the early 1990s and talk about the operating system situation at that time. There were two clear separations in terms of operating systems: personal computers and everything else.

- The personal computer market was dominated by two players: Microsoft Windows (Windows 3.x and MS-DOS 5.0) and Apple Macintosh (System 7). There were, of course, other players, but they were minor in terms of market share: AmigaOS, Atari TOS, IBM DOS, DR-DOS, OS/2, BeOS, MINIX, Xenix, and so forth.

- In the remaining areas of computing (professional workstations, minicomputers, mainframes, and so on), there were a number of other contenders:

  - **UNIX-Based**: NeXTStep, IRIX, Xenix, AIX, SunOS, Ultrix, HP-UX, SCO, BSD, and UNIX. There were many operating systems based on UNIX, and the number was growing. Also, there was an increasing number of migrations and new installations of these operating systems in a variety of machines. This family of operating systems likely had the largest market presence at that time.

  - **Others**: Multics, OS/8, TOPS-X, OS/400, and so on. Today there are still machines running some of these operating systems; however, a lot of installations have migrated over time to a UNIX-based OS.

As you know, today the Microsoft Windows and Mac OS operating systems are the main players in the personal computer niche. In other computing areas, however, the UNIX family still has the biggest market share. Moreover, at this time, Linux is the most common UNIX variant, and it is growing faster and replacing a lot of older UNIX installations. So, why has Linux succeeded so well in the face of so many alternatives?

---

[1]www.top500.org/statistics/details/osfam/1

There are four main reasons for Linux's success:

1. **Linux was based on the existing UNIX OS**. Linus Torvalds was already using MINIX at home, and he wanted to use a similar OS to the UNIX-based one installed on the campus' mainframe at the university he attended. As mentioned, buying a new computer with an 80386 processor forced him to develop his own OS since he wanted to use a UNIX-based OS on that machine. Given the success and broad presence of the UNIX family of operating systems in the world, there were a lot of people willing to adopt a new alternative for their personal computers. There were only a few ones back then, MINIX and Xenix being the main ones, and each had its disadvantages.

2. **Linux was aimed at personal computers**. As mentioned, the main UNIX-based operating systems available for microcomputers at that time were MINIX and Xenix. (There were other minor actors, such as the IBM PC/IX, Venix, Coherent, and Idrix). But MINIX and Xenix had the following inconveniences, which opened the door to other competitors:

   - MINIX had a low-cost license, and the source code was made available by its developer, Andrew S. Tanenbaum (a computer science professor), who created it for educational purposes. However, it was only available for the 8086 PC and the 80286 PC AT machines, and its license prevented use of its source code to develop a new OS based on it.

   - Xenix, originally developed by Microsoft, was a Santa Cruz Operation (SCO) product at that time. Even when it was available for 386 systems, its license was very restrictive and expensive (it originally was an OEM product) and its source code was not accessible. This UNIX-based OS, however, was the most commonly installed one in the personal computer market.

   - Simultaneous with Linux development by Torvalds and others, there were a number of people working to port a UNIX version called the Berkeley Software Distribution (BSD) to 386 machines. This resulted in a series of BSD-based operating systems for personal computers. Torvalds didn't know at the time about the BSD project. If he did, perhaps he would never have started to develop the Linux kernel. (He has stated this many times in public.) I will cover this topic more in Online Chapter.

3. **The way in which Linux was distributed: free and open source**. Since Torvalds had few resources (and thought that $169 for MINIX was way too much), if he wanted others to use it, comment on it, and perhaps improve upon it, the best way to distribute Linux was to give it away for free. Torvalds developed his Linux kernel in a MINIX OS environment using the GNU C compiler, and later included the GNU tools, so you were obliged to use the GPL license (more on that later) and distribute its source code. This fact, plus free distribution, helped propel the early adoption of Linux by a bunch of "hackers" (in the original meaning) who were willing to play with the kernel and the code. Heretofore, you could not play with the Xenix code, and even if you could contribute to MINIX or make your own version or port of it, you could not distribute it freely and legitimately. (There were, in fact, several unofficial ports of MINIX to various machines.)

4.   **The Internet**. The Internet was essential to the success of Linux. Without the Internet, e-mail, FTP, and newsgroups, it would have been impossible to join so many people together and to be able to work collectively on a project like this. People from all over the world became enthusiasts of Torvalds' pet project, and they started to collaborate voluntary in its development. The number of Linux supporters grew at an astounding pace, and today there are thousands of developers and numerous enterprises working together to make Linux a better OS with each new release. Shortly after its introduction, the original assembly code for Linux was ported to C by Torvalds and others, and soon ports would appear for machines other than the 386.

---

■ **Note**   If you are curious about what the first release of the Linux code looked like, you can download it from `www.kernel.org/pub/linux/kernel/Historic/linux-0.01.tar.gz`.

---

Torvalds initially began by developing a few utilities for MINIX OS, including a terminal emulation program to connect to the university's mainframe, a disk driver, and a file system drive. Soon he realized that if he continued along this path, he would wind up making his own OS, so he made the decision to get rid of MINIX and make a better UNIX-based OS himself.

On October 5, 1991, less than two months after he started work, Torvalds made the following announcement about version 0.02 of his kernel in the `comp.os.minix` Usenet newsgroup[2]:

*Do you pine for the nice days of minix-1.1, when men were men and wrote their own device drivers? Are you without a nice project and just dying to cut your teeth on a OS you can try to modify for your needs? Are you finding it frustrating when everything works on minix? No more all-nighters to get a nifty program working? Then this post might be just for you :-)*

*As I mentioned a month (?) ago, I'm working on a free version of a minix-lookalike for AT-386 computers. It has finally reached the stage where it's even usable (though may not be depending on what you want), and I am willing to put out the sources for wider distribution. It is just version 0.02 (+1 (very small) patch already), but I've successfully run bash/gcc/gnu-make/gnu-sed/compress etc under it.*

*Linus*

Soon many other programmers joined to the cause. The quality and fast pace of the kernel development was achieved in a naïve and very unusual way—simply by releasing a new version on a weekly basis and getting feedback from users and volunteers. Thus it evolved in the strictest definition of the word: by selecting only the changes and improvements that worked and discarding the rest. As a result, by the end of 1993, the Linux OS was stable and reliable enough to compete with almost all of the commercial versions of UNIX, and it even began to serve as the foundation of a lot of commercial applications. In a short period of time, Linux became the predominant UNIX alternative.

As mentioned, the rate of growth of Linux was amazing, and by March 1994, Linux version 1.0 was released. In a brief span of time after the release of the first Linux distributions (1992-1994), it became a component of the toolbox of numerous enthusiasts, professionals, and academics.

---

[2]`https://groups.google.com/forum/#!topic/comp.os.minix/4995Siv0l9o`

Torvalds continued to lead the development effort, and he is still making the final decisions on the shape of the Linux kernel today. He now works at the Linux Foundation, a non-profit institution created to promote, care for, and standardize the development of the Linux OS. It is supported by a number of leading Linux and open source companies around the world as well as by individual developers globally.

It's important to remember that Linux is only a kernel, not a complete OS, so Torvalds put together this kernel and the tools from the GNU project to realize that first version of the GNU/Linux OS. But what was the GNU Project?

---

■ **Note**    A kernel is the core, or central, component of an operating system. It basically connects the hardware and the application software. There are two main architectures involved in constructing a kernel: the microkernel (a lot of small pieces) and the monolithic kernel (a unique large piece).

Without getting too deep into those concepts, a curious historical aspect of the Linux kernel is that was developed as a monolithic kernel, while MINIX was based on a microkernel. This was the reason for a comment made about Linux by A. S. Tanenbaum (the original developer of MINIX) in 1992, which stated that Linux was obsolete by concept. That spurred a debate between Tanenbaum and Torvalds, and demonstrated Torvalds' obstinacy, which has become legendary, as he continued to support the monolithic kernel architecture in his OS.

Tanenbaum also maintained that Linux would become obsolete in a few years, and the GNU Hurd kernel (a sort of UNIX-based microkernel) would be its replacement. It turned out that he was completely wrong about this prediction. Linux is more alive than ever and GNU Hurd is still under development and never delivered on its promise.

The Linux mascot, shown in Figure 1-2, has a funny history behind it. The community was looking for a logo/mascot, and after several suggestions, Linus talked about being bitten by a "ferocious fairy" penguin in an Australian zoo in 1993. Thus it was settled. Larry Ewing made the original drawing. The name Tux came from Torvalds **UNIX,** and it's also the beginning of the word tuxedo (frequently associated with penguins).

---

*Figure 1-2.*  *Tux, the official mascot of the Linux kernel and its de facto logo*

# GNU Project

Earlier I mentioned that Torvalds is kind of stubborn, and his obstinacy was in play in retaining the kernel architecture of Linux, a major factor in its success. The GNU Project exists because of the obsession and determination of another legendary character, Richard M. Stallman of MIT, who resisted culture changes in software development, deciding to turn back the clock to its origins.

*Hacker* is a word that has been abused and distorted from its original meaning. Almost no one outside of the computing world knows the real concept behind that term, and even a lot of people in the IT sphere don't realize its true meaning.

The hacker subculture was born in the 1960s at MIT (Massachusetts Institute of Technology) by a very clever group of people (engineers and physicists) who found solving day-to-day problems with the computer systems of that time to be fun and intellectually rewarding. They discovered workarounds to avoid and circumvent the limitations and failures of those systems, and they challenged themselves and others to extend the limits of those computer systems and achieve smarter paths to doing so.

The goal was to always achieve excellence and have fun in the process, and the pranks among them were a great part of that culture. The quintessential part of the hacker's subculture, however, was the sharing of information and achievements, rather than keeping these to themselves. This was done in part for pride and glory, and in part because they wanted to help to improve the world. They saw themselves as a sort of a mix between rebel heroes and mythical Robin Hoods, willing to give away their spoils. They had a strong sense of ethics and responsibility, even when they seemed to act as children in the eyes of computer corporations and institutions. This subculture expanded to other areas as well. In Silicon Valley, for example, one of the icons of this movement was the Homebrew Computer Club, a computer hardware hacker's club, where later the first Apple computer was presented by member Steve Wozniak.

> "What they had in common was mainly love of excellence and programming. They wanted to make their programs that they used be as good as they could. They also wanted to make them do neat things. They wanted to be able to do something in a more exciting way than anyone believed possible and show 'Look how wonderful this is. I bet you didn't believe this could be done.'"
>
> —Richard Stallman in the 1985 TV documentary, *Hackers: Wizards of the Electronic Age*

It was this subculture that gave birth to some big technological achievements like the UNIX OS, the TCP/IP protocol (the backbone of the Internet itself), and the GNU Project. You can honestly say that Linux was a byproduct of the last strains of that original movement, before it evolved into a somewhat different and wider approach, the Free Software initiative. Going back to the GNU project, however, Stallman is sometimes called "the last of the true hackers" (he even saw himself as that for a period of time), and by that I am referring to original group of hackers at MIT.

---

■ **Tip** If you want to know more about the origins of hacking and computers as we know them today, you may be interested in an excellent book called *Hackers: Heroes of a Computer Revolution* by Steven Levy (Anchor Press/Doubleday, 1984). It is the best and most accurate chronicle about those early and interesting times.

---

Richard Stallman (see Figure 1-3), a mathematical prodigy and student at Harvard in 1970 (he would graduate from Harvard *magna cum laude* in Physics in 1974), soon joined MIT's Artificial Intelligence (AI) Lab and became part of this subculture. He had grown up as a professional systems programmer in that environment, and he had internalized those ethics so much that they become part of his way of living.

***Figure 1-3.*** *Richard Stallman, founder of the GNU project, at Oslo, Norway on February 23, 2009*

In the early 1980s, however, a series of events would break down that environment and destroy the idealism and freedom that had so influenced Stallman's life. So in 1983, Stallman decided to start a new project called the GNU's Not Unix (GNU) Project to try to create a completely new operating system that could be freely distributed, inspired by the hacker subculture and ethics. His initial goal soon became a full-time job, so he abandoned MIT in 1984 and began writing the GNU software. He also wanted to avoid the possibility that MIT could claim any rights to his code. Two of the first programs he wrote were the multi-language and multi-platform gnu compiler, or gcc, and the Emacs text editor. These two programs are still in use today. gcc is one of the most used software compilers in the world, and Emacs is still the favorite text editor of a lot of computer professionals (myself included).

To attract people to help him develop the GNU OS, he published the GNU Manifesto in 1985, which would become one of the pillars of a software revolution, six years before the initial Torvalds message to the com.os.minix newsgroup. This manifesto stated some fundamental liberties that should apply to all software:

- Freedom to run a program for any purpose.

- Freedom to study the mechanics of a program and modify it to suit your needs.

- Freedom to redistribute copies free or for a fee.

- Freedom to improve and change modified versions to use by everybody.

As more people read the manifesto and began embracing its principles, a set of new needs appeared: a way of sharing and distribution and a way to preserve the hacker's ethics that Stallman so much appreciated. FTP and traditional mail solved the distribution problem, and the creation of the GPL solved the ethical issues and legal matters. *GPL* stands for General Public License, and Version 1, written in 1989, was a compendium of similar attempts made in the early versions of GNU Emacs, GNU compiler, and GNU debugger. The license basically solved two problems:

- **The distribution of the software as a binary**. The GPL prevented this by forcing the distribution of the software under this license, which is always accompanied by the source code in a human-readable format.

- **Avoiding additional restrictions**. Under the GPL, the software can be combined with other software programs that have license agreements with minor restrictions in them unlike the GPL itself, but never with software programs with more restrictive licenses unless the whole package is distributed under the GPL.

The GPL was a complete success, and later the Linux OS would adopt the GPLv2 and become one of its major beacons throughout the world. This license would eventually be complemented with the LGPL in order to support the software libraries. The third, and current, iteration of both licenses was adopted in 2006. Some believed that it was too restrictive; Linus Torvalds and other notable Linux developers were some of the most vocal critics. However, it's difficult to calculate the exact number of programs developed under this license; estimates are that the GPL family of licenses cover about 55% of all free software available, so it has clearly had a huge impact.

---

■ **Tip**　If you want to read the original GNU Manifesto, you can do so at www.gnu.org/gnu/manifesto.en.html. You can read the original version of the GPL License at www.gnu.org/licenses/old-licenses/gpl-1.0.html.

---

As stated earlier, the GNU Project (see Figure 1-4) was a main contributor to the Linux OS, as a complement of the kernel, in the same way that the Linux kernel covered the lack of one in the GNU project, because the Hurd kernel was still unavailable. (The first "usable" version would appear in 1996.)

*Figure 1-4.　The logo of the GNU Project is obviously a gnu*

In the early days of Linux, these GNU tools made up a large percentage of the OS (the GNU Project produced thousands of utilities like the shell, Emacs, the GIMP, GNOME, and the initial file system). Stallman always remembered this, and he claims that the proper name for Linux is GNU/Linux (some distros, such as Debian, still maintain this name) to recognize the priceless contribution of the GNU Project. The name suggested by Stallman and the Free Software Foundation never had any great impact. I personally just call the OS Linux, as do most people today.

However, it wouldn't be fair not to recognize that without the GNU Project, the Linux OS may have never existed. But it would also be reasonable to state that the GNU tools are today a minor part of the Linux OS, and with the great changes that the cloud, virtualization, and the systemd project (a new init system for Linux that is slowly replacing a lot of tasks heretofore done by a collection of small tools) are making in the OS, perhaps in the future the GNU Project elements will be completely gone from the Linux OS.

Thus the GNU project was critical for the development of Linux, and it was the key to arriving at a new way of developing software. It is certainly the reason why we had so many software projects and developers in those days. It was clearly a revolution, but it is sometimes is forgotten, underestimated, and even criticized. I'm absolutely sure, however, that if the GNU Project had not existed, the software world today would be radically different from what we have now.

# The Birth of Linux Distros

Once the Linux kernel became a reality and the GNU tools formed the missing piece to build the entire operating system, you still had to assemble, compile, and package them. It was a difficult, complex, and large job, well suited to enthusiasts ("geeks," as we call them today). However, if your intention was to introduce the OS to a larger audience, it was clearly necessary to simplify this process. With the development of a number of new programs built with the new OS in mind by an ever-increasing army of new developers, this need became an urgent one. Some of those enthusiasts developed the first Linux distros initially for their personal use, but they soon started to share them because they quickly realized that the job required a large number of interested individuals.

Thus, in 1992, the first Linux distributions were created. None of these distributions (MCC Interim Linux, Yggdrasil, H. J. Lu's "Boot-root," and Softlanding Linux Systems) still exist, but in 1993, the first two of the great Linux distributions were born: Slackware and Debian. Slackware was based on the SLS (Softlanding Linux System) and Debian was a new creation by Ian Murdock, because he was dissatisfied with SLS distribution. New distributions kept appearing, such as Red Hat, SUSE, Caldera, Conectiva, Mandrake, and so on, until the "big expansion" at the start of the new century when a large number of new distros were introduced.

I cover this history in a detailed manner in Chapter 3 and also in the subsequent chapters dedicated to the major Linux distros. Those distros were a convenience to less-experienced users, but they also met the basic requirements of the most experienced hackers, who adopted them even if they chose to work with more complex versions specifically suited to their needs.

As stated at the beginning of the book, there are an astounding number of distributions, and many of them offer different versions for different architectures, purposes, tastes, and so forth. You may ask yourself, "Why so many distros?" Read on! The answer to this question follows.

# Why So Many Distros?

The reasons behind the awesome set of different Linux distributions are in the roots of the Linux OS itself and the GNU Project. The conditions that cultivated the success of the Linux OS also nurtured the huge ecosystem that we have today with Linux. The possibility of changing nearly anything within the OS and distributing those changes for free contributed to the tremendous growth in the installed base of Linux users. Anyone who didn't like how something worked could simply change it, assuming they had the knowledge, motivation, and means to do so. Add to this the tweaker mentality of the hackers and you have what is available today: a distro for every taste.

New distros appear every year. And a vast number of nonconformist Linux users still like to tweak every minor aspect of their Linux installations. As if that isn't enough, some of them take it a step further: it is entirely possible to make a one-off Linux distro (and there are many examples).

While the majority of Linux distros are sustained by a group, or perhaps even a community of developers, most of the major distros are supported by corporations with a number of employees dedicated to its development.

> *The GNU Project and the GPL represented just the beginning of a new, larger, and more important movement: Software Libre, which translates to "Free Software." When Stallman started the GNU Project, he also introduced the concept of "copyleft" (as opposite of "copyright"), which would become the major component of the GPL and some other licenses with similar concepts of more or less restrictive use. As Stallman described it, "The central idea of copyleft is that we give everyone permission to run the program, copy the program, modify the program, and distribute modified versions — but not permission to add restrictions of their own. Thus, the crucial freedoms that define "free software" are guaranteed to everyone who has a copy; they become inalienable rights. For an effective copyleft, modified versions must also be free. This ensures that work based on ours becomes available to our community if it is published."*

> —Richard Stallman in *Opensources: Voices from the Open Source Revolution* by Chris Dibona (O'Reilly Media, 1999)

In 1985, as a part of the plan to support the GNU Project, Stallman founded the Free Software Foundation (FSF), a non-profit organization with the goal of supporting the development of free software in general. The GPLs that FSF created soon went viral in the programming community, and the movement surrounding free software began to grow. This movement quickly gained mindshare in the software world, and those who generally liked the idea but not the restrictions imposed by the GPL created other licenses such as Apache, BSD, MIT, Public Domain, Mozilla, and so on. In 1989, a group of people, including Bruce Perens and Eric Raymond, tried to unify the BSD and GPL licenses under the umbrella of a new movement called the *Open Source Initiative* (OSI). Others used the term FOSS, for *Free and Open-Source Software*, as a means to unite both movements. In any event, the fact is that the mindset of sharing and opening up source code is here to stay, and the number of developers writing code under these terms will not cease to grow. Software forges[3] and central repositories like GitHub, Bitbucket, GNU Savannah, and others are testimonials to the vitality of the Free Software movement. A large part of the Internet itself is built on the foundation of Free Software projects.

Although Free Software today has not achieved the high level of ethics and the culture of the early hacker's movement, and although software patents are a constant menace to its goals, it is true that it provides us with the privilege of using and enjoying a great number of software projects that we can fork[4] and modify at any time.

This is the environment in which a great number of communities continue to develop Linux distros, creating new ones daily, and without the Free Software movement, and if all software were closed-source, doing so would literally be impossible. Contrast this with the Microsoft and Apple operating systems. Linux represents more than an OS; it is also about freedom. Even though most people refuse to use the term GNU/Linux, the truth is that the success of Linux is also the success of the GNU Project, the FSF, and Free Software.

---

[3]A web-based platform designed to host and share computer program source code, generally FOSS (Free and Open Source Software). You can learn more about it at `https://en.wikipedia.org/wiki/Forge_(software)`.
[4]Fork in the sense of bifurcation. It's a common term used in programming when a copy of a source code is made to work on its own as an independent project. You can learn more at `https://en.wikipedia.org/wiki/Fork_(software_development)`.

> ■ **Note** You may have noticed that the term "Software Libre" was used before. This term is preferred by some people, and Richard Stallman himself has also used it, because the word "libre" in Spanish avoids the ambiguity of the same word in English (free). Those who prefer Software Libre simply do not want you to confuse free, as in a free beer, with free, as in free speech. Software Libre is always linked to freedom, but it could be commercialized and sold, as it frequently is. You can learn more about this at `https://en.wikipedia.org/wiki/Gratis_versus_libre`.

## Do I Have to Choose One? Aren't They All the Same?

This is a common question. Why choose a particular Linux distribution? Can't you achieve the same goal with all of them? The answer is clear and simple: NO.

There are many different reasons for choosing a Linux distribution, just like there are many different reasons and ways to create one. Yes, you can tweak and customize almost any distro, but the effort to do so can be huge in some cases, and sometimes it's nearly impossible to achieve your goal.

If you need to embed a Linux distro in an electronic device with scarce resources, for example, you cannot simply install the last Ubuntu distro for desktops because it does not work that way. Similarly, if you try to use the elementary distro as a Linux server, it probably will not end well, and you will get a huge headache for your trouble.

## Summary

I hope that you now have a clear idea about what a Linux distro is and the reasons leading up to the current multitude of available Linux distributions. Perhaps you were wondering why I was spending so much time talking about the GNU Project and Software Libre when this is book about Linux. However, by now you should understand that Linux is linked by birth, nature, and definition to the GNU Project and the Software Libre movement.

The more important point, and the theme of this book, is that it is impossible to choose just one Linux distribution for all situations. This is precisely the reason behind this whole book; you would have nothing to read and I would have nothing to say about this topic if the choice of a Linux distro did not matter.

I cover the decision criteria for selecting a Linux distro in the next chapter in order to help you understand the variety of purposes, tasks, tastes, and so forth that form the basis for choosing a Linux distro. The rest of the chapter explores the different factors that have to be taken into account when choosing the right distro for your needs.

# CHAPTER 2

■ ■ ■

# Linux Distro Selection Criteria

Now that you know what a Linux distribution is and why there are so many, the next step is to find a way to compare and screen them. The best way to do this is by choosing a series of factors that you can use to measure and classify the various Linux distros objectively, without bias in your reasoning. It is OK to listen to the opinion of a colleague or a Linux expert, or to read an article or review, and so on, but it is very rare to find a source that is completely unbiased or that matches your particular situation. I strongly advise you to take these factors into account and weigh the most important ones based on your needs. Then you can choose the distribution that is the strongest based on those needs. This book will help you make an informed decision.

In this chapter, I name some distributions in each category, but don't take this as a way to easily choose the right distro (also, I don't name all of the distributions that fit for a particular point). You should choose your Linux distro on the basis of a number of factors, not just one (except in very particular cases like task-oriented ones). This goal of this chapter is to help you evaluate each distribution by knowing what factors you should consider when doing so.

In the next chapters I introduce you to many distros in detail. I have chosen a sample of the most popular, reliable, and secure, but also a few ones to illustrate some points like the current state-of-the-art Linux distributions or ones that fit particular needs. In certain chapters I refer back to the factors that I mention here to see how each distro rates. Although it is impossible to cover all of the alternatives available to you, I try to cover as much ground as possible.

Also, note that I do not take a deep dive technically. I think that is beyond the scope of this book. There are some technicalities and concepts that I must cover to give you precise information, but if you are new to Linux, I don't want you to get distracted or intimidated by me being too technical. When I analyze the different distros, I will get as technical as necessary to explain how they perform.

---

■ **Note** I mention many factors to consider when choosing a Linux distro. By the end of the chapter you may have come up with some factors that I did not mention. Please note that I covered the most critical ones for making the right decision, and I discarded some because I think they overlapped ones that were mentioned or were less specific.

---

© Jose Dieguez Castro 2016

J. Dieguez Castro, *Introducing Linux Distros*, DOI 10.1007/978-1-4842-1392-6_2

# Factors to Consider when Choosing a Linux Distro

Figure 2-1 shows the important factors to consider when choosing a Linux distro. The first step in choosing a system, whatever it is, is to ask yourself how you are going to use it. Using your new operating system to compose letters and track your finances is not the same as using one to serve a marketplace on the Internet. You could use the same distro for both purposes, and some people do, but it most cases this would be a very bad decision. Even if you are new to computers, you probably know that is generally not a good idea to use the same tools for domestic purposes and for professional work.

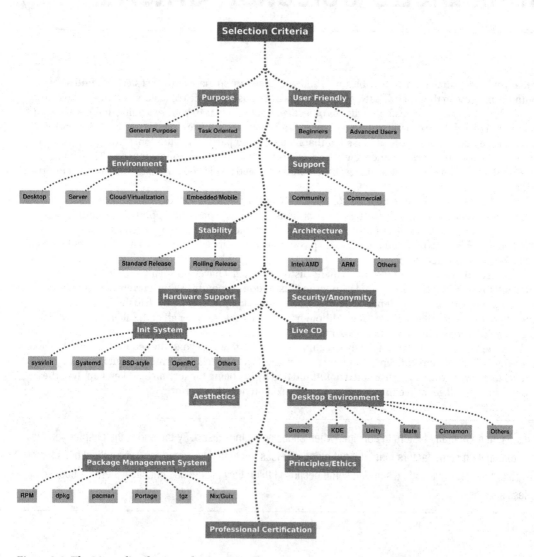

*Figure 2-1. The Linux distribution selection criteria graph*

Let's divide the category of basic workflow into two large categories: general purpose and task-oriented.

# General Purpose

We can include in this category the majority of the Linux distros and we can think about them as the equivalent of the other big competitors of Linux: MS Windows and Apple OS X. They are not oriented to doing any specific task; rather they try to fulfil common and diverse jobs from writing documents to editing videos, etc. These tasks are what everyone thinks of when they think about an operating system. The majority of people who want a Linux distro for their own use also want to perform such tasks.

You expect a distro to be able to use whatever category of software you need for your daily work at home or work. In this category are the most popular distros: Ubuntu, Fedora, Debian, and Mint.

# Task-Oriented

Why would you need a specialized Linux distro? This is an interesting question, and there is no simple answer to it. The most common cases are the following:

- You want to use the distro for something specific and the general Linux distros lack a necessary feature. It could be as simple as a heavy customization and the ability to add specific software repositories. Educational and children-oriented distros are good examples.

- You want to focus on only one task and eliminate all features and software that are not needed. There are several reasons for this, such as the following:

  - Hardware constraints: It could be for space on disk or in memory, or architecture, like distros oriented for networks devices like routers or other embedded devices. You could need to reduce the software in the distro to the minimum required; often the kernel is also customized. A distro suited for a mobile device is another example, like Android.

  - Security: If you want to run a Linux distro in a firewall or similar device, you want the minimal software overhead possible for non-vulnerability and performance reasons. And you only want to use software and libraries that you can trust. Alpine is a good example, as is Tails.

  - Ease-of-use: A distro to manage a home theater PC does not need a word processor or a spreadsheet, but an easy-to-use interface oriented for use with a remote is a desirable feature. Likewise, the Chrome OS distro for notebooks is focused on apps and storage in the cloud.

There are a lot of tasks and distros in this category; so many that I devote all of Chapter 17 to this topic. In advance, I will enumerate here some of the tasks and distributions for the sake of completeness.

- Multimedia/Arts: Ubuntu Studio, ArtistX

- Media PC/Home Theater: Kodi (formerly known as XBMC), Mythbuntu

- Security/Forensics/Anonymity: Kali, Tails, DEFT

- Storage: FreeNAS

- Mobile: Android, Tizen, Ubuntu Phone

- Cloud Apps: Chrome

- Routers: OpenWrt

- Gaming: SteamOS

- Cloud/Data Center: CoreOS

I think you get the idea. You can jump to Chapter 17 if you are looking for a distro of this type but a better idea is to keep reading and see what other factors you should consider when choosing a distribution that fits you.

## Environment

Another question that you should consider when looking for a Linux distro is the environment where you are going to run it. I've broken it into four main environments where you could run a Linux distribution (I tried to keep it simple): desktop, server, cloud/virtualization, and embedded.

## Desktop

The desktop environment is what most people think of when they think about a Linux distro; ironically, it is precisely this one on which Linux has the least success. Although there are some estimations of tens of millions of Linux OSes installed on the desktop (and some estimates go as high as over one hundred million), the truth is that there is a huge gap between Linux and the leaders in this field, Windows and Apple (in that order). Some people believe that the Linux desktop user count is very similar to Apple worldwide. The majority of Linux distros are oriented to this environment (the big ones have specialized versions for each environment), and ironically many people think that this is the reason behind the lack of success of Linux in this area. Anyway, Linux started as a desktop OS and it remains the first Linux experience for most users.

Here we could talk about SoHo users (Small Office, Home) and about corporate and workstations users. Usually a Linux distro oriented to this environment is a general purpose one that is focus on ease of use and offers a familiar graphical interface. These distros also contain administrative tools and services more proper for a server purpose, but they are not suited to this task like servers are, and when people use them in environments other that the desktop it usually requires a lot of customization and knowledge to make them work properly. Debian is a classic example of this.

In this category are almost all of the most popular distros: Ubuntu, Fedora, Mint, Debian, OpenSUSE, etc.

## Server

When you need to serve a database or a web site, you use a Linux distro oriented to the server environment. These distros are especially suited for this task, incorporating tools, services, security, customizations, and specialized kernels. They usually lack a graphical environment. Security, performance, and stability are the main features in this category and usually these distros are a bit outdated compared to the desktop distros. These Linux distros are meant to be running on a 365/24 basis and they usually are not rebooted for years at a time. Considering the critical aspects of this category, to rely on a Linux distro not especially designed for this task may work for a short period (usually with great effort and many headaches) but it could be a nightmare in the long run. I would rather use a server distro on my desktop (which is also an unpleasant experience) that use a desktop distro in a server. (Debian is a notable exception).

In this category are popular and well-recognized distros like Red Hat Enterprise Linux, SUSE Linux Enterprise Server, CentOS, and Oracle (the last two are forks of Red Hat) as well as the corresponding server versions of the most popular desktop distros like Ubuntu Server or Debian.

## Cloud/Virtualization

This is a subcategory or a super-specialization of the server category, but its importance and how is shaping the future of Linux is enough to claim its own place. You will find here distros that are suited to work in the cloud where they need to be reliable, secure, scalable, easy to automate and deploy, etc.

Most of the big and popular distros are used in this environment, like Red Hat, CentOS, Ubuntu, and Debian. Some offer specialized versions to fit new needs, like Ubuntu Cloud and Amazon AMI (one fork of Red Hat suited to work with AWS), and some even offer their own cloud services like Red Hat OpenStack or OpenShift. There are also extremely light and minimal Linux distros created especially for this environment like CoreOS, which makes use of new technologies like containers (Docker, rocket and Kubernetes). Other new initiatives like that are at last beginning to appear point, together with systemd, to the future of Linux and servers in general.

And although virtualization is supported by default nowadays in the kernel, there are some distributions that focus only on it, like Oracle VM Server or Proxmox VE (Debian based), which work like bare-metal hypervisors.

## Embedded/Mobile

The distros in the embedded/mobile category are very specialized, aimed to fit in mobile devices, consumer electronics, network appliances (routers, firewalls), machine controls, industrial automation, road vehicles, medical instruments, etc. The best known ones are employed on mobile devices, such as Android, Ubuntu mobile, and Tizen. Others like OpenWrt and Alpine are focused on network devices. And of course, there is a Debian distro for embedded devices.

## Support

For some users, like professionals, the level of support can be a threshold point to filter which Linux distros are suitable for them and which are not. Good documentation or support by the community of users (wikis, irc, forums, mailing lists, etc.) can be enough for experienced or domestic users, but for the corporate world you may desire commercial support to keep the systems running without trouble. So, as you maybe already suppose, there are two categories in this group: community and commercial support.

## Community

Traditionally, because of the origins of Linux itself, the help documentation needed to install and troubleshoot the OS is created and maintained by the community of users and developers. If the distro has a big community, the quantity and quality of the documentation and support is better. When the support is better, it attracts new users to the community. A traditional example of this is Debian. However, even some distros that are oriented to advanced users and are hard to install and administrate to newcomers have excellent documentation and a very supportive community, like Arch Linux or Gentoo.

What you can expect from the community in the majority of distros is some documentation (in a webpage, a wiki, or a CD) and several ways in which the users can communicate with each other in order to answer questions. Almost every Linux distro has a mailing list, and most of them also have irc channels and forums; the bigger ones also have some system for users to submit bugs to the developers. There are often separate resources of the same type to drive developers and normal users into sub-communities that sometimes overlap on some topics.

## Commercial

When corporations and institutions began to replace their UNIX installations with Linux, some people saw the opportunity to do more than sell and distribute the software; they could also offer commercial support from experts to assist in the process of migration and maintenance of Linux. Thus the first commercial distributions of Linux supported by a company were born. Today two of them still represent a major number of corporate Linux installations: Red Hat and SUSE.

There are different approaches to offering commercial support. Companies like Red Hat have an entirely commercial distribution. Red Hat also has a separate distro named Fedora that is supported by the community; some Red Hat programmers contribute to its development, and it is where they introduce the most recent technologies and test a lot of changes that are later incorporated into the commercial distro. The company Canonical has a main distribution, Ubuntu, that is essentially the same for all users and is partially supported and developed by the community, but it also offers commercial support to SoHo and corporate users and some tools especially fit for the corporate world, like an Ubuntu Server version.

This commercial support can be offered in different channels, such as the community one, from personal support offered by experts directly on the site (by direct employers or consulting firms that are official partners) to telephone hotlines or web sites offering help.

Usually this commercial support is linked to a maintenance contract paid annually. And some companies, like Red Hat and SUSE, also offer certification programs and exams to provide external professionals the knowledge and competence to maintain these distro installations. I'll explain this in detail later in this chapter.

# User Friendly

I'm going to split the user friendly section into two groups: beginners and advanced users. Yes, this is a little unfair: using an "easy" Linux distro does not imply that the user does not have profound and advanced knowledge about Linux. Take Apple, for example; their OS X is famous for its ease of use even for beginners but it is also the OS chosen by a lot of IT professionals, even Linux Kernel developers. Some people don't want their OS to get in the middle of their work; they want an OS that simply works, so they choose a distribution that is very easy to install and maintain, and one that requires very little time to keep current. Others are just the opposite; they want to tweak every minor detail of their OS and feel that they are in total control of their machines. Thus, choosing a distro based on its ease of use is not always a question of knowledge or capability; most of the time it is a question of personal preference.

So, when talking about the friendliness of a Linux distro, there are two questions to consider: your level of experience with Linux and how much time you want to spend maintaining, customizing, and learning about your OS.

# Beginners

Is this your first rodeo with Linux, or do you have a little experience with it? Do you want to spend very little time tweaking your distro? Do you want to avoid as much as possible the use of the terminal? Do you have little interest in learning about Linux? If you simply want to install the OS and then spend very little time keeping it updated, you should consider a "beginner" Linux distro. Keep in mind that ease of use does not mean inferior quality, stability, or capabilities. In fact, the bigger distros try to make the experience with the OS as pleasant possible, hiding all of the nuts and bolts from the user, as a way to attract the biggest number of users possible.

Saying what is easy to use is not always as clear as you might think. There is a large amount of subjectivity here. However, there is some common ground that allows us to establish a certain agreement on which Linux distros are friendlier than others, such as how easy it is to install the distro and how easy it is to update and install new programs and hardware.

Some examples of this kind of distro are Ubuntu (which, in fact, had a great impact in this aspect), Mint, and elementary OS.

# Advanced Users

As in the previous category, there is no direct relation between experience and this kind of distro; some users who are new to Linux begin with an "advanced" distro because they want to learn as much as they can about the OS and want to have an OS suited to their needs. I strongly discourage this approach because desire and willingness do not always come together, and this approach usually ends in frustration. If you are coming from Windows or OS X and you decide to start your Linux experience with a distro focused on advanced users, you must be ready to learn a lot, and I mean a huge amount, of concepts that cover a big span, from the internals of your machine to the internals of your OS. And Linux is not like Windows in that you will not have a GUI to tweak any aspect of your OS (in fact, this is true for some things in Windows); you must use the terminal to write some complex, arcane, and often very long commands as opposed to editing simple text files. It is not a walk in the park. But it could be a very funny and pleasant experience if you are willing to do it. So, it is up to you, but if you have little experience with Linux I strongly recommend that you start first with a "beginners" distro to get a glimpse of how the OS works and to learn the general concepts.

On the other hand, all of the distros (well, most of the desktop ones) allow you to tweak them at a very deep level through the terminal. This is counterproductive in many "beginner" distros; they work very well as installed. If you customize them too much at critical points, you may end up regretting it. This is one of the main reasons why distros for advanced users exist. If you want to deeply customize your Linux OS, you must use a distro that allows you to do so without breaking things in the long term. Anyway, distros like Debian have a friendly way to customize the distro as you wish (and sometimes break it too).

Some of the distributions in this category are Arch Linux, Gentoo, NixOS, and Slackware.

# Stability

Stability is another crucial factor for professional users who needs the MTBF (mean time between failures) of their OS to be minimal. For professional users, time is money. Failures in their Linux installation could cause other serious problems like data loss/corruption or security breaches. When I talk about stability here, I'm talking about how often a distro updates the packages and kernel.

Traditionally this factor is divided into two categories: standard release distros and rolling release distros, but in some distros this division is more like a blurred line where no clear model exists and both can be used at the same time.

# Standard Release

The standard release model is the desirable model when you need a Linux distro for a professional environment. This release cycle is based in versions (with a fixed period or not) and the core base of the distro is kept stable until the next release, which only contains bug fixes or security patches. When a new version is launched, the kernel and packages are not fresh ones; they are stable versions, well tested and arguably secure. This is the model of Red Hat, for example. Versions are normally linked to the development or upgrading of important features and do not have a specific interval of time between releases; they are released when they are ready. The Linux kernel itself follows a similar model with its version releases.

Others distros like Ubuntu have a time-based release, which is currently two times a year (a six-month period). Every fourth release (a two-year period) is a special one named LTS (long-term support) that aims to be a stable release maintained for a long time (five years versus the nine months in normal releases). The LTS is the one oriented to professional environments.

Debian goes a step further. It has three different models: Stable, Testing, and Unstable. The Stable model follows the standard mode, the Unstable model is a rolling release distro, and the Testing model covers some ground in the middle. Debian Stable is a very common Linux distro used in many web servers and other reliable services.

With this model, once a new version is released you usually have two options:

- Upgrade your distro to the new version. This is the most comfortable option, when all goes well. However, even when some distros take special care to make this process go as smoothly as possible, it does not always work perfectly. Sometimes this is due to errors in the process, but most of the time it is due to heavy customizations from users. Remember to always make a backup of your data before any distro upgrade (you should make backups regularly).

- Make a backup of your data, make a fresh install, and restore your backup. This requires more work and time compared to the upgrade option (if all goes well, obviously), but it does minimize the problems that you could find. Some users end up doing this due to experience gained after various broken distro upgrades.

## Rolling Release

Rolling release distros try to keep pace with the development of the Linux kernel and the different software packages so they always have latest version available. In order to do so, some distros also tend to minimize the customization of those packages and kernel, so they are almost vanilla packages. They are geared to advanced users and those who are eager to have bleeding-edge technology. Once you install one of these distros, if all goes well, you usually only have to do periodic updates.

These distros are considered not as stable and harder to maintain, but the truth is not as severe as it sounds. You can work on a daily basis with one of these distros without problems; some people even use them in servers. Many of these distros offer solutions for keeping a certain stability, like different repositories separating the latest software versions from the ones that are a little outdated (frequently a matter of days or weeks) but are more reliable.

There is a controversial opinion that a rolling-release distro is always more reliable in terms of security terms because the latest version has more holes fixed and is less prone to having zero-day vulnerabilities because there is no time to discover them. I think that you should take this theory with a grain of salt: some vulnerabilities exist in version after version because nobody noticed them.

There are many distros that follow this model; the most popular ones are Debian Unstable, Arch Linux, and Gentoo.

---

■ **Tip**   I am trying to be as objective as possible in this book. If you are curious about my software choices, I use a rolling release distro on a daily basis on my laptops and workstations but I always use a standard release distro on my servers and critical machines.

---

## Hardware Support

The question of hardware support is usually as simple as how many resources are available to the team responsible for maintaining and developing the Linux distribution. Much hardware is supported by the kernel directly, but the distro controls how good the automatically detection and enabling of this hardware is. Also, there are binary drivers that some distributions do not add to their distros for ethical or licensing reasons, which makes it very hard to support certain hardware. Printers, graphic cards, network cards, and wireless devices are usually problematic devices, and even some laptops are poorly supported by Linux.

Happily there has been a huge improvement in this field over the last few years, and often there is no problem at all with common hardware. But specialized devices usually require the company behind them to develop a driver for Linux. Although this is common today, there is another problem: usually the companies only develop drivers in .rpm and .deb packages, forcing the user to make conversions or to compile from the source in other distros. Sometimes this does not work very well because they are customized for a certain distro, normally Red Hat/Fedora and Debian/Ubuntu.

Thus you must know before you buy any hardware if it is completely compatible with Linux; this is especially important with laptops. There are some websites dedicated to covering this issue. The best way to ensure that you will have minimum problems with hardware in Linux is to do your research and choose one of the big distros (Ubuntu, Fedora, Debian, Mageia, OpenSUSE) that normally have a lot of resources or a company behind them. You may think that the derivate distros of these big ones will offer the same support, but this is not always the case; and if it is supported, it is not always as simple as adding the same hardware in their mother distro.

## Aesthetics

Aesthetics is a very subjective topic, but here is one thing that you can take from a completely objective point of view: whether the distro takes care of its design or not. Usually, as in the previous factor, this is directly related to the level of resources available to the team behind it. Having some community developers try to make a distro look pleasant is not the same as having a team of designers focus on it. There is one notable exception: elementary OS, a community-driven distro that aims to offer the best design experience possible with only a small team behind but tons of good taste (it is an Ubuntu-based distro; they focus mainly on usability and design). It has the same goals as OS X: ease of use and being a pleasure to the senses (in fact, it's been criticized for taking heavy inspiration from OS X). There is a new project called Ozon OS that looks to follow the steps of elementary OS but with its own sense of design; it is still in the early stages but it seems promising. Other distros that have a very good design (I do not have to like them, but I recognize the effort) are Ubuntu, OpenSUSE, Mint, Mageia, and Fedora.

But to be honest, once you have chosen one of the main desktop environments, KDE or Gnome, you do not have too much room for improvement. Even if you customize it and the main programs that are installed by default, there is so much software in the repositories with its own design and aesthetic, and this software does not use the API of those common desktops. So it is hard to keep a homogenous aesthetic within the OS. This problem is common to Windows too, and also in very minor way to OS X, but in Linux it is more obvious. It does not matter if elementary OS is beautiful and homogenous in all of its (few) native apps if you install an awful software that comes with its own design. If design matters very much to you, keep in mind that a Linux distro like Mint that has a really good aesthetic but with minor customizations would be always more homogenous in its design if you are willing to install more software that the few developed apps that elementary OS offers.

It would be stupid for me, even when I love and support Linux, to not recognize that a nice design and a homogenous look is still far from being ideal for the most of the Linux distros out there.

## Desktop Environment

The desktop environment is also a question of taste. Some people strongly prefer a desktop environment and even dislike others. The most commonly used and known are Gnome and KDE, but there are some alternatives like Unity, Mate, Cinnamon, Xfce, LXDE, and Enlightenment.

Usually you can have several different desktop managers installed in your distro, even at the same time (choosing the one you want to work in at login time), but is normal for each distro to have a predefined one by default. Some people choose OpenSUSE over Fedora, for example, because they prefer to work with KDE instead of Gnome. But some of the big distros let you choose what DE you want to use when installing them.

To measure the impact that a desktop manager can have in a distribution, consider Linux Mint. When the Gnome project released the version 3 of its desktop environment, there were huge changes; as a result, many detractors wanted to keep working on version 2. Mint decided to develop two desktop environments to please those users: Mate is based on Gnome 2 and Cinnamon is a fork of Gnome 3. The distro gained a

25

lot of users because of this decision. Later, Ubuntu developed its own desktop environment, Unity, which also created a lot of controversy and a great number of people who did not liked it, so they migrated mainly to Mint. Those two great migrations of users and the excellent work made in both environments means that today Linux Mint is the most popular distro on distrowatch. So, clearly the DE matters a lot to a huge number of users.

I will cover this in more detail in the chapters dedicated to the distros, showing the DE available (and predefined options) for each distro.

---

■ **Tip**   I do not use any desktop environment. I use a windows manager instead, a tiling window manager to be more precise (Awesome WM in particular). This is a very trendy option for a lot of advanced users and there are plenty of possibilities, the most well-known being OpenBox, FluxBox, xmonad, i3, Awesome WM, and dwm.

---

## Init System

Until very recently I did not consider the init system as a factor in a decision because almost all of the distros were using the same init system, init (SysV). But in 2006, the Ubuntu distribution (and all of its derivatives) implemented a new init system, Upstart, that was also adopted as the default by Red Hat and Fedora. And five years ago, a new init system was born to become a revolution in the Linux ecosystem, and a very controversial one. This new init system, systemd, created by Lennart Poettering at Red Hat, not only was a revolutionary init system, it soon become something more that an init system, in fact much more than that. And that made a lot of people angry, creating many polarized opinions on the matter.

The systemd init system broke some of the traditional UNIX principles, and that is not acceptable to some people, both distro developers and system administrators. The current reality is that almost all of the big Linux distributions adopted systemd, and others are totally opposed to taking that step. Two cases became famous and controversial: Ubuntu discarded its own init system in favor of systemd, and Debian adopted systemd after a very contentious debate among the members of the Debian Technical Committee. This created an outburst in the Debian community and resulted in the resigning of some members. The situation is still hot, and recently a new distribution forked from Debian called Devuan was created to allow to those who hate systemd to still continue to use Debian (only as Devuan). In 2014, some users started a boycott campaign against systemd but it has not had a huge impact.

Thus, as mentioned, some distros are reluctant to abandon sysvinit or adopt systemd, and as a result you can now choose between different alternatives. Since this topic is so controversial, the type of init system has clearly become a factor for many people when choosing a Linux distro.

### sysvinit (Traditional Init)

Some distros are still using the traditional init system, also known as SystemV init, and others offer it as an option. Devuan is one of them, as are PCLinuxOS and LFS. There are a few more, but basically none are very popular distributions. We are at the end of an era for sysvinit.

### systemd

Almost all of the popular distros and derivatives are supporting the systemd init system as the default option these days. It is included by default in Red Hat, Fedora, Ubuntu, Debian, Arch Linux, and OpenSUSE.

## BSD-style

The BSD-style init system was used by Arch Linux for many years, but it was abandoned in favor of systemd. CRUX is still using it, however, as is Slackware.

## OpenRC

Created by a former Gentoo developer, Roy Marples, OpenRC is still the init system used by that Linux distribution. Gentoo also allows systemd as an option, the same way that you can still continue to use sysvinit if you want. That's the very nature of the distro itself: do whatever you want. Other than the ones based on Gentoo and Alpine, I do not know of any other Linux distros using the OpenRC init system.

## Others

There are a few other init systems, but they are merely testimonial, such as GNU dmd for Guix, Mudur in Pardus, BootScripts in GloboLinux, or busybox-init suited to embedded systems.

As you can see, there are not many options if you are a systemd detractor, but it's Linux, so you always have a few options.

## Package Management System

In Linux, you install/update software using a package manager, usually from official repositories on the Internet or directly from a package. These days it's rare to have to compile a package by hand (but it happens). A package manager is a fantastic, centralized, and secure way to manage the software of your operating system. But, as usual in Linux, there are many different package managers.

I'm not going to get into my opinion of whether one is better than the others; all of them have advantages and disadvantages. The truth is that it is very difficult, if not impossible, to use one as a complete replacement for the one that comes by default with the distro. So we can divide the Linux distros by their package management systems. Also, distros that share the same package management system often have different tools to manage them; Mageia uses urpmi to manage its rpm packages, while Fedora uses DNF (previously YUM).

## RPM

RPM is the acronym for Red Hat Package Manager and is obviously the one used by that distribution and its derivatives. It was also adopted by SUSE and Mandriva and thus their derivatives. It's the de facto official packaging system, and it's the one most frequently supported by corporate developers. These packages have the .rpm suffix.

Some of the Linux distros that support this system are Red Hat, CentOS, Oracle Linux, Fedora, SUSE, OpenSUSE, Mageia, and PCLinuxOS.

## dpkg

The package management system created by Debian is called dpkg, and it is the second most used after rpm. The suffix of these packages is .deb. When corporate developers release a version of their software for Linux, they normally offered .rpm and .deb packages, and sometimes also the source.

Some of the many distros that use this system are Debian, Ubuntu, Mint, and all of the Debian/Ubuntu derivatives.

## pacman/AUR, Portage/emerge, and tgz

pacman/AUR, Portage/emerge, and tgz are the package management systems of Arch Linux, Gentoo, and Slackware, respectively. The first two are sophisticated and advanced systems because they support advanced and rolling release distros. The last is used almost exclusively by Slackware.

Pacman/AUR is used in Arch Linux, Manjaro, Parabola, Antergos, Chackra, and ArchBang. Portage is used in Gentoo, Sabayon, Chrome Os, and Funtoo.

## Nix/Guix

Nix/Guix is a new type of package management system. It is based in a purely functional model, which allows a series of unusual features like multiple versions of the same package, atomic upgrades and rollback, garbage collection, etc. Nix is the original concept; Guix has a similar approach and comes from the GNU Project.

Currently, as it is the state of the art in this field, there are only two distros that support these systems: NixOS with Nix and GuixSD with Guix.

## Architecture

Since the decline of the RISC processors (except ARM), there are not very many different architectures in modern machines. Intel processors are the clearly dominant actor in the market, followed by AMD. The ARM processors are getting more and more popular, thanks to mobile systems. But there are many other architectures out there, such as folks who still carry around old Apple PowerBooks with a PowerPC processor, servers with Intel Itanium cores, workstations such as SUN UltraSPARC, IBM mainframes, etc.

The Linux kernel by default supports a lot of different hardware architectures, but not all of the distros support them. In fact, the majority of the distros only support the major ones: Intel and perhaps ARM.

## Intel

In the Linux kernel, the denomination i686 (a.k.a. 586) is for the 32-bit processors after the 386 (deprecated in the kernel), and x86-64 (a.k.a. amd64 or intel64) is for the 64-bit processors from Intel and AMD. Almost all of the distros currently support the x86-64 architecture and i686 as well, but some of them are abandoning the i686 architecture, like Sabayon Linux.

Ubuntu, Debian, Fedora, openSUSE, Mint, Mageia, ... as said, practically all of them support both architectures.

## ARM

The ARM processor is the king of consumer electronics and mobile devices; its omnipresence is astounding. However, ARM is not as well supported as the Intel/AMD processors, and currently only a few distributions have ports for it. Some of these distros are Ubuntu, Debian, Fedora, Arch Linux, Gentoo, Slackware, Kali, and of course Android and Chrome OS. Perhaps the fact that ARM is becoming as an interesting actor in the low-consumption server world will change the adoption by the big actors in this field (Red Hat and SUSE are the first ones making some movement in that direction).

## Others

Other architectures are still less supported, as expected. The commercial ones have good support for mainframes and PowerPC. If you are looking for other architectures, even exotic ones, your decision is a clear one: Debian. Debian supports a lot of different architectures, about ten officially and more as unofficial ports. You can even find images for older architectures and install them as if were the 1980s.

## Security/Anonymity

If you are concerned about security (and you should be), you must know that some Linux distros are more conscious about this topic than others. Usually the big ones that have more resources, especially the commercial ones, are the most dedicated to this matter. Distros like Red Hat, CentOS, SUSE, and Fedora are the most secure by default. Linux is a reasonably secure system by default, but usually the Linux distros do not come with a default hardened security; you can make it this way if you have the knowledge, but still you must rely on the security of the distro for things like the software repositories. For example, you can make Arch Linux a very secure system, but until recently the software packages not were signed, and the AUR packages can be a security concern if you don't know what you are doing.

There are a few distros that are focused entirely on security from different perspectives. Some of these are

- Tails (The Amnesiac Incognito Live System): It is based on Debian and its perspective is to provide security through anonymity, preserving your privacy.

- Pentoo: It is a Live CD Gentoo-based distro hardened by default.

- Kali (formerly BackTrack): It is also based in Debian and is focused on digital forensics and penetration testing.

- Alpine: A lightweight distro that focuses on being secure by default. A tiny and very secure distro, it is primarily designed for x86 routers, firewalls, and similar.

- Qubes: Its approach provides a secure system based on the isolation of its components via virtualization. It is based on Fedora.

## Principles/Ethics

In the previous chapter you learned how the GNU Project took an important view on principles, and how the FSF created a new way to license software based on a series of solid principles and ethics. The FSF has a series of guidelines (which you can read at www.gnu.org/distros/free-system-distribution-guidelines.en.html) that establish when a Linux distribution is a Free system.

> *This means these distros will include, and propose, exclusively free software. They will reject nonfree applications, nonfree programming platforms, nonfree drivers, nonfree firmware "blobs," nonfree games, and any other nonfree software, as well as nonfree manuals or documentation.*

### Free Software Foundation: About Free Linux Distributions

There are a few distros that embrace these guidelines and thus are endorsed by the FSF. If you want to support these guidelines, you may want to choose one of those distros. But I must advise you that in this case (when not?) freedom comes with a price, and you are probably going to be very restricted in the hardware that you can use. The major problem here is with graphic cards, network cards, and printers.

Some of the distros endorsed as Free by the FSF are Trisquel, gNewSense, Dynebolic, and Parabola. You can get the complete list at www.gnu.org/distros/free-distros.en.html.

# Live CD

A Linux Live CD is a Linux distro contained on a CD-ROM (or DVD) that can be booted and run as if was installed on the system but without writing anything to the hard disk. There are three main reasons why you would want to use a Linux distro in a Live CD:

- To test a Linux distro without installing it.

- To use it like a rescue tool to recover a system. There are Live CD distros that specialize in this approach.

- For anonymity/security reasons. A Live CD does not leave any footprint in the system and you can be sure that the distro was not altered (e.g. trojans) because of the only-read medium. Distros like Tails are a perfect example of this use-case.

Not all distros have a Live CD version, but Ubuntu, Fedora, Mageia, Debian, OpenSUSE, and Mint do. Laptops and workstations often lack a DVD reader these days, so these Live CDs are also usually available as an image to install on a USB flash drive and boot from it.

# Professional Certification

Some commercial distros have a program to certificate professionals with the necessary skills to perform administrative and engineering tasks on their operating systems. There are also certifications offered by third parties that are not linked to any distribution of Linux in particular. A Linux professional certification is often a mandatory requirement to work in companies with a Linux infrastructure, so it could be a good investment for any System Administrator that wants to works with Linux installations.

There are currently five major Linux certifications, three tied to a specific distro and the others not (Ubuntu offered one in the past, but was discontinued in 2010):

- LPIC by the Linux Professional Institute is a very well recognized certification not linked to any distro, but their exams and questions are based both in Red Hat and Debian. They currently offer three levels of certification:

  - LPIC 1: Linux Server Professional - Junior Level. It requires you to pass two exams: 101 and 102.

  - LPIC 2: Linux Server Professional - Advanced Level. It also has two exams (201 and 202) and requires you to have a LPIC 1 Certification.

  - LPIC 3: Linux Server Professional - Senior Level. It consists of one exam from one of the three available specializations:

    - 300: Mixed environment (Linux and Windows)

    - 303: Security

    - 304: Virtualization and High Availability

- Linux Certification by the Linux Foundation. The Linux Foundation recently began to offer two different certifications (these certifications are based on CentOS (Red Hat), Ubuntu, and openSUSE):
    - Linux Foundation Certified System Administrator (LFCS) - Advanced Level
    - Linux Foundation Certified Engineer (LFCE) - Senior Level
- Novell offers certifications to administer systems with SUSE Linux. The current Novell certifications are the following (each one of them requires one exam):
    - SUSE Certified Linux Administrator (CLA) - Junior Level
    - SUSE Certified Linux Professional (CLP) - Advanced Level
    - SUSE Certified Linux Engineer 11 (CLE) - Senior Level
- Red Hat has three levels of certifications to qualify as an expert system administrator of their distro. This is the most recognized Linux certification (and one of the most in all of the IT world qualifications too) and their owners are in much demand.
    - Red Hat Certified Systems Administrator (RHCSA) - Advanced Level. It requires one exam.
    - Red Hat Certified Engineer (RHCE) - Senior Level. It requires one exam.
    - Red Hat Certified Architect (RHCA) - Master Level. It requires five exams from within nine different specializations.
- Oracle, which has a Linux distro that was originally a fork of Red Hat, offers their own certification programs at two levels: OCA and OCP.

As an IT professional, you should pursue any of these certifications and therefore choose any of the distros involved in one of these certifications. As a company IT manager, you may want to find a Linux professional that has one of these qualifications to be sure of her competence. Earning these certifications can be expensive (about $4,000 for the RHCA exams) and can require a high level of experience. The most valuable certifications are the Red Hat and LFC ones because they are hands-on exams based on real experience, not just theory.

# Linux Standard Base

By now you should realize that not all Linux distros are equal. Obviously they have a lot in common, but at the same time they have many particularities that make them different from each other. In order to make this "mess" something bearable and manageable to software developers (and ultimately the users), the LSB[1] was created.

The Linux Standard Base is a project supported by several Linux distros that aims to offer some common ground between the different distributions. It provides standards for things like the file system hierarchy, libraries, printing system, run levels, and so on.

---

[1] www.linuxfoundation.org/collaborate/workgroups/lsb

*The goal of the LSB is to develop and promote a set of open standards that will increase compatibility among Linux distributions and enable software applications to run on any compliant system even in binary form. In addition, the LSB will help coordinate efforts to recruit software vendors to port and write products for Linux Operating Systems.*

The project originated in 2001 and the current version of its standards is 5.0. But its impact is very small; only a few Linux distros follow it, like the commercial ones: Red Hat, SUSE and Ubuntu. So it is currently only a beautiful idea embraced by a small percentage of all Linux distributions. Also, it has been criticized by some distros like Debian over some controversial decisions. As always, Linux gives you freedom at the cost of its big diversity.

# Summary

In this chapter, I showed you several factors that you should consider before choose any Linux distro. Use the factors that most concern you to compare distros. Also, a cruel reality was revealed to you in this chapter: not only is there a huge number of distros, but they are very different. And although there are some people working to "unify" Linux, there is still a long, long way to go. Maybe there is no need to unify Linux; maybe things like containers, Nix, and systemd are going to make that unnecessary in the future.

In the next chapter, I introduce you to the genealogy of the current "families" of distros.

# CHAPTER 3

■ ■ ■

# The Linux Distro Family Tree

The first Linux distributions were created from scratch, having only the Linux kernel and a bunch of dispersed tools (like the GNU Project ones) with which to work. It was necessary to create a series of new tools and scripts to compose what we consider a Linux distro. Over time they would become more sophisticated, advanced, and useful, but the very first distros were created in this way, from zero.

But once there were some distros that were good enough, and because some of them were Free Software, it began to make sense to create new distros based on these early ones, rather than going through all of the work to recreate the required nuts-and-bolts software. Thus, soon there were new distros based on prior ones, but with various tweaks to achieve the goal(s) of the creators. As with the kernel, the user communities and the free licenses allowed for the fast adoption of this model.

This model is still the most used, and it has given birth to a series of "families" of Linux distros. In fact, only a few Linux distros are created and maintained based on the original approach from the kernel. The majority of distros today are derived from ones that existed before, sometimes from the "original" ones and sometimes from ones that were derivatives themselves.

The reasons to create derivatives are obvious:

- You already like most of a specific Linux distro, but you want to change some things. The best way to do this is to create a fork of the distro and make the changes you need. If you maintain synced all of the things that you left intact, it helps to develop your distro through the years.

- You have a different or personal view of what a Linux distro should be, and you want to create a personal distro, but you (or your team) do not have enough resources to perform all of the necessary work. Taking a previous distribution and selecting what fits your project is an excellent starting point.

- You want to create a task-oriented distribution but you don't want to deal with the hard work that creating an entire distro from scratch entails, so you pick a distro that you like because most of the job is already done.

Sometimes forks originated within the distro's community itself because of a difference of opinion or irreconcilable disagreements between members. There are some famous examples of this in the history of Linux distros.

© Jose Dieguez Castro 2016
J. Dieguez Castro, *Introducing Linux Distros*, DOI 10.1007/978-1-4842-1392-6_3

# Linux Distro Genealogy

In this chapter, I want to give you a brief idea of how the Linux distro genealogy evolved from the time of the birth of the Linux kernel itself. You can see the popularity of a distro by how many forks it has or how old it is. Also, the genealogy explains why some distros do the things the way they do. I don't pretend to include all of the current distros; that would be an astounding task and, except from an academic point of view, not a great help; it might even be boring and confusing.

I have divided this genealogy into three periods to help you assimilate the information, and I created three graphical timelines to show a quick view of this evolution. In those graphics, the distros are represented as originals or as derivatives. Some of the distros that were created as a fork of one may switch over time to a completely original approach or become based on a distro different from the original one. The same happens with names; I use the current name (or the last one, if it has been discontinued), but sometimes the name changed more than once during its lifetime. The date you see is the date of the first release of each distribution; I do not list the end date of the distribution for the sake of clarity.

Also, I don't get into a detail discussion on every distro because this would be pointless given the quantity of distros. Some distros did not have a significant impact on history or were not different enough to rate discussion. As for the historical distros, there is so little information available. Profound research into this topic is beyond the goal of this book and not my intention anyway.

By the way, there is very little information (and it is often contradictory) about the history of Linux and the distros in particular. Somebody should take up the torch, do the research, and publish it[1].

Let's begin with the early Linux distro timeline shown in Figure 3-1.

---

[1]I only know about one book onto this topic, *Rebel Code: Linux and the Open Source Revolution* by Glyn Moody for Basic Books, but it only cover in detail the first years of Linux.

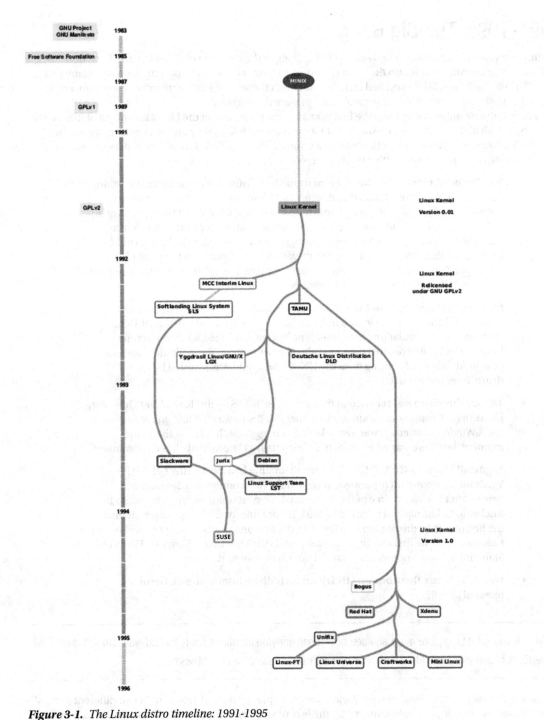

**Figure 3-1.** *The Linux distro timeline: 1991-1995*

# 1991-1995: The Big Bang

The first five years of Linux history represents the Big Bang in the Universe of Linux Distros, from none to the first ones appearing. This is also the crucial time when four of the most important distros in history were born: Debian, Slackware, SUSE, and Red Hat. And although there were some derivatives even then, this is the period when distros based on an original concept were the majority.

The first distros appeared in 1992, the first year after the beginning of the Linux kernel. All of them were pioneers, and all of them are extinct today. The first distros were released by one or two developers. They were the foundation of the main four (Debian, Slackware, SUSE, and Red Hat), either as derivatives or as a source of inspiration. Let's learn a little about these pioneers.

- **MCC Interim Linux**: This was not exactly the first distro to try to achieve something similar to the goals of a Linux distribution, but it's the first one that we can name properly as a Linux distribution. It was released in February of 1992 at the University of Manchester (England), more specifically at the Manchester Computer Centre, hence the name. A set of end-user and programming tools plus the kernel could be installed through a primitive menu-driven installer. Thanks to the work of its developer, Owen Le Blanc, non-experts in Linux could install the OS in their systems for the first time. It is currently discontinued.

- **Softlanding Linux System (SLS)**: This name is very representative of the intentions of the first distros. It was released by Peter McDonald in Canada in May of 1992. It was the most popular one for a brief time but was criticized for its numerous bugs. It was the first distro to use a graphical environment, the X Window System (still used today and coming from the UNIX world) and was inspired by the MCC distro. It ceased to exist.

- **TAMU**: This distro was released at the same time as SLS by the Texas A&M University Linux Users Group. Some sources claim that this distro was the first one to include the X Windows System. It was also, like SLS, a buggy one. It is not active at the moment, but there was an attempt to resuscitate it as late as 2010. It is discontinued.

- **Yggdrasil Linux/GNU/X (LGX)**: The first distro that had a company behind it, Yggdrasil Computer Incorporated, making it the first commercial distro. It was named after the World Tree of the Norse mythology. It was developed by Adam J. Ritcher in California and released in 1995. It's notable for three big achievements: it's the first one to be distributed as a Live CD, the first one to auto-configure and detect hardware, and the first one that was compatible with the UNIX Filesytem Hierarchy Standard. It's also another one that did not survive those days.

- **Deustche Linux Distribution (DLD)**: An early distro from Stuttgart, Germany, released in 1992.

---

■ **Tip** If you want to explore more and see how those early distributions really looked, you can still download old versions of some of them at `www.oldlinux.org/Linux.old/distributions/`.

---

Now let's look at the big four. Almost at the same time (the summer of 1993) but in two different parts of United States, two developers, both annoyed by the lack of stability of the SLS distro, had the same idea: to begin their own distribution.

- **Slackware**: Created by Patrick Volkerding in 1993 and originally a fork of the SLS distribution, it is the oldest distro still maintained actively. Perhaps with the intention of avoiding the errors of SLS, this distro focused on stability and simplicity. It was created with no further intentions and even its name was based on a joke, but is the most mature, one of the most popular, and the basis for another big distro. It was the first one that was really popular. It is probably the most representative of how those early distros were at that time, because of its conservative nature.

- **Debian**: Ian Murdock created this distro in 1993 and named it after his then-girlfriend, Deborah, and himself. It was originally inspired by SLS but it was not a fork. Its big contribution was the Debian Manifesto, which was included very early in the first release and was aimed at maintaining and developing the distro in a free and open way, like Linux, creating the first Linux distro community. This idea is still at the core of the distro and it continues to have strong values about freedom and sharing through the Debian Social Contract. Over time it would become one of the most forked distro in history.

Not too much later the other two big ones were born:

- **SUSE**: A German distribution, still active, that was first released in September of 1992. The first big, commercial one, SUSE was one of the most used distros in Europe for a long time. It was based originally on Slackware but soon it began its own distro based on another one, Jurix (now discontinued), also a German distro.

- **Red Hat**: Red Hat started by selling Linux and UNIX software accessories, and then it released its own distro in 1994. It was the big commercial one in United States (as SUSE was in Europe) and is still the most important distro in the USA, and also worldwide. It was the first to adopt the RPM package management system, based on a previous development in the Bogus distro.

The middle era in Linux distribution history is explained in the next section. I have split it into two groups visually, Figures 3-2 and 3-3.

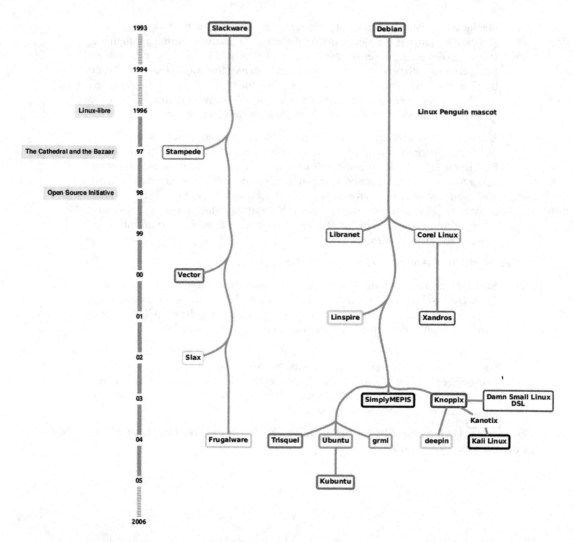

*Figure 3-2.* *The Linux distro timeline: 1996-2005, Part I*

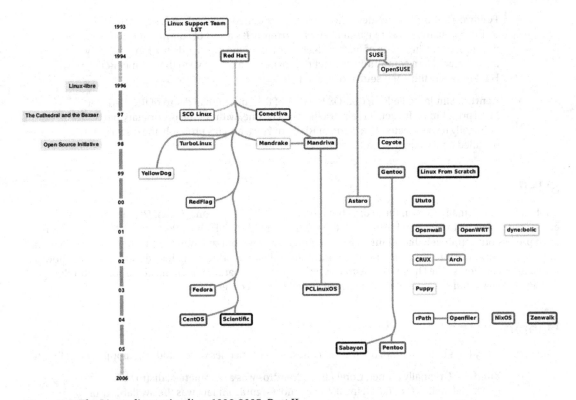

*Figure 3-3. The Linux distros timeline: 1996-2005, Part II*

# 1996-2005: The Expansion of the Linux Universe

The period of 1996-2005 is characterized by the crowning of the big four as the most popular distros and the expansion of their family trees. This is the era in which the fork mode was popularized, and the big four were the most forked ones, especially Red Hat and Debian. It's also notable as the time when three distros, which would become the source of many forks, were born: Gentoo, Arch, and Ubuntu.

## Red Hat

One of the most popular distros in this era is also one of the most forked. Some of the most relevant distros based on Red Hat (RH) are

- **SCO**: Originally named Caldera, it was the first distro fully oriented to the corporate world. It was based on the German LST distro but also much inspired by Red Hat. It's not properly a fork of RH, but it adopted much of RH's solutions. It showed other distros how to be an alternative to the corporate desktop, making it very popular for years. It's currently defunct.

- **Mandriva**: A French distro released in 1998, Mandriva was very popular in Europe and was considered very friendly and easy to install and manage. It was greatly used as an alternative to the Windows desktop. It is currently discontinued.

- **Fedora**: The community-developed alternative to Red Hat, Fedora is supported by the company. It was released in 2003. Currently it's a sort of community lab for developing/testing some of the new technologies of the mother distro, but originally it was created as a community project to provide an alternative to the defunct Red Hat Linux, the full open source distro of RH.

- **CentOS**: Similar to Fedora, CentOS is a fork of the commercial distro of RH, Red Hat Enterprise Linux. In fact, it is almost like the last one, without the proprietary parts. Originally it was created as a clone of RHEL in 2004, and it's probably the distro most installed on corporate servers around the world.

## SUSE

SUSE did not have many forks in these days but it had a very significant one, OpenSUSE, which is the equivalent of Fedora in Red Hat. It was really the successor of the SUSE Linux Personal distro. SUSE was the most professional approach that a Linux distro had in those days, but that implied that much of the code was private and only available as free after a few months, that affected seriously on his adoption and therefore a small number of forks. The OpenSuse distro was a change of that paradigm and it gained some popularity through the years, but never enough to be a rival of Red Hat and other distros.

## Debian

Debian had many forks in this period, but the three most significant ones were Xandros, Knoppix, and Ubuntu.

- **Xandros:** Originally named Corel Linux, Xandros was a commercial distro based on Debian and first released in 1999. The most significant fact was the availability of Corel WordPerfect Office on Linux. It was a clearly an attempt by Corel to compete with the Windows/Office duo. It's discontinued.

- **Knoppix:** This is a German Live CD/DVD distro that was distributed with many computer magazines, a popular trend at the time. It was released in 2000 and soon become very popular because of its approach. Given that it didn't need to be installed to run/test it, it was tested and used by many users that were new to Linux.

- **Ubuntu:** Clearly the big revolution of this era, Ubuntu was the distro that helped the most to popularize the Linux OS. To a great number of people it is a synonym for Linux. It was the most forked one of this era and still is. Originally released as a Debian fork in 2004, many Debian users switched to it.

## Originals

This period also had some new, original distros, and some of them would become very popular years later and the base of many forks.

- **Gentoo**: It was released in 1999 by Daniel Robbins. Its goal was to create a distro without precompiled binaries that could be specifically tuned to the current hardware and tailored by the user's needs. Advanced users received this new distro very well.

- **Linux from Scratch (LFS):** This was never a popular distro, but its unique approach made it a significant input in this era. It is not properly a Linux distro; instead it is a kit to make your own Linux distro. It was originally released in 1999.

- **Arch**: Inspired by CRUX (another distro of this period), Arch became very popular among advanced users and was later a base for many forks. Its goals were minimalism and simplicity as well as power and the ability to stay up-to-date. It was released in March 2002.

- **NixOS**: A distro built around a revolutionary package manager, Nix, it is still a state-of-the-art distro. It was not well known, and it is without forks, but it still was a significant event of that era.

## Slackware

Slackware continued to have fans who were very loyal to the distro, but it was not as popular as Debian or Red Hat. It had some forks, like Slax and Vector, but far less than the number of forks from Debian/Red Hat.

Figures 3-4 and 3-5 show the last period in the history timeline of Linux distros. This period is explained in the next section.

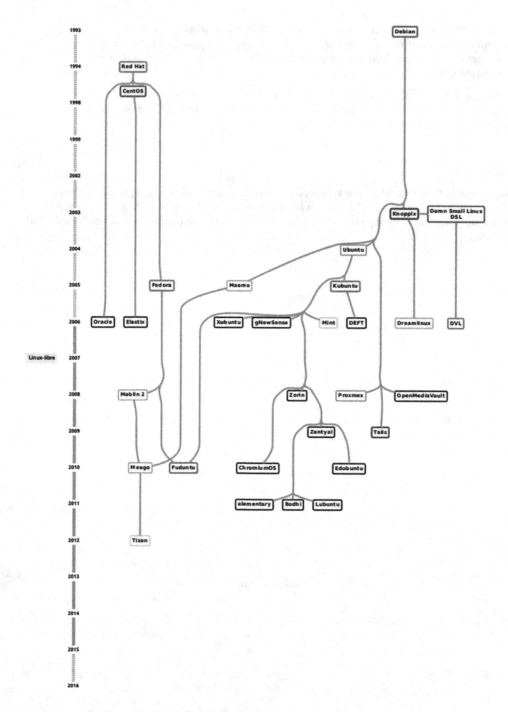

***Figure 3-4.*** *The Linux distro timeline: 2005-2015, Part I*

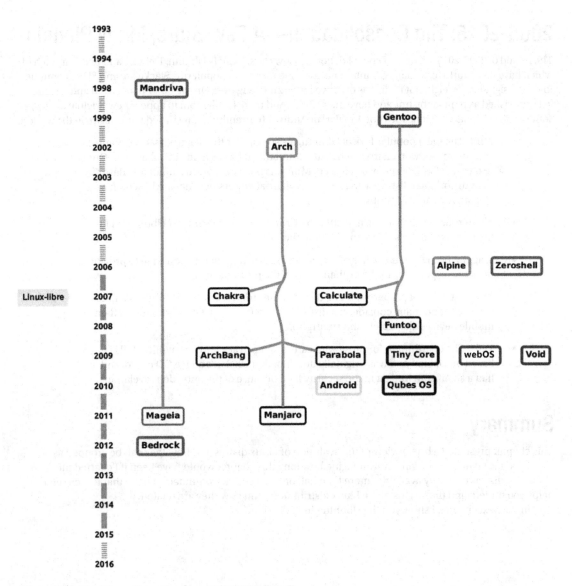

*Figure 3-5.* *The Linux distro timeline: 2005-2015, Part II*

# 2006-2015: The Consolidation—A Few Stars, Many Planets

The period of 2006-2015 is a time of consolidation of a few stars, namely Ubuntu, Debian, and Red Hat, each of which have many forks (especially Ubuntu) and continue to grow in popularity. Slackware and SUSE continue to have a significant weight but their eras of active forking are long over. On the other hand, Arch and Gentoo get established as popular distros and have many forks. And there is still room to appear new original distros, some as revolutionary as QubesOS (not popular) or Android (currently the most-used Linux distro in the world).

- **Mint**: The most popular fork of Ubuntu, it's so popular that it surpassed the fame of Ubuntu recently on distrowatch (but I doubt that it has as many installations). Only two years after Ubuntu was released, Mint was born to provide a different "flavor" than the original distro. Currently, it has alternative versions that are based on Debian instead of Ubuntu.

- **elementary OS**: It was born in 2011 to provide a nicer and simpler Ubuntu. In fact, the origins of the distro are in a Gnome theme.

- **Mageia**: Born from the ashes of Mandriva in 2010, its goal is to continue to provide the same experience to the orphan users of the previous distro.

- **Android**: It is not properly a Linux distro in the strictest definition, but it is a Linux-based OS, and many consider it a distro. It was released in 2008 and is focused on mobile devices like tablets and smartphones.

- **Tails**: The distribution for those who care about privacy and anonymity, Tails is based on Debian and was originally developed in 2009. It's a Live CD distro, and it had a significant impact in the security field because of the Snowden revelations.

# Summary

This chapter presented a brief review of the evolution of Linux distros and how they can be grouped as "families" based on their origins. Now imagine how long this chapter would have been if I charted the about 700 distros currently available (more than half of which are discontinued). I hope that this chapter helps you understand the origins of the Linux distributions and how they are related.

In the next chapter, I show you the Ubuntu Linux distribution.

■ ■ ■

# PART 2

# General Purpose Distros

In this part of the book, I cover ten Linux distributions in detail. All of these are general-purpose distributions, which is the most common type. This is the core of the book; these chapters give you a better perspective on each distro and provide a good demonstration of how one distro compares to another. These chapters also provide real-world examples of the crucial decision points presented in Chapter 2. Plus, these chapters save you a lot of time testing distros in order to pick the right one for you.

The following chapters provide a brief description of each of the distros as well as some of the history and philosophy of them. You also learn how to install a Linux distro, maintain it, and discover its pros and cons. Finally, I include a brief compilation of all of these points for each particular distro.

## Why Only These Particular Distros?

I cannot analyze in detail all of the available Linux distributions if I want to keep this book at a reasonable length and price. Thus I had to be selective: I chose to cover the main distributions in depth, but I also wanted to show you a wide spectrum of what is available. To that end, I picked the popular distros plus two advanced ones and even one "experimental" distribution. The Linux distributions covered in detail in this book are (in order):

1. Ubuntu
2. Fedora
3. Debian
4. OpenSUSE
5. Mint
6. Mageia
7. elementary OS
8. Arch
9. Gentoo
10. Slackware
11. NixOS

After covering these distributions, I dedicate one additional chapter to some of the other distros in a summary fashion; the idea here is to give you a glimpse of these distributions without going into the amount of detail provided on the others.

■ ■ ■

# CHAPTER 4

# Ubuntu

Ubuntu is one of the most famous Linux distributions (and the most used, too), so it's probably the first one to come to mind among people who are not advanced Linux users. In fact, many people think Linux and Ubuntu are the same thing. This is particularly remarkable because Ubuntu is a relatively recent distribution (only 11 years old as compared to its "parent" distro, Debian, which is 22 years old). Obviously, Ubuntu has done something very well in order to achieve such recognition. I can safely say that when it comes to Linux history, you can divide it into the era before Ubuntu and the one after it. I think this is reason enough to start my distro analysis with Ubuntu.

## History

In the mid-1990s, a South African entrepreneur named Mark Shuttleworth (see Figure 4-1) founded a digital certificate authority and Internet security company called Thawte, which would become the second largest company on the Internet (until its main rival, VeriSign, purchased it in 1999 for several hundred million dollars). Suddenly rich, Shuttleworth decided to use the money to achieve some of his dreams. After founding a non-profit organization (The Shuttleworth Foundation, or TSF), a venture capital firm (HBD for "Here Be Dragons"), and becoming one of the first space tourists (all in the first three years after the sale), he took a step in 2004 that would make him one of the most recognizable figures in the Linux world, and the catalyst of some of the actions would shape how Linux would be seen by the rest of the world in the future.

*Figure 4-1.* Mark Shuttleworth at Linuxtag 2006 at Wiesbaden, Germany

© Jose Dieguez Castro 2016

J. Dieguez Castro, *Introducing Linux Distros*, DOI 10.1007/978-1-4842-1392-6_4

As a long-time Debian user, maintainer, and developer (and general open source advocate), Shuttleworth firmly believed that Linux (as a distro) could be brought into the mainstream and thus compete with the major operating systems of the time, meaning Windows and Mac OS. He had a strong commitment to open source and Software Libre, and wanted to give back to the community, as it was the basis of his former company and its success. However, he thought that bringing big and radical changes to Debian would be a huge enterprise given its community management nature. So, the easiest and best solution was to use Debian as the base for a new distribution.

In April of 2004, he met with about a dozen developers from the Debian, GNU Arch, and GNOME projects to outline a better Linux distribution. They called themselves "the Warthogs" and in six months they would shape what would become the first Ubuntu release, the "Warty Warthog."

Shuttleworth also founded and funded Canonical Ltd., a UK-based company to provide the commercial support and services for Ubuntu. The name of the company is a clear message: they want to be the canon for all other. The name chosen for the distribution, Ubuntu, is also a statement. Ubuntu is word of Zulu origin (one of the South Africa tribes) that means "humanity to others;" it also means "I am what I am because of who we all are." This is the spirit behind Ubuntu.

Ubuntu soon won several prizes and recognition from the specialized media, and then it quickly became the most famous distro. I personally used the distro as my main OS from 2005 to 2012, and I remember it was already on the tongue of almost every advanced Linux user. Today, Canonical estimates that there are 40 million Ubuntu desktop users and counting. Ubuntu is also very prominent in the server market, especially in the cloud, where it is one of the most installed distros. Moreover, Dustin Kirkland from Canonical recently claimed that there are over a billion people using Ubuntu, both directly and indirectly, through servers, cloud instances, virtual images, phones, and so forth[1].

# Criticism and Controversy

Ubuntu has had to confront a lot of criticism and controversy. Shuttleworth and Canonical have a particular vision of the path Ubuntu must follow to be a competitor in the desktop market and other areas, and they have not hesitated to make innovations and changes that move away from the Linux and Free Software tradition of other distributions. Some users are very conservative and they do not like abrupt changes, especially if they love Ubuntu.

As a result, Ubuntu has gone from being the one of the most loved Linux distro to one of the most criticized, and it has lost many users. I suppose this is the price you pay when you are the king of the desktop Linux distributions. I feel that in the past few years, since the decision to make Ubuntu a ubiquitous distro in search of convergence, it seems to have lost its way a little. I hope that in the future Ubuntu gets back to being the amazing and revolutionary distro that changed the Linux world forever.

# Philosophy

The original philosophy of Ubuntu was to create the best Linux distro available, and to compete with the other major actors in the OS arena: Windows and OS X. Today the philosophy has not changed too much, but these days Canonical wants to conquer the desktop and server markets as well as mobile devices, the cloud, and the Internet of Things. Ubuntu wants to be everywhere and to be the best.

Originally Canonical wanted to offer a distro that was easy to use, accessible, localized, and driven by the community. It also wanted to be predictable, so frequent releases were a crucial point. This is still true today, and this goal has expanded to offering a ubiquitous experience where you can have the same distribution in almost every device.

---

[1]http://insights.ubuntu.com/2015/12/22/more-people-use-ubuntu-than-anyone-actually-knows/

# Distro Selection Criteria

Now that you know its origins, let's look at how Ubuntu does against the distro selection criteria discussed in Chapter 2.

## Purpose and Environment

Ubuntu is mostly a general purpose distribution, but lately Canonical is looking to be a distro that can be installed on all types of hardware far beyond the traditional laptop/desktop arena, like mobile devices (smartphones and tablets), the cloud, servers, and the IoT (the Internet of Things, meaning electronic devices connected to the Internet). To achieve this goal, it has created different versions of the same distribution, fitted for particular tasks. Thus we can say that Ubuntu is a general purpose distro and a task-oriented one as well, depending on which flavor you use.

Currently Ubuntu has "versions" of its distribution for different environments, but not all are available for download.

- **Desktop**: This is the traditional version of the distro, which is general purpose and oriented to workstations, desktops, and laptops.

- **Server**: This version is installed in servers, so it is a task-oriented one.

- **Cloud**: Available as images for the most common public clouds such as Amazon AWS, Google Cloud, or MS Azure, this version also has a complete OpenStack product. As part of its orientation to the IoT, there is also Ubuntu Core, which can be used in cloud environments.

- **Kylin**: This is an adaptation of the desktop version for the China market and it complies with the Chinese government's procurement regulations.

- **Phone (Mobile)**: This version is not available for download from the web site but it comes with some smartphones and tablets as an OEM OS. This is a recent adventure for Canonical and it is still in its first stages, so the devices available are limited.

## Support

Ubuntu is a well-supported distribution, offering both commercial and community support (even when they have the same distro for both cases). For enterprises, there is Ubuntu Advantage service, which includes tools for management, automation, deployment, and assistance like Landscape (an exclusive technical library), 24/7 telephone support, and optionally an on-site dedicated Canonical support engineer. For that, you have to pay a quota annually based on your installation size. You can learn more about Ubuntu Advantage at www.ubuntu.com/management/ubuntu-advantage.

As for the free support from Canonical, you can use two resources:

- **Documentation**: https://help.ubuntu.com/

- **Technical Answer System**: https://answers.launchpad.net/ubuntu

Also, you can get free community support from various channels:

- **Wiki**: https://wiki.ubuntu.com

- **Forums**: http://ubuntuforums.org/ or http://discourse.ubuntu.com

- **Ask Ubuntu**: https://askubuntu.com

- **IRC**: https://wiki.ubuntu.com/IRC/ChannelList

- **Mailing lists**: http://community.ubuntu.com/contribute/support/mailinglists

Of course you can contribute to the community and give back as much as you want/can to help to sustain it at http://community.ubuntu.com. Ubuntu is so widely used that you can also contact and participate in one of the many local communities (LoCo) all around the world; go to http://community. ubuntu.com/help-information/meeting-other-ubuntu-users/local-communities.

This level of support, huge not only in size and means also in quality, is something that you cannot find in other distributions. This is one of the strongest points about Ubuntu.

## User Friendliness

User friendliness was always a core goal of the distribution. Ubuntu is a very easy-to-use Linux distro; it is especially recommended for newcomers to the Linux world. It has its ways of doing things, and not all people like the Unity desktop environment, but once you get accustomed to it, it is very easy to use and intuitive. Also, it tries to be transparent and automate as much as possible, from hardware detection to maintenance updates. This plus the great support make it one of the distros that I recommend to beginner Linux users.

## Stability

Out of the box, Ubuntu is a very, very stable Linux distribution. You can install a normal release (not a LTS one), and use, maintain, and upgrade it without problems for several years without needing to do a fresh install. There's also the option of using a LTS release to get an extra assurance of stability and security. The LTS (long-term support) versions are oriented to those who need a headache-free OS install for their systems because they depend on it for their job or simply because they don't like to spend too much time maintaining their OS.

Canonical uses a variant of the standard release scheme for their distro. There are normal releases, with a period of six months, and there are LTS releases with a longer period (about four standard releases in two years). The standard releases have a maintenance period of nine months, after which they cease to be officially supported. The LTS releases are supported for five years, and are generally more stable because they lack experimental or partially finished functionalities. You can see a calendar and list of releases at https://wiki.ubuntu.com/Releases.

The Ubuntu releases have a double denomination of a number scheme and a codename. The number scheme is in the format YY.MM, corresponding to the year and month of the release. Usually the releases happen in the 04 and 10 months (April and October). The codename is always composed by an adjective and an animal, usually funny, like the current one, the 16.04 or "Xenial Xerus" release.

## Hardware Support

Ubuntu's hardware support is probably one of the best. The most common hardware is detected automatically; even when it is a graphic card you can usually choose between installing an open source or a private driver for it. When the hardware is not known, it is often easy to find an alternative source for a driver from the hardware's company or from the community because Ubuntu is such a popular distro; smaller distros don't usually get specific drivers made for them. And in a worst-case scenario, you can often use a Debian driver.

When a computer company decides to sell its machines with a Linux distribution as their OS by default (or optional), usually Ubuntu is the chosen one. This is true for companies as big as Dell, HP, Asus, and Lenovo to the specialized ones such as System76.

As a whole system, laptops are the most problematic hardware, but there are companies that make laptops that work particularly well with Linux, such as Lenovo, HP, and Dell. Canonical has a site and a program to certify hardware that runs without problems with Ubuntu; it's called Ubuntu certified hardware, and the site for desktops is http://www.ubuntu.com/certification/desktop.

## Aesthetics

Shuttleworth tried from the first version to create a good-looking distro, and Canonical continues this effort. The logo is a very recognizable icon in the Linux world and even outside it, and it is also a clear symbol of its principles. It is easy to see that Canonical takes care of the aesthetics in every aspect of the distro, from the web site to the distro itself. In the past, when the company freely sent CDs to your home, the CD envelope was always very well designed. The design has changed over time, and it's obvious that it continues to evolve. But this is a very subjective topic and many people don't like the color palette, which is several tones of orange and aubergine. This color palette forms part of the corporate image and it is strongly linked to Ubuntu, so it will probably never change, but it has more than one or two detractors.

## Desktop Environment

From the very beginning, Ubuntu used the Gnome desktop environment. The first derivatives, Kubuntu and Xubuntu, used KDE and Xfce for the desktop by default as the main difference. But since the 11.04 release, Ubuntu uses its own Unity desktop interface. It was conceived initially for the purpose of having a unique interface that could be used on all of the devices available (originally notebooks but now laptops, tablets, and smartphones).

The launch of Unity was a great controversy in the Ubuntu community. Many users migrated to other distros (like Mint) because they disliked the new interface. This is still a problem today. Two new official flavors, Ubuntu Gnome and Ubuntu MATE, exist only for those who love Ubuntu but hate Unity.

If you want to see all the different official flavors available, go to https://wiki.ubuntu.com/UbuntuFlavors (not all of them are based on a different desktop environment).

## Init System

Until very recently, in fact until the 15.04 release, Ubuntu used its own init system named Upstart, which was also adopted by other distros like Fedora. (Actually, in the first few years, it used the classic sysv init, System V).

But in the last releases Ubuntu decided to join to the majority of distros and adopt the new kid on the block, systemd. You could find Upstart in their penultimate LTS release (14.04) but it's now deprecated in the current LTS release (16.04).

You still can use Upstart in the last release by installing it and switching to use it permanently, but this is not something that I recommend to any non-advanced user. In the end, the future seems to be a systemd one in almost every Linux distro out there (with honorable exceptions).

## Package Management System

Because it was initially a derivative of Debian (it still depends a lot on this distribution), the package management system is the same as the one used there, dpkg. Ubuntu, of course, has its own package repositories and its own graphical tools, but it uses the classical shell tools of Debian, apt-get and aptitude. The typical user will use the graphical tool for this job, Software (actually gnome-software), but is not unusual to need to use the shell tools when you have to install a very rare package or when you want to use a PPA (you can do this graphically, too).

The PPAs (Personal Package Archive) are a unique characteristic of Ubuntu (there are similar things in some distros, but not exactly like this). They are a way to keep your own packages maintained by you in a personal repository. This is frequently used to add software that is not in the official repositories, but it is also a big source of headaches and problems when upgrading, and it could cause big security risks. You have to trust in the owner of that PPA if it is not yours and vice versa. Usually people use PPAs to run the latest versions of software not yet available in the repositories; it's a way to emulate rolling releases in a certain way, but it's wrong.

Another innovation in package management that Canonical introduced recently is Snappy; it was previously only supported in Ubuntu Core and Phone, but now is part of the Desktop versions, since the 16.04 release. Snappy is sort of a mixture of the Nix (and Guix) package managers, and the Apple OS and Android ones. Basically Snappy uses transactional updates (which can be rolled back) and atomic packages, reducing the complexity and the conflicts between packages.

## Architecture

The Desktop version of Ubuntu Linux officially supports only the 32 and 64-bit Intel/AMD architectures. The Server version offers releases for the ARM and IBM Power8 platforms. This covers the majority of use cases for the normal user, but if you need to use Ubuntu in other platforms you must rely on older or unofficial versions. Obviously tablets/smartphones that use the Phone version are supported but there it comes as a bundle item (Ubuntu as OEM).

## Security/Anonymity

Ubuntu is a reasonably secure Linux distro out of the box. It is not a paranoid-level security distro, but it uses the AppArmor security module and its defaults are enough for the majority of users. Of course, you can always make it more secure; you can install the tools and configure them, but you need to know what you are doing because you can easily make it worse. You can take some extra measures during the installation itself, like encrypting your home directory or the entire disk and always using a password (and a strong one). The official documentation offers great advice; go to `https://help.ubuntu.com/lts/serverguide/security.html`.

In fact, the major risks that an Ubuntu user could suffer in terms of security result from user behavior. Things like not using a password to log in, using a weak password, or using unofficial repositories or PPAs are the most common threats.

As for the anonymity part, Ubuntu is generally respectful in this matter, leaving it up to the users whether they send their information to the company to help to improve the distro. However, over the past few years there has been a great controversy because of the integration of Ubuntu Search with Amazon and the inclusion of a direct link to the store. Later there was an option to deactivate the Amazon search; finally, in the current release of 16.04, the online searches are deactivated by default. From a financial point of view, I suppose Amazon's financial support for this feature helped Canonical to balance its books.

## Principles and Ethics

From the beginning, Shuttleworth and Canonical had a strong sense of ethics and principles based on Software Libre and open source. The name and the logo are a strong declaration of their principles. But as the years went by, Canonical and Shuttleworth adopted a more flexible and pragmatic approach to these matters in order to achieve its main goal, to be an alternative in the desktop market and gain a bigger share of users. This flexibility meant that the distro could ship both binary and proprietary drivers for things like graphics and network cards. Also, the user was given the option of installing proprietary or even commercial software from the installation (like mp3 support) or from the Software Center.

Last year there was some criticism about how Canonical was moving away from its core community. There is some truth in this because canonical did lose a bit of focus when it shifted to making a ubiquitous OS for all types of devices. But Canonical is a company and it has to make money.

## Live CD

The desktop version of Ubuntu is also a Live DVD that you can use to test Ubuntu without needing to install it. You can also use it for security reasons, such as accessing the Internet without leaving any footprints in the system or if your current OS (for example, Windows) is infected or insecure. Advanced users can also use it to fix/repair problems with a current Ubuntu installation. Older versions usually fit onto a CD but current versions require a DVD.

## Professional Certification

In the past, Canonical offered a professional certification for their systems, but this has been discontinued. That certification was equivalent to the current LPIC-1 from the Linux Professional Institute and was a very basic one. As Ubuntu is based on Debian, there are some certifications that are generic and valid for this distro, such as the previously mentioned LPIC series or the offerings from the Linux Foundation.

# Installation

Installing this distro, or any other, is never a straight path. There are multiple options that allow you to personalize your installation to your needs or preferences. I am going to cover the most common installation for this particular distro, but I will show you other ways in other distros throughout this book, with the purpose of giving you a wider spectrum of what Linux (as a distro) is; I won't just stick to the almost automatic "push next ➤ push next" procedure.

The first thing you have to do is download an installable ISO image of the desktop version of the distro from www.ubuntu.com/download/desktop. You can also purchase a USB stick from the shop at http://shop.canonical.com, but the only option there is to get the last LTS release of the distro for 64-bit Intel/AMD architectures, as you can see in Figure 4-2.

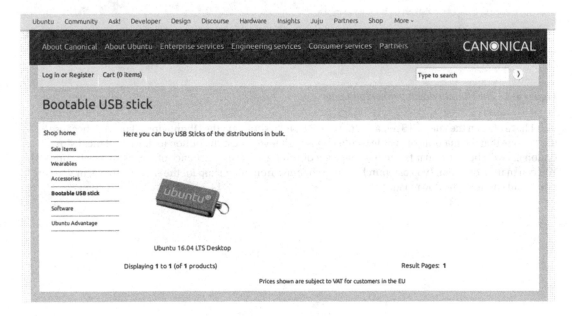

*Figure 4-2.* *The Canonical shop, where you can purchase a Ubuntu LTS release on an USB stick*

Figure 4-3 shows the download page. There are usually two main options to choose from: the latest LTS release and the latest normal release (they are called "versions" instead of "releases," but I will stick to the term "release" for consistency). If you use your computer for work or you do not need to have the latest versions of the software, I strongly recommend that you install the LTS release; in other cases, choose the latest normal release and you are good to go. At the time of writing this book, the corresponding release is the 16.04 LTS.

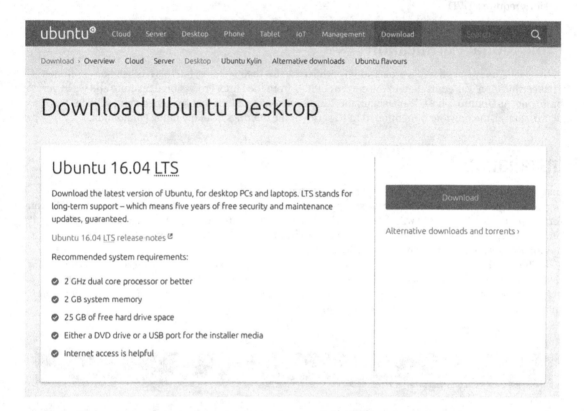

*Figure 4-3.* *The Ubuntu desktop download page*

I have chosen the latest LTS release, 16.04 for 64-bit, to show you the Ubuntu install process because it is the one that the majority of people would choose. After you press the button to download the distro, Canonical will show you an intermediate page to contribute to the maintenance of the distro (see Figure 4-4). You can make a donation (you can purchase merchandise from their shop for the same purpose) or you can skip it and continue the download.

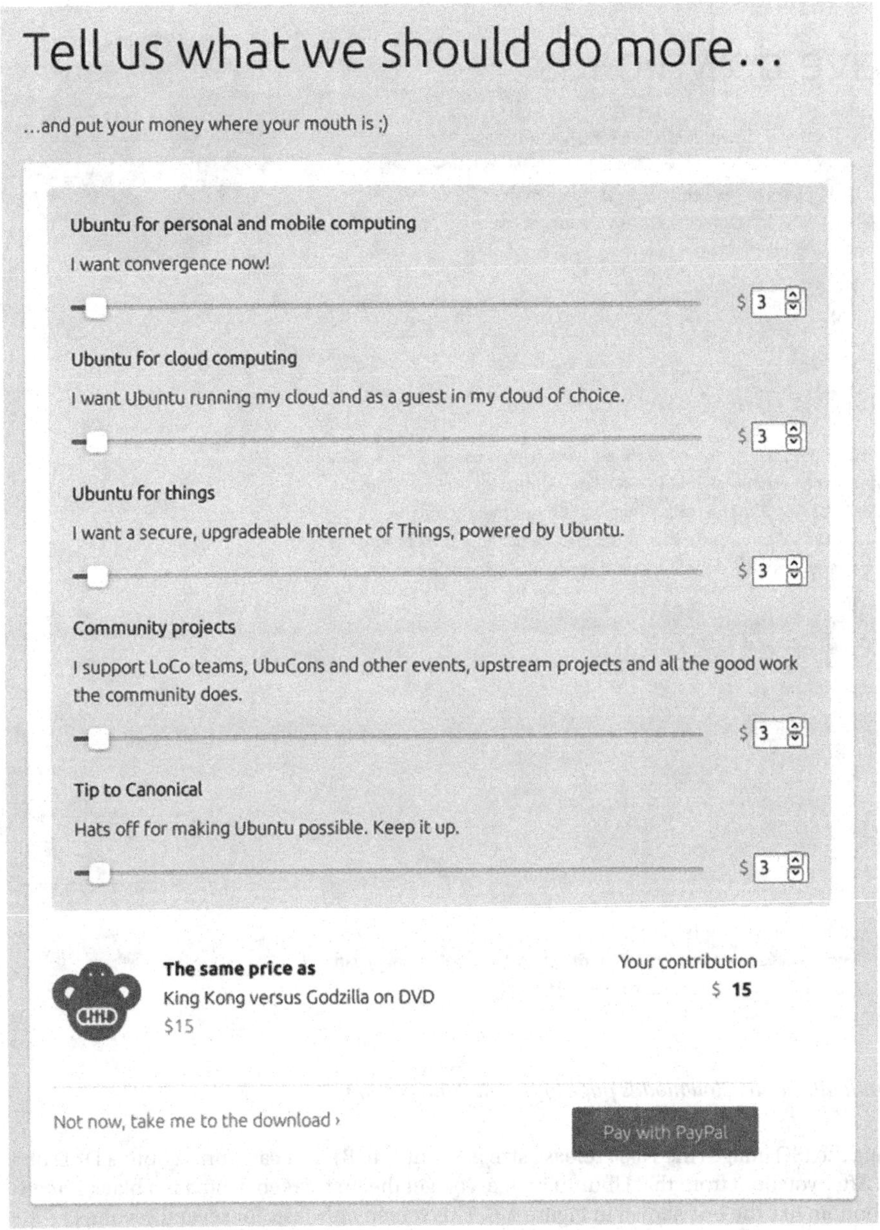

# Tell us what we should do more…

…and put your money where your mouth is ;)

Ubuntu for personal and mobile computing

I want convergence now!

$ 3

Ubuntu for cloud computing

I want Ubuntu running my cloud and as a guest in my cloud of choice.

$ 3

Ubuntu for things

I want a secure, upgradeable Internet of Things, powered by Ubuntu.

$ 3

Community projects

I support LoCo teams, UbuCons and other events, upstream projects and all the good work the community does.

$ 3

Tip to Canonical

Hats off for making Ubuntu possible. Keep it up.

$ 3

**The same price as**
King Kong versus Godzilla on DVD
$15

Your contribution
$ 15

Not now, take me to the download ›

Pay with PayPal

***Figure 4-4.*** *The intermediate page where you can donate to the project*

You can also choose an alternative download (there is a link on the download page) in case you need an older release, a network installer (to download all you need from the Internet at install time; this is only recommended for fast online connections), or you want to use the BitTorrent protocol to download the ISO image (see Figure 4-5).

# Alternative downloads

There are several other ways to get Ubuntu including torrents, which can potentially mean a quicker download, our network installer for older systems and special configurations and links to our regional DVD image mirrors for our older (and newer) releases. If you don't specifically require any of these installers, we recommend using our default installers.

## Network installer

The network installer lets you install Ubuntu over the network. This is useful, for example, if you have an old machine with a non-bootable CD-ROM or a computer that can't run the graphical interface-based installer, either because they don't meet the minimum requirements for the live CD/DVD or because they require extra configuration before the graphical desktop can be used, or if you want to install Ubuntu on a large number of computers at once.

- ✓ Download the network installer for 16.04 LTS ☑
- ✓ Download the network installer for 14.04 LTS ☑
- ✓ Download network installer for 12.04 LTS ☑

## BitTorrent

BitTorrent is a peer-to-peer download network that sometimes enables higher download speeds and more reliable downloads of large files. You will need to install a BitTorrent client on your computer in order to enable this download method.

*Figure 4-5.* *The Ubuntu alternative downloads page for the desktop version*

After downloading the ISO image (the 16.04 release size is about 1.4GB), you can burn it onto a DVD or put it on a USB drive. After you boot from that Ubuntu image, you get the first screen, which is a black screen with an image at the bottom like the one shown in Figure 4-6. This screen only lasts for several seconds.

*Figure 4-6.* *The first screen that appears in the boot process*

If your press any key in this screen before it disappears, you will jump to a screen like the one shown in Figure 4-7.

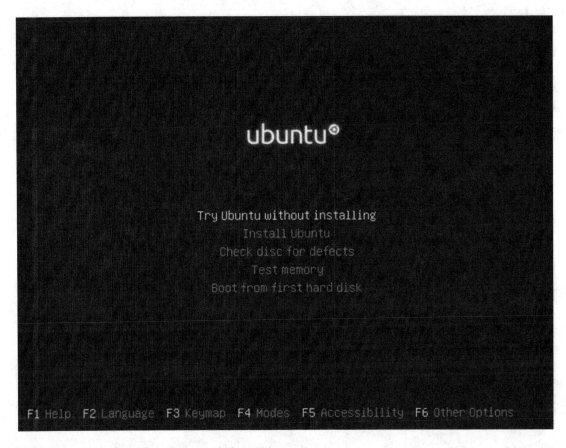

*Figure 4-7.* *The text installation menu of Ubuntu*

This screen is a text menu that allows you several options that are not available in the regular graphical installation process. It allows you to test your DVD disk or your memory, usually to diagnose some problem that happened in a previous installation attempt. But you can also set other advanced options using the function keys, as shown in the bottom menu, like making an OEM or an expert installation, or avoiding certain hardware detection problems, or changing the default language of the installation. These options are intended for intermediate/advanced users and I don't recommend trying any of them, so do not press any key in the previous screen and let's continue the booting process.

The next screen that appears is another black screen with an image in the center with an animated graph that shows you the activity while it is booting (see Figure 4-8).

*Figure 4-8.* *Image shown on the boot progress screen*

At the end of the boot process you get your first screen in the graphical environment, which is shown in Figure 4-9.

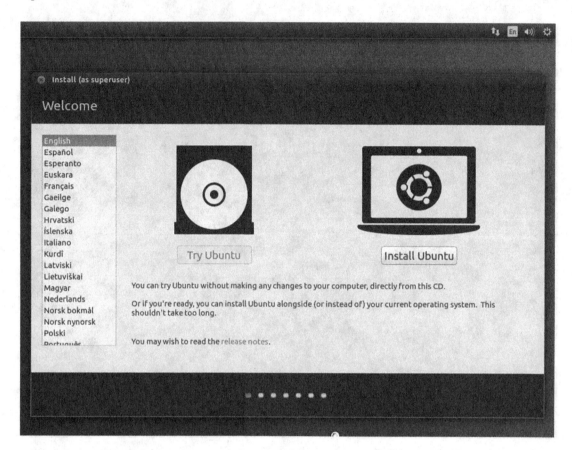

**Figure 4-9.** *The Welcome screen after booting the Ubuntu ISO image*

This screen offers two main options: "Try Ubuntu" and "Install Ubuntu." You can also set the language used in the install process. In the menu bar at the top you can also set other options (some of them are equal to the text menu I showed you before) like network or accessibility options. If you choose "Try Ubuntu" you are going to initiate a Live session of Ubuntu in which you can test a lot of things without writing anything in your hard disk, and you can always continue the install process from there. Skip that process. Instead, press the "Install Ubuntu" button.

The next screen (Figure 4-10) checks if your computer has enough disk space and a connection to the Internet. An Internet connection is not necessary to install the distro, but if you have one available and you check the option "Download updates when installing," the distro is going to install the available updated packages instead of the old ones in the ISO image. I recommend checking this option for two reasons:

- If you want to keep your Linux up-to-date (and I strongly recommend that you do so) you must spend extra time to download the packages after the installation when you make your first update anyway. So, if you're not in a hurry and you have a good Internet connection, do it now.

- If any of the updates are security updates, the first time that you boot up your new Linux and go to use the Internet you will avoid any security holes that could affect your system/data because you hadn't updated the system yet.

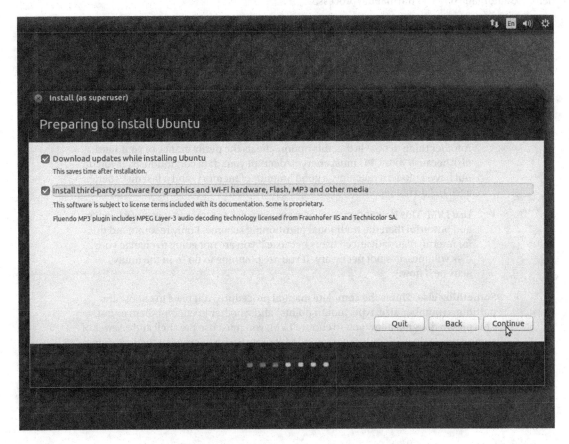

*Figure 4-10.* *The first step in the Ubuntu installation process*

After releasing a new version of the distro, even the day after, there are often new package updates. In Linux and generally in open source, it is very normal to have regular updates, even daily ones. If you use a distribution like Ubuntu perhaps you won't have updates every day, but if you use a rolling release distro you can count on one hand the days without any updates (of course it depends on the number and variety of packages that you have installed in your system).

The last option on this screen is to install proprietary software like graphics cards and wireless drivers, Adobe Flash, or the mp3 Fluendo plug-in (to allow several applications to reproduce .mp3 files). The reason why this is optional is that this software is not under a free license and some people do not agree with that. It is up to you to install it or not; however, for example, due the prevalence of the mp3 format in audio files, I chose to install the plug-in so I can play those files.

Press the Continue button. The next screen that appears is the one in Figure 4-11. This is the most complex part of the installation because you have to make a few critical decisions. Basically this part is deciding how you are going to manage your hard drive(s) to install Ubuntu. There are two main options here: the automatic one and the manual process.

- **Erase disk and install Ubuntu**. This is the automatic process. Ubuntu is going to erase your entire hard disk (and all of the data) and make new partitions with an automated calculated size. This is only recommended when installing on a fresh machine. In this option you have two other choices:

    - **Encrypt the disk**. This encrypts your entire hard disk, and only you can access its contents with a password. CAUTION! With this, if you forget your password, you lose all of your data. I only recommend this for intermediate/advanced users with experience with Linux. Also, always make backups of your data! Another thing to note is that this option affects the performance of your hard disk because your CPU must encrypt/decrypt your data continuously. If you do not have a modern machine, a good amount of memory, and a fast disk (better, a SSD), I do not recommend activating this option.

    - **Use LVM**. This is a modern way of managing disk volumes that is more flexible and powerful than the traditional partitioning scheme. I only recommend this for intermediate/advanced users because if you are not going to change your disk volumes, it is not necessary. If you are planning to do so in the future, activate it now.

- **Something else**. This is the complete manual procedure. You have to choose the partitions (number, size, type, mount points) and whether to encrypt them or not. This option does not allow you to choose LVM; you must use the shell and a series of commands to do it. It's only recommended for those who know what they are doing.

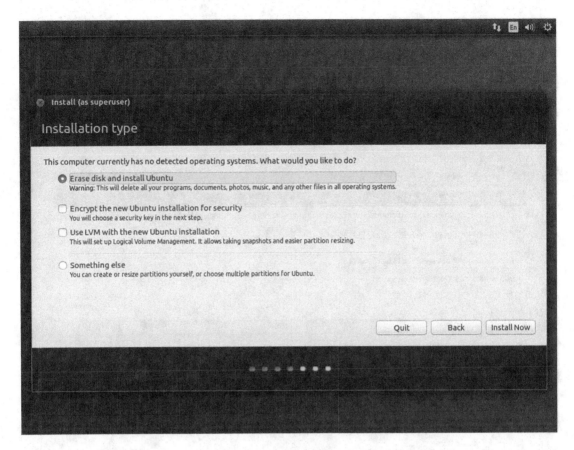

**Figure 4-11.** *The installation type screen where you choose how to manage your disk*

In this first review of a distro, my intention is to show you how easy it can be to install a new Linux distribution in a fresh system. Later, in different distros, I introduce you to other ways to install a distro, to avoid being boring and repetitive, and to show you how to do certain things in Linux. Because of that I'll skip any advanced options here.

If you press the Install Now button, it will show you a resume (Figure 4-12) of the changes that are going to be made to the hard disk(s). This operation is irreversible and that's reason enough to show you the information. Usually it will create two partitions: a root one in the ext4 format and a swap one. Because I am installing Ubuntu in a fresh system, I can press the Continue button without worry.

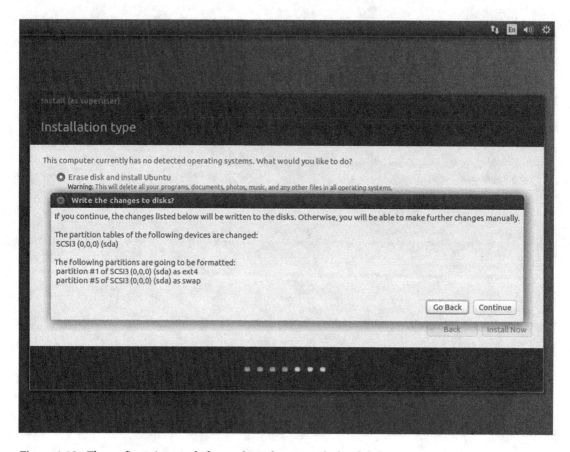

*Figure 4-12.* *The confirmation step before making changes to the hard disk*

Figure 4-13 shows an interactive map for choosing your time zone to correctly adjust the date and time. Usually Ubuntu will automatically detect your current time zone, but you can always choose it manually by navigating to the appropriate area in the map.

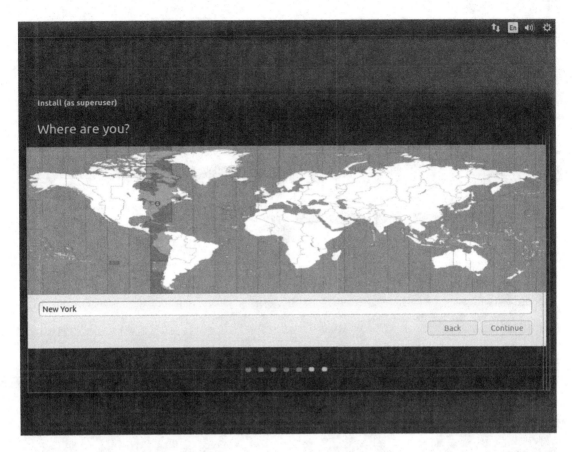

***Figure 4-13.*** *Interactive time zone selection*

After selecting your time zone and pressing the Continue button, you must choose your keyboard layout and language (Figure 4-14). Usually this is automatically detected, too. Otherwise, you can push the button to try to detect it again interactively (it is going to ask you to press some keys and maybe ask some questions) and then test the results in the interactive text field. Once you have finished, you can press the Continue button.

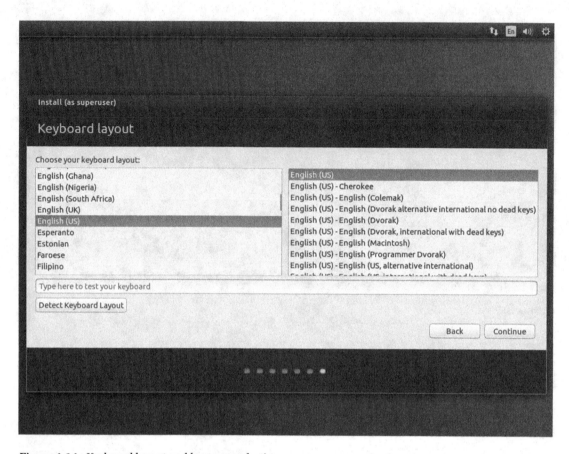

***Figure 4-14.*** *Keyboard layout and language selection screen*

Figure 4-15 shows the last screen where you have to make any decisions. You basically have to decide your name and password. Actually, I recommend deciding these things BEFORE you begin your installation. I suggest you pick a username (put your real name, if you want, in the first text field) that is easy to type in any keyboard, so avoid any non-English alphanumeric characters. If your keyboard ever breaks or your installation fails and does not detect your keyboard layout, you are going to thank me for this, believe me.

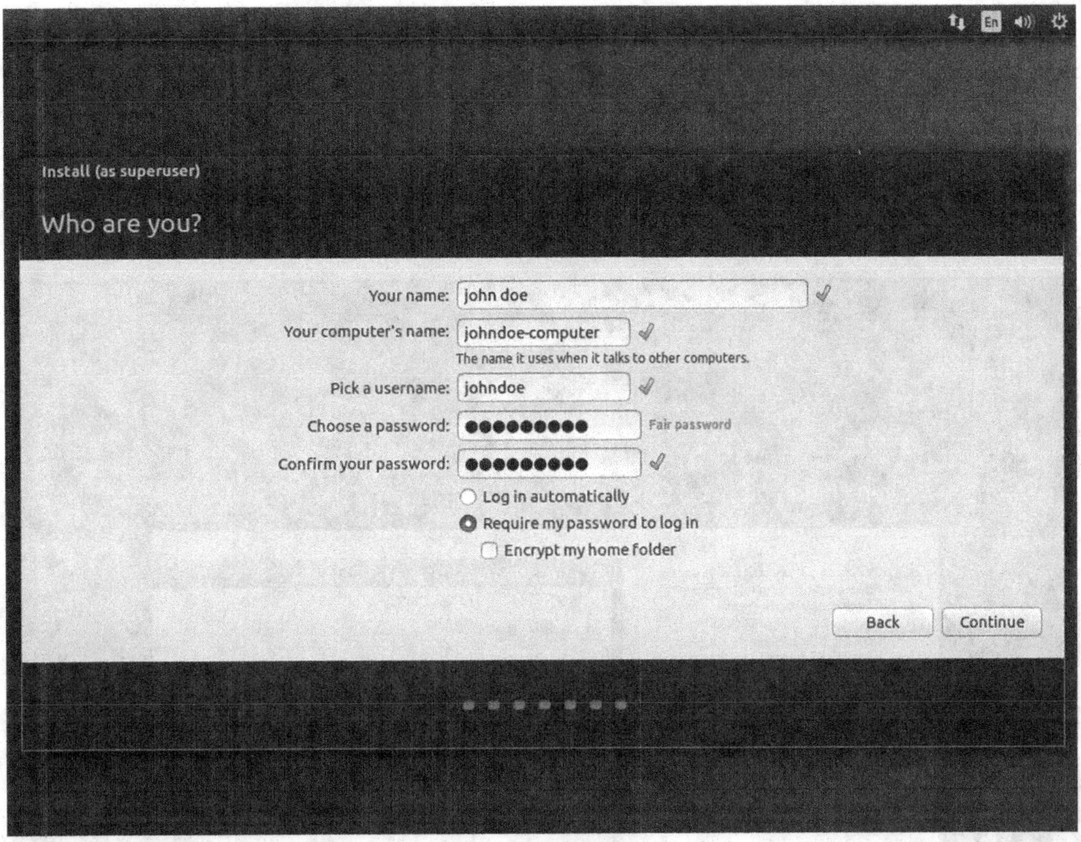

*Figure 4-15. Identity screen where you enter your user name and password*

Next you must choose a password. It's best to choose a strong one, and this means using lowercase and uppercase letters, numbers, and symbols. But there is a way to do this easily. I suggest the following: pick a sentence from a poem, a song, or a book that you like and you can remember easily. Then pick the first letter of each word, add a pair of numbers and symbols, and you have a very strong password that is easy to remember. For example, consider this famous sentence:

*O Captain! my Captain! our fearful trip is done.*

—Walt Whitman, Leaves of Grass, 1891

You can easily compose a very strong password by taking the first letter of each word, adding two different symbols to separate the different parts (make them easy to find on any keyboard), adding the first letter of the last name of the author and two numbers from the year when the poem was first published.

### Ocmcoftid.W-91

Now you have to decide if you want to log in automatically when you turn on your computer or use your password. If you are installing Ubuntu on a desktop computer that only you can access now or in the future, you can log in automatically. Likewise, if this computer is for an elderly person who may not be able to remember a password or is open to the public, you can pick this option. Otherwise, I strongly suggest against this option.

As for encrypting the home folder, I give you the same advice as with the encryption of the hard disk. And again, remember, you must always do backups periodically. (I learned by experience that you can never recommend this too many times.)

Pressing the Continue button begins the real process of the installation. The screen is now a carousel that introduces you to the possibilities of your new OS at the same time that is doing the install process (see Figure 4-16). At the bottom is a progress bar and the step where you are at the moment (in text). The amount of time this process takes depends of your computer and your Internet connection speed because it is going to download several packages from the Internet.

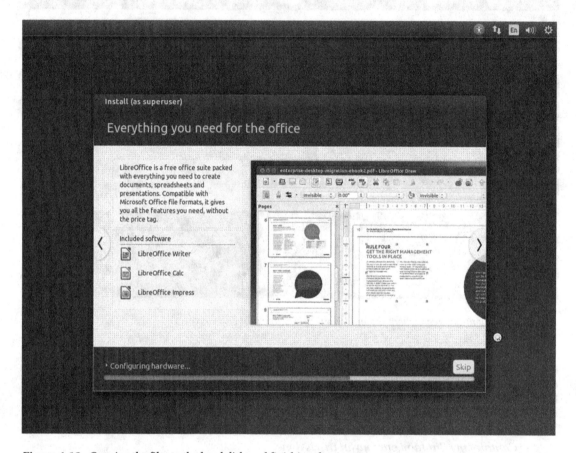

***Figure 4-16.*** *Copying the files to the hard disk and finishing the setup*

At the end of the installation of Ubuntu on your hard disk, you will see a dialog that informs you that the installation is complete and you need to restart your computer to be able to enjoy your new Ubuntu Linux OS (see Figure 4-17).

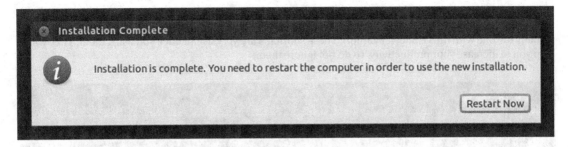

*Figure 4-17. The installation is complete. Restart your computer*

So restart your computer. After booting, the first screen that appears is the login one to start a new session (see Figure 4-18). Here you need to introduce your password (I hope that you did not forget it. You are going to need this password for every administration process). You could log in as a guest if you want to do a few things in the system (like browse the Internet or use any already installed app) but all of the data from this session will be temporary and you won't have access to your data on your hard drive. This is an ideal option, however, for any visitor to your system.

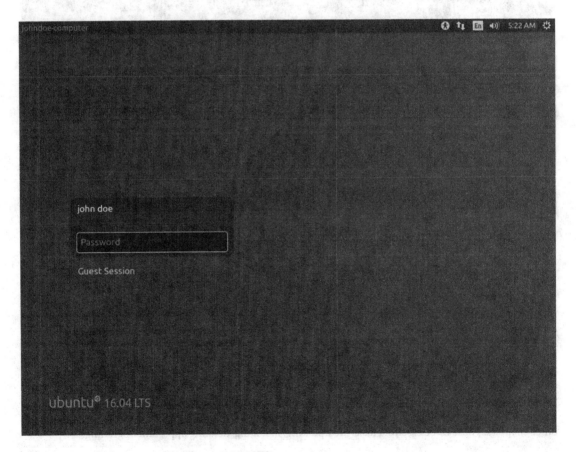

*Figure 4-18. The login screen to Ubuntu 16.04 LTS*

So enter your password. Now you can enjoy Ubuntu. The first screen you will see is a list of keyboard shortcuts (see Figure 4-19). This screen can always be shown by pressing and holding the "Super" key (usually the one with the Windows symbol). These shortcuts are very useful once you learn them. They will help you to increase your productivity, so do not ignore them.

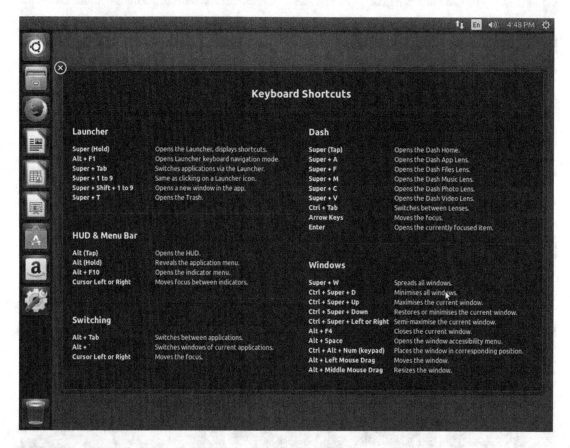

*Figure 4-19. First screen after you successfully install Ubuntu*

As you can see, the install process is very easy. Don't be swayed by those rumors that Linux can be very difficult to install and use. These days that is not true; you can install and use Linux in a very easy way, and Ubuntu is a great example. Of course, you can choose a more complicated or sophisticated one, and you can install the same Ubuntu from a text menu and in expert mode, but that is up to you and your knowledge and experience.

# Maintenance

There are three essential tasks to maintain your Linux OS, and Ubuntu makes them very easy to do. As with the install process, I'm going to show you the easy way to do these things; I'll cover the advanced options in other chapters. These three essential tasks are updating, installing/deleting apps, and upgrading.

# Updating

Usually Ubuntu will notify you when new updates are available (see Figure 4-20) and you only have to follow the steps. But if you want to manually check if new updates are available and then install them, it is very easy; you only have to execute the Software Updater application (see Figure 4-21).

*Figure 4-20.*  *Ubuntu updates notification dialog*

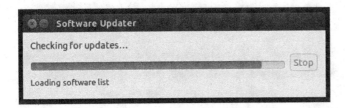

*Figure 4-21.*  *The Software Updater application checking for updates*

Usually this process won't give you any problems, but sometimes bad things happen. If you frequently tweak your OS (by following tutorials from the Internet) or use PPAs to install programs, you will probably experience problems with this process sooner or later. It is very rare that any problem will appear if you only use the graphical apps of Ubuntu and follow the established way of doing things. Bad things happen when you play with fire. If you get burned, look for help in the available ways; this is usually enough to solve any problem. From time to time, some hardware driver updates, like the graphic cards, can give you some headaches, but this is rare and usually you can reinstall a previous version.

Some LTS versions have an .x suffix where x is a number, for example in the 14.04.3 LTS release. This suffix refers to the LTS enablement stack that is available at the moment. These enablement stacks are the way that Ubuntu chooses to bring the updates to the kernel and X windows systems in the LTS releases. This is included by default in the latest ISO images of a LTS release, but if you have one already installed and want to update it to that point, you have to do it manually through commands in the shell. You can get more information about this topic at `https://wiki.ubuntu.com/Kernel/LTSEnablementStack`.

# Managing Apps

Sooner or later you are going to want to install new software or remove packages that you not use or like. To do so, Ubuntu gives you a very simple and complete app named Software, which is the official application management tool of Gnome (Figure 4-22). From it you can remove or add any application available in the official repositories, and there are many. You can also check for package updates and perform them from there.

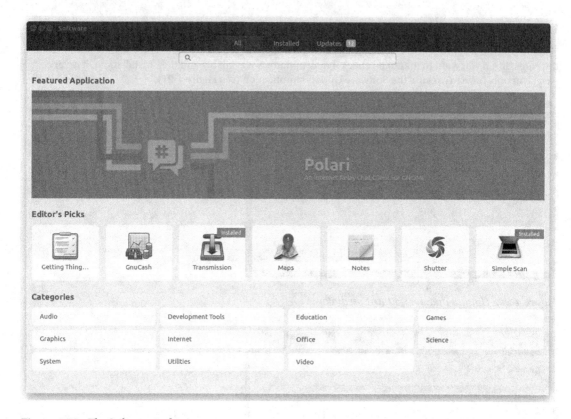

***Figure 4-22.*** *The Software tool*

The applications are organized by categories (and subcategories). If you click over to one of them, you get a detailed resume of the app and sometimes even screenshots (see Figure 4-23). The installation/removal process is very simple and intuitive.

***Figure 4-23.*** *The Software tool showing information about an application*

## Upgrading

As in the updating case, you will usually be notified when a new release is available. However, you can select the "Software & Updates ➤ Updates ➤ Notify me of a new Ubuntu version" option of the System Settings tool if you want to be notified only of a new LTS release (the default) or when a normal release is available. The application used is the same as in the update case; you can also invoke it by hand. The difference here is the duration of the task and this is more critical; you can easily end up with an unusable system if something goes wrong during this process. If you tweak your system a lot and use external PPAs, very often the upgrading process will fail at some point and you'll end up with a half-upgraded and normally non-bootable OS. Enthusiasts who like to do those things with their Linux systems normally make a fresh install of the new releases by preserving only their data (or restoring it from a backup). I recommend you always make a backup of all of your data before you upgrade your distribution to a new release.

# Pros and Cons

I'm going to list some of the things that I personally see as pros and cons of the Ubuntu distribution. Of course there is always room for discussion in this matter, but I'll do my best to be as objective as possible.

# Pros

- Ubuntu is one of the easiest to use.

- It is without a doubt the most used and installed of all of the Linux distros.

- It has great official support from the distro (and others) and a very big community willing to help you.

- It has great hardware support. And if a company only supports a few distros, Ubuntu or Debian will probably among them.

- As for applications, if they only support a few package managers, probably dpkg is going to be included.

- It offers a regular release scheme. You always know when the next release is going to be launched, which is an advantage when scheduling maintenance. LTS releases offer extra quality and stability.

- You can use Ubuntu on a smartphone or a tablet with almost the same experience as on your laptop or desktop.

# Cons

- Not everybody likes Unity. But you can always choose another flavor of Ubuntu.

- Canonical has a particular vision of Linux. The company has made things its way, and certain people do not like that.

- Sometimes Canonical introduces changes in a normal release that are immature or not well thought out. To avoid this, you can use a LTS release, but you lose the new innovations.

- If you prefer a totally free Linux distro with only free software, Ubuntu is not your distro (but there is an option in the text menu to only install free software).

- Sometimes the commercial aspects of the distribution overrule the community aspects, like the integration with Amazon.

- The big goal of creating a Linux distro available on all type of devices meant a loss of focus on the desktop and other areas. Instead of having the best distro for the desktop, they could have ended with a regular one on all of the scenarios.

- Ubuntu makes big use of the Debian distro work but it does not give back much; the same with the Linux kernel.

# Summary

I analyzed in detail here the best-known Linux distribution of all, Ubuntu, from its origins and philosophy to the installation and maintenance. The section on pros and cons and the decision criteria give you a series of arguments to compare this distro to others in a more objective way.

In the next chapter, I do the same with Fedora.

# CHAPTER 5

# Fedora

Fedora is always in the top five of the most popular Linux distributions, and part of that merit comes from its "big brother," Red Hat, which not only uses Fedora as the community edition of its distro but also uses it as a prototype for development. But it's unfair to ignore the merits of Fedora itself. It has a large and expert community. It is not a favorite of newcomers to Linux, but many experienced Linux users, developers, and systems administrators use it as their day-bay-day default distro. And because of Red Hat, although it has lately been losing traction in favor of easier to use or trendy distros, it still has great future.

## History

The Fedora Project was founded on September 22, 2003 when Red Hat decided to split Red Hat Linux into Red Hat Enterprise Linux (RHEL) and another OS based on a community, Fedora. At the same time, another distro, the Red Hat Professional Workstation, was created with the intention of filling the place RHL had once occupied but without a clear route sheet. Non-enterprise RHL users soon switched to Fedora instead. The first release of the Fedora distribution appeared on November 6 of the same year.

The Fedora name came from a former volunteer project, Fedora Linux, which made additional software; it's inspired by the hat worn by the character of the Red Hat logo (shadowman).

## Philosophy

The philosophy of Fedora is a mix between two goals: to serve as the community edition of Red Hat Enterprise Linux and to serve as a sort of laboratory for new technologies that might later be integrated into Red Hat. In fact, the new releases of Red Hat come from a stabilized, secured, and improved version of a release of Fedora (they also offer technologies and software exclusive to Red Hat). As a result, Fedora focuses on innovation and on contributing and collaborating with the Linux kernel itself. Fedora aims to be the leader of innovation and the distro that creates the path that Linux takes. Thanks to Fedora, the new init system, systemd, was widely adopted by almost every distro. Linus Torvalds uses Fedora on his computers, probably because of the tight relationship between the Fedora community and developers with the Kernel communities and core developers.

© Jose Dieguez Castro 2016
J. Dieguez Castro, *Introducing Linux Distros*, DOI 10.1007/978-1-4842-1392-6_5

# Distro Selection Criteria

Now that you know a brief history of Fedora, let's see how it fares on the selection criteria from Chapter 2.

## Purpose and Environment

Because it has the support of Red Hat, Fedora, even though it is a general purpose distro, has versions for different environments and for task-oriented purposes. Along with Ubuntu, Fedora offers the most versions/flavors available with official support.

The following are the main official versions of Fedora:

- **Workstation**: The general purpose version oriented to the desktop/workstation. This is the one that I will show you here.

- **Server**: For installing on servers, it's a task-oriented version.

- **Cloud**: To use in cloud environments, it's a specialized and minimal server version.

Like Ubuntu and its different flavors (which really only differ in their desktop environment), Fedora offers Fedora Spins, which are versions of Fedora with a DE different from the default one. You'll see them in the "Desktop Environment" section.

Fedora also offers another series of images that are made with a specific task in mind, the Fedora Labs (https://labs.fedoraproject.org). Thus, Fedora is a task-oriented distro in the following scenarios:

- **Design Suite**: Oriented to publishing, multimedia, and visual design.

- **Games**: A collection of games ready to run under Fedora.

- **Jam**: To create, edit, and produce music and audio.

- **Robotics Suite**: Packages aimed at beginners and experts in robotics.

- **Scientific**: Tools used in scientific research and numerical computing.

- **Security Lab**: For security auditing, system rescue, and forensics.

And finally, Fedora has special images for the ARM architecture, for servers and desktops. For desktops, there is the official version for that processor, and all of the Fedora Spins are available as well. For servers, there is a regular one and a minimal one (which you can think of as the Cloud equivalent, a core version). You can get all of them at https://arm.fedoraproject.org.

## Support

Fedora is reasonably well-supported distro (not as well supported as Ubuntu, but well enough). This support comes only from the community and Fedora developers; there is no commercial support for this distro. The Red Hat company sponsors Fedora but only offers commercial support for its commercial distribution, Red Hat.

Also, the Fedora community is big, but it's not as big as the Ubuntu one. However, it does not lack ways of supporting its users. The following are the channels to get help from the community:

- **Documentation**: http://docs.fedoraproject.org/

- **FAQs**: https://fedoraproject.org/wiki/FAQ

- **Wiki**: https://fedoraproject.org/wiki

- **Ask Fedora**: https://ask.fedoraproject.org/en/questions/
- **Fedora Forum**: http://fedoraforum.org/
- **Community**: http://fedoracommunity.org/
- **Mailing List**: https://lists.fedoraproject.org/mailman/listinfo/users
- **IRC**: #fedora channel at freenode

## User Friendliness

From the point of view of an Ubuntu user, you could say that Fedora is less user friendly, but from the point of view of an Arch Linux/Gentoo user, it is a very easy-to-use distro. Depending on what you want to do with it, Fedora occupies a middle point. For example, Fedora has a very good installation tool, Anaconda, which makes that process a comfortable experience. But when you need to do any administration/maintenance tasks, you need to know how to use command line tools. This was the norm for years in Linux, and is probably the same case as Debian, for example, but the truth is that there are other distros that are easier to use than Fedora.

## Stability

Although Fedora is always on the bleeding edge of technology and innovation, it is a very stable distribution. From my point of view, it is more stable than Ubuntu, if you do things in the manner intended (in other words, don't use external repos, don't tweak it too much, etc.). Fedora offers a shorter period of support for its releases than Ubuntu (13 months versus 18 months for regular releases of Ubuntu). As with Ubuntu, Fedora uses a variation of the standard release scheme; both have the same cycle for new releases; 6 months. You can learn more about the Fedora release cycle at https://fedoraproject.org/wiki/Releases.

## Hardware Support

As a result of its policy of not including private drivers, the hardware support in Fedora is not as good as in Ubuntu. However, it gets the benefits from being the community version of Red Hat, because a lot of hardware supports Red Hat. Also, a great number of companies develop drivers in the .rpm package format, which is supported in Fedora. And if you are willing to use alternative, non-official repositories for the distro, you can use various private drivers (especially graphics and network cards).

Note that using the most recent kernels helps detect new hardware supported by it. This is especially important with laptops.

## Aesthetics

Apart from the logo, colors, and backgrounds, Fedora does not make a great effort to customize the design of its distro. It ships the standard and current versions of Gnome without customizations, which is the opposite of Ubuntu, Mint, and others. If you like the out-of-the-box designs of the current DEs, you will like Fedora; otherwise you should look for customizations.

# Desktop Environment

The default and official desktop environment of Fedora is Gnome, currently version 3 of this DE. But as mentioned, the Fedora Spins provide alternatives to this in the form of available ISO images that use other DEs as defaults. Currently, the available Fedora Spins (`https://spins.fedoraproject.org`) are the following:

- **KDE Plasma**: Uses the KDE Plasma DE.

- **XFCE**: The XFCE DE is used here.

- **LXDE**: The lightweight LXDE desktop for this option.

- **MATE-COMPIZ**: Combines MATE (sort of the classical Gnome 2) with Compiz composition effects.

- **CINNAMON**: Uses the GTK3+ toolkit from Gnome 3, but with a more classical look.

- **SOAS**: Sugar on a Stick combines the Sugar Learning platform with the mobility of being able to fit on a USB drive. It is oriented as an education/learning platform.

# Init System

If the majority of the Linux distros have recently adopted the systemd init system, obviously the distro that developed it (from Red Hat developers) and first adopted it continues to use it.

# Package Management System

Fedora uses the same package management system as Red Hat, rpm, and the same tools for it. Although there is a GUI app to manage the software apps, named Software (gnome-software), the proper way to manage packages in Fedora is via the `dnf` command (formerly `yum`) in the terminal. Also there are tools to manage the `.rpm` packages directly.

The official repository (there is only one) of Fedora has an inferior number of packages compared to Debian or Ubuntu (about 5,000 packages less), and third party packages that are non-free are also absent from it. Thus, there is a tradition of external, non-official repositories that provide more packages and non-free ones. As I said in the Ubuntu chapter, this practice compromises not only the stability of the OS, but it's also a clear security risk because you must trust the repository maintainers.

Fedora benefits from the `.rpm` format from all of those companies and developers who create software that maybe not be in any repository, but is usually available in `.rpm` or `.deb` packages (or as source tarballs).

# Architecture

As with many distros, the two main Intel architectures are supported, the 32-bit version and the 64-bit version. Fedora recently announced that they are going to focus only on the 64-bit version in future releases, leaving the i686 architecture on a second plane and perhaps not synced in the release cycle. ARM is also supported.

# Security/Anonymity

Fedora has a well-deserved reputation of being one of the most secure distributions. For example, a firewall, PolicyKit, and SELinux are enabled by default, among other security features. Also, you can use encryption on all of your disk or by volume or file; Fedora is the leader in this field. See `https://fedoraproject.org/wiki/Security_Features` for more information.

On the anonymity side, you can configure those options when you first start the Gnome Initial Setup or later in the Settings app. You can decide what information is shared and what information is sent back to Fedora or Gnome.

## Principles and Ethics

Fedora has a strong focus on only using free and open source software, but that does not mean that they don't distribute private blobs (non-free binary firmware) in the kernel. Other than that, Fedora is very strict with its policy of not using proprietary software of drivers. It doesn't include the proprietary drivers of graphics cards, mp3 software, the Flash player, etc. Users who want to use some of this software normally must rely on alternative, non-official repositories. The official Fedora policy about this matter can be seen on its wiki at `https://fedoraproject.org/wiki/Forbidden_items`.

## Live CD

The ISO images of Fedora work well as Live editions of the distribution, so you can use them to start a Live session of Fedora without touching anything on your storage devices.

## Professional Certification

Fedora itself has no professional certifications, but its supporting company, Red Hat, has several of the most prestigious ones, as outlined in Chapter 2. Thus, because Fedora is the base for Red Hat, you should be able to apply the knowledge gained by passing those certification exams to Fedora without a problem.

# Installation

As stated in the previous chapter, I will deviate in this installation (and in the next ones) a bit from the "predefined" way that is given as the default workflow by the installation tool. As you will see later, this little change in Fedora doesn't make a great difference, but it does in other distros (e.g. Ubuntu).

The first step is always to download the ISO image of the distro to be able to install it. Obviously I chose the Workstation version of the distro to install here, because it is the one used by the majority of users. So go to the download page of the Fedora distribution, `https://getfedora.org/en/workstation/download/`, and you will something similar to Figure 5-1.

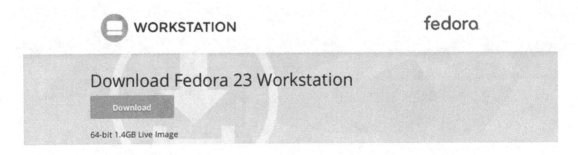

***Figure 5-1.*** *The download page of Fedora 23 Workstation*

If you click the Download button, the download begins automatically. The release at the time of writing is 23 and the default architecture is 64 bits. The current size of the image, 1.4GB, only fits on a DVD or a USB drive. If you need a different architecture, image, or flavor, you can go to the bottom of the page where you will see something similar to Figure 5-2.

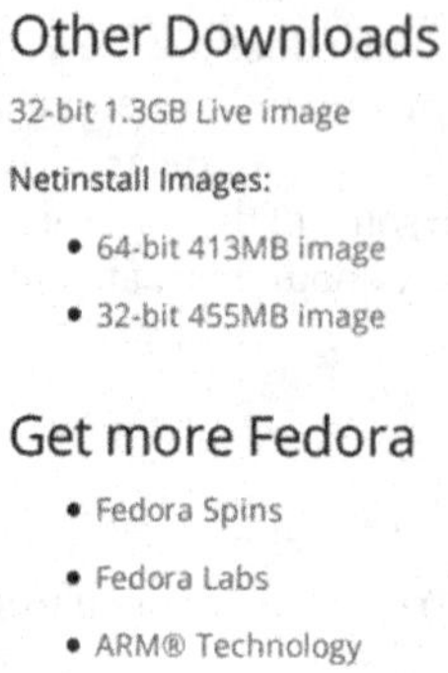

## Other Downloads

32-bit 1.3GB Live image

**Netinstall Images:**

- 64-bit 413MB image
- 32-bit 455MB image

## Get more Fedora

- Fedora Spins
- Fedora Labs
- ARM® Technology

*Figure 5-2.* *Alternatives for downloading Fedora's ISO images*

You can get the 32-bit ISO image (i686) or the netinstall images for both architectures. You can also access the Spin and Labs versions and the ARM versions. This page also links to the Fedora Wiki to locate online or local vendors that sell DVD copies of the distribution or to their Free Media Request program for those who can't afford the purchase. Another alternative is to use a BitTorrent tracker to download the ISO image. These options are at `https://torrents.fedoraproject.org/`.

Fedora provides access to the release notes (I recommend always reading these notes when upgrading to a new version) and the documentation for the installation process for that release, which is very good (`http://docs.fedoraproject.org/en-US/Fedora/23/html/Installation_Guide/`). However, you only need this guide for the very first steps of the installation process; for the rest of the steps, good documentation is available directly from the installation program.

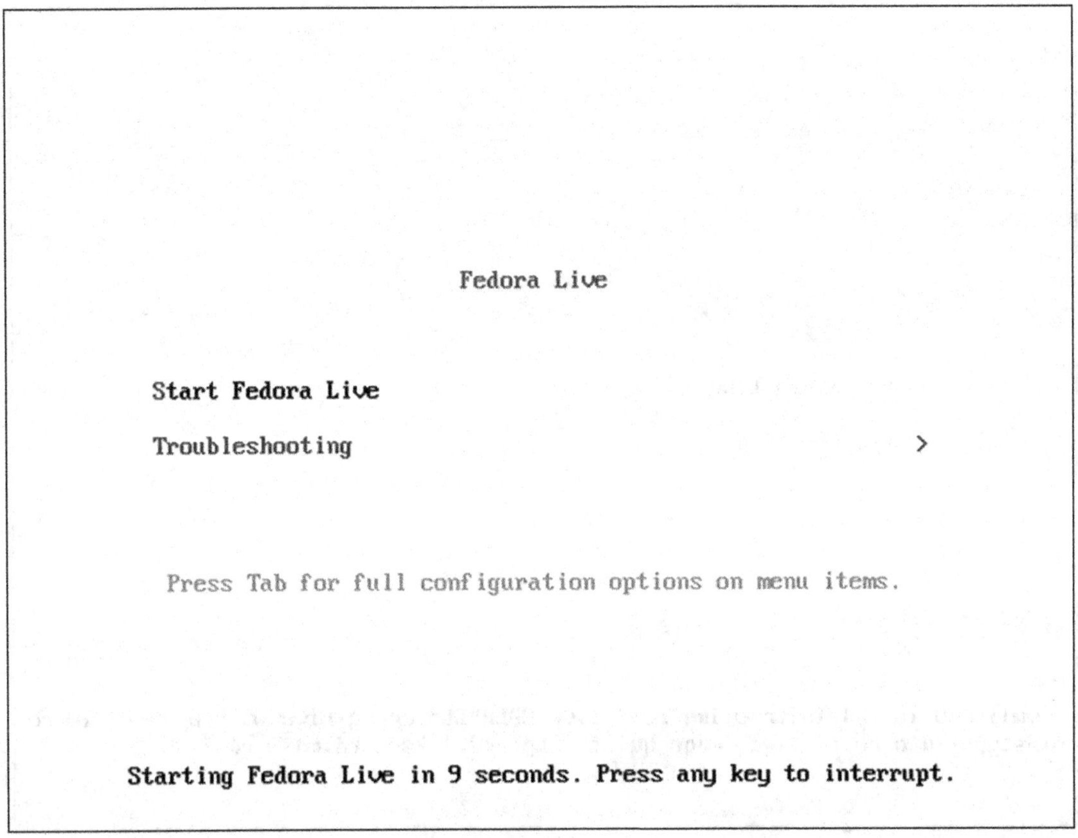

```
                          Fedora Live


      Start Fedora Live

      Troubleshooting                                           >



      Press Tab for full configuration options on menu items.




      Starting Fedora Live in 9 seconds. Press any key to interrupt.
```

**Figure 5-3.** *First screen of the Fedora installation process*

Once you have the ISO image of the distro, you can boot up your system with it for the first time. The first screen that appears is the one in the Figure 5-3; it is a classical text menu (which is common in Linux). You may think that it's less polished that the Ubuntu one, but don't let its appearance trick you. This screen only lasts 10 seconds before it starts Fedora Live automatically unless you press any key. Thus, from here you can do four meaningful things:

- Nothing. The Live version of Fedora will start after 10 seconds.

- Start Fedora Live immediately by pressing Enter.

- Press Tab to access to the configuration options, as you can see in Figure 5-4. This is for advanced users who usually customize the installation because of hardware or deployment requirements.

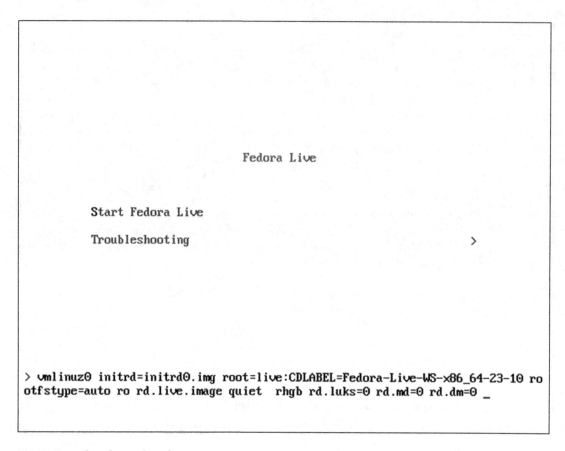

*Figure 5-4.* *The advanced configuration options of the installation boot*

- Go to the other menu option, Troubleshooting (Figure 5-5), which allows you to test your installation media or memory, or both, from your hard drive. It also allows you to start the Live version, avoiding problems with your graphics card (which is common in laptops). Do this when you experience rare things on your screen (like distortions or lines) with the default option.

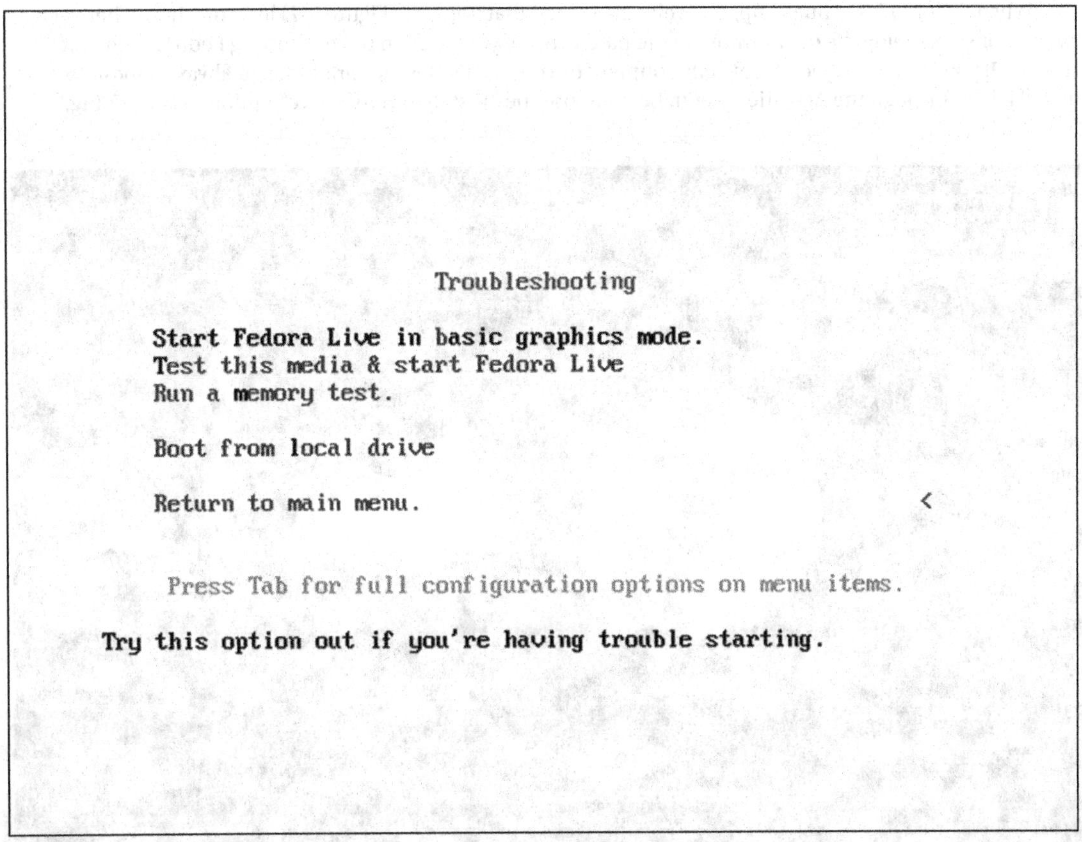

```
                        Troubleshooting

        Start Fedora Live in basic graphics mode.
        Test this media & start Fedora Live
        Run a memory test.

        Boot from local drive

        Return to main menu.                                    <


          Press Tab for full configuration options on menu items.

        Try this option out if you're having trouble starting.
```

*Figure 5-5.* *The troubleshooting menu of the Fedora Live boot process*

The obvious choice is to continue with the default option, then wait 10 seconds or press Enter to go to the next step. The next screen that is going to appear in front of you is a black one with a sort of animated progress bar at the bottom and the Fedora release version at the end of this step, as you can see in Figure 5-6.

*Figure 5-6.* *The bottom of the screen when Fedora Live is booting up*

When Fedora Live is finally up, the welcome screen that appears (Figure 5-7) lets you choose between two options: installing the distribution on the hard drive of your system or keep testing Fedora in the Live session. If you are new to the Gnome environment or you want to test Fedora, you can always choose to install it later through the Activities menu. Let's choose the "Install to Hard Drive" option to keep going.

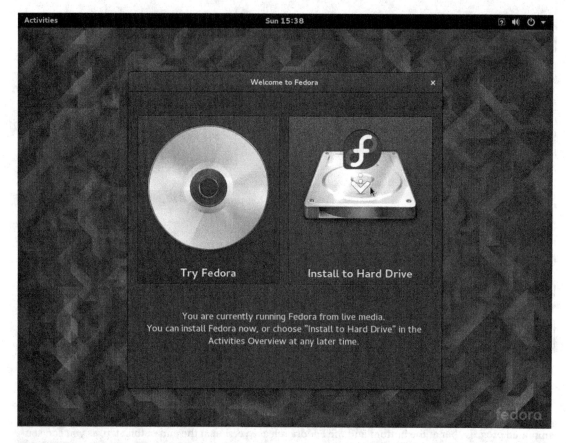

*Figure 5-7. Fedora Workstation Live welcome screen*

This is the first real step of the installation process, and the first thing to do is to choose the language to use in all of the next steps (and by default in the distro). If you have an Internet connection, it will try to auto-detect your region (time zone, to be exact) through your IP WAN address and set the language automatically for you. Otherwise, it will pick English (USA) by default and you must change it manually if necessary. There is also a button named Help!, which is a context help that can guide you in the process. After you pick your language, press the "Continue" button (Figure 5-8).

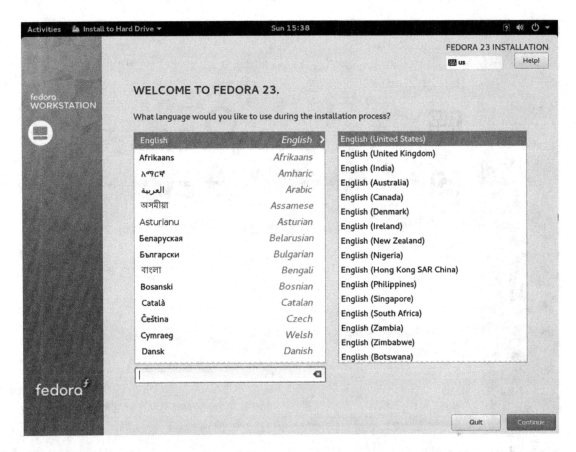

*Figure 5-8.* *The language selection screen*

The next screen includes almost all of the rest of the choices that you must make to complete the process. As in the previous screen, Anaconda (the Fedora installation program), is going to try to make all the decisions for you, and in a big number of cases they will be the right ones. However, even if all the choices are right, as in Figure 5-9, the program won't allow you to continue until you complete the Installation Destination section. The reason is obvious: before you make any changes on your hard disk, you want to check them out. Let's take a tour through all of the four sections included here. If you press the Help button, you'll get the help dialog shown in Figure 5-10.

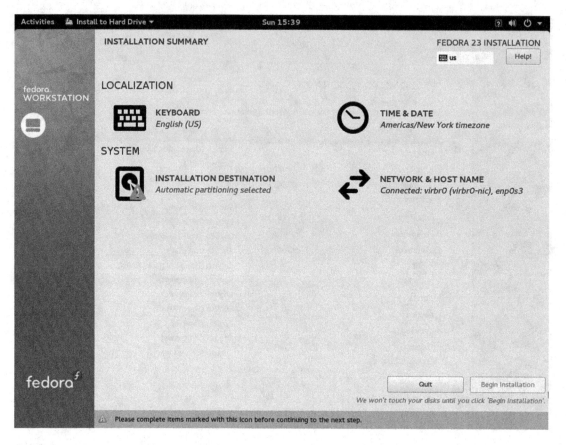

***Figure 5-9.*** *The installation summary screen*

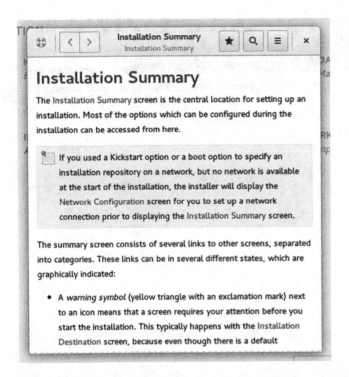

**Figure 5-10.** *The context help that can guide you through all of the installation*

In the Keyboard section (Figure 5-11) you can choose the keyboard layout(s) that you want to use in your distro. As usual, there is a big probability that the correct one was chosen automatically; if not, you must choose it manually. There are two interesting options here. First, if you select with your mouse any layout from the list, you will see an interactive representation of it (to help you identify it visually). Second, if you added more than one layout, you can pick from a list the keyboard combination that you want to use to switch between them. To do the latter option, you must use the Options button.

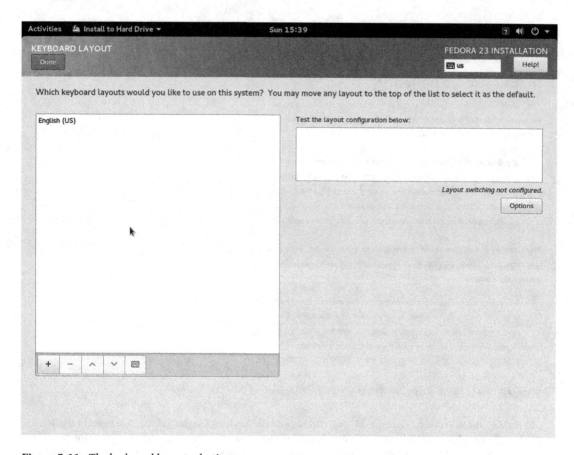

***Figure 5-11.*** *The keyboard layout selection screen*

The Time & Date section allows you to select your time zone interactively on a map and set both time and date manually (Figure 5-12). If you are online, this is probably automatically selected correctly. One of the differences from Ubuntu is that, apart from being able to manually adjust the clock and calendar, you can also toggle the network time and even configure it. The NTP (Network Time Protocol) means that your system clock will always be correct because it's adjusted regularly by checking a time server on the Internet. You can also set your NTP servers via the gear icon if you want a different one from the Fedora default. This is turned on by default in Ubuntu, but you can see that Fedora has a different approach to the matter. As part of the Red Hat legacy and also as part of its different philosophy, you will continue to see how Fedora, although it is easy to use and install, gives the user more responsibility. I recommend you stick with the default NTP option. Make the necessary adjustments or simply check that all is correct, and then press the Done button.

***Figure 5-12.*** *Selection of time and date by region*

The Network & Host Name section (Figure 5-13) is a little tricky since you can only change the host name here. The rest of the network configuration is under the configuration options in Gnome. If you are not on a local network or you don't understand the option, keep the host name value as the default one. The rest of the configuration is accessible via the icons to the right of the top Gnome menu bar, where you can see the volume, net, and power icons. If you click this icon, you will see a dialog like the second one in Figure 5-14. In this dialog, you will see the current network configuration detected by Anaconda; it can be a wired or wireless connection. You'll also see the user and volume settings and the icons to access the configuration, screen lock, and power settings. If you click the network connection icon, it will show you two options: to toggle the connection on/off and to access the settings. Click the settings and you access a pop-up dialog with all the network settings, as shown at the bottom of Figure 5-14.

***Figure 5-13.*** *The first part of the network configuration*

***Figure 5-14.*** *How to access the network settings in the installation process*

On the left is a list of all the available connections detected (you can add more) and the proxy configuration. On the right is the information about the current connection selected and a button to toggle it on/off. If you are connected to the Internet with a router (wired or Wi-Fi) with a DNS server or via a local network, all of this will be correctly configured automatically. If not or if you want to tweak something, you can always change the settings via the gear icon. Also, you can manage different profiles via the Add Profile button, which is very useful for laptops to connect to different networks (automatically or by asking for password every time; it's your choice).

The last section of this Installation Summary screen is the Installation Destination part. This information is unique to you and it must be reviewed (it's mandatory). As you can see in Figure 5-15, this screen has four important parts:

- **Local standard disks**. Here you will find the normal hard disks (HDD, SDD, USB) currently available on your system. For now, there's only one regular 1TB HDD disk; in other examples, I'll show you other situations.

- **Specialized and network disks**. This is where you will find LAN disks like iSCSI and FCoE ones. These are usually for advanced users working on a local network. I'll skip this part here.

- **Other storage options**. This is where you decide to accept the automatic settings already made for you or customize them. This is the part that I will explore next.

- **Full disk summary**. It appears unimportant because it's just a link at the bottom, but it's a summary of your disks and you can select from which one you want to boot (usually you don't need to change it).

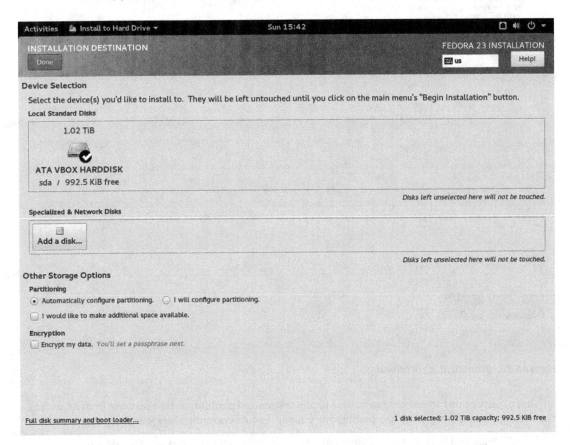

*Figure 5-15.* *The Installation Destination section*

The Other Storage Options section is where you must take special care about what you are doing. You can decide here if you want to encrypt your data (the entire disk) or not, as I explained in the Ubuntu chapter. I'll skip this step in this installation example. It's the partitioning topic where I want to take a moment to explain the options. As mentioned, this configuration is usually automatically taken care of, so you could simply press the Done button and begin the installation. I would recommend doing this only if you have one disk and it's empty (or if you don't mind losing the data currently there). But if you want to leave some disk space empty (e.g. to install another OS), you must choose the "I would like to make additional space available" option.

Let's ignore all of that and manually configure the partitions by selecting the "I will configure partitioning" option. Once you select that option, press the Done button. You'll get the screen shown in Figure 5-16.

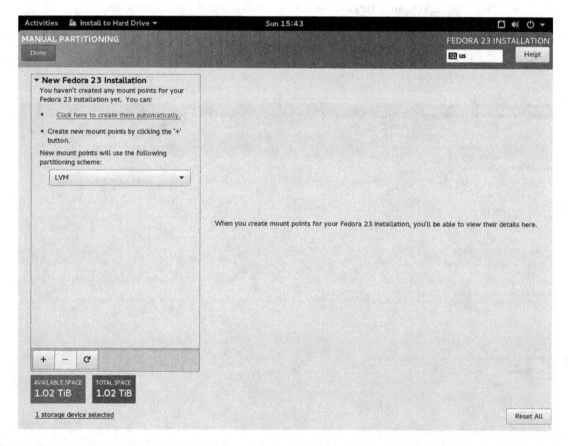

**Figure 5-16.** *Manual disk partitioning*

It is a blank canvas where you can make a totally customized partition or get assistance from Anaconda. The most important thing here is the partitioning scheme. Fedora currently offers four alternatives:

- **Standard Partition**: The traditional scheme with regular partitions and the ext4 file system by default.

- **Btrfs**: Because it's on the bleeding edge of technology, Fedora offers Btrfs. Btrfs is a file system with volume managing and error tolerance capabilities based on a binary tree similar to Solaris ZFS.

- **LVM**: The Logical Volume Manager offers you more flexibility and ease of use than the traditional partitions (among other advanced functionalities).

- **LVM Thin Provisioning**: This is an advanced feature of LVM that dynamically allocates disk space for the logical volumes when needed. If you are not an advanced user, ignore this.

Fedora by default chooses the LVM scheme because it is more balanced in features/performance/easiness. If you prefer the traditional way, you can choose the Standard one. Btrfs offers you a good number of additional capabilities versus LVM but it is still experimental and its performance is worse than ext4 fs. So if you don't have any particular requirements, keep the LVM scheme.

---

■ **Note**    Consider one particular thing when choosing LVM or BTRFS as your partition scheme: although both offer more flexibility to manage your partitions (like allocation or resizing), there are only a few GUI tools to manage this properly (and they're not very good) so you should manage this volume through the command line.

---

After you chose your partition scheme, you have two options: to manually add your volumes or let Fedora manage this automatically. Fedora differs here from the traditional way of doing this task; usually you should first define your partitions or logical volumes, then your file system for each one, and then choose the mount points. Anaconda makes you first choose your partition scheme, then your mount points, and the rest is decided automatically (you can change it later). From my point of view and experience, this is a much better approach, especially for non-advanced users.

If you decide to manually add the mount points, you must use the + icon at the bottom of the screen. A dialog similar to Figure 5-17 should appear. You choose a mounting point like /, /boot, /swap, or /home and then the disk space you want to assign to it. You can create as much as you need while there is free space available (you can always change the initial settings by selecting that mount point). And here is where I want to introduce you to the partition scheme that I recommend (it differs from Ubuntu's, which I told you I didn't like).

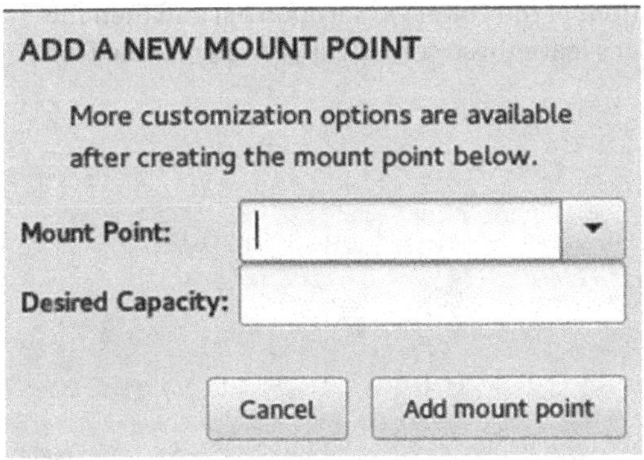

**ADD A NEW MOUNT POINT**

More customization options are available after creating the mount point below.

Mount Point:

Desired Capacity:

Cancel    Add mount point

*Figure 5-17.* *Dialog to add a new mount point*

To refresh your memory, Ubuntu only creates two partitions with two mounting points, one for the swap partition and other for the root (/) partition. All of the files from the system plus your personal data are in the same partition, the root one. This way is easy to manage and wastes less disk space, but only in the short term. I don't like it because in the long term it usually gives you more headaches and problems, so it's not worth it. For example, if you want to upgrade your Linux distribution to a new release and the upgrading process does not work well, you are bound to make a backup/delete/restoration cycle of all your data (at least the /home directory) in a mandatory way (although I recommended doing it regularly) if you want to do a fresh installation and not end up with an unmanageable mess. So I recommend that you separate the / mount point into two different ones: the / itself for all of the system files and the /home one to store your personal files and program configurations. And I recommend adding an additional /boot partition to manage the boot files and avoid future problems with system upgrades, migrations, or certain BIOSes. In order to do this, I recommend a minimum of 500MB for the boot partition (and use a standard partition) and 15GB for the / mount point.

If you let Anaconda do this for you, the result will look like Figure 5-18. It also shows the default automatic partition that Fedora would apply if you choose the default automatic way instead of this pseudo-manual one. As you can see, Fedora chooses the same partition scheme that I recommended you, and it is way better than the one that Ubuntu chooses by default. Fedora always chooses this scheme, regardless of whether you choose Standard, LVM, or BTRFS. Thus, Fedora makes one standard partition for the /boot mount point with an ext4 fs and a LVM volume group named fedora for the rest as a logical volume with an ext4 fs (swap for the swap mount volume). The final free available space is tiny, less than 1MB, so it works very well in that matter. The amount of space dedicated to the swap volume is assigned as a function of how much physical RAM you have in your system, because if you want to hibernate your system, the data in your memory is going to be stored in that partition. In each of the volumes/partitions, you have a series of data/options that you can change, from the mounting point and capacity to the file system and name. I like to change the amount of disk space dedicated to the / volume; 50GB is a bit conservative and safe, so maybe 35GB is enough. You can decrement that space in the / volume and press the Update Settings button, and then increment the /home volume. As you can see, you can encrypt individual volumes here, instead of the previous screen option that does it globally. Additionally, you can set other advanced features like RAID via the Modify button of the Volume group (this settings affects all of the logical volumes). You can also do things like mix LVM volumes with BTRFS ones, or use a file system other than ext4. One last thing: if you make any changes and don't think they are good, you can always start again from scratch by pressing the ↻ button at the bottom of the volumes/partition list and then the Rescan Disks button in the new dialog that appears. Well, let's leave these settings as is and press the Done button in the left top corner of the screen.

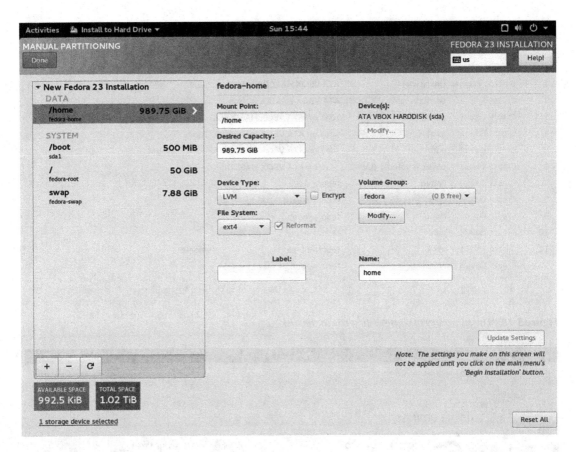

**Figure 5-18.** *The automatically defined partition scheme for LVM*

A dialog appears, showing you the changes that are going to be done to the disk; if they are OK, press the Accept Changes button (Figure 5-19). You will return to the Installation Summary screen. The Begin Installation button is enabled; press that button and the installation process will write the changes to your disk and begin installing the OS on your system. However, even when the process of partitioning and installing Fedora is going on, you still need to set two more things (Figure 5-20).

**SUMMARY OF CHANGES**

Your customizations will result in the following changes taking effect after you return to the main menu and begin installation:

| Order | Action | Type | Device | Mount point |
|-------|--------|------|--------|-------------|
| 1 | Destroy Format | Unknown | ATA VBOX HARDDISK (sda) | |
| 2 | Create Format | partition table (MSDOS) | ATA VBOX HARDDISK (sda) | |
| 3 | Create Device | partition | sda1 on ATA VBOX HARDDISK | |
| 4 | Create Format | ext4 | sda1 on ATA VBOX HARDDISK | /boot |
| 5 | Create Device | partition | sda2 on ATA VBOX HARDDISK | |
| 6 | Create Format | physical volume (LVM) | sda2 on ATA VBOX HARDDISK | |
| 7 | Create Device | lvmvg | fedora | |
| 8 | Create Device | lvmlv | fedora-swap | |
| 9 | Create Format | swap | fedora-swap | |
| 10 | Create Device | lvmlv | fedora-home | |
| 11 | Create Format | ext4 | fedora-home | /home |
| 12 | Create Device | lvmlv | fedora-root | |

Cancel & Return to Custom Partitioning    Accept Changes

***Figure 5-19.*** *The summary of changes to write to the disk*

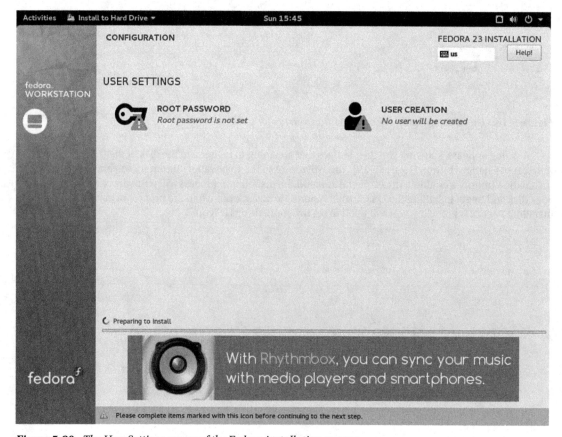

***Figure 5-20.*** *The User Settings screen of the Fedora installation process*

Another big difference here from Ubuntu is that you need to set a password for the root user (the main account and the default admin account); this is disabled by default in Ubuntu (you use your regular user, requiring your password for admin things). This is the right thing to do, although it is less easy and takes responsibility from the user. If you want to emulate the Ubuntu behavior, you can always add your user to the wheel group later. Let's establish the root password in the Root Password section (Figure 5-21).

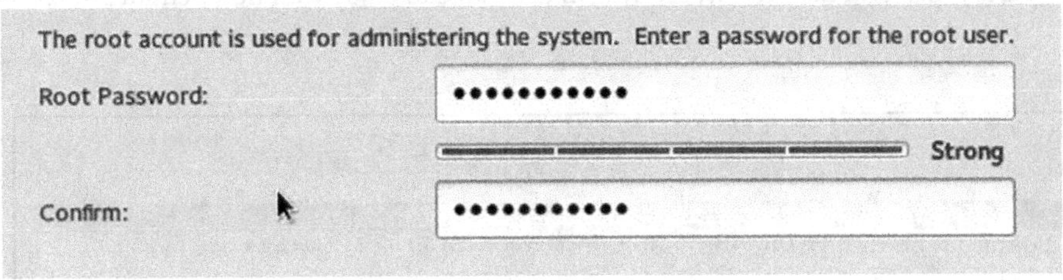

*Figure 5-21.*  *Setting the root password*

Take care here to set a strong password because this is one of the most crucial points of attack when we talking about security. If someone knows your root password, he can own your entire system, Caution! After setting this password and returning to the previous screen, you may notice something weird. The User Creation section is now OK and you are good to go without needing to create another user. You could proceed, but I strongly recommend that you never, but never, use your system with the root account. Always use another regular user to work with your system. It's a serious security flaw (and the main one for many years for Window users). I suppose that Fedora does this in order to allow OEM installations. (You can always create your own later; in fact, you will do it in the Gnome setup if you don't do it now). Anyway, let's create a new user that will be the default one for your computer Figure 5-22).

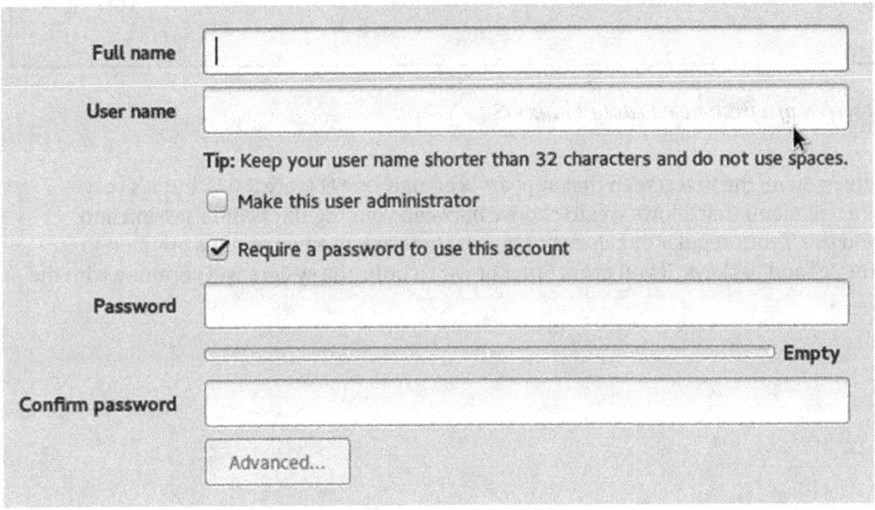

*Figure 5-22.*  *Create a new user account*

Here you have two main options: to make that user an administrator, and toggle on/off the need of a password. If you want to emulate the Ubuntu behavior, set the first option; the second option should be never set (only to create Guest accounts). Never, absolutely never, set the first option without setting the second one; a user with admin capabilities without a password is a straight route to disaster (especially if your system is connected to the Internet). In the Advanced section, you can adjust these settings, but don't touch them if you don't understand them. After setting this new user and returning to the previous screen, you only have to wait for the installation to finish and then restart the system to be able to enjoy your new Fedora Linux OS (Figure 5-23).

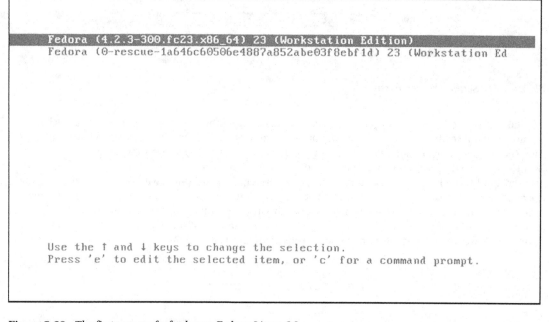

```
     Fedora (4.2.3-300.fc23.x86_64) 23 (Workstation Edition)
     Fedora (0-rescue-1a646c60506e4887a852abe03f8ebf1d) 23 (Workstation Ed




















     Use the ↑ and ↓ keys to change the selection.
     Press 'e' to edit the selected item, or 'c' for a command prompt.
```

***Figure 5-23.*** *The first screen of a fresh new Fedora Linux OS*

After you restart the system, the first screen that appears is an ugly one (Figure 5-24), but it's very common in Linux; it's a text menu that allows you to choose between your regular Fedora session and a rescue one (which you use if your regular one does not boot). There are also two options oriented to advanced users, like the "e" and "c" keys. If you press Enter or wait a little, the system will continue with the boot process.

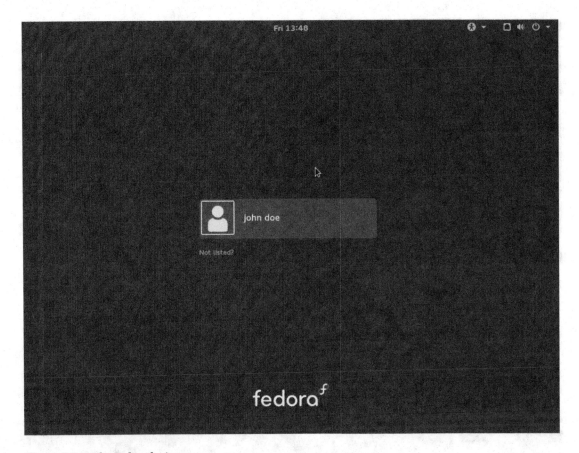

***Figure 5-24.*** *The Fedora login screen*

When Fedora finishes the boot up process, you'll get the Gnome login screen (Figure 5-24) with all of the users listed (at this moment, you only have one). If you select your user, it will ask for your password. When you enter your password, you'll see a gear icon to the right of the Sign In button. This icon (Figure 5-25) lets you to choose between the available desktop environments installed on your system. By default you only have three: Gnome (Gnome 3), Gnome Classic (Gnome 2), and Gnome on Wayland (Gnome 3). I recommend you keep the default one, Gnome, because Classic can cause problems with some applications. Wayland is another example of Fedora's use of new technologies; Wayland aims to be the substitute of the venerable and old X window system, but it's still too new and it may crash with some apps and especially with some graphics cards.

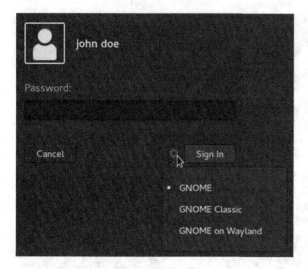

***Figure 5-25.*** *The desktop environments available to you*

So now you're logged in to your new operating system but a new surprise awaits you: the Gnome initial setup. This is where you set up the Gnome configuration for language, keyboard layout, privacy settings, and online accounts (and a local account if you didn't create a user in the installation process). These settings are usually set by default, and if you don't want to change anything, you can skip all of them. At the end, a Getting Started manual (Figure 5-26), part of the Gnome Help system, will be shown to help new users become familiarized with how to do things with Gnome.

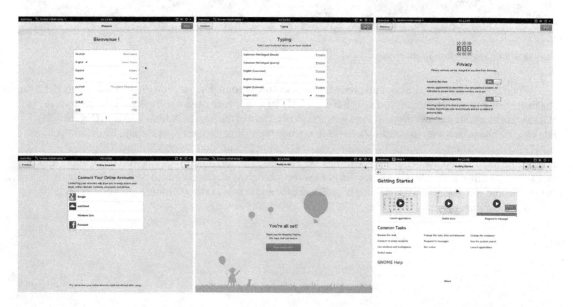

***Figure 5-26.*** *The Gnome initial setup and the Getting Started Help*

And that's it! You can now freely enjoy your Fedora Linux OS. In the next Linux distro installations, you will continue to explore different things.

# Maintenance

As with Ubuntu (and in general), there are three essential tasks to maintaining your Linux distro: update and upgrade your distro and manage your applications. But unlike Ubuntu, with Fedora these tasks require the user to use the terminal, something most users dread.

## Managing Apps

In Fedora, managing apps is at first an easy task; you can use the Software app (gnome-software) to install and remove applications. It's a very easy-to-use application and it is very similar to the one in Ubuntu. You can see it in Figure 5-27. But you can't find all of the Fedora apps there; for the majority of Fedora's own packages, you must use the command line, like it or not.

*Figure 5-27.* *The Software manager application of Gnome*

# Updating

Figure 5-27 shows an Updates tab, so you might think that you can update your Fedora from here. Wrong. This is yet another time where you must use the terminal and command line apps. To manage packages in Fedora from the command line, you must use the command dnf (formerly yum), and you must open the terminal for that. If you want to update the packages of your Fedora OS, you should use this command:

```
$ sudo dnf update
```

Basically this command refreshes the information about the packages (metadata) from the repositories online. If there are updates available, it will show you a list and a summary, and request your confirmation to update all of them. Obviously you should do this regularly to keep your OS up to date (at least to avoid security problems).

---

■ **Note**  I'm using the sudo command here to perform an administration task (update the packages) because I'm assuming that you created your default user at installation time with administrative permissions (as I suggested). If this is not the case, you need to use the root user to do this task. To do so, use this code:

```
$ su root:       # you are going to switch here your user with root
Password:        # you have to introduce here the root password
# dnf update:    # then you can update, don't forget to log out (exit) after end
```

---

■ **Tip**  If you don't want to use the user root anymore, you can add your user to the wheel group to be able to use the sudo command and your password. Use this code (from the root user):

```
# usermod -a -G wheel youruser
```

---

Figure 5-28 is graphical proof of what I'm telling you. The Software app says that there are no updates and that everything is up to date, and the $ sudo dnf update command tells you a completely different story. So, you have to update 552 packages (which also requires installing 11 new ones), adding up a total of 799MB. You cannot trust the gnome-software app here. If you choose Fedora as your Linux distro, learn how to use the dnf package. It's not that hard and you'll have more control over your system.

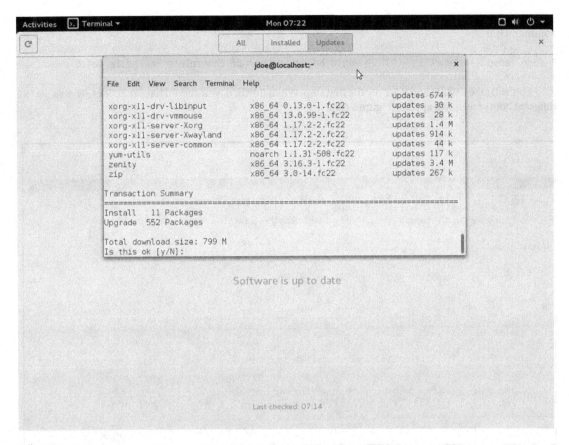

**Figure 5-28.** *The gnome-software vs. the dnf package updates search results*

You can also set up automatic updates from dnf, but it's not recommended because you lose control of what and when is updating.

# Upgrading

If you want to upgrade your current release of Fedora when a new one arrives, the command line and the terminal are your friends. You can use the dnf package to do this, too, but I'll show you a better way. There is a package exclusively dedicated to this task, FedUp (for Fedora Upgrader). It's not installed by default, so the first thing to do is install it.

```
$ sudo dnf install fedup
```

After that, you must update your system (which I just showed you). It's important to do this to avoid any problems with the upgrading process (a very delicate one, as I told you in the Ubuntu chapter; the same applies here). I strongly recommend that you make a backup of your data, because even if you have a dedicated /home volume for all of your personal files, bad things happens and you would not be the first one who, after a failed upgrade, tried a fresh install and forgot to not format his current /home volume. If I only had a dollar for every time that I saw that...

Now it's time to do the upgrading. In order to do this, you need to have an Internet connection. The command is this:

```
$ sudo fedup --network 23     # 23 would be the number of the relese to update to
```

This will take a while and it is only the first step. When finished, you should have to reboot. Then a different boot screen will appear (Figure 5-29).

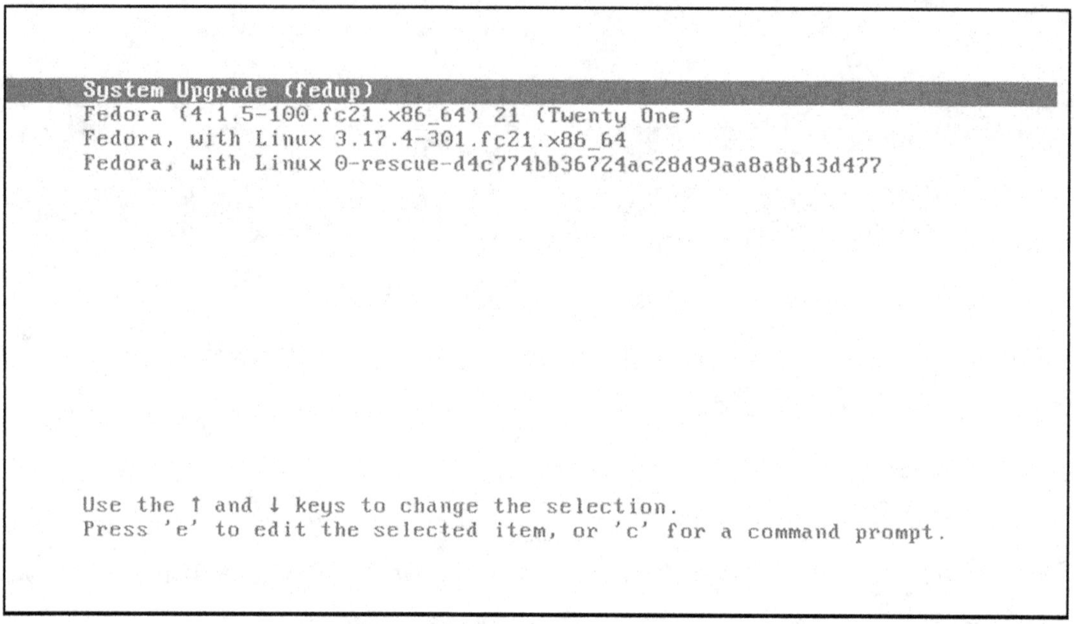

```
System Upgrade (fedup)
Fedora (4.1.5-100.fc21.x86_64) 21 (Twenty One)
Fedora, with Linux 3.17.4-301.fc21.x86_64
Fedora, with Linux 0-rescue-d4c774bb36724ac28d99aa8a8b13d477




            Use the ↑ and ↓ keys to change the selection.
            Press 'e' to edit the selected item, or 'c' for a command prompt.
```

*Figure 5-29.* *The boot screen that appears after upgrading (21 to 22)*

You should select the first option (or do nothing and wait) to continue to the second step, which will take a while too. If all goes well, you can now enjoy your new release of Fedora. You should also execute a series of commands to make a cleanup and avoid problems when you update your packages:

```
$ sudo rpm --rebuilddb
$ sudo dnf distro-sync --setopt=deltarpm=0
$ sudo dnf install rpmconf
$ sudo dnf install rpmconf
```

More information about this process is at the Fedora wiki page, https://fedoraproject.org/wiki/FedUp.

# Pros and Cons

The following is a list of things that I personally see as pros and cons of the Fedora distro. There is always room for discussion in this matter, but I've done my best to be as objective as possible.

## Pros

- Fedora has a good balance between ease of use and advanced features.

- It's a very secure distribution by default.

- It uses only free and open source software.

- It has a regular release scheme, so you know when a new release is coming.

- It uses the latest technologies and innovations, and gives a lot back to the Linux community and the rest of the distros.

- It has a large and talented community behind it, which drives it.

- Red Hat is behind Fedora, and Fedora is the base for Red Hat.

- It uses one of the most extended package managers, rpm.

- It is an original distribution, not a derivative.

- There are many task-oriented predefined images (music, games, etc.).

- It has a very good installer application.

- Its DevAssistant tool, with its Docker and virtualization tools integration, provides one of the best environments for software developers.

## Cons

- It does not offer much in the way of aesthetics.

- It has no commercial support.

- It has no proprietary drivers by default, so the hardware support in some cases is not good.

- There's a lack of proprietary third party software.

- Because of the two previous points, many people use alternative repositories. This introduces security and instability risks.

- The Gnome Software manager is a buggy and slow application.

- You must use the terminal for a lot of administrative tasks.

# Summary

Fedora is the second Linux distro that I analyzed for you. In this chapter, you got to see how Fedora handles certain issues. Now you can see how two distros are not necessarily the same thing. This contrast will grow in further chapters and you will gain an understanding of why there are so many distros and why it is so important to know what you need.

In the next chapter, I put the Debian distro under the microscope.

# CHAPTER 6

# Debian

Debian is not only one of the most famous, charismatic, and oldest Linux distribution, it is also the perfect example of an independent and community-driven distro. There is a saying among Linux users, "If all other distros disappear, we'll always have Debian." It is the favorite distro of many system administrators, developers, and users, and this is not just due to its long life; it's also because Debian's community, philosophy, and management make it a unique distro. Its "genealogy tree" is the biggest one of all the distros. Debian is the parent of many distros. In fact, almost half of the currently active, maintained distros are based on Debian, either directly, like Ubuntu or Knoppix, or two or three generations removed, like elementary OS or Mint.

## History

Since Debian is one the two oldest Linux distros, we could say that the history of Debian is a fundamental part of the history of Linux itself. Let's focus on the beginning. As I said in Chapter 3, Debian was born as an alternative to SLS, the distro that inspired Ian Murdock (then an undergraduate at Purdue University) to make something better. He released the first release of Debian in August 1993. He coined the name by pairing the name of his then-girlfriend (later wife and currently ex-wife) and himself: **Deb**orah + **Ian** = Debian.

With the birth of Debian also came *The Debian Manifesto*[1] (later revised in 1994), which was a declaration of what Debian should and wanted to be. Although it names the Free Software as a fundamental pillar (in fact, Debian was sponsored by the GNU Project for the first year) and the importance of the community, these guidelines focus mainly on the development and maintenance of the distribution.

> *The Debian design process is open to ensure that the system is of the highest quality and that it reflects the needs of the user community. By involving others with a wide range of abilities and backgrounds, Debian is able to be developed in a modular fashion. Its components are of high quality because those with expertise in a certain area are given the opportunity to construct or maintain the individual components of Debian involving that area. Involving others also ensures that valuable suggestions for improvement can be incorporated into the distribution during its development; thus, a distribution is created based on the needs and wants of the users rather than the needs and wants of the constructor. It is very difficult for one individual or small group to anticipate these needs and wants in advance without direct input from others.*
>
> *The Debian Manifesto*, Ian Murdock, 1993-4.

---

[1]www.debian.org/doc/manuals/project-history/ap-manifesto.en.html

© Jose Dieguez Castro 2016
J. Dieguez Castro, *Introducing Linux Distros*, DOI 10.1007/978-1-4842-1392-6_6

In June of 1997, two Debian developers, Ean Schuessler (who had the initial idea) and Bruce Perens (who coordinated its creation), created the *Debian Social Contract*[2] to complement the initial manifesto. This contract addresses the moral agenda of the Debian project to preserve the project as independent, free, driven by the community, and under the umbrella of the Free Software. These written guarantees would shape the future of the distro but at the same time would preserve its unique identity. This contract also contains the *Debian Free Software Guidelines* which would serve as the basis of the *Open Source Definition*[3].

Also in 1997, the Software in the Public Interest was created as a non-profit organization by Bruce Perens to allow the Debian Project to accept donations and support it. Over the years it would become the supporter of other Free Software projects.

# Philosophy

There is no other distro with its purpose and philosophy as clearly and well defined as Debian (well, maybe Fedora). The initial *Debian Manifesto*, the *Debian Social Contract*, the *Debian Free Software Guidelines*, together with the *Debian Constitution*[4] and the *Debian Code of Conduct*[5], clearly define the guidelines of the distro. This strong commitment to the morals and ethics of Software Libre is the best definition of its philosophy, but let's look at the main points of the *Debian Social Contract* to understand this better:

> *"Social Contract" with the Free Software Community*
>
> *1. Debian will remain 100% free.*
>
> *2. We will give back to the free software community.*
>
> *3. We will not hide problems.*
>
> *4. Our priorities are our users and free software.*
>
> *5. Works that do not meet our free software standards* [are supported; *see the* Contract].

*The Debian Social Contract*, version 1.1, April 2004.

# Distro Selection Criteria

Now that you know a little history of Debian, let's see how this particular distro fares on the selection criteria from Chapter 2.

## Purpose and Environment

Debian is essentially a general purpose distribution with a unique version for all purposes, thus the same image is used both in the desktop and server environments (among others). The user is responsible for using it in one way or another, and there is almost no graphical and easy help to do so. However, there are several ways to install it, from Live CDs or DVDs to netinstall ISOs. Also, you can opt for different kernels: the standard and official Linux one, a FreeBSD one, and an experimental and unofficial microkernel, the "Hurd" from the GNU Project.

---

[2]www.debian.org/social_contract.en.html
[3]http://opensource.org/docs/osd
[4]www.debian.org/devel/constitution.en.html
[5]www.debian.org/code_of_conduct.en.html

# Support

Obviously, all of the support come from the Debian community, and like Fedora or Ubuntu, it has multiple channels:

- **Debian Documentation**: www.debian.org/doc/index.en.html
    - **The Debian Administrator's Handbook**: www.debian.org/doc/manuals/debian-handbook/
    - **Debian Reference**: www.debian.org/doc/manuals/debian-reference/
- **Wiki**: https://wiki.debian.org/FrontPage
- **Mailing Lists**: www.debian.org/MailingLists/index.en.html
- **Forums**: http://forums.debian.net/ and www.debianhelp.org/
- **Q&A site**: http://ask.debian.net/
- **IRC**: #debian at irc.debian.org

Although the Debian support comes from the community, the web site provides links to third party consultants (people/companies) that can provide unofficial commercial support (see www.debian.org/consultants/index.en.html).

# User Friendliness

Debian is not a particularly friendly distro. You must know the basics of what Linux is and how to manage the usual administration tasks. It's harder to use than Fedora or Ubuntu but not as hard as Arch or Gentoo. Still, it was the starter distro for many people for a long time, before Ubuntu arrived, and it still is because it continues to be one of the most recommended distros. You will see in the installation process how, although it's not difficult to install, it gives more space to the user. The installer is less friendly than the Fedora and Ubuntu ones. Obviously, if you use the same desktop environment in all of them, it balances things a little, but in the end, the perception of how things work is fundamental. You can see the same phenomenon in Android smartphones: there are so many different phones and the differences between them are minimal, yet people still have strong feelings and preferences for one instead of another.

# Stability

Debian has a very particular approach to stability. It can be a very stable distro and it can be a very unstable and up-to-date one. To do this, it has three main branches: Stable, Testing, and Unstable.

- **Stable:** The main and current version. It is the most stable, with only well-tested software, and it is very conservative (the packages may be very old by regular distro standards, except Red Hat/CentOS). It only receives security and major fixes. It follows a standard release model and has a cycle of about two years, but this is not written in stone; a new major version is only released when is finished. The Stable version is the one normally used in servers and workstations.
    - **OldStable:** It's the former Stable version. It is supported until one year after a new Stable is released and then it is archived.

- **Testing**: It is the future new Stable version, where all of the packages, changes, and innovations are tested before deciding that a new version is needed. It receives continuous updates, and when it is time to prepare a new version, it "freezes" and then only bug fixes and improvements are made until it is ready to become the new Stable.

- **Unstable**: Here is where the development of Debian happens; the packages are almost up-to-date and it can be very unstable. It is intended for Debian developers and people that like to always have the latest technology, but this comes at a cost: broken systems. You cannot find any ISO image for this branch (the opposite of the others); you have to change the repositories to a testing installation and then upgrade the distro. It is a sort of rolling release distro, but technically it is the development branch of the distro, unlike true rolling release distros like Arch or Gentoo where it is the main branch.

  - **Experimental**: A sort of staging area for packages that are experimental and with a high probability of breaking your system. It is the only repository oriented to the Unstable branch.

Since 2014, Debian has also adopted a derivation of the Ubuntu LTS releases system for the Stable version of the distro with a LTS repository mainly for security updates. In this way, each Stable release is supported for five years. (The regular support is only for three years.)

A curiosity about Debian it is that uses code names based on characters from the Toy Story films. The current Stable version is called Jessie, the Testing and future Stable is Stretch, and the Unstable version is called Sid (and obviously that never changes). You can learn more about Debian releases at `www.debian.org/releases/`.

## Hardware Support

Debian is in the middle ground between Fedora and Ubuntu in terms of hardware support because although Debian supports only Free Software, non-free software is also available in their repositories, like binary drivers for network cards and graphics cards. You can also find private blobs in the kernel. Thus, Debian has reasonable good hardware support.

## Aesthetics

The aesthetics of Debian are the default of the desktop environment that you choose; the only aspects that are taken care of are the logo and the desktop background. Despite this and the installer, you may have to customize the DE in order to have something that you like if that is not the default aesthetic.

## Desktop Environment

The de facto standard desktop environment of Debian has always been Gnome, but others are available in the DVD ISO image or in dedicated CD images for each DE alternative (but not all of them). Currently these are the DEs that can be installed from the DVD image directly (you can choose another from the repositories):

- Gnome (version 3)

- XFCE

- KDE

- Cinnamon
- MATE
- LXDE

## Init System

Until 2015, the init system was the traditional SysV, but now it is the same as almost all of the others distributions: systemd. This decision was the cause of great controversy, and it even caused the creation of a new fork, for the sole purpose of continuing the Debian distro with the old SysV init system: Devuan[6]. Debian still offers SysV as an alternative in their repositories, but installing it and making it work is not an easy or pleasurable task. It requires considerable effort, especially with some DEs.

## Package Management System

The package management system of Debian is the same as Ubuntu, since Debian is its original creator: dpkg (as the basis of apt). Its repositories hold the most number of packages of any distribution, currently about 50,000 packages.

## Architecture

Debian is the distro that supports the most hardware architectures, but some things (like the LTS support for security upgrades) are only available for the amd64 and i386 architectures. The current officially supported architectures are amd64, i386, ARM, i64 (Intel Itanium), MIPS, PowerPC, SPARC, S390, and some variations of those. Debian also unofficially supports other architectures; some of them are not actively developed, but you can find images for those machines. Because Debian has a big community and a focus on freedom, it can afford to maintain some architectures that are not "profitable" for other projects.

## Security/Anonymity

Debian offers the regular level of security out of the box. There is a special security team that takes care of finding and fixing security vulnerabilities in its packages, but the distro itself does not come with any extra security features enabled by default. Of course, you can have a very secure distro with Debian but you have to harden it by yourself. There are guides to do this, but you should know what you're doing. In this matter, Fedora and Ubuntu are more secure by default (in that order). You can learn more about Debian security at www.debian.org/security/.

## Principles and Ethics

Although Debian has a clear focus on and commitment to the Software Libre, it also has a pragmatic view of non-free software. As stated in the *Debian Social Contract*, all of the non-free software available for Debian should work in the distro, and it encourages this. The intention behind this is to let users who may not share the same vision of freedom still use Debian as their distro. On this point, its position is more relaxed than Fedora's. Although the non-free software is not officially supported, it can be installed from their repositories; in Fedora you must use third party repositories to achieve this.

The morals and ethics of the Debian Project and its community can be further researched via the links provided in the "Philosophy" section.

---

[6]https://devuan.org/

## Live CD

There are dedicated Live ISO images available for the i386 and amd64 architectures. These are only available for the Stable branch.

## Professional Certification

Debian does not offer any professional certification, but it is one of the distros that the Linux Professional Institute endorses in its certifications, the well-known LPIC.

# Installation

Installing Debian is not as hard as people say (there is a joke that says that Ubuntu means "I do not know how to install Debian") but, as you are going to see, it is clearly more difficult than the previous installations I've showed you. Don't let this intimidate you. It's perfectly doable by anyone; in the past, almost every Linux was installed in this manner.

Let's begin, as always, by obtaining the ISO image to do the installation. You have to go to the Debian downloads page at `www.debian.org/distrib/`. You'll see something like Figure 6-1.

## Getting Debian

Debian is distributed freely over Internet. You can download all of it from any of our mirrors. The Installation Manual contains detailed installation instructions.

If you simply want to install Debian, these are your options:

### Download an installation image

Depending on your Internet connection, you may download either of the following:

- A **small installation image**: can be downloaded quickly and should be recorded onto a removable disk. To use this, you will need a machine with an Internet connection.

64-bit PC netinst iso, 32-bit PC netinst iso

- A larger **complete installation image**: contains more packages, making it easier to install machines without an Internet connection.

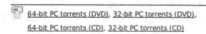
64-bit PC torrents (DVD), 32-bit PC torrents (DVD),
64-bit PC torrents (CD), 32-bit PC torrents (CD)

### Try Debian live before installing

You can try Debian by booting a live system from a CD, DVD or USB key without installing any files to the computer. When you are ready, you can run the included installer. Provided the images meet your size, language, and package selection requirements, this method may be suitable for you. Read more information about this method to help you decide.

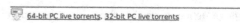
64-bit PC live torrents, 32-bit PC live torrents

***Figure 6-1.*** *The downloads page from the Debian project*

You can choose from several options: a netinstall image if you have a good Internet connection to install almost all the packages from the Internet, a Live image, or a complete image. With the complete images, you can download all of them (there is a collection of them) to be able to install any package offline, or you can download only the first image to do a basic installation (you can always install anything from the repositories later). This is an interesting alternative if you want to install and have a "hard" offline CD/DVD repository for those places where an Internet connection is not available. Below, on the same page, Debian also offers you options to buy the DVD/CDs or a Debian pre-installed computer from third parties.

Let's choose the most common option, the complete installation image, so click the link and go to a new web page, like the one in Figure 6-2.

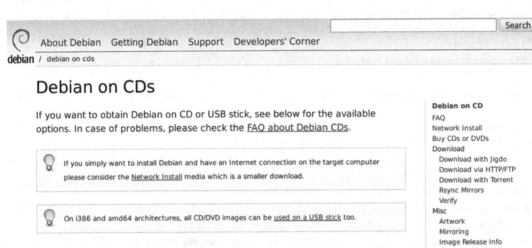

**Figure 6-2.** *The Debian options to download a complete ISO Image*

More options to choose from! Basically you can download the images using the traditional HTTP/ FTP way, using Bit Torrent or jidgo. The best option to not saturate the Debian servers is the Bit Torrent one (especially when a new version is released) or jidgo (a tool to download a file from several simultaneous locations/files, a sort of Bit Torrent based on a client/server model). Let's choose the traditional way. Click the "Download CD/DVD images using HTTP or FTP" option and you will be send to the page seen in Figure 6-3.

## Official CD/DVD images of the *"stable"* release

To install Debian on a machine without an Internet connection, it's possible to use CD images (650 MB each) or DVD images (4.4 GB each). Download the first CD or DVD image file, write it using a CD/DVD recorder (or a USB stick on i386 and amd64 ports), and then reboot from that.

The **first** CD/DVD disk contains all the files necessary to install a standard Debian system.
To avoid needless downloads, please do **not** download other CD or DVD image files unless you know that you need packages on them.

**CD**
The following links point to image files which are up to 650 MB in size, making them suitable for writing to normal CD-R(W) media:

**DVD**
The following links point to image files which are up to 4.4 GB in size, making them suitable for writing to normal DVD-R/DVD+R and similar media:

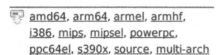 amd64, arm64, armel, armhf, i386, mips, mipsel, powerpc, ppc64el, s390x, source, multi-arch

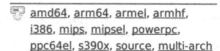 amd64, arm64, armel, armhf, i386, mips, mipsel, powerpc, ppc64el, s390x, source, multi-arch

***Figure 6-3.*** *Debian Stable ISO images*

Now you can select the Stable version or the Testing one. Choose the Stable one; it's available in two formats: CD and DVD. The CD is currently is a collection of eight pieces; there are only three in the DVD format. Get the image corresponding to your computer architecture; in my case, I got the amd64 version. Click it, and you go to the page shown in Figure 6-4, where you actually can download the image that you need.

| Name | Last modified | Size |
|------|---------------|------|
| Parent Directory | | - |
| MD5SUMS | 2015-06-08 00:17 | 893 |
| MD5SUMS.sign | 2015-06-08 00:32 | 819 |
| SHA1SUMS | 2015-06-08 00:17 | 1.0K |
| SHA1SUMS.sign | 2015-06-08 00:32 | 819 |
| SHA256SUMS | 2015-06-08 00:17 | 1.3K |
| SHA256SUMS.sign | 2015-06-08 00:32 | 819 |
| SHA512SUMS | 2015-06-08 00:17 | 2.2K |
| SHA512SUMS.sign | 2015-06-08 00:32 | 819 |
| debian-8.1.0-amd64-DVD-1.iso | 2015-06-06 17:33 | 3.7G |
| debian-8.1.0-amd64-DVD-2.iso | 2015-06-06 17:33 | 4.4G |
| debian-8.1.0-amd64-DVD-3.iso | 2015-06-06 17:33 | 4.4G |
| debian-update-8.1.0-amd64-DVD-1.iso | 2015-06-07 02:41 | 4.1G |

*Figure 6-4.* *The Debian DVD images currently available for amd64*

After you select the first DVD (you only need the first one), it starts the download. When it's done, you can boot up your computer for the first time with that image (Figure 6-5).

*Figure 6-5.* *The first screen of the Debian installation*

After your computer has completely started, the first screen will be very familiar to you because it's the same as you saw in the Ubuntu/Fedora installations. However, it offers some unusual options. There are three installation options (Install, Graphical install, and Install with speech synthesis). Additionally, the advanced options include Expert install, Rescue mode, Automated install, and the graphical versions of them. You can see both menus in Figure 6-5. The options without the word "graphical" at the beginning are text interfaces, which are very useful for systems where the auto-detection of the graphic card does not work well or for a faster option for those used to it (it's the one that I prefer). The graphical one is the friendliest one, and you can use the mouse. You can see the difference between them in Figure 6-6. So choose the Graphical install option and begin the installation process.

113

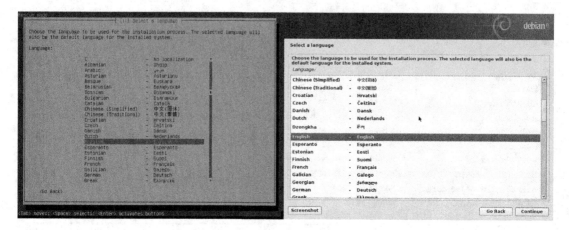

**Figure 6-6.** *Both versions of the installation process: text-based and graphical*

The first screen (Figure 6-6) ask you for the language that you want to use in the rest of the process, and then your location and your keyboard template, as you can see in Figure 6-7.

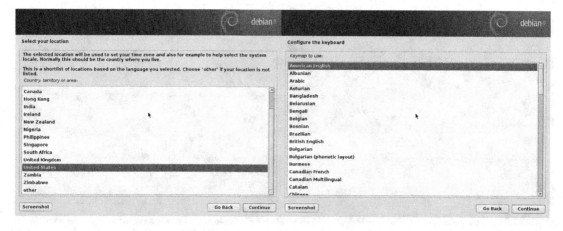

**Figure 6-7.** *Location and keyboard selection*

Next, the installer will show you progress bars, the first to detect and mount your CD-ROM (or the ISO image on a USB drive), the second one to load the rest of the installer components from the image. A third one will appear to detect and auto-configure the network; if not, it will prompt you for your network values.

The next screen (Figure 6-8) is about the hostname of your system; it suggests "debian" by default (and I left it) but you can choose whatever you want. Next, it asks for a domain name, but you can leave it blank, as I did in Figure 6-9.

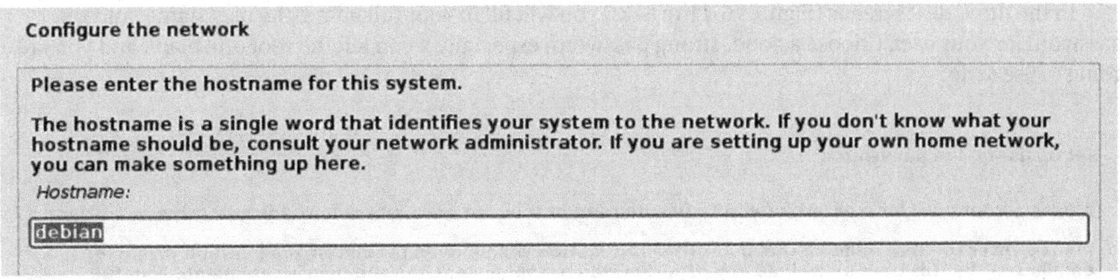

**Configure the network**

Please enter the hostname for this system.

The hostname is a single word that identifies your system to the network. If you don't know what your hostname should be, consult your network administrator. If you are setting up your own home network, you can make something up here.

*Hostname:*

debian

*Figure 6-8. The hostname value*

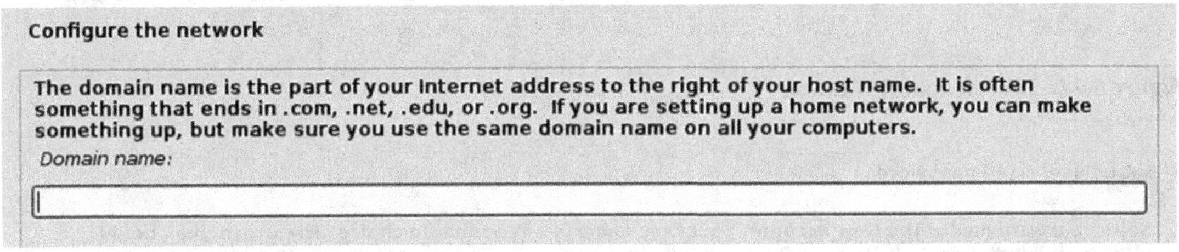

**Configure the network**

The domain name is the part of your Internet address to the right of your host name. It is often something that ends in .com, .net, .edu, or .org. If you are setting up a home network, you can make something up, but make sure you use the same domain name on all your computers.

*Domain name:*

*Figure 6-9. The domain value*

Now you have to set the password for the root user (Figure 6-10). Remember the advice I gave you in the preceding chapter and choose a strong one here, or leave it blank to disable this user and use your regular user and the command "sudo" like in Ubuntu; it's up to you. I set one here because old habits die hard, but the latter option is completely fine (some prefer it because the bad guys must guess two things, the user name and the password, to attack the system remotely).

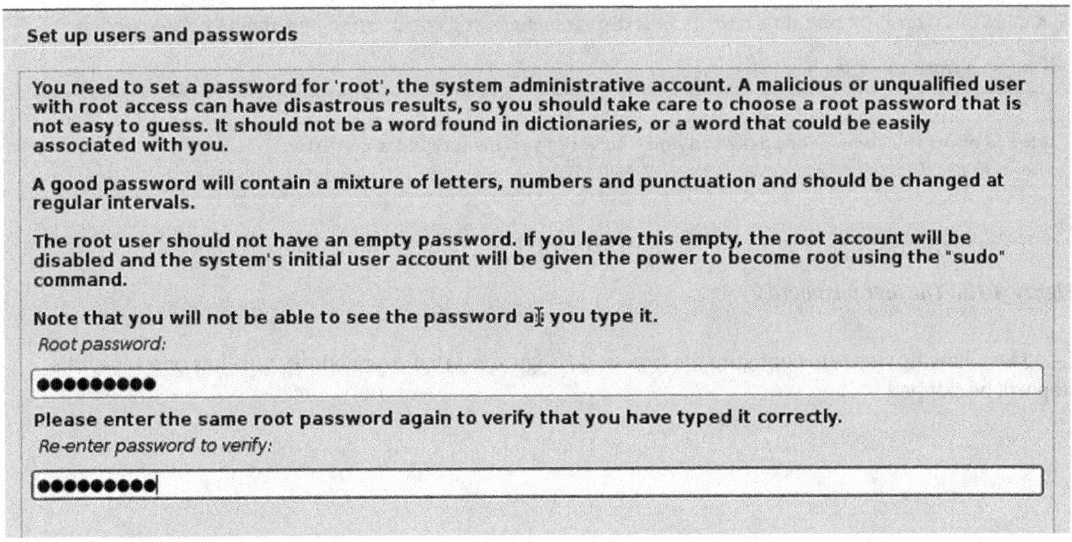

**Set up users and passwords**

You need to set a password for 'root', the system administrative account. A malicious or unqualified user with root access can have disastrous results, so you should take care to choose a root password that is not easy to guess. It should not be a word found in dictionaries, or a word that could be easily associated with you.

A good password will contain a mixture of letters, numbers and punctuation and should be changed at regular intervals.

The root user should not have an empty password. If you leave this empty, the root account will be disabled and the system's initial user account will be given the power to become root using the "sudo" command.

Note that you will not be able to see the password as you type it.

*Root password:*

●●●●●●●●●

Please enter the same root password again to verify that you have typed it correctly.

*Re-enter password to verify:*

●●●●●●●●●

*Figure 6-10. The root password*

In the three next screens (Figures 6-11 to 6-13) you will fill in your full name, the user name, and the password for your user. Choose a good, strong password, especially if you left the root one blank and you are going to use sudo.

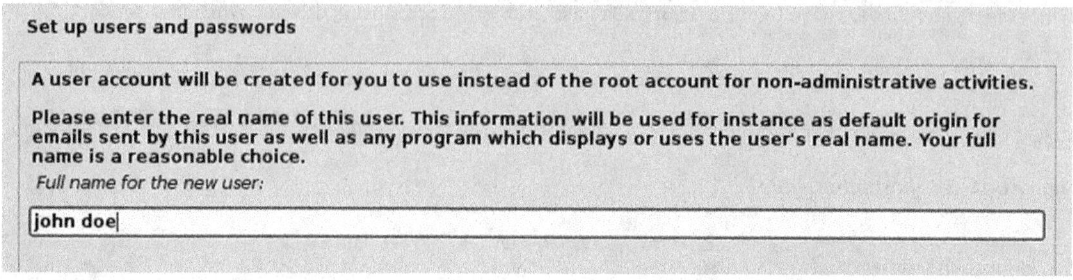

**Set up users and passwords**

A user account will be created for you to use instead of the root account for non-administrative activities.

Please enter the real name of this user. This information will be used for instance as default origin for emails sent by this user as well as any program which displays or uses the user's real name. Your full name is a reasonable choice.

*Full name for the new user:*

john doe

*Figure 6-11.* *The full name of the user*

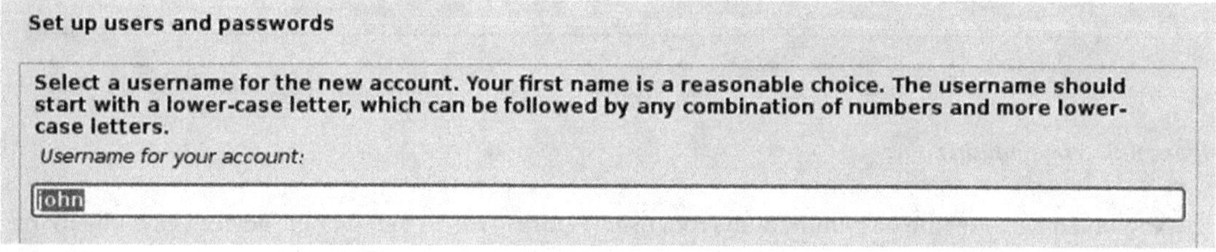

**Set up users and passwords**

Select a username for the new account. Your first name is a reasonable choice. The username should start with a lower-case letter, which can be followed by any combination of numbers and more lower-case letters.

*Username for your account:*

john

*Figure 6-12.* *The user name for the account*

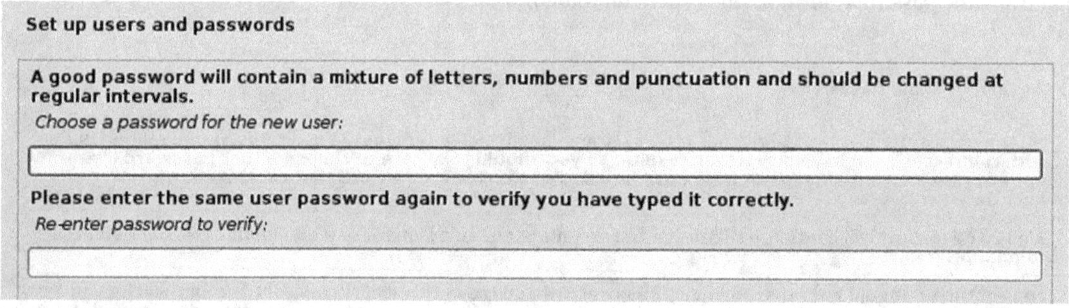

**Set up users and passwords**

A good password will contain a mixture of letters, numbers and punctuation and should be changed at regular intervals.

*Choose a password for the new user:*

Please enter the same user password again to verify you have typed it correctly.

*Re-enter password to verify:*

*Figure 6-13.* *The user password*

The following step is to configure the time zone (Figure 6-14); if your country only has one zone, this step will be skipped.

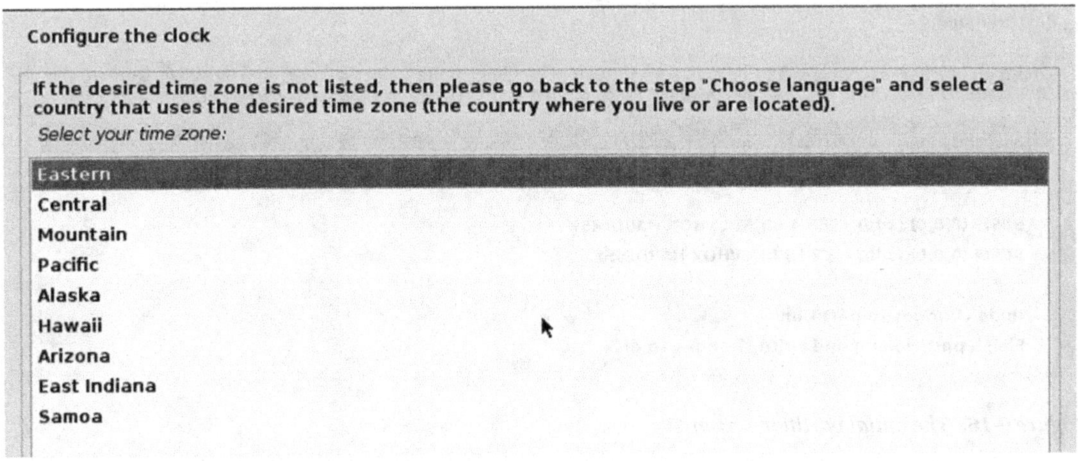

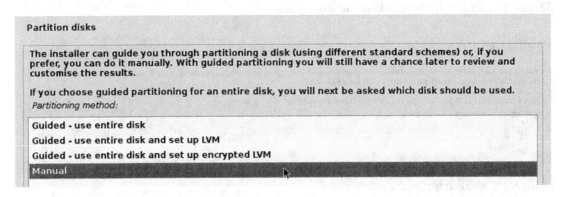

**Figure 6-14.** *Configuration of the time zone*

Now you begin the hard part of the installation: using the partition manager. After it detects your disks, you will see a screen like Figure 6-15.

**Figure 6-15.** *Selecting the partition method*

I'm going to show a different scenario from the previous ones. Let's imagine a very common situation: a desktop system with two hard drives, one SDD (250GB) and one HDD (2TB). To get the best of both drives, you probably want to have the system and configuration files on the SSD for good general performance and your personal files and data on the HDD for good storage capacity. To do this, you must choose the Manual option on the menu.

The screen in Figure 6-16 is what you should find in a scenario like the one I propose. You can see the two disks; you can differentiate them by the capacity and how both don't have any partitions yet. Take a good look at them. In fact, I suggest that you write this info down on paper because you will need it later. Now you must make the partitions. I will show you how to make one of them and you can figure it out how to make the rest.

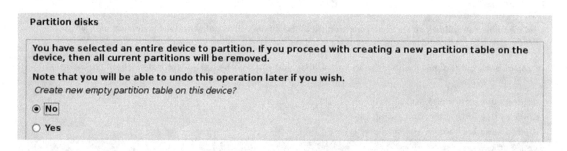

**Partition disks**

This is an overview of your currently configured partitions and mount points. Select a partition to modify its settings (file system, mount point, etc.), a free space to create partitions, or a device to initialize its partition table.

Guided partitioning
Configure iSCSI volumes

SCSI3 (0,0,0) (sda) - 268.4 GB ATA VBOX HARDDISK
SCSI4 (0,0,0) (sdb) - 2.2 TB ATA VBOX HARDDISK

Undo changes to partitions
Finish partitioning and write changes to disk

***Figure 6-16.*** *The initial partition screen*

From my point of view, this is the weakest part of the install program, because it's not that intuitive and it's hard for newcomers to understand how the interface in this part works. I will show you the easiest way possible.

Let's begin with the first partition of the SDD. To do this, click the description of the disk. You'll get a screen similar to Figure 6-17. It asks for confirmation to create a new empty partition table on the disk. In this case, let's assume that both disks are new, so say yes.

**Partition disks**

You have selected an entire device to partition. If you proceed with creating a new partition table on the device, then all current partitions will be removed.

Note that you will be able to undo this operation later if you wish.
Create new empty partition table on this device?

◉ No

○ Yes

***Figure 6-17.*** *New empty partition confirmation*

In Figure 6-18, you can see how the SSD disk has a new empty partition table. You can also see that you have new options in the superior menu. To simplify things, I will avoid any LVM, RAID, or encryption settings. Thus, to create your first new partition, click the partition table.

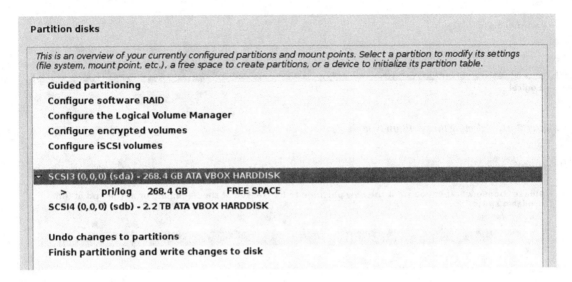

*Figure 6-18.* *A new partition table is created*

Another screen appears (Figure 6-19). Select the "Create a new partition" menu entry.

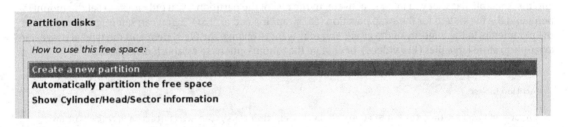

*Figure 6-19.* *Choosing the action on the free disk space*

The first partition that you are going to create is the boot partition with a size of 500MB (Figure 6-20).

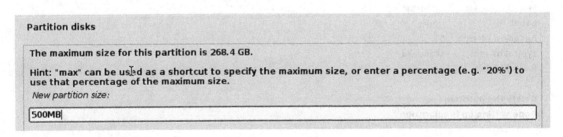

*Figure 6-20.* *Size of the partition*

Next, you must set the type of the partition (Figure 6-21), Primary in this case, and then you must say where you want to allocate the partition, at the beginning or at the end of the free available space (Figure 6-22). Obviously you want to allocate this partition at the beginning (actually, being an SSD, this is not as important as in the hard disk case, but it is the norm).

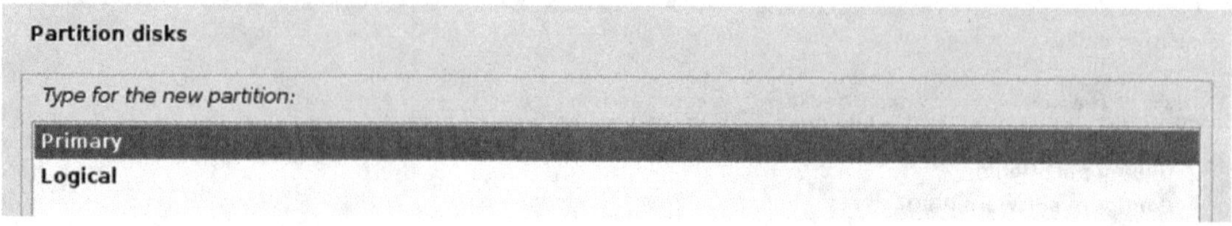

**Partition disks**

Type for the new partition:

Primary

Logical

*Figure 6-21.* *Selecting the partition type*

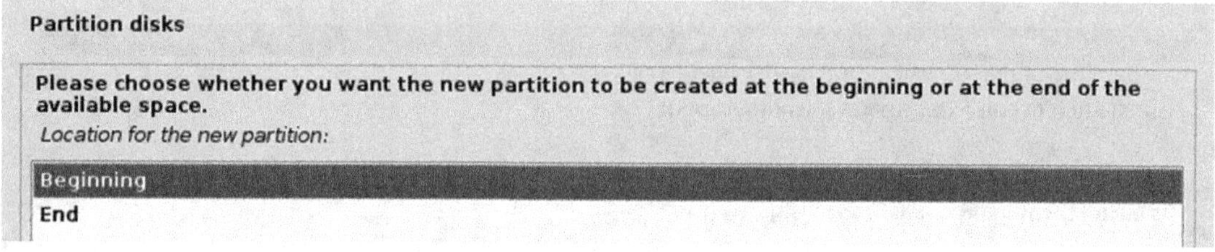

**Partition disks**

**Please choose whether you want the new partition to be created at the beginning or at the end of the available space.**
Location for the new partition:

Beginning

End

*Figure 6-22.* *Where the partition is allocated*

The screen that appears will show the default settings of this partition (Figure 6-23). Each one of them can be customized; in this case, let's keep the defaults except for the mount point, which you set to /boot, and the bootable flag that you need to activate. In the rest of the partitions, you only need to set the mount point and the file system for the swap partition (as "swap" instead of "Ext4"). You can safely ignore the rest of the parameters in the majority of the cases. You may want to change the file system and the typical usage, for example to store large files (like videos), or change the mount options to establish disk quotas.

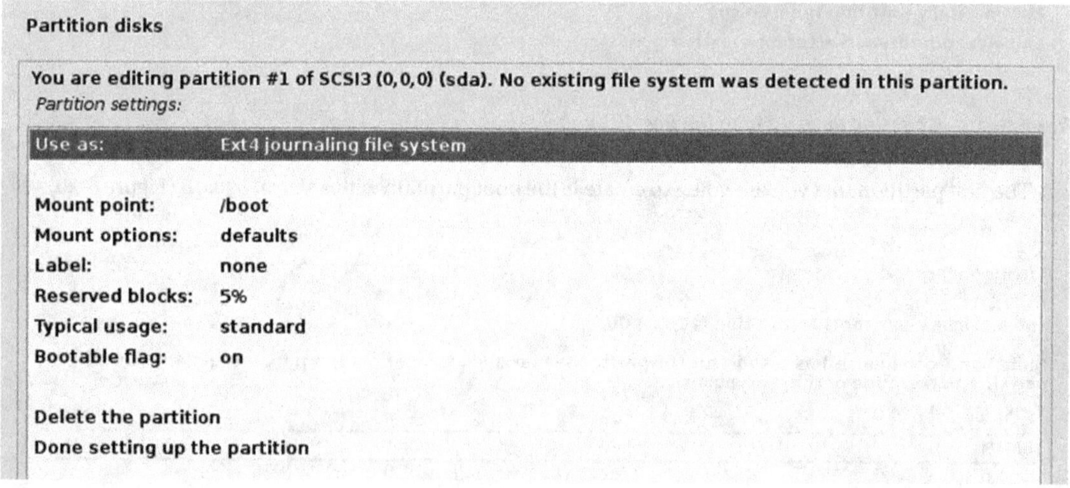

**Partition disks**

**You are editing partition #1 of SCSI3 (0,0,0) (sda). No existing file system was detected in this partition.**
Partition settings:

Use as:                Ext4 journaling file system

Mount point:          /boot
Mount options:        defaults
Label:                none
Reserved blocks:      5%
Typical usage:        standard
Bootable flag:        on

Delete the partition
Done setting up the partition

*Figure 6-23.* *Partition settings*

As you can see, this method is a little less friendly than the graphical installers of Fedora and Ubuntu, but it's not as hard as the rumors said. Actually, comparing it to both previous distros, it's not that hard to install it. The maintenance is where things change a bit versus Fedora and a lot versus Ubuntu.

Once you set the partition settings, you can see how the partition table has changed to reflect that (Figure 6-24). All of the important parameters are shown here: number, type, size, boot flag, format flag, file system, and mount point. And you can see the amount of free space that remains after creating the new partition.

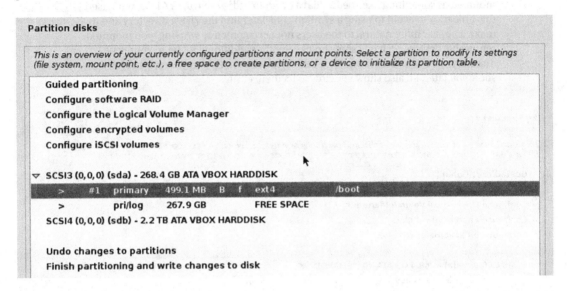

**Figure 6-24.** *A new partition is created*

You can proceed in the same manner to create the rest of the partitions to achieve the goal shown in Figure 6-25. At the end, you should have the following partitions/mount points:

- /boot: The partition where you store the files needed to boot the system. It is the only one with the boot flag "B" activated.

- /: The root partition, where the system files are stored. This is located in the SSD to improve the performance of the read/write operations.

- swap: The size of this partition depends of the amount of memory that you have; these days, a good option is to make it almost as big as your RAM memory (to allow the system to suspend to disk or hibernate). Some people think it's a bad idea to put this partition on a SSD drive; well, the days when they easily wear out are behind, and when you have enough memory, this partition is usually only used to store the contents of your RAM when hibernating. So it's not a problem to locate this partition here.

- /home: Where your configurations files are going to be stored. By default, this partition should be used to store your data files too, so why not create this partition in the HHD? For same reason you created the data partition in the HDD, to achieve a balance between speed and big storage capacity. You want to have a big space available to store your files (especially multimedia, like your pictures or your videos), but at the same time you want your programs to start quickly and have good performance. The binary files of your programs are going to be in the / partition, but the configuration files for a lot of those programs are stored by default in the root folder of the /home partition. So, no matter how fast your program starts, if it has to wait to read the configuration file in the HDD, it's a problem. You should store only these files and the files that you want to speed up because you use them frequently, such as work files like spreadsheets, etc.

- /home/john/data: This is where you should store all of your big files as well as files that you do not use regularly. It has the disadvantage of worse performance but it has great capacity. Notice that I used the following scheme for the mounting point, /home/youruser/data, where john is the user I created before. Usually this would be mounted as something like /media/data or /run/media/youruser/data, but I used this little trick to avoid to using a symbolic link later into the /home directory and to make it appear more natural to the users not accustomed to working with mounted/removable devices, so it will show up like another additional folder in your home directory. All of these methods have little inconveniences/annoyances that I will show you later; I'll also show you how to fix them easily.

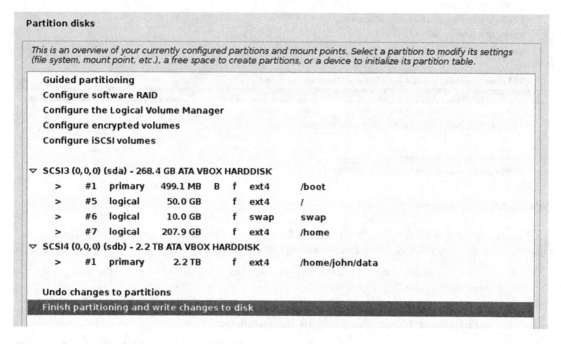

**Figure 6-25.** *The final partition settings for both disks*

Finally, after you create all of those partitions, the installer will ask you to confirm the writing of these changes to your disks by showing you a resume of them (Figure 6-26). If everything is OK, you can continue with the installation.

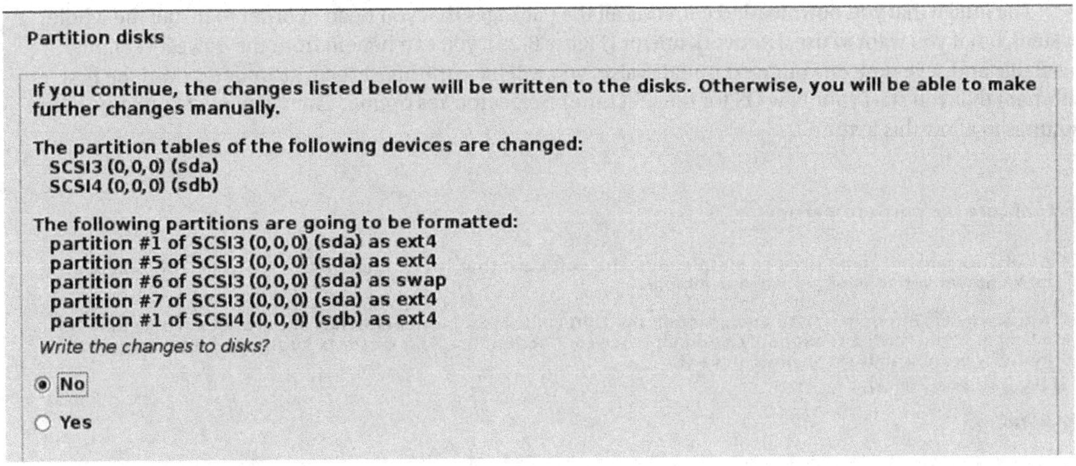

**Partition disks**

If you continue, the changes listed below will be written to the disks. Otherwise, you will be able to make further changes manually.

The partition tables of the following devices are changed:
  SCSI3 (0,0,0) (sda)
  SCSI4 (0,0,0) (sdb)

The following partitions are going to be formatted:
  partition #1 of SCSI3 (0,0,0) (sda) as ext4
  partition #5 of SCSI3 (0,0,0) (sda) as ext4
  partition #6 of SCSI3 (0,0,0) (sda) as swap
  partition #7 of SCSI3 (0,0,0) (sda) as ext4
  partition #1 of SCSI4 (0,0,0) (sdb) as ext4

*Write the changes to disks?*

◉ No

○ Yes

*Figure 6-26.* *Disk changes confirmation screen*

The installer is going to create the partitions, format them, and then begin to install the base system. This will take some time (Figure 6-27).

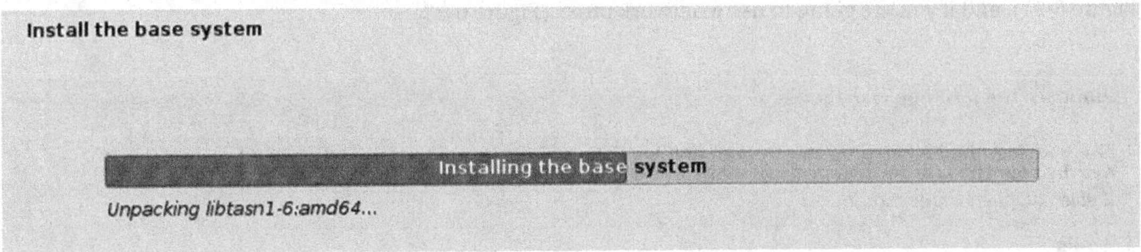

**Install the base system**

Installing the base system

*Unpacking libtasn1-6:amd64...*

*Figure 6-27.* *Installing the base system*

After a while you have the option of scanning more CD/DVDs (images) if you already downloaded them. This can be very useful when there is no Internet connection available. In this case, select the No option and continue (Figure 6-28).

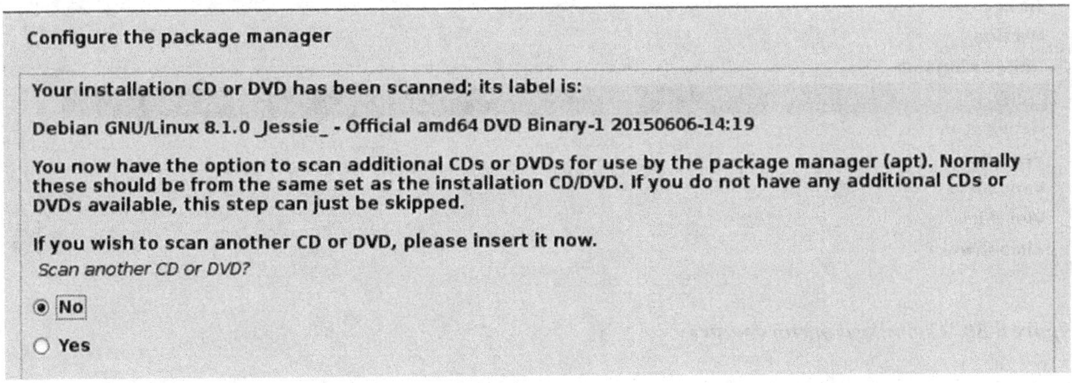

**Configure the package manager**

Your installation CD or DVD has been scanned; its label is:

Debian GNU/Linux 8.1.0 _Jessie_ - Official amd64 DVD Binary-1 20150606-14:19

You now have the option to scan additional CDs or DVDs for use by the package manager (apt). Normally these should be from the same set as the installation CD/DVD. If you do not have any additional CDs or DVDs available, this step can just be skipped.

If you wish to scan another CD or DVD, please insert it now.

*Scan another CD or DVD?*

◉ No

○ Yes

*Figure 6-28.* *Optional scanning of another CD/DVD*

The image that you downloaded contains all the packages that you need in order to install the whole system, but if you want to use a network mirror (Figure 6-29), you can benefit from the newest versions available and save time on your next update (also, you will have the latest security updates from the first moment that you start your new OS for the first time). Select the Yes option. Then you must configure some settings to allow this feature.

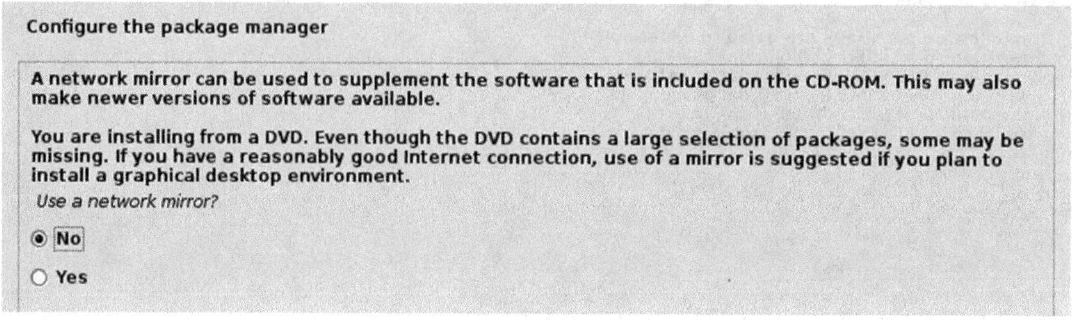

**Configure the package manager**

A network mirror can be used to supplement the software that is included on the CD-ROM. This may also make newer versions of software available.

You are installing from a DVD. Even though the DVD contains a large selection of packages, some may be missing. If you have a reasonably good Internet connection, use of a mirror is suggested if you plan to install a graphical desktop environment.

*Use a network mirror?*

⦿ No

○ Yes

*Figure 6-29.* *Deciding to use a network mirror*

You need to select the country where the mirror server is located (Figure 6-30), the actual mirror server (Figure 6-31), and if you are going to use a network proxy (Figure 6-32).

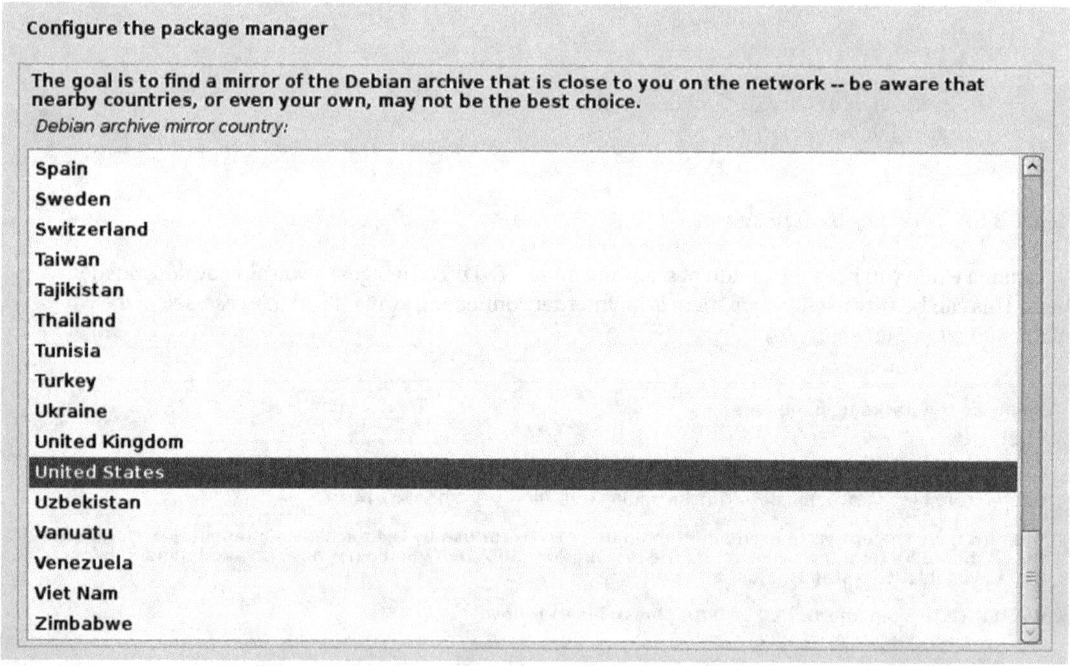

**Configure the package manager**

The goal is to find a mirror of the Debian archive that is close to you on the network -- be aware that nearby countries, or even your own, may not be the best choice.

*Debian archive mirror country:*

Spain
Sweden
Switzerland
Taiwan
Tajikistan
Thailand
Tunisia
Turkey
Ukraine
United Kingdom
United States
Uzbekistan
Vanuatu
Venezuela
Viet Nam
Zimbabwe

*Figure 6-30.* *Choosing a mirror country*

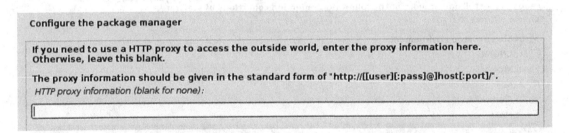

**Figure 6-31.** *Choosing an archive mirror*

**Configure the package manager**

If you need to use a HTTP proxy to access the outside world, enter the proxy information here. Otherwise, leave this blank.

The proxy information should be given in the standard form of "http://[[user][:pass]@]host[:port]/".

*HTTP proxy information (blank for none):*

**Figure 6-32.** *Configuring an HTTP Proxy*

The next step (Figure 6-33) questions if you want to send information (anonymously) from the packages that you are going to install on your system. This is up to you, but it's very helpful to Debian to be able to collect data to make usage statistics.

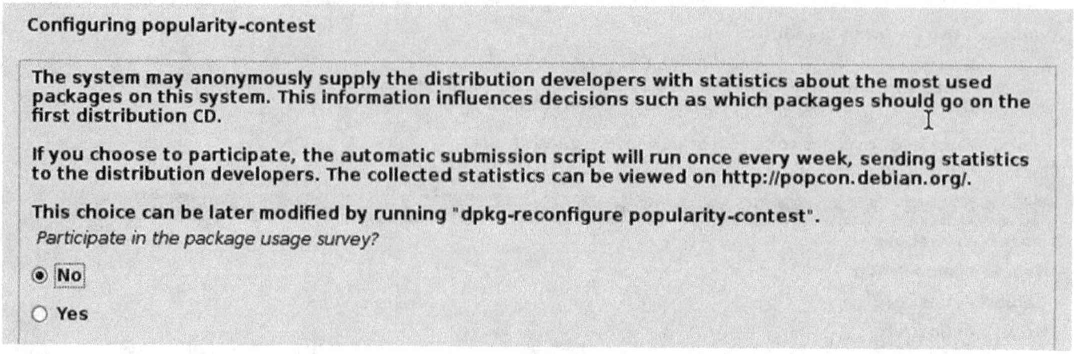

Configuring popularity-contest

The system may anonymously supply the distribution developers with statistics about the most used packages on this system. This information influences decisions such as which packages should go on the first distribution CD.

If you choose to participate, the automatic submission script will run once every week, sending statistics to the distribution developers. The collected statistics can be viewed on http://popcon.debian.org/.

This choice can be later modified by running "dpkg-reconfigure popularity-contest".

*Participate in the package usage survey?*

◉ No

○ Yes

***Figure 6-33.*** *Participating in the package usage survey*

Now you must select what predefined collections of software you want to install (Figure 6-34). Here you see mainly the desktop environments that Debian supports and a few more things, but if you had scanned another CD/DVD you would see more collections. Although the de facto DE of Debian is Gnome, I want to choose one that you won't see in any other distro installation: LXDE. So choose it and leave the other options selected by default. If you choose the SSH server, you better know how to secure it because it is one of the most frequent vectors of attack in a Linux system.

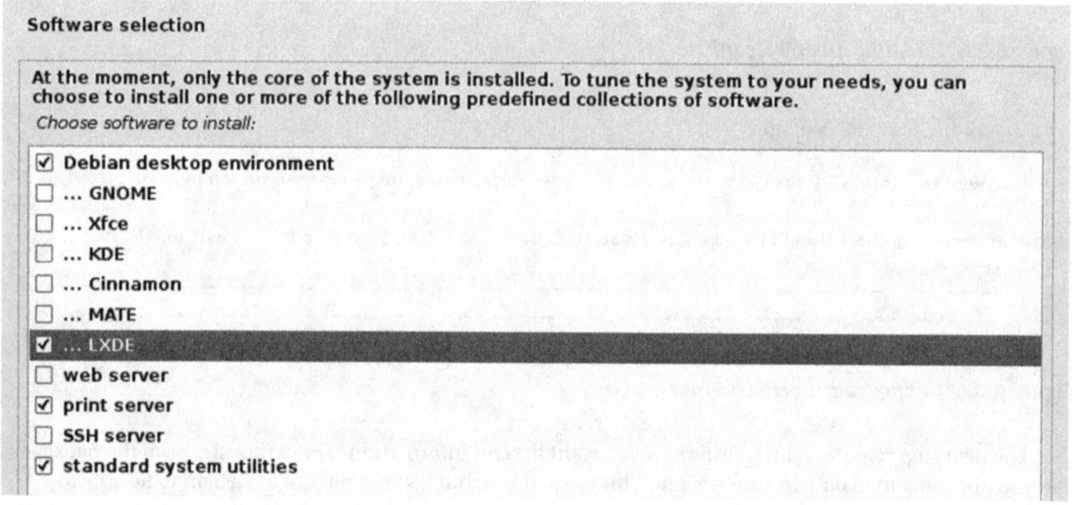

Software selection

At the moment, only the core of the system is installed. To tune the system to your needs, you can choose to install one or more of the following predefined collections of software.

*Choose software to install:*

- ☑ **Debian desktop environment**
- ☐ ... GNOME
- ☐ ... Xfce
- ☐ ... KDE
- ☐ ... Cinnamon
- ☐ ... MATE
- ☑ ... LXDE
- ☐ web server
- ☑ print server
- ☐ SSH server
- ☑ standard system utilities

***Figure 6-34.*** *Selecting the software to install*

Once you select the software, the longest step (Figure 6-35) of the installation process begins, the installation (and download) of the packages to your SSD drive.

**Select and install software**

Select and install software

*Preparing python-notify (amd64)*

***Figure 6-35.*** *Installing the software*

Finally, you have to decide (Figure 6-36) whether to install the boot loader (Grub, in this case) on your hard drive to manage the boot up of your system. In this case, pick Yes and continue.

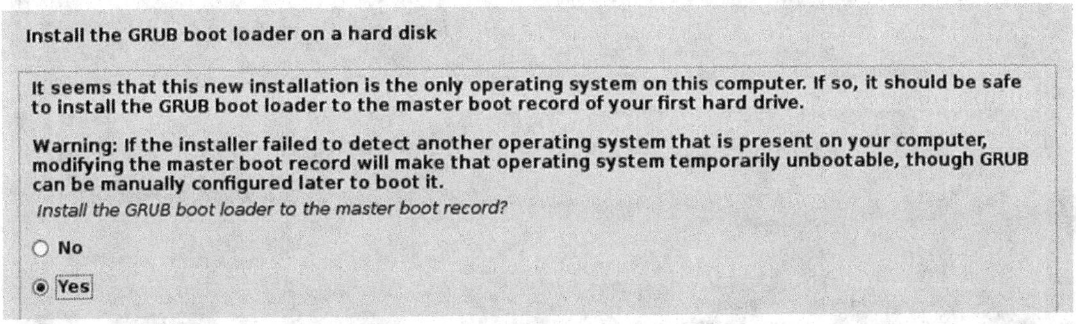

**Install the GRUB boot loader on a hard disk**

It seems that this new installation is the only operating system on this computer. If so, it should be safe to install the GRUB boot loader to the master boot record of your first hard drive.

Warning: If the installer failed to detect another operating system that is present on your computer, modifying the master boot record will make that operating system temporarily unbootable, though GRUB can be manually configured later to boot it.

*Install the GRUB boot loader to the master boot record?*

○ No

◉ Yes

***Figure 6-36.*** *Deciding to install Grub*

The final decision to make is upon which disk you want to install Grub (Figure 6-37). You must install it on the drive that has the bootable partition (/boot, in this case), which is the SSD one. I told you before to write down the references of the disks (sda and sdb) because it was going to be helpful later; well, that's now. You can see that the only references to identify both drives are the UUID (Universal Unique Identifier) and the device path (e.g. /dev/sda). You could figure it out by the order, but it's always better to know for sure, isn't it? Well, your SSD is the /dev/sda device, so choose it and continue.

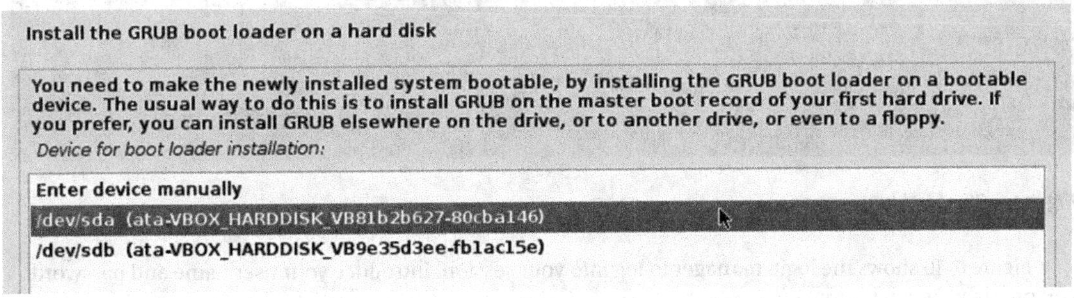

**Install the GRUB boot loader on a hard disk**

You need to make the newly installed system bootable, by installing the GRUB boot loader on a bootable device. The usual way to do this is to install GRUB on the master boot record of your first hard drive. If you prefer, you can install GRUB elsewhere on the drive, or to another drive, or even to a floppy.

*Device for boot loader installation:*

**Enter device manually**

/dev/sda (ata-VBOX_HARDDISK_VB81b2b627-80cba146)

/dev/sdb (ata-VBOX_HARDDISK_VB9e35d3ee-fb1ac15e)

***Figure 6-37.*** *Choosing the disk upon which to install Grub*

That's it! Your Debian OS is installed (Figure 6-38). It wasn't that hard, right? You must reboot your system now.

**Finish the installation**

 *Installation complete*

**Installation is complete, so it is time to boot into your new system. Make sure to remove the installation media (CD-ROM, floppies), so that you boot into the new system rather than restarting the installation.**

***Figure 6-38.*** *The installation is finished.*

The first screen that you see when you boot up your system for the first time is the already familiar Grub screen, which you saw in the Fedora install (Figure 6-39). Press Enter or wait to boot your new Debian OS.

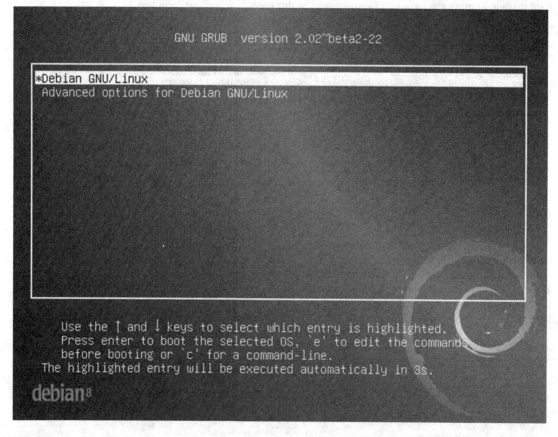

***Figure 6-39.*** *First boot screen*

Figure 6-40 shows the login manager to log into your session. Introduce your user name and password, and press the Log in button.

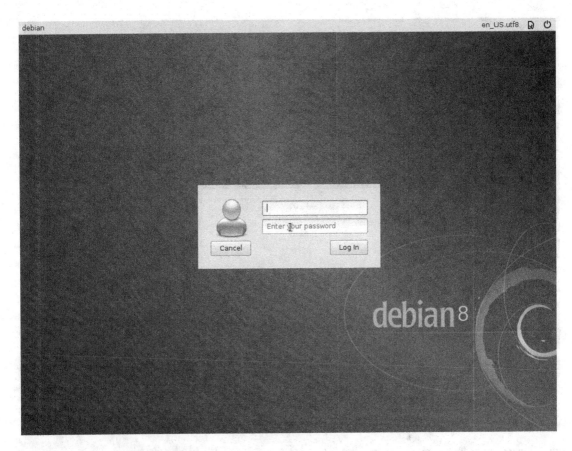

***Figure 6-40.*** *First login in Debian*

You are logged now in the LXDE desktop environment. The first thing that you can see in the middle of the screen is a pop-up dialog (Figure 6-41) that gives you advice about ClipIt and the security risks of saving that information in plain text. It's up to you; I don't even use ClipIt, so I don't recommend activating it. (I use a clipboard without history, with only the current data in it.)

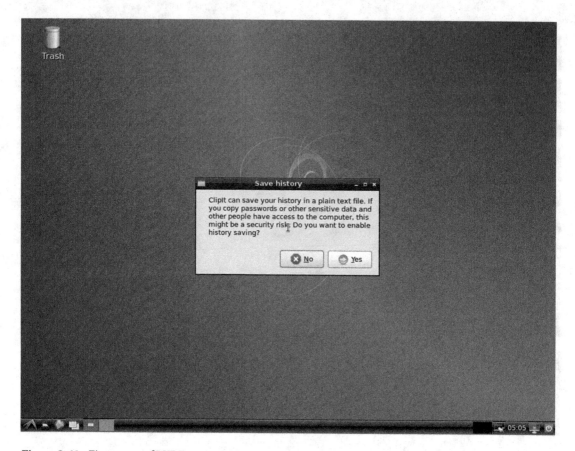

*Figure 6-41.* *First screen of LXDE*

I told you before that mounting the data partition would have a little inconvenience/annoyance, and this is it. The partition is created with the root user permissions, and you are not allowed to write anything in there (and therefore you must create a new file, as you can see in Figure 6-42). But this is easily fixable.

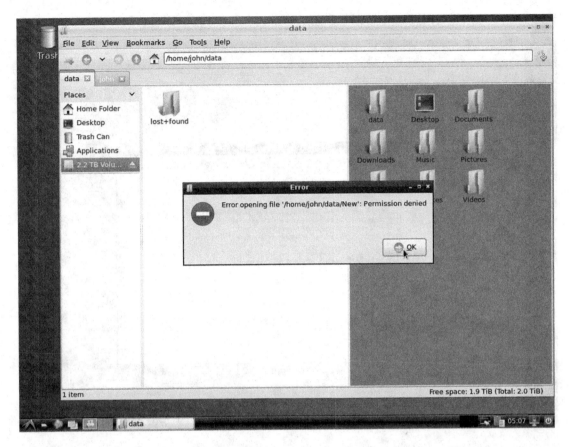

*Figure 6-42.* *Wrong permissions in data partition*

You have to change the permissions for the mounted partition to the user that you created. You can see how to do this in Figure 6-43, but I repeat it here where it's easier to read.

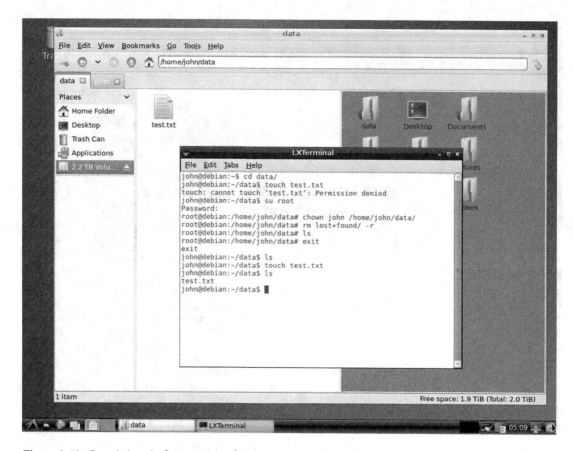

*Figure 6-43.* *Permissions in data partition fixed*

If you gave a password to the root user, you have to do it like this:

```
$ su root
Password:                              # enter the root password
# chown john /home/john/data/  # user your username instead of john
# rm lost+found/ -r            # delete the lost+found folder
# exit                         # never let the root user log in
$
```

If you left the root password blank, you have to use the sudo command:

```
$ sudo chown john /home/john/data/  # user your username instead of john
Password:                           # enter your user password
$ sudo rm lost+found/ -r            # delete the lost+found folder
$
```

And that's it! Your new Linux Debian OS is ready to use! Enjoy it!

You can read an installation guide at www.debian.org/releases/stable/amd64/index.html.en.

# Maintenance

Again, the three essential tasks are updating, installing/deleting apps, and upgrading. Like Fedora, you must deal with the command line, like it or not, and be familiar with the essential apps to do the job.

## Managing Apps

To install/delete applications you can use a graphical application, as is the case with Ubuntu/Fedora, like Synaptic. But almost every Debian user users the command line to do this. You can use the typical apt tools or you can use the friendlier aptitude. For example, if you want to install an app (such as gnome-chess), you should use this command:

```
# aptitude install gnome-chess
```

To remove it:

```
# aptitude remove gnome-chess
```

It's as simple as that, and you have a level of control over what you're doing that is superior to what you get with the graphical application (it's hard to see from a simple example like this, but it's true).

## Updating

The same happens with the package updating process: there's no easy way. You can use Synaptic, but the best way to do it is to use aptitude. To do so, you only need to type this:

```
# aptitude update
```

That's it!

---

■ **Note**   Note that the DVD that you used to install the distro is still considered as a source of packages, so whenever you use any package command, Debian will search the DVD for the packages first. If you have an Internet connection, you don't want this to happen. You always want the freshest packages, so you must fix this behavior. Again, Debian does not provide an easy way to do this (well, that's not entirely true; you can do this with the Synaptic application in a graphical way), so you must edit a plain text configuration file. Here I use the graphical text editor that comes with LXDE (I would use Vi(m) or Emacs, but that's another story) to edit the file:

```
# leafpad /etc/apt/sources.list    # open the file with Leafpad
```

And now you must locate two lines at the beginning of the file that begin with something similar to this:

```
# deb cd rom:
deb cd rom:
```

The only thing you need to do is comment the second line by preceding the line with the "#" character, like the first line. Save the file, close Leafpad, and that's it.

---

# Upgrading

To upgrade the distro, you must update the currently installed packages. You should also make a backup of your data first, because this is a critical process. Let's see how it's done:

```
# apt-get update           # update the current packates using apt tools
# apt-get upgrade          # a first minimal upgrade to avoid conflicts later
# apt-get dist-upgrade     # the full upgrade of the distribution
```

This is enough in desktop installations and in a majority of cases. If this is a server or another critical machine, there are additional steps that you should take, but that's a story for another book.

# Pros and Cons

The following is a list of some things that I personally see as pros and cons of the Debian distro. Of course there's always room for discussion in this matter, but I've done my best to be as objective as possible.

## Pros

- The *Debian Manifesto*, the *Debian Social Contract*, the *Debian Constitution*, plus its long longevity and big community are guarantees that Debian is going to be among us for a long, long time.

- The stability of the Stable branch is one of the best of all the Linux distros; it's always a bit outdated but stable as a rock.

- Although there's no company behind Debian, its community is one of the friendliest and most willing when it comes to helping its users, so you will have very good support.

- The size of its community.

- The big number of available packages.

- It uses one of the most extended and best package managers: dpkg.

- It is an original distro, not a derivative.

- It is widely adopted by a lot of professionals and organizations.

- It supports many architectures and even various kernels.

## Cons

- There is no regular/fixed cycle of releases for the Stable branch, so you could wait for a long time for the next one.

- Aesthetics and design are greatly ignored in this distro.

- It has no official commercial support.

- You must know how to use the terminal to perform admin tasks.

- The installer program is unfriendly and outdated.

- It is not the easiest distro to manage and configure. You have to use the terminal too much. It's for advanced users or those willing to learn.

- The Stable branch has outdated packages even when it is released.

# Summary

With the analysis of Debian, you have the third example of a Linux distro. As you could see, Debian has many points in common with Fedora and Ubuntu, but there are clear differences that make Debian unique.

The next chapter on openSUSE will introduce you to another way of doing things in Linux.

# CHAPTER 7

■ ■ ■

# openSUSE

openSUSE, as its name implies, is an open distro and the base of the SUSE Linux Enterprise commercial one. SUSE was the top European distro and the alternative to Red Hat, at least until the arrival of Ubuntu. SUSE adopted Red Hat's idea of having a community version of its commercial distro, and openSUSE received a good reception from the community, so good that it eventually displaced SUSE as the chosen distro for regular users. The SUSE family of distros have always been very well maintained, designed, and finished products. openSUSE was for years one of the few distros that was sold in a box, accompanied by a large printed manual; you can still purchase openSUSE in this manner in Germany (only in the German language, however).

## History

Although SUSE started as a German company in 1992, the openSUSE project didn't start until 2004. SUSE was purchased the American company Novell, and openSUSE was released in October of 2005. In 2011, Novell was acquired by The Attachmate Group (which merged with the British firm Micro Focus in 2014); it decided to make SUSE an independent company with its headquarters back in Germany, specifically Nuremburg. As a result, Germany and United States are the main zones where openSUSE is very popular; these locations account for almost half of the installation base.

## Philosophy

openSUSE is the community version of SUSE's commercial distro, similar to Fedora/Red Hat. openSUSE, like Fedora, is also a kind of test laboratory for new ideas and technologies. Also, both have a strict policy of only using open and free software in its official repositories/installation images. As for differences, openSUSE uses KDE as its default desktop environment, while Fedora uses Gnome. Fedora offers better security and innovation, while openSUSE provides advanced tools and services like OBS, openQA, and SUSE Studio to its community. In other words, both distros have the same initial purpose, but their results differ mainly due to the influence of their mother distros and community (in size, the Fedora community is larger than the openSUSE one). You can read about openSUSE's guiding principles at https://en.opensuse.org/openSUSE:Guiding_principles.

© Jose Dieguez Castro 2016
J. Dieguez Castro, *Introducing Linux Distros*, DOI 10.1007/978-1-4842-1392-6_7

# Distro Selection Criteria

Now that you know a little history of openSUSE, let's see how this particular distro fares on the selection criteria from Chapter 2.

## Purpose and Environment

openSUSE is a general purpose distribution, but there are a few unofficial versions developed by the community that are task-oriented ones[1]. Like Debian, there is no special version for server purposes (SUSE has one). It offers only two official versions of the distro:

- **Leap**: The regular release version of the distro and the main one. Leap is the stable version.

- **Tumbleweed**: A rolling release version of the distro, with frequent updates of the newest packages, this is a bleeding-edge version.

Also openSUSE (more specifically, SUSE) offers a unique service, SUSE studio, which allows you to create your own derivative or customized image of openSUSE. It is a very powerful tool with advanced features that lets you create images for a DVD, virtual machines, the cloud, etc. You even can deploy your images to the cloud directly or test the result online. You can find SUSE Studio at `https://susestudio.com/`.

## Support

Similar to Fedora, openSUSE only offers community support, even though SUSE is behind this distro as a sponsor. The community is far from the size of Ubuntu's or Debian's, but, as with Fedora, it is big enough to offer good support. As with the majority of distros, you can access this help through numerous channels:

- **Documentation**: `https://en.opensuse.org/Portal:Documentation`

- **Wiki**: `https://en.opensuse.org/Main_Page`

- **Forum**: `https://forums.opensuse.org/forum.php`

- **Mailing Lists**: `http://lists.opensuse.org/`

- **IRC**: `https://en.opensuse.org/openSUSE:IRC_list`

## User Friendliness

You can see in openSUSE the influence of its mother distro's orientation (to the corporate world) by how many advanced settings you can configure in your OS via graphical interfaces (and in the installation process). Still, it's reasonably easy to use.

It claims that its unique configuration and installation tool, YaST (Yet another Setup Tool), is the best and easiest to use in the Linux ecosystem. The rest of the usability of the OS is due to the default desktop manager utilities. I personally think that YaST is a very good tool, but nothing replaces the command line when you want to manage your OS. In comparison, it is comparable to Fedora (maybe a little easier); it's less easy than Ubuntu, but more than Debian. Moreover, YaST is a very powerful tool but because of this, it's perhaps is not the easiest one for beginners. Thus, I don't recommend this distro for beginners; they may get overwhelmed by so many advanced options.

---

[1] `https://en.opensuse.org/Derivatives`

# Stability

openSUSE is a very stable distribution. It also has a unique (at least as a public service) characteristic: an automated testing tool to test the build of packages, the installation process, and several features of the OS like GUI actions or if a program works as expected. With this tool, openQA (https://openqa.opensuse.org/), they can test several combinations of hardware and installation options automatically each time a new build is ready (the builds are made through another automated open tool, openSUSE Build Service). Of course it is impossible to cover all possible errors and fails with tests, but it helps greatly to build a very stable release. This tool is used for both versions of the distribution, the regular one (Leap) and the rolling release one (Tumbleweed).

The release cycle of the Leap version, the one that follows the standard release model, is intended to be a year for each minor release and three years for a major release. The support life of each version is around 18 months after the release date for each minor release and three years for a major release. Also, as of the current release, openSUSE is based on SUSE Linux Enterprise (SLES).

Also, the community selects several openSUSE versions to support (by the community) for a long time (not a fixed period) through the Evergreen program. If you want to know more about openSUSE releases, go to https://en.opensuse.org/Lifetime.

# Hardware Support

In terms of hardware support, openSUSE is in a similar place as Fedora. Because of the strict policy of not including private drivers, hardware support is not as good as that of Ubuntu by default. This can be solved partially thanks to several community repositories and the use of the rpm package system (many drivers are in this format).

# Aesthetics

Like Fedora, the aesthetics of openSUSE are the default ones of the desktop environment chosen, except for the desktop background, colors, and the installer (YaST).

# Desktop Environment

Traditionally SUSE (and openSUSE) have always offered the two main desktop environments (Gnome and KDE) as an option in the installation process, but KDE is the default/official one. openSUSE also offers the option to choose XFCE or LXDE in the installation process.

# Init System

The init system of openSUSE is the most common these days among all the distributions: systemd. openSUSE was the third big distro to adopt systemd, after Fedora (its creator) and Mageia.

# Package Management System

The package management system is the same as Fedora: rpm. Thus, it benefits from the wide distribution of this package system from third party developers. To manage the packages, it includes graphical and command line tools: YaST and zipper.

# Architecture

Until very recently, openSUSE supported two hardware architectures, 32 and 64 bits, but since the current release, Leap 42, only the Intel/AMD 64-bit architecture is supported. This is a decision that many distros are looking to make soon; Fedora and Ubuntu make this change in the near future.

# Security/Anonymity

openSUSE is a secure distro. Like Ubuntu, it enables AppArmor by default and a firewall. It is less secure than Fedora, but through YaST you can customize AppArmor, the firewall, and configure other options to harden the OS. Also, you can encrypt your partitions or your home folder.

# Principles and Ethics

Like Fedora, openSUSE provides only free and open source software by default, even drivers. But there are non-official community repositories where you can find software, which can easily be added through YaST. You can read more about openSUSE's policies at https://en.opensuse.org/Restricted_formats.

# Live CD

openSUSE offers two Live DVD ISO images, one for each desktop manager (KDE and Gnome).

# Professional Certification

Like Fedora, openSUSE does not offer any professional certification program, but its mother distribution, SUSE, does (detailed in Chapter 2).

# Installation

The first thing you must do before installing openSUSE is choose between the regular release version and the rolling release version. Here I will show you how to install the distro using the Leap version (the standard release) because it is the main one and the most probable selection by the majority of users.

As in the previous distros, you must go to the project page to download the ISO image to use it to install the OS. If you go to www.opensuse.org/, you will see a screen like Figure 7-1.

***Figure 7-1.*** *The OpenSUSE project web page*

Click the Install Leap button for the Leap version. You will go to a screen like Figure 7-2, where you can directly access the ISO image that you need by pressing the Direct Link button. You can also choose another download method such as Bit Torrent.

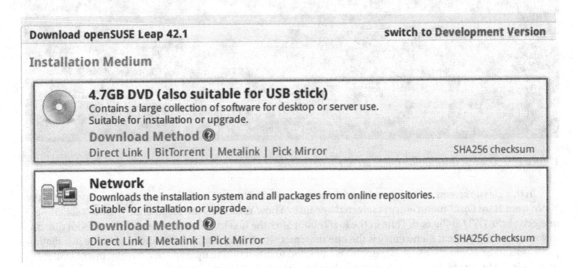

***Figure 7-2.*** *The downloaded ISO image dialog*

This screen shows two interesting options:

- The *Switch to Development Version* allows you to download the current Beta or Development version of the distro.

- The *Network* version is the minimal installation base and it relies on an Internet connection to download all of the packages.

After you download the current ISO image of the Leap version and boot up your system, you will see a screen where you can see how openSUSE takes care of certain things like design (Figure 7-3).

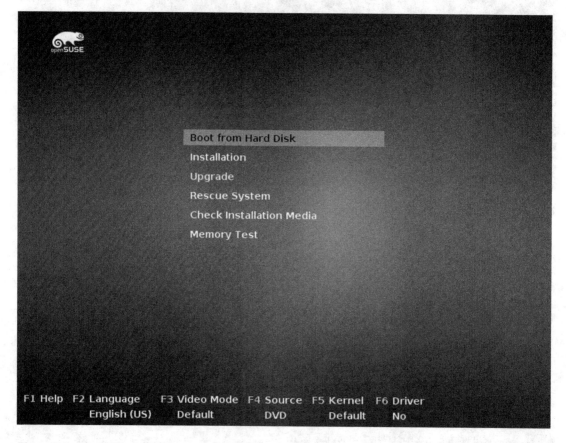

*Figure 7-3. The text installation menu screen of openSUSE*

In this classic screen, you can see (apart from the beautiful openSUSE logo) your options. By default, the "Boot from Hard Disk" menu entry is selected because of how YaST ends the installation, without soliciting or ejecting the DVD at the end. Thus in the first reboot after the first installation, openSUSE will boot directly to your new OS. The next menu entry is the one that interest us: "Installation" is going to start the installation process as soon as you choose it. "Upgrade" is intended to do an offline upgrade of a current openSUSE installation. The rest of the menu entries are the same as you saw in other distros.

Note the lines at the bottom of the screen. One line lists the usual advanced options; the line below it shows the current values selected (in this case, they are the default ones). It is worth mentioning that if you press Esc and then OK in this screen, you will be sent to the text version of this screen (the installer still is a graphical one).

So press the Installation option and then begin the installation on the first screen of YaST (Figure 7-4).

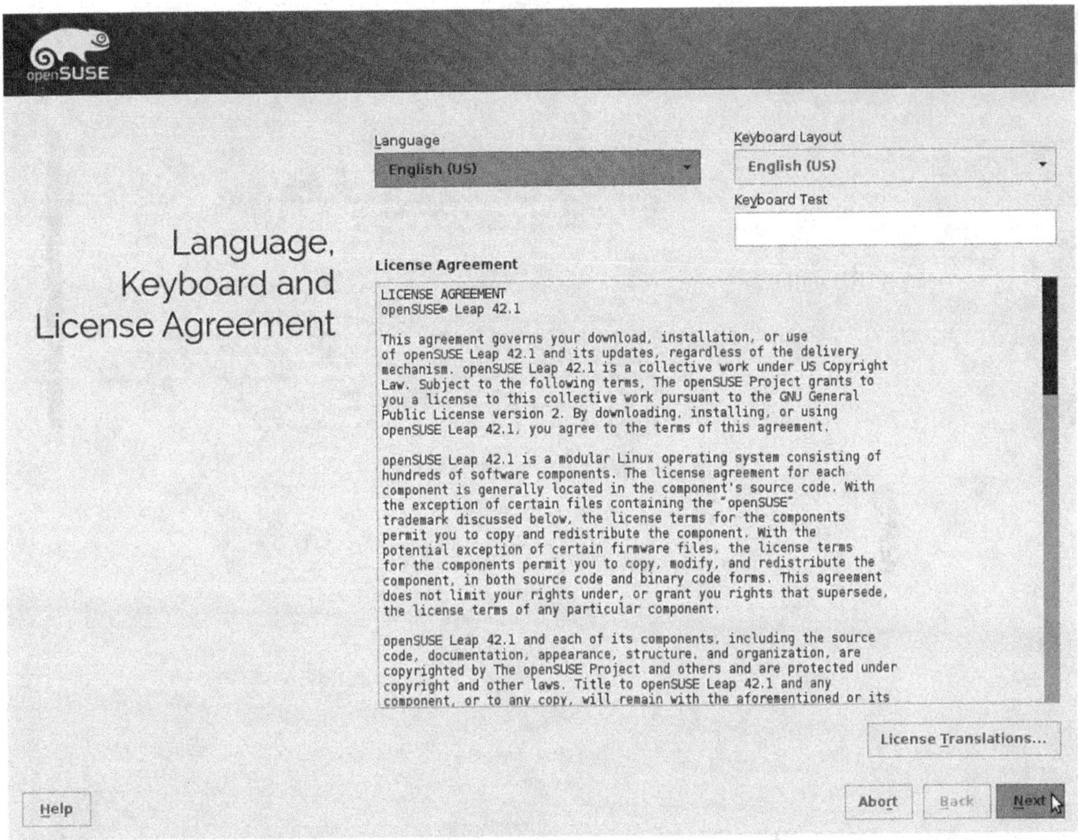

**Figure 7-4.** *The first screen of YaST is where you select the language, keyboard layout, and agree to the license*

On this first screen you see the traditional options to select a language and a keyboard layout, a Help button, and for the first time, a License Agreement. This is a peculiarity of openSUSE; it is very rare to see this in a Linux distribution, since this is Free Software under a GNU license and the majority of distros want to avoid this step to differentiate themselves from other OSes and their EULAs.

Select your language and keyboard layout, and press the Next button to jump to the next step, shown in Figure 7-5 (after a brief hardware system auto-detection process).

**Figure 7-5.** *Source installation options*

This screen offers the option to choose additional sources of packages for the installation, like the default repositories or other media (online or offline). If you have a good Internet connection, add the online repositories to get always the most recent versions of the packages. The next step is shown in Figure 7-6.

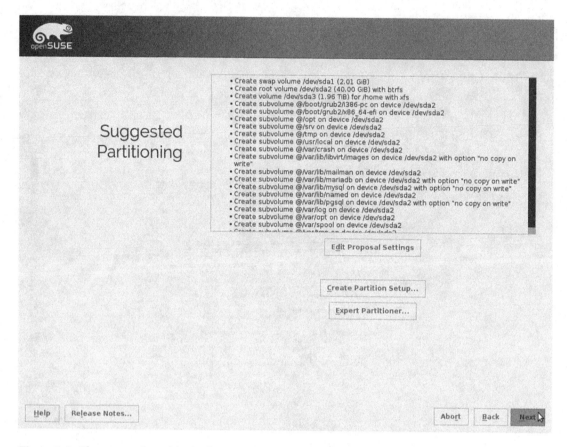

*Figure 7-6. The suggested partitioning by YaST*

This is the drive partitioning step. The suggested partition from openSUSE is far more complex than you've seen so far in this book. This is because it uses by default the btrfs file system in the root partition. openSUSE uses a tool called Snapper that takes snapshots (manual or automated) of that partition. This tool works with btrfs, ext4, and thin-provisioned LVM volumes. And the reason why xfs is used for the /home directory is because SUSE adopted this file system because it offers advantages like error handling and support of big volumes of data that suit corporate environments better. Plus, it creates a lot of subvolumes, making use of the advantages of btrfs to do so.

There are three ways to edit the settings that are proposed to you; the first two are semi-automated ones and the third is completely manual.

- **Edit Proposal Settings**: This allows you to make a few changes to the already proposed scheme, like opting to use LVM and encryption and the file systems of the / and /home partitions.

- **Create Partition Setup**: This is very similar to the previous option, but here you can choose the disk and partition/free space (which is useful in cases when other OSes are already installed) where you want to install the OS.

- **Expert Partitioner**: This is the completely customized manual procedure. Here you can see one of the best things about YaST; the partitioner program is one of the best and most powerful in all Linux distros. You can take a glance at it in Figures 7-7 and 7-8.

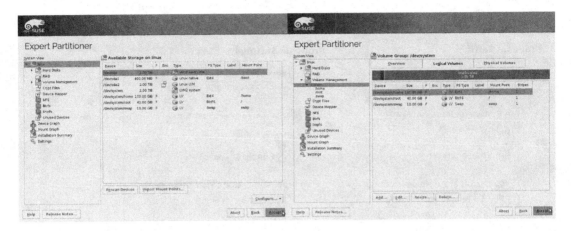

***Figure 7-7.*** *The Expert Partitioner from YaST*

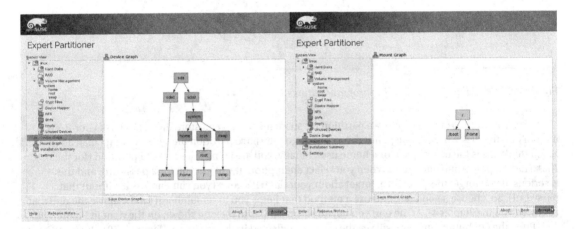

***Figure 7-8.*** *Another view of the Expert Partitioner*

If you are an expert or want to completely customize your partitions, the last option is for you; otherwise the other two are fine. Instead of dealing with the Expert Partitioner, which I think that is an awesome tool, let's customize the default scheme a little by choosing the first button. If you press the Edit Proposal Settings button, you will see a dialog like the on the left in Figure 7-9. It's the default setup, but you're going to change it a little to see how small changes can create a perfect setup.

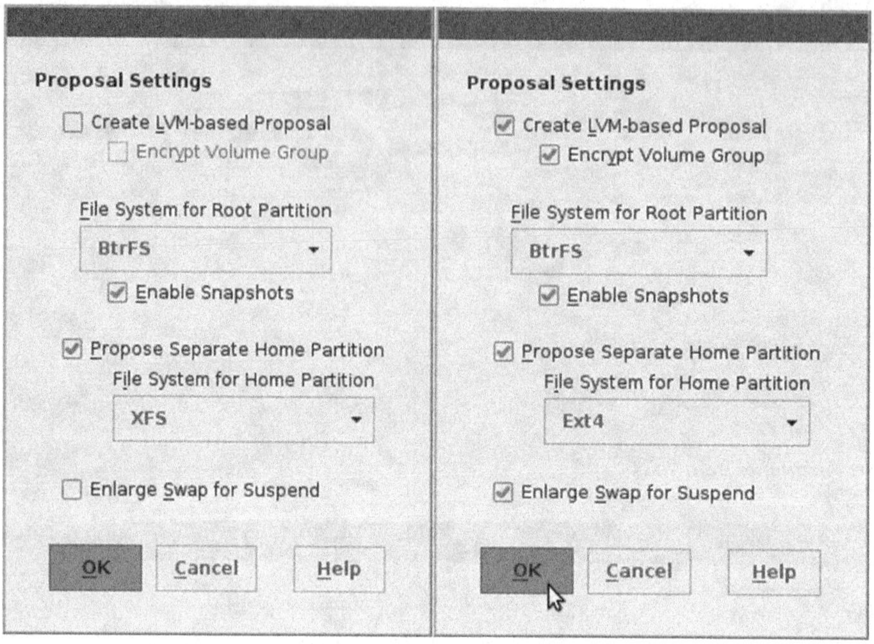

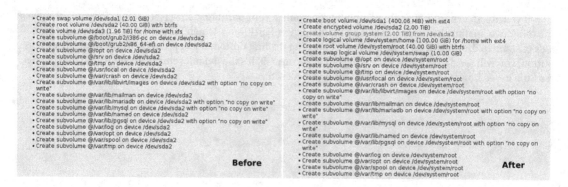

**Figure 7-9.** *Changing the partitioning proposal settings*

First, you want to enlarge the swap partition for suspend, so you can store the contents of your RAM memory on the disk when it is suspended. Next, change the /home partition file system to ext4 instead of XFS; I think this is the best choice for a home user. Finally, you are going to use a LVM partition (for the /home mount point) and encrypt it. When you select encryption, it will ask you for a password, and this is serious. If you forget this password, forget about your data: it's gone (you can't access it without that password). So, choose a good one and use a method that helps you to remember it (you can use the one that I showed you in Chapter 4). At the end you have a setup similar to the one shown on the right in Figure 7-9.

Press the OK button and you will see the changes reflected in the summary (Figure 7-10). Press the Next button to go to the next step.

**Figure 7-10.** *The summary of partition actions before and after change the proposal settings*

146

This is the usual step where you configure your clock and your time zone (Figure 7-11). As with Fedora, you can also customize advanced options like synchronization with an NTP server via the Other Settings button. You should know already how to complete this step. When finished, press the Next button again.

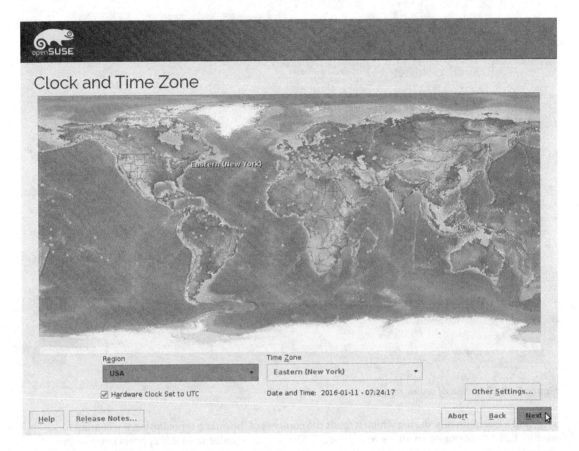

***Figure 7-11.*** *The clock and time zone settings*

If in the first step you added the online repositories as suggested, now you must select which ones you want to use here to do the installation (Figure 7-12). I suggest that you choose the first four, which are selected by default. If you are not going to compile any packages, you don't need the sources (or read the source code), and the debug ones are intended for developers of openSUSE. Select them and go to the next step.

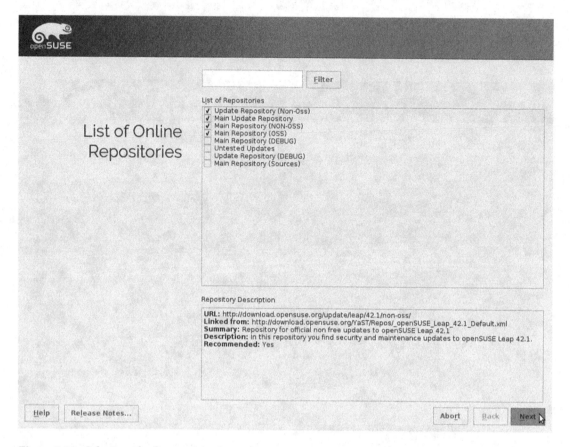

***Figure 7-12.*** *Selection of online repositories*

After a few moments, during which it reads the contents of the online repositories, it will jump to another EULA license agreement, as you can see in Figure 7-13. I understand this appears because the contents of the main repository may have changed from the ones on the DVD, but I suspect that you will find this as annoying as I do. Regardless, it's due to the philosophy of the distro, so press the Agree button and continue with the process.

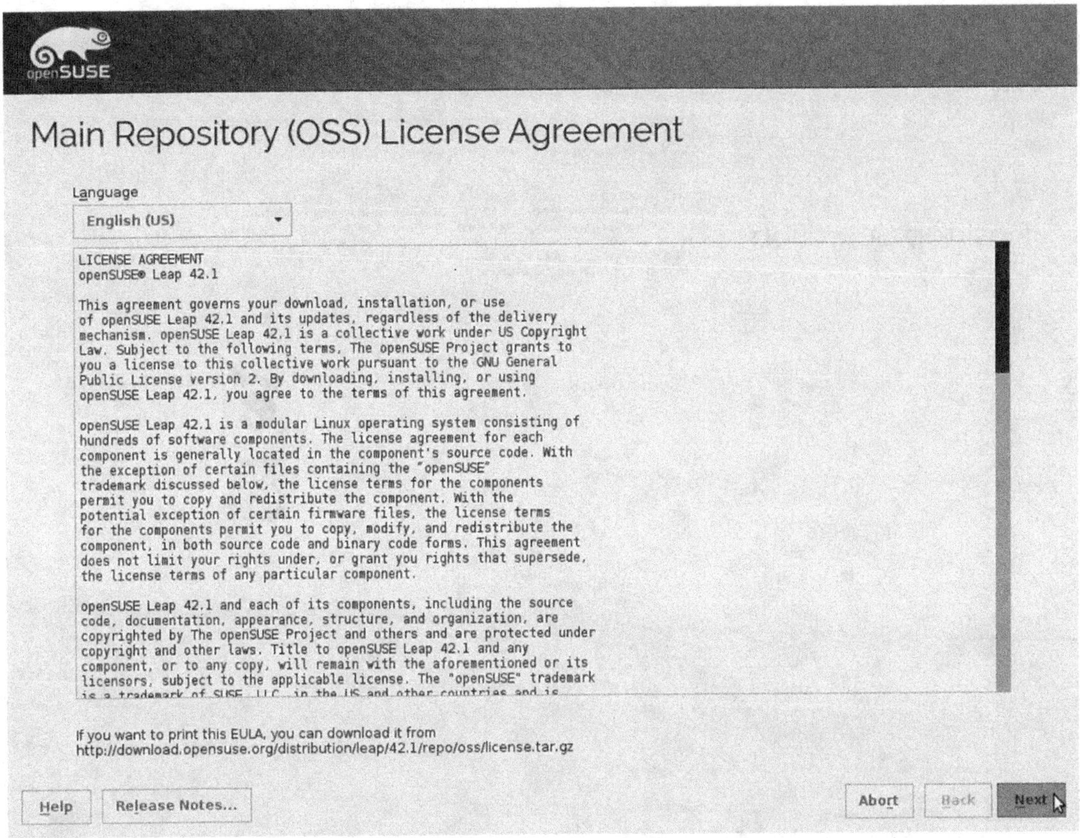

## Main Repository (OSS) License Agreement

Language

English (US)

LICENSE AGREEMENT
openSUSE® Leap 42.1

This agreement governs your download, installation, or use
of openSUSE Leap 42.1 and its updates, regardless of the delivery
mechanism. openSUSE Leap 42.1 is a collective work under US Copyright
Law. Subject to the following terms, The openSUSE Project grants to
you a license to this collective work pursuant to the GNU General
Public License version 2. By downloading, installing, or using
openSUSE Leap 42.1, you agree to the terms of this agreement.

openSUSE Leap 42.1 is a modular Linux operating system consisting of
hundreds of software components. The license agreement for each
component is generally located in the component's source code. With
the exception of certain files containing the "openSUSE"
trademark discussed below, the license terms for the components
permit you to copy and redistribute the component. With the
potential exception of certain firmware files, the license terms
for the components permit you to copy, modify, and redistribute the
component, in both source code and binary code forms. This agreement
does not limit your rights under, or grant you rights that supersede,
the license terms of any particular component.

openSUSE Leap 42.1 and each of its components, including the source
code, documentation, appearance, structure, and organization, are
copyrighted by The openSUSE Project and others and are protected under
copyright and other laws. Title to openSUSE Leap 42.1 and any
component, or to any copy, will remain with the aforementioned or its
licensors, subject to the applicable license. The "openSUSE" trademark
is a trademark of SUSE, LLC, in the US and other countries and is

If you want to print this EULA, you can download it from
http://download.opensuse.org/distribution/leap/42.1/repo/oss/license.tar.gz

Help    Release Notes...                                    Abort    Back    Next

*Figure 7-13.* *Another license agreement screen*

After adding the repositories, you get to choose the desktop environment (Figure 7-14) that you want
to use for the installation. The default one is KDE (the openSUSE tools are written for this environment; if
you use another, it will install the minimal components of KDE, Qt, to be able to use it), but you can choose
Gnome or other. Let's select KDE here. Now for the last steps!

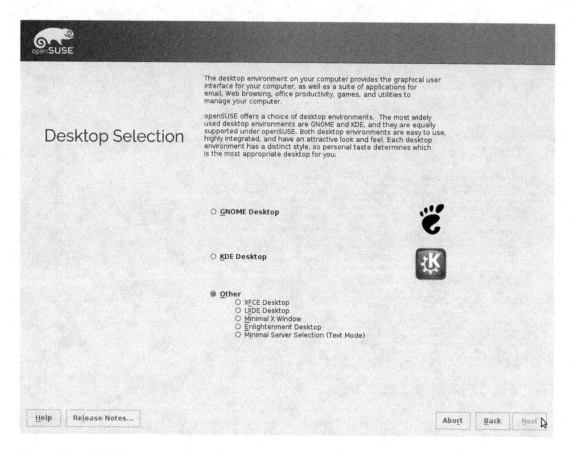

**Figure 7-14.** *The desktop environment selection screen*

As you can see in Figure 7-15, now you must create the user that you are going to use in the OS, as usual. As in Fedora, there are a series of advanced options. The first one is "Receive System Mail," to be able to receive the mail destined to the root user into this account. Also, you can change the authentication method with the Change button. The default options in this case are the most secures ones, so I suggest that you don't change them. The option "Use this password for systemd administrator" is exactly that it says; don't confuse this with the sudo command. So fill in the fields with your name and the password (please use a strong one) and then you can continue.

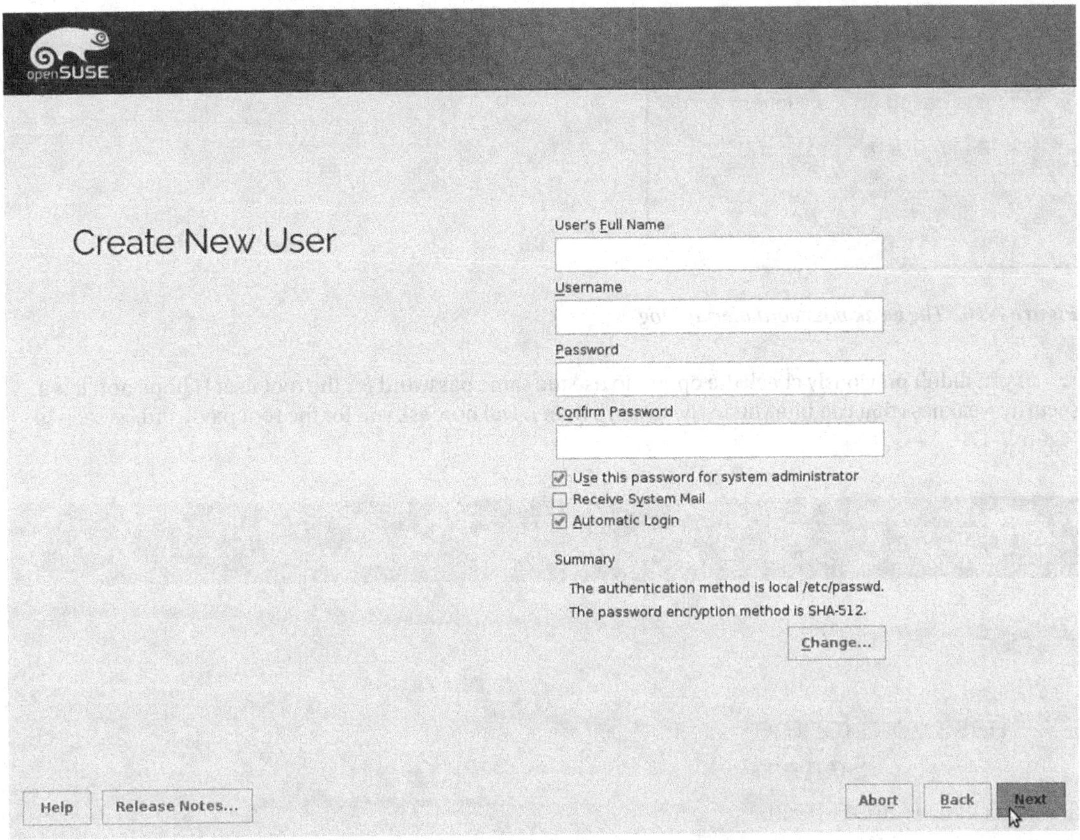

***Figure 7-15.*** *The user creation screen*

---

■ **Note** I'm using a virtual machine manager, VirtualBox, to install the distros that I'm showing you in this book, for two main reasons. The first one is convenience; I can create a new machine or delete it in a matter of seconds (so I can have several machines for the same distro with different scenarios). If I had to do that with a real machine, it would be impossibly tedious. The second reason is because it's much easier to take screenshots in this scenario.

In order to manage several machines and distros in a reasonable way, I'm using the same password in all of them. And from the beginning I intended to use a short and easy password, because it helps to make the task less annoying. Also, by using a weak password I can test how the different distros manage this situation. Until now, only Fedora considered my password as weak. But openSUSE was the first one (Figure 7-16) to advise me against using a weak password. It was also the first one to alert me that it was very weak because it was based on a dictionary word (and that is true). If you are curious, the password is pas$wor.d. So never, ever use a password like this or you will be owned very fast. Kudos to openSUSE for taking care of things like this.

---

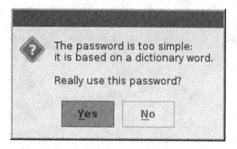

***Figure 7-16.*** *The weak password alert dialog*

If you didn't previously check the option to use the same password for the root user (I hope not; it is a security weakness that can bite you in the future), then it will now ask you for the root password, as seen in Figure 7-17.

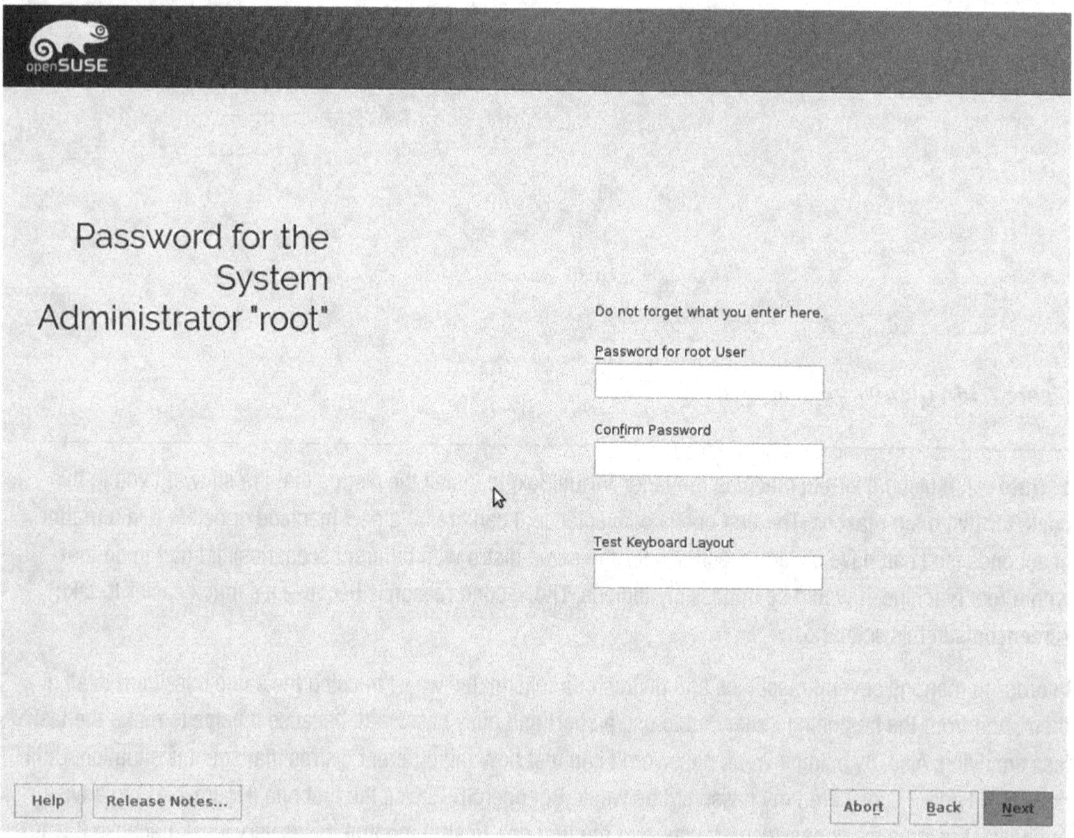

**Password for the System Administrator "root"**

Do not forget what you enter here.

Password for root User

Confirm Password

Test Keyboard Layout

Help    Release Notes...                                          Abort    Back    Next

***Figure 7-17.*** *The administrator password form*

Before beginning the installation, you will get a summary of the installation settings (Figure 7-18). Note one important point here—this is an interactive summary, so you can click the links (underlined in green) to access to some options and change them. For example, you can change the software that is going to be installed (Figure 7-19), an option that you didn't have before. Also, you can export this configuration to be able to do other installations exactly like this one in a complete unattended and automated way with AutoYaST. One thing worth mentioning is that you can see the size of the packages that you are going to download from Internet. If you don't have a fast connection and the size is too big, you can always go back and deselect the repositories.

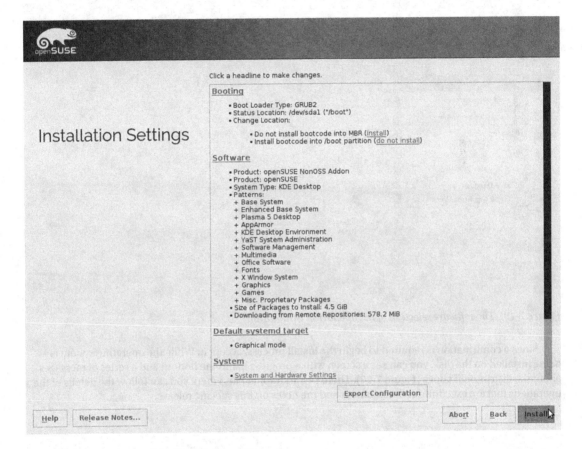

*Figure 7-18. Summary of the installation settings*

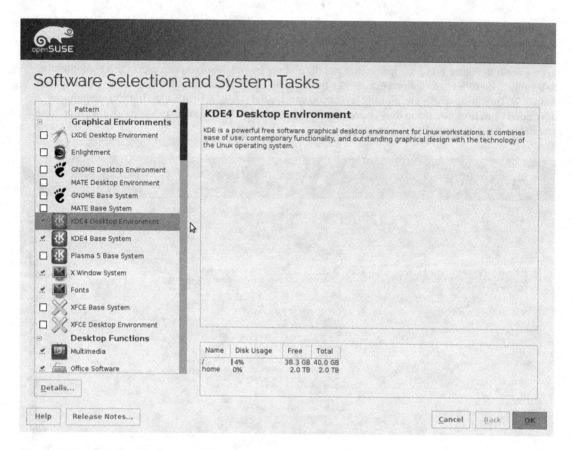

***Figure 7-19.*** *The software selection of the openSUSE installation*

Since a confirmation is required to begin the install process, accept it. While the operating system is being installed on the disk, you can see a screen with a progress bar in the bottom and a series of messages about the distribution above (Figure 7-20). There two additional tabs where you can follow the details of the operations that are executing at that moment and the notes on this specific release.

**Figure 7-20.** *openSUSE is installing*

When the process of installing all the packages on the disk is done, it will tell you that it is going to reboot. After the reboot, you will end up on the first screen again. If you do nothing, it will boot from the hard disk, thereby booting your fresh install of openSUSE. When booting from disk, the first screen that you will see is the already-familiar Grub boot manager, shown in Figure 7-21.

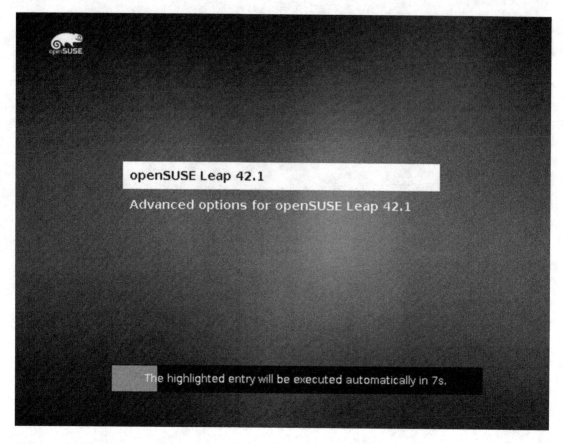

**Figure 7-21.** *The Grub boot loader of openSUSE*

The next screen is the most critical one: the encryption password to decrypt the contents of your hard disk. If you forgot that password, bad luck! You can't continue (Figure 7-22).

*Figure 7-22.* *The decrypt password for your files. I hope you remember it!*

If you successfully entered the password, the booting process will continue. And if you did not select the automatic login (I hope not), then you will see the screen in Figure 7-23. Once you introduce your name and your password, you can start your first KDE session.

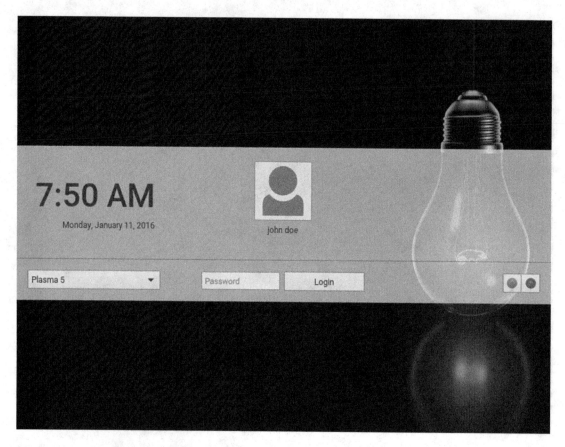

*Figure 7-23.* *The openSUSE login screen*

And voila! You can enjoy your new operating system (Figure 7-24).

**Figure 7-24.** *The openSUSE KDE desktop*

# Maintenance

Well, in a manner between the Ubuntu one and the Fedora one, openSUSE is intended to be maintained in an easy way, centralized in the YaST tool. So, let's see how these tasks are performed in openSUSE.

## Updating and Managing Apps

Although you can use the command line and the tool zypper to update and install/remove your apps, the default goal is to do all of this using YaST. YaST has a complete section for manage software, as you can see in Figure 7-25.

**Figure 7-25.** *The software section of YaST*

openSUSE, like Ubuntu, will alert you when new updates are available (Figure 7-26), so you can use that dialog to perform the updates directly from it.

***Figure 7-26.*** *New updates available notification*

But you can always check the updates manually by using the Online Update option from YaST (Figure 7-27) to perform the update. It is the regular software manager from YaST, but only the patches tab is selected by default. This is the same tool that you must use to remove or install software. It is a very powerful tool indeed, but I think that it's not intuitive, so beginners may find it hard to use at first. Personally, I find this tool and Synaptic (one that you can use in Debian or Ubuntu) to be very poor in terms of usability; I prefer to use command line utilities for these tasks because they are easier to control and use once you know how. However, openSUSE is focused on the corporate world and advanced users, so these tools are what their users expect to find.

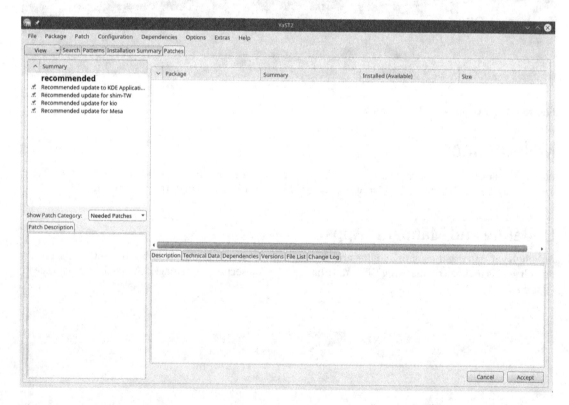

***Figure 7-27.*** *The YaST software updater*

## Upgrading

There are two ways to perform a release upgrade in openSUSE: the online method and the offline one. To perform the online method, use the command line, the zypper command, and the online repositories. The offline method only needs an ISO image of the new release, and then you pick the Upgrade option on the first screen instead the Installation one. The command to perform the online method is very easy to use at first sight, # zypper dup, but you need to perform a series of operations first to change the repositories, update your packages, and so on[2]. So, if you are a new user to the distro, I recommend you choose the offline method and follow the instructions.

# Pros and Cons

The following is a list of some things that I personally see as pros and cons of the openSUSE distribution. Of course there's always room for discussion in this matter, but I've done my best to be as objective as possible.

## Pros

- YaST is one of the best and powerful tools to configure and install a Linux OS.

- openSUSE is a secure distribution and can be hardened directly from YaST.

- It takes care of a lot of little things.

- You have the option of a rolling release version if you like to have the latest updates or you have the option of a very stable version.

- openSUSE supports only free and open source software but lets you access proprietary software easily if you want.

- The developers contribute and collaborate with the upstream versions of packages and are great contributors to the kernel.

- It is an original distribution, not a derivative.

- It uses one of the most extended package formats, rpm.

- SUSE is behind openSUSE, and openSUSE is part of the base of SUSE.

- It is well documented, and if you know German, you even can buy the boxed version and get a printed manual.

## Cons

- openSUSE is focused on the corporate world and advanced users. It's not user friendly for beginners.

- YaST is powerful but not intuitive, and it is not the best way to configure some things.

- The hardware support by default is not as good as other distros; you may have to manually use proprietary drivers.

---

[2]https://en.opensuse.org/SDB:System_upgrade

- The regular release scheme of the main distro is not as regular as the Ubuntu or Fedora ones, but it's not as bad as the Debian one.

- It has no commercial support.

- It only supports one architecture.

- The installation base is not as big as Fedora, Debian, or Ubuntu.

# Summary

Another distro, openSUSE, was put under the microscope. It takes a different approach to many common matters. There is no equivalent to YaST in any of the distros seen in previous chapters, and I assure it is not going to be the last new thing that you will see in this book.

Thus, in the next chapter you will see how Linux Mint approaches various topics.

# CHAPTER 8

# Linux Mint

Linux Mint is the new sensation. It's been the most popular distro for the past four years, even more popular than Ubuntu, the distro upon which it is based. This is ironic, because Ubuntu was the most popular distribution for the prior six years and it was based on another one, Debian[1]. However, there's popularity and there's install base, and in the latter, Ubuntu still has a bigger number by far. So, what makes Linux Mint so successful? The main reason is that Linux Mint goes a step further than Ubuntu in making the distro easier to use, and it listens to its user base about what direction to take in its development.

## History

Linux Mint was started by a French developer, Clement Lefebvre, in 2006. It was based on Kubuntu (only for the original release; after that one, Ubuntu was the base distro). Lefebvre's goal was to create a more elegant distro. After its release, it was slowly but continuously adopted by a growing community, largely based in Europe. However, two events would make a big difference in expanding the popularity and adoption of Mint in a short period of time.

Around 2011, the Gnome desktop environment made a radical change in its version 3. A big number of Gnome users did not like that change, and began to search for an alternative. At that time, KDE was also transitioning from version 3 to 4, with frequent bugs due to the immaturity of the new version. Of the few distros that did not change to version 3 of Gnome, Mint was the friendliest, most stable, and most polished. The other event was when Ubuntu switched from Gnome to Unity, a desktop environment even more hated and unwelcomed that Gnome 3; this provoked a great migration of users from Ubuntu to Mint.

Mint was able to take advantage of this avalanche of users coming into its community and develop its own desktop environment, Cinnamon, as an alternative to Gnome 3; it also adopted and helped develop MATE as an alternative to Gnome 2. And Mint listened to its users again: it created an alternative version based on Debian Stable that works as a semi-rolling release version of Mint.

Through the years, Linux Mint would usurp the throne as the top European distro from the venerable openSUSE distribution.

## Philosophy

When Clement Lefebvre defined the goal of Linux Mint as an elegant distribution, what he meant was a distro focused on ease of use, appealing design, stability, and feedback from its users. The focus on usability is reflected in things like the full multimedia support out of the box, something that is not easy to achieve in

---

[1]Popularity ranks based on DistroWatch (http://distrowatch.com)

© Jose Dieguez Castro 2016
J. Dieguez Castro, *Introducing Linux Distros*, DOI 10.1007/978-1-4842-1392-6_8

other distros. Listening to feedback from its users is the reason behind the development of Cinnamon and the adoption of MATE and other software contributions. Also, Linux Mint is known as a very polished distro, where everything works and the little details are taken care of.

As a result, in terms of ease of use, Linux Mint is probably one of the top three. Another thing worth mentioning is that Linux Mint is focused only on the desktop user, and this obviously helps it end up with a more polished product.

# Distro Selection Criteria

Now that you know a little history of Mint, let's see how this particular distro fares on the section criteria from Chapter 2.

## Purpose and Environment

Linux Mint is a general purpose distro focused only on the desktop user. It comes in two versions:

- **Linux Mint**: The main distribution, it is a regular release version and is based on Ubuntu. There are different images for each desktop environment supported (Cinnamon, MATE, KDE, Xfce). Moreover, the two main DEs offer versions with no codecs, for use in countries where multimedia codecs are patented.

- **LMDE**: A version based on Debian (LMDE means Linux Mint Debian Edition), it has a semi-rolling release cycle.

## Support

Obviously, without a company behind it, Linux Mint offers only community support, and since it has the smallest community of all the distros seen in this book so far, the support is not as good. The available channels to get this support are the following:

- **Documentation**: www.linuxmint.com/documentation.php

- **Forum**: http://forums.linuxmint.com/

- **Mailing Lists**: http://librelist.com/browser/linuxmint/ linuxmint@librelist.com

- **IRC**: #linuxmint-help at irc.spotchat.org

Because Linux Mint is based on Ubuntu, some things can be resolved via Ubuntu's support channels, so you can always try those channels if you don't find help in the Mint ones.

The feedback from the users is collected, discussed, and often implemented from the Ideas section of the community web site, http://community.linuxmint.com/idea.

## User Friendliness

As mentioned, Linux Mint is one of the easiest Linux distros to use, and you can see this from the start. It takes the best parts of Ubuntu and adds its own features to make the general experience a very pleasant one. There are a lot of little details that intend to minimize friction with the OS, things like the domain blocker (not having to deal with the firewall to set parental controls) or the Upload Manager (for managing FTP and SCP services). In the "Maintenance" section, you'll see how far Linux Mint goes to make certain things easier. This is one of the distros that I would recommend to beginners.

# Stability

Linux Mint is a very stable distribution. I think it's more stable than its mother one, Ubuntu, because Mint uses the Long-Term Support releases of Ubuntu, and it only offers "safe" updates by default. And by "safe," the Linux Mint developers mean that these updates will not break your OS. Thus, this distro does not have the latest packages (in fact, it is usually more outdated than Ubuntu), but it offers a better balance between stability and freshness than Debian Stable, for example.

Mint follows a standard release model (at least with the Ubuntu-based one), and it is based on the LTS releases of Ubuntu. Thus, after an Ubuntu LTS release (every two years) is released, so is a major version of Mint, and after each regular Ubuntu release (every 3 months), a minor version of Mint (without too many changes) is released. Each version has a code name, which is always female name ending with "a." They follow an alphabetical order and the first letter of the code name is in the alphabet position that corresponds to the version number.

Obviously, because it depends on the Ubuntu releases, Linux Mint cannot be as regular as Ubuntu because its developers need some time to prepare their own release, and this amount of time varies per release.

# Hardware Support

Being an Ubuntu derivative, the hardware support is almost as good as Ubuntu's, but Mint always gives priority to open source drivers over private ones. (You can always install private ones later through the driver's manager.)

# Aesthetics

A good global aesthetic is one of the major goals of Linux Mint. Mint develops its own desktop environment, which is made with design in mind. You can see this in every corner of the distro, from the colors, the desktop, the logo, the theme, the icons, to the wallpaper. There is a general consistency throughout the desktop and it is easy on the eyes. Linux Mint is often cited as the most appealing of all of the distros (of course this is a very subjective matter, but there is a global consensus about it).

# Desktop Environment

There are two main official desktop environments for Linux Mint: Cinnamon and MATE. The first one is a fork of Gnome Shell (Gnome 3) and the second a fork of Gnome 2. As mentioned, Cinnamon was developed by the Mint community; it is the most popular, and it is the de facto official Mint DE. Other desktop environments like KDE and Xfce are provided in separate ISO images.

# Init System

Currently Linux Mint still uses Upstart (and SysV in LMDE) as its init system, but this will change in the next release (which will happen soon after the next Ubuntu LTS release) when it will adopt systemd, something the majority of distros have done already.

## Package Management System

Since it's based on Ubuntu, obviously the package management system is dpkg, so it uses .deb packages. And even though Linux Mint has a repository for its own packages, it uses the Ubuntu repositories as well, so it gets the benefits of the packages available for Ubuntu. You can configure other popular sources for Ubuntu packages like the PPAs or the Getdeb repository. Linux Mint offers a good graphical tool to manage those packages, the Software Manager (mintinstall) but you can also use Synaptic for the same task.

## Architecture

Mint only supports the two major architectures: Intel and AMD in 32- and 64-bit versions.

## Security/Anonymity

Mint is based on Ubuntu and so it is reasonable secure by default. However, it is not as secure as Ubuntu because it does not implement AppArmor out of the box. Also, the levels update policy can make the OS a bit unsafe because the kernel updates (some of them with security patches) are not made by default. As always, there's a balance between ease of use and security; normally you need more knowledge to maintain a more secure distro.

## Principles and Ethics

Linux Mint gives preferences to free software over proprietary software, but it does offer proprietary software like Adobe Flash support and multimedia codecs. Even though the graphic drivers are set by default to open source drivers, it has tools like the Driver Manager to deal with proprietary drivers, and you can always find some in the repositories.

## Live CD

Like Ubuntu, the ISO images of Linux Mint are also Live DVD images.

## Professional Certification

Linux Mint does not offer any professional certification.

# Installation

Because Linux Mint is based on Ubuntu, the Mint installation process is very similar to the Ubuntu one (in fact, it's the same one with little, aesthetic changes), so I'm going to introduce another scenario here to show you something different from the installation in the Ubuntu chapter.

The first of all, as usual, go to the download page of the distribution, www.linuxmint.com/download.php, where you will see something similar to Figure 8-1.

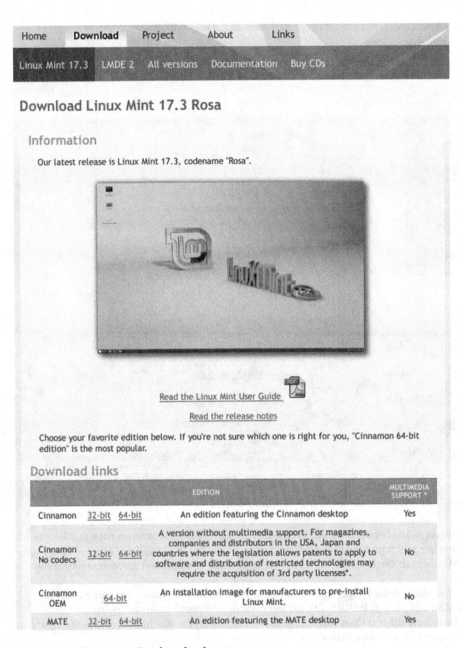

Figure 8-1. *The Linux Mint downloads page*

Select the main version (the Ubuntu-based one) that is current; at the time of writing, it was the 17.3 release. You can select different images depending on the desktop environment that you want to use; Cinnamon is the default one. Also, there are different versions for each of the main DEs (Cinnamon and MATE), so you can choose if you want a version without multimedia codecs or an OEM image. Let's choose the most popular one, the Cinnamon 64-bit version. After you click that link, you will see the screen in Figure 8-2.

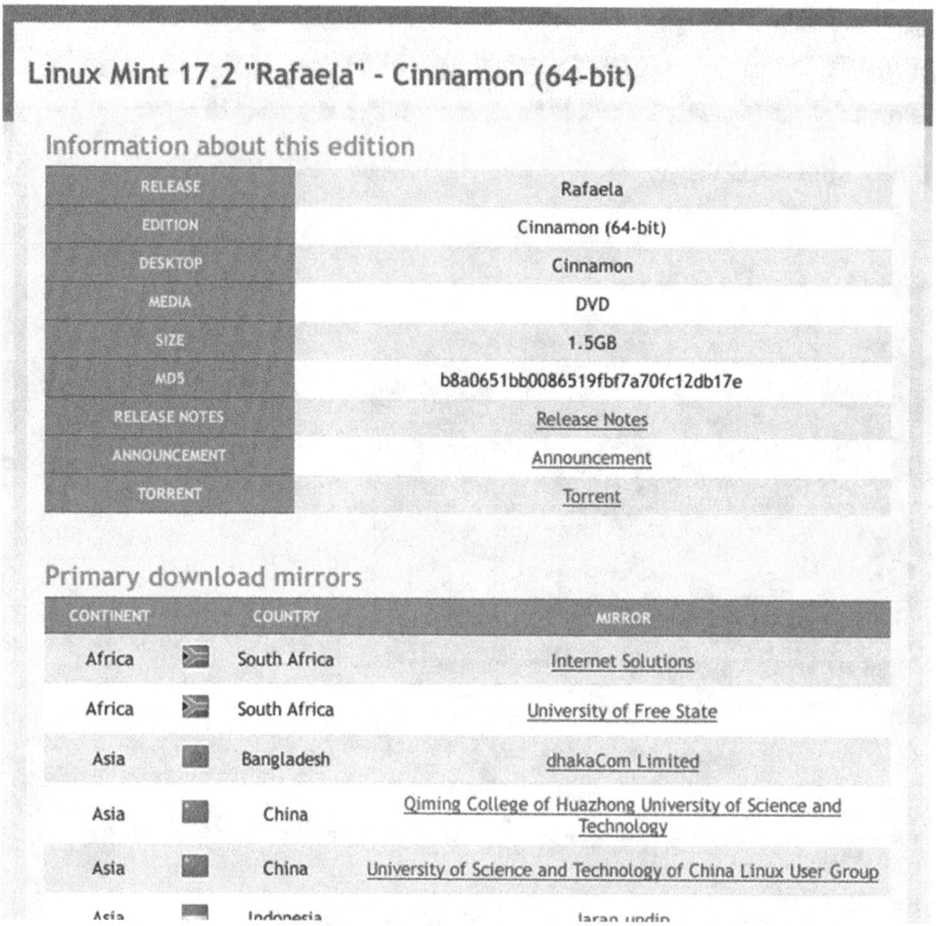

## Linux Mint 17.2 "Rafaela" - Cinnamon (64-bit)

### Information about this edition

| | |
|---|---|
| RELEASE | Rafaela |
| EDITION | Cinnamon (64-bit) |
| DESKTOP | Cinnamon |
| MEDIA | DVD |
| SIZE | 1.5GB |
| MD5 | b8a0651bb0086519fbf7a70fc12db17e |
| RELEASE NOTES | Release Notes |
| ANNOUNCEMENT | Announcement |
| TORRENT | Torrent |

### Primary download mirrors

| CONTINENT | | COUNTRY | MIRROR |
|---|---|---|---|
| Africa | | South Africa | Internet Solutions |
| Africa | | South Africa | University of Free State |
| Asia | | Bangladesh | dhakaCom Limited |
| Asia | | China | Qiming College of Huazhong University of Science and Technology |
| Asia | | China | University of Science and Technology of China Linux User Group |
| Asia | | Indonesia | Jaran undip |

*Figure 8-2. The download options for the ISO image of Linux Mint*

The first option that you see here is to download the ISO image via Bit Torrent, the most suitable option for a Linux distribution like this, with little economic resources. Below this is a long list of mirrors where you can download the ISO image through HTTP. It is up to you, but I chose to download the torrent file for the image.

Once you have downloaded the image, you can start the installation. In my case, I'm going to install Linux Mint in a machine that has a 2TB HDD with a default Windows 8 installation occupying the entire hard drive. The goal is to have the two OSes installed at the same time on the machine and have the ability to choose the one you want to use at boot up time.

The first screen that appears when you boot from the Linux Mint ISO is a little different than in other distros (a ten-second countdown). If you don't wait those ten seconds, a live session of Linux Mint starts; otherwise, if you press any key, you will see the screen shown in Figure 8-3. It's the common menu that you see in other distros, but here Mint hides it in order to make the installation process easier and less intimidating.

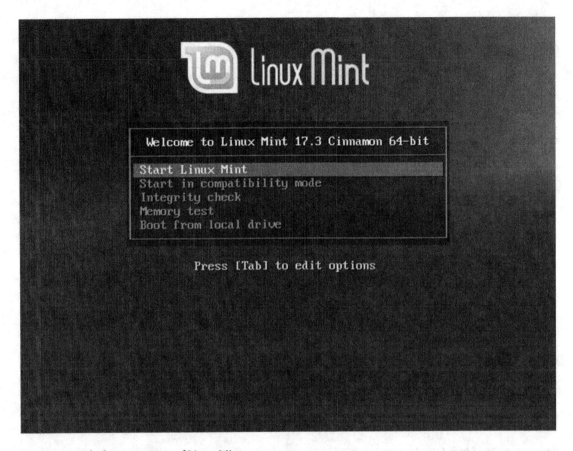

*Figure 8-3.* *The boot-up menu of Linux Mint*

Once you are in the Live session of Linux Mint (Figure 8-4), you can play around a little; at the end, click the "Install Linux Mint" icon to start the actual installation (see Figure 8-5).

***Figure 8-4.*** *The Linux Mint Live session*

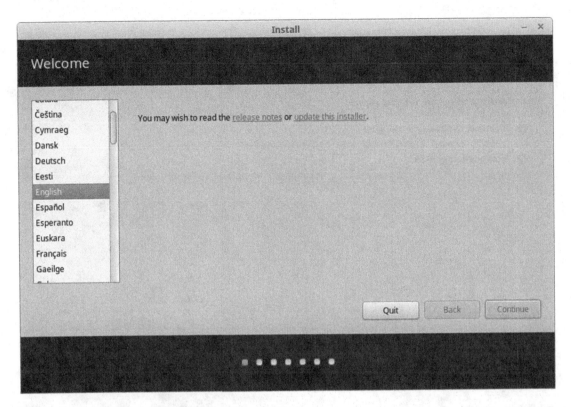

*Figure 8-5. The first step of the Mint installation*

The first step is the one where you must select the language to use in the process and your OS. You can also read the notes on the release or update the install software itself (this option only appears if necessary, after you check for an upgrade). Then comes the easy part (Figure 8-6).

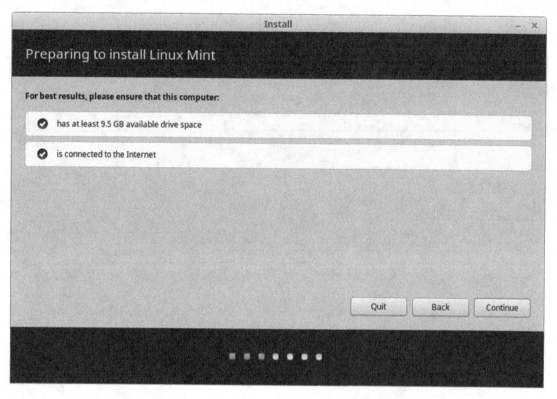

***Figure 8-6.*** *Checking for prerequisites*

Nothing is required of you here. It's just testing the system to make sure that it has the hardware necessary for the installation. Continue to the next step.

You can see in Figure 8-7 that the Windows OS was detected; you are offered the option to install Mint alongside it or delete all of the data on the hard disk and install Mint. As I said at the start, the intention is to have both OSes available at the same time. This option is selected by default, so press Continue to go to next step (Figure 8-8).

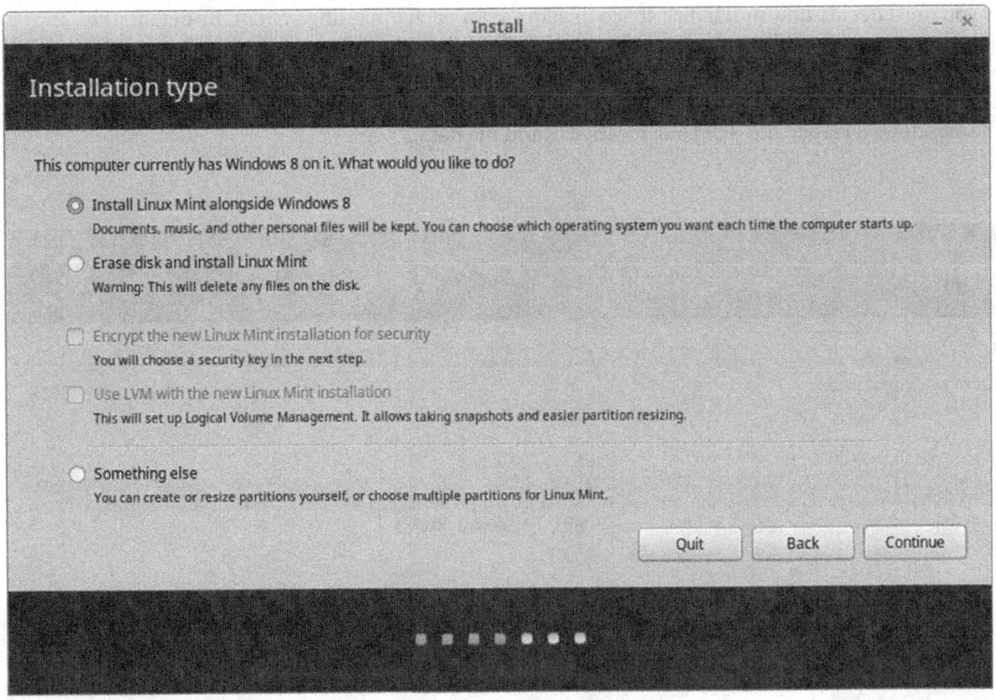

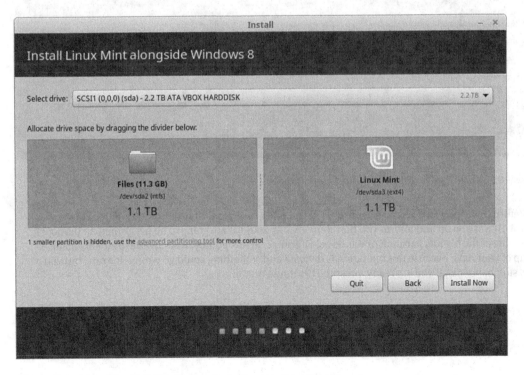

**Figure 8-7.** *Installation type screen*

**Figure 8-8.** *Size of the disk distribution for both operating systems*

Now you must decide how much disk space to allocate for each operating system. By default the installation program uses a 50/50 split, but you can modify this by simply moving the bar that appears between both green squares. You can also access the advanced partitioning tool via a link.

You can see the current status of my disk in Figure 8-9. There are currently two partitions, a very small one for the Windows 8 loader and a big one for the OS and the data.

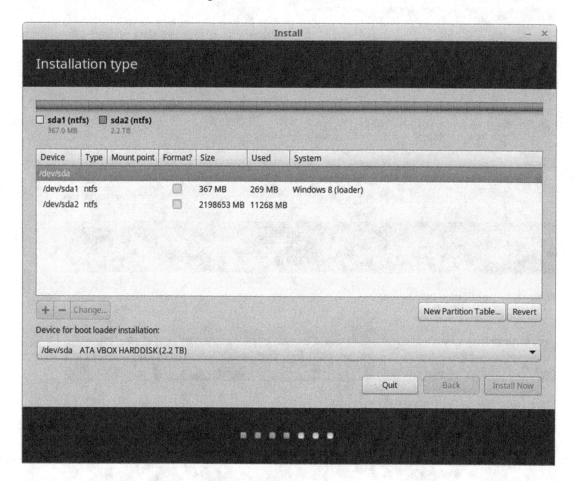

***Figure 8-9.*** *The current partitions of the disk with Windows 8*

Return to the previous screen (Figure 8-8). If you press the Install Now button, the dialog shown in Figure 8-10 will pop up and inform you that some disk operations are going to be performed, in particular the resizing of the big ntfs partition of Windows. Of course, at this point you should have already made a backup of your data, because this operation is delicate and something could go wrong (it's rare, but you know, stuff happens). If you are ready, press the Continue button.

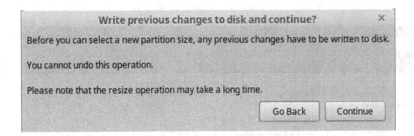

***Figure 8-10.*** *The warning dialog about the resize operation*

Once the partition is resized, and before it creates the new partitions to allocate your Linux Mint installation, a pop-up dialog appears to show you the changes that will be made and ask for your confirmation (Figure 8-11). At this point, you should know that the default proposed partition (a root partition and a swap one) is not the best plan for the long term. So, instead of continuing from here, let's go back and set up a better partition scheme.

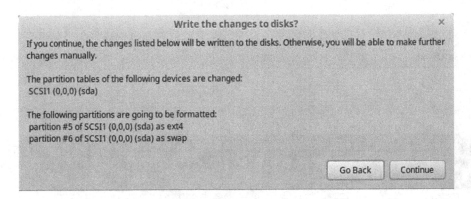

***Figure 8-11.*** *Are you sure you want to write the changes to the disk?*

If you go back, you'll land in the Figure 8-7 screen again. This time, choose the "Something else" option to create your own partition scheme. The advanced partitioner now shows something like Figure 8-12, where the Windows partition was already made smaller. So now you have half of the disk as available space. In that space, let's create new partitions similar to Figure 8-13. Yes, they could be different, but this is good enough without being too complex.

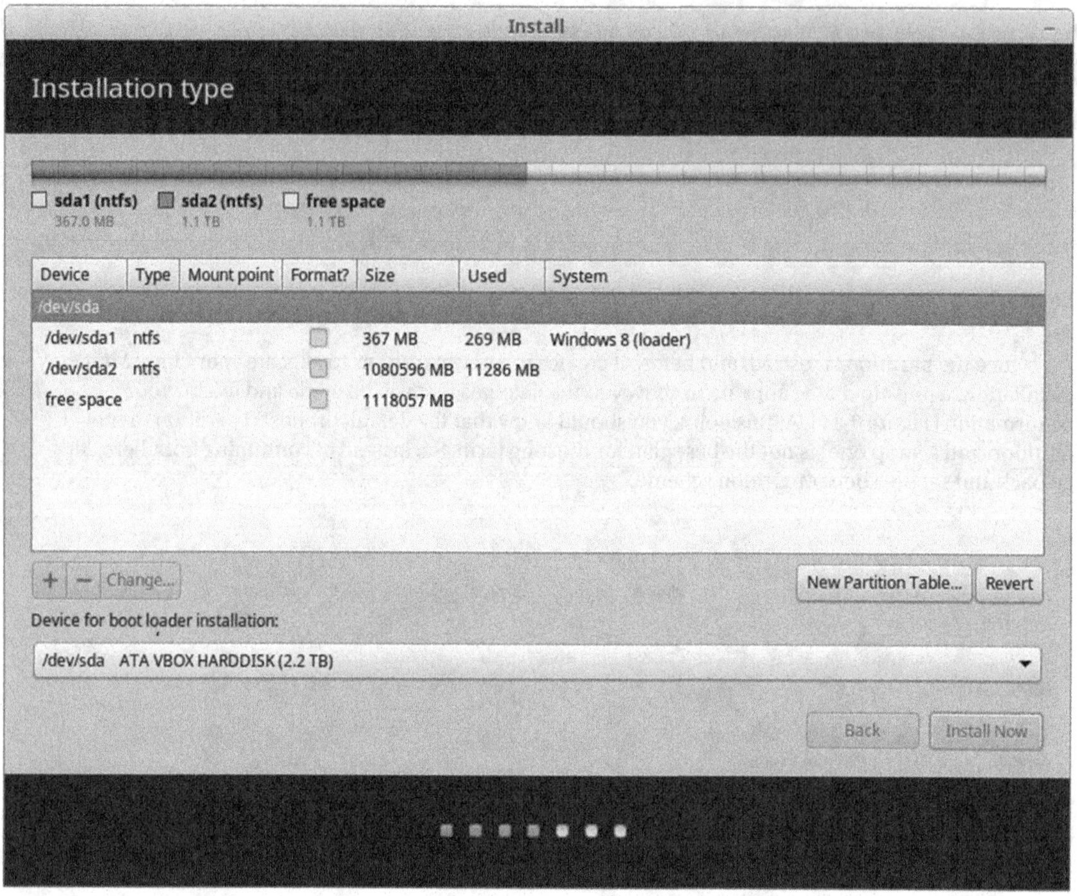

*Figure 8-12.* *The Windows partition already resized*

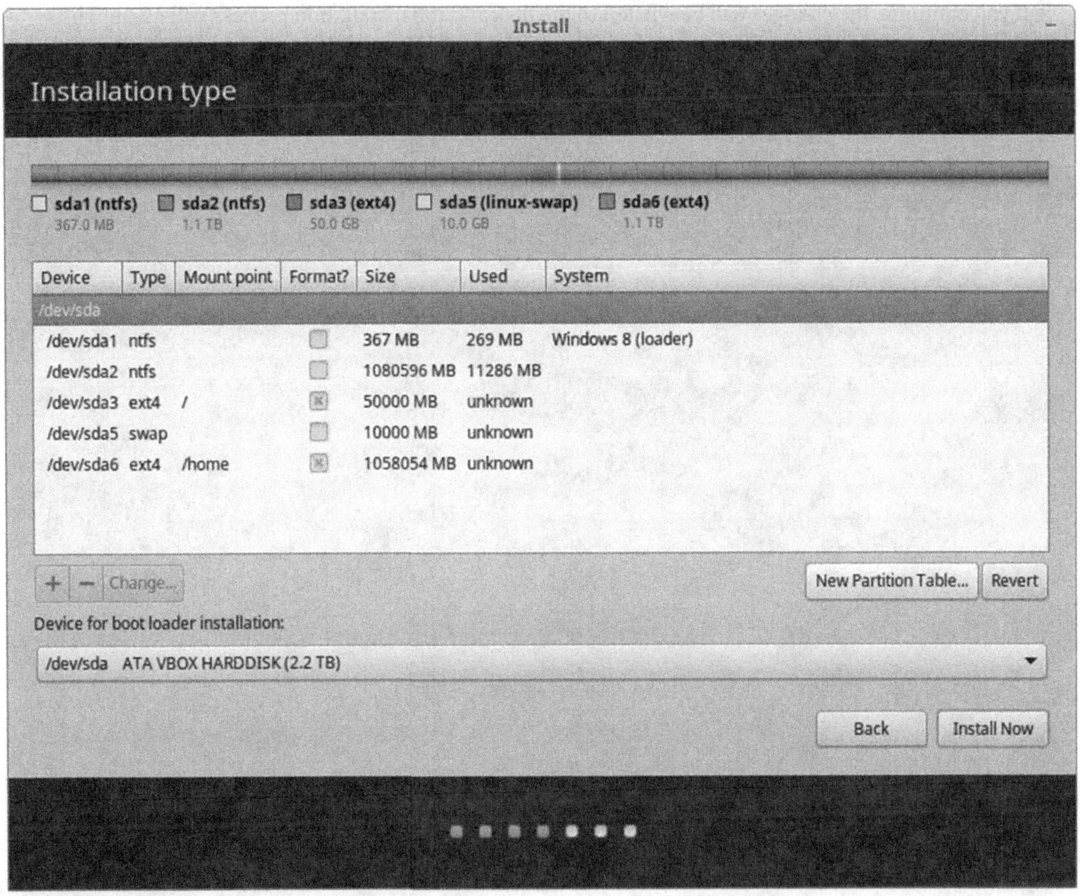

*Figure 8-13.* *The new partition scheme to install Linux Mint*

If you press the Install Now button, you'll see the summary shown in Figure 8-14.

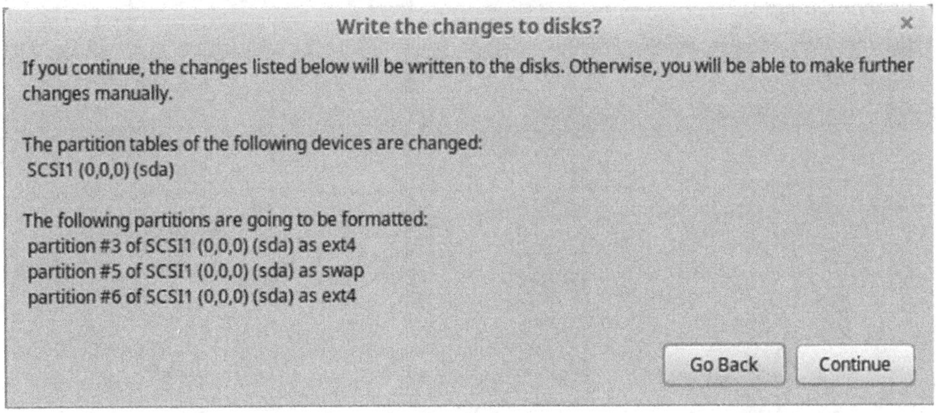

*Figure 8-14.* *The summary of the new partition scheme*

If you continue, the changes will be written to the disk and the installation process will go on. The next steps are to set the current time zone where you are located (Figure 8-15) and the keyboard layout (Figure 8-16).

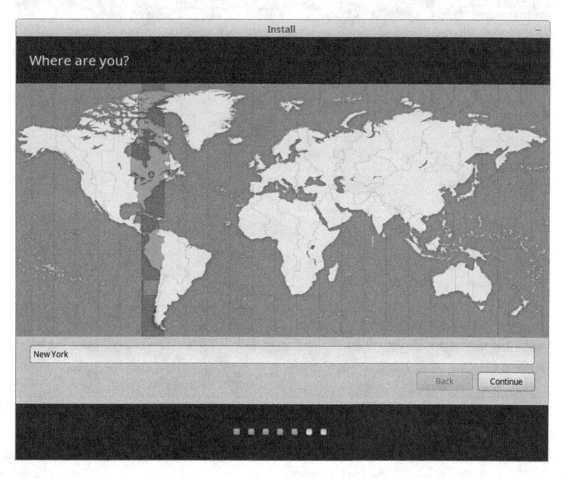

***Figure 8-15.*** *Time zone settings*

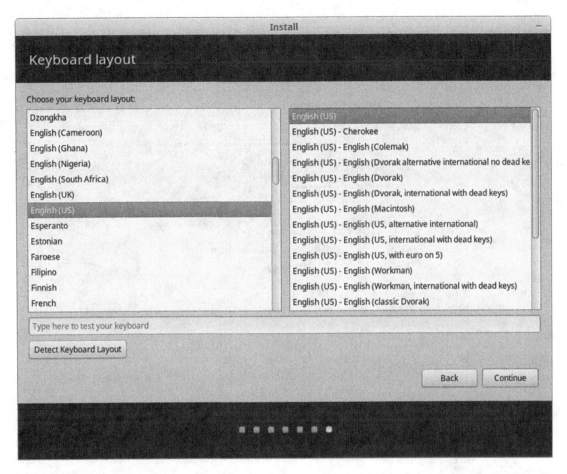

*Figure 8-16.* *The keyboard layout settings*

In Figure 8-17, you can observe the user settings; these are the same ones I have used all along. However, the password that Fedora and especially openSUSE found as weak is seen here as a fair one. Well, press the Continue button anyway.

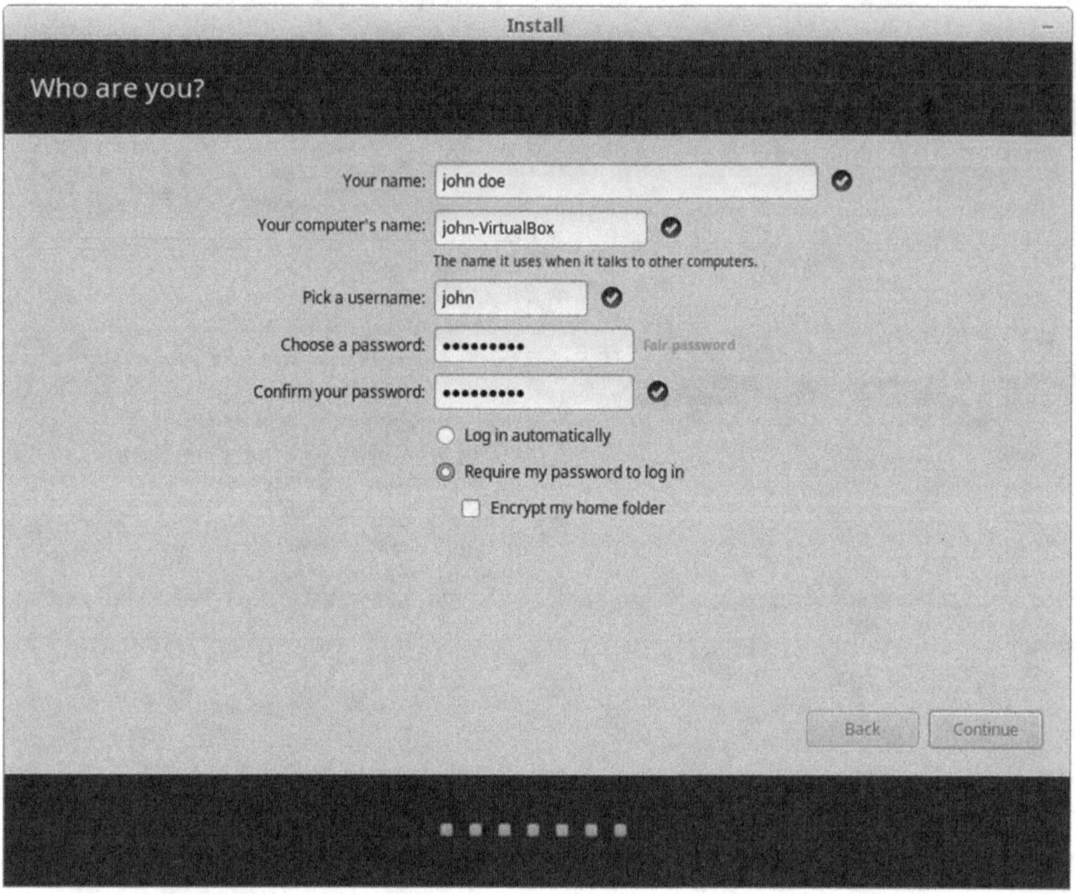

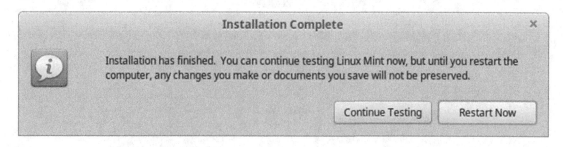

*Figure 8-17.* *The user settings*

The boring part of the installation, the copying of the files of the OS to the disk, will begin. At the end, you get the dialog shown in Figure 8-18. When you press the Restart Now button, the Live session will shut down and ask you to remove the ISO image file from the system (Figure 8-19).

**Installation Complete** ✕

Installation has finished. You can continue testing Linux Mint now, but until you restart the computer, any changes you make or documents you save will not be preserved.

Continue Testing     Restart Now

*Figure 8-18.* *The installation is complete*

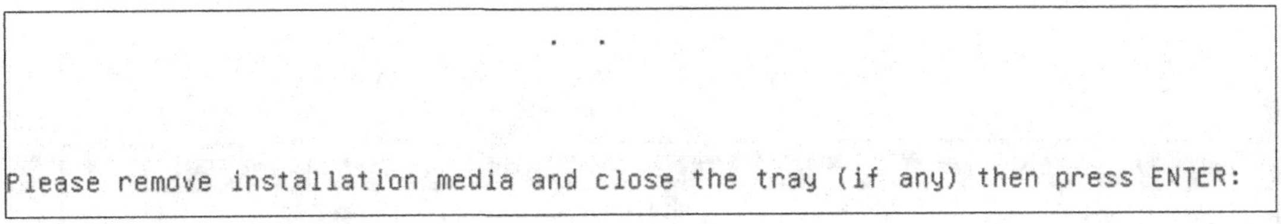

```
                              .   .




Please remove installation media and close the tray (if any) then press ENTER:
```

***Figure 8-19.*** *Remove the image from the DVD/USB to restart the system*

The OS is now installed and this is the first time that you will boot up the machine with it. The first screen, as usual, is the Grub one, shown in Figure 8-20.

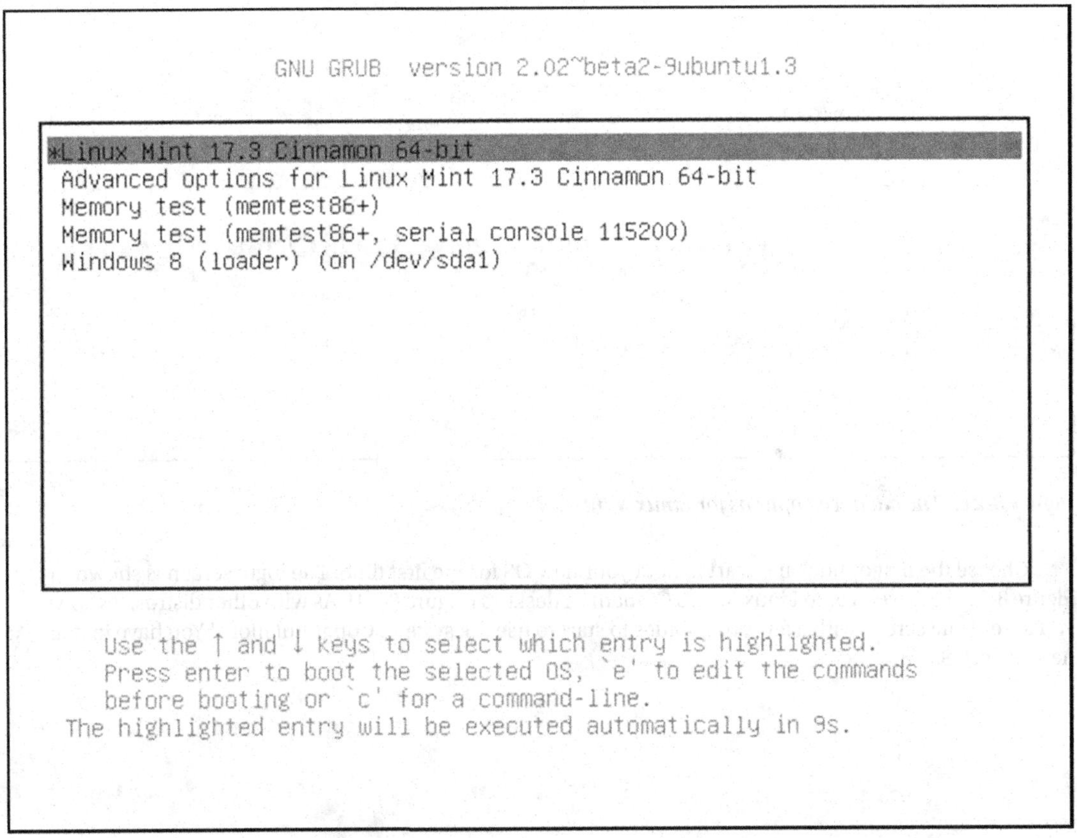

```
              GNU GRUB   version 2.02~beta2-9ubuntu1.3

 ┌──────────────────────────────────────────────────────────────┐
 │*Linux Mint 17.3 Cinnamon 64-bit                                │
 │ Advanced options for Linux Mint 17.3 Cinnamon 64-bit           │
 │ Memory test (memtest86+)                                       │
 │ Memory test (memtest86+, serial console 115200)               │
 │ Windows 8 (loader) (on /dev/sda1)                              │
 │                                                                │
 │                                                                │
 │                                                                │
 │                                                                │
 │                                                                │
 │                                                                │
 └──────────────────────────────────────────────────────────────┘

     Use the ↑ and ↓ keys to select which entry is highlighted.
     Press enter to boot the selected OS, `e' to edit the commands
     before booting or `c' for a command-line.
  The highlighted entry will be executed automatically in 9s.
```

***Figure 8-20.*** *The Linux Mint Grub screen*

You can observe various things here. First, at the top, in the very first line, you can read that the version of the Grub used here is an original Ubuntu package, a little detail that the Linux Mint people left behind. Also, you can see that you can opt to boot to Linux Mint (as the default option) or you can boot to the Windows 8 OS. If you choose Windows 8, it will boot as usual, as if you hadn't made any changes to the disk. And finally you should notice that there are two options to boot Mint; the second one is shown as "Advanced options …" (see Figure 8-21). In reality, the usual two entries that are seen in almost all distros are the normal and the recovery ones. I suppose that the Mint developers took this approach to make it easier for newcomers to use.

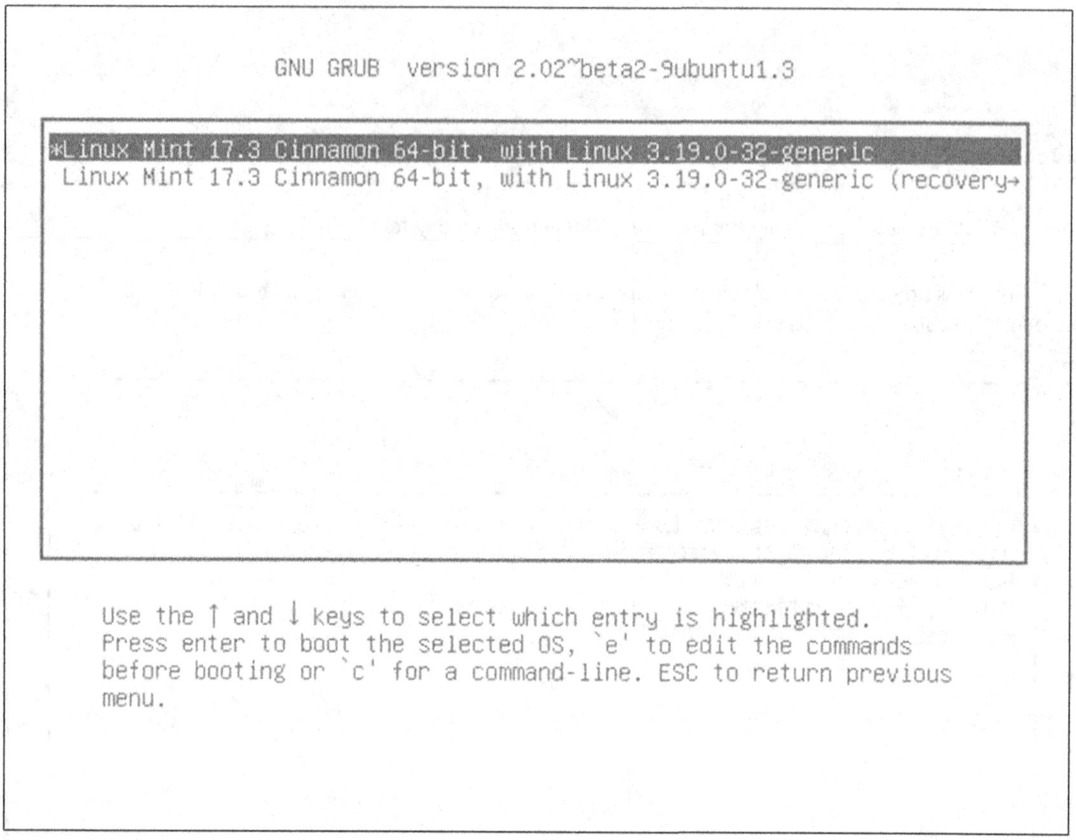

```
              GNU GRUB  version 2.02~beta2-9ubuntu1.3

 ┌──────────────────────────────────────────────────────────────────┐
 │*Linux Mint 17.3 Cinnamon 64-bit, with Linux 3.19.0-32-generic      │
 │ Linux Mint 17.3 Cinnamon 64-bit, with Linux 3.19.0-32-generic (recovery→│
 │                                                                    │
 │                                                                    │
 │                                                                    │
 │                                                                    │
 │                                                                    │
 │                                                                    │
 │                                                                    │
 │                                                                    │
 │                                                                    │
 └──────────────────────────────────────────────────────────────────┘

      Use the ↑ and ↓ keys to select which entry is highlighted.
      Press enter to boot the selected OS, `e' to edit the commands
      before booting or `c' for a command-line. ESC to return previous
      menu.
```

*Figure 8-21.* *The advanced options for Linux Mint*

Choose the first option, and start to boot your new OS for the first time. The login screen is shown in Figure 8-22. Then you get to Linux Mint's Cinnamon desktop (Figure 8-23). As with other distros, it shows you a welcome screen with a few possibilities to start to use the system. Congratulations! You have installed a new Linux OS.

*Figure 8-22.* *Mint's login screen*

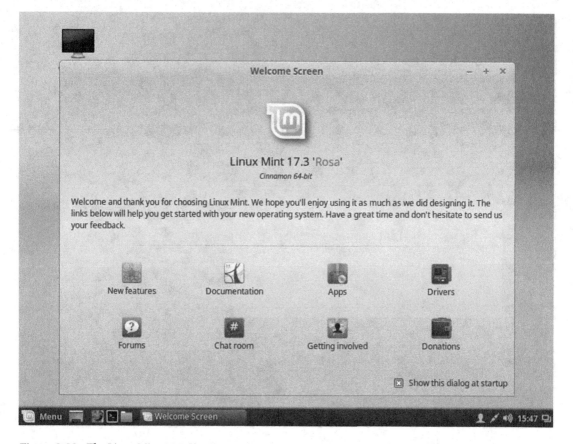

***Figure 8-23.*** *The Linux Mint 17.3 Cinnamon screen*

# Maintenance

As per its founding philosophy, Linux Mint is one of the easier distributions to maintain. You can do it all from graphical interfaces, which makes Linux Mint well suited for beginners.

## Managing Apps

If you want to install or remove applications in Linux Mint, you have the same alternatives as in Ubuntu: you can do so via a dedicated graphical application, via the Synaptic tool, or in the terminal with the common command line tools for .deb packages (apt-get, aptitude, dpkg). The only difference here is that the dedicated graphic app is different from the Ubuntu one.

The Software Manager app (Figure 8-24) is a simple, easy-to-use, and intuitive application, in the same spirit as the Ubuntu equivalent, grouping apps by category. But once you start to use it, the first thing that you will notice is that the search and navigation is much faster than its Ubuntu counterpart; in fact, it has less bugs and works a little better. The Mint developers made a good thing with this app.

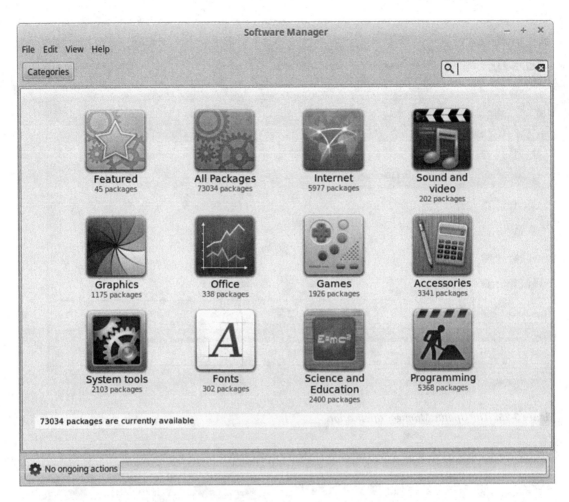

*Figure 8-24.* *The Software Manager application*

This application will help beginners manage their apps in an easy way, without having to deal with the terminal.

## Updating and Upgrading

In Mint, the package updates and distro upgrades are managed with the same tool: Update Manager (mintupdate), shown in Figure 8-25. Linux Mint has a particular way of managing updates; it doesn't follow the same manner as Ubuntu, even though it is based on that distro and use the same packages and repository. Mint divides the updates into various levels based on function, stability, or security. This is not a popular classification system with many people because they consider kernel updates unsafe to update by default (because they can break some configurations like hardware drivers). I personally think that this is good thing for newbies to Linux and to keep the OS more stable, but it can be a security risk. If you don't like this policy, you can always configure it to show those updates; it is up to you (you can see this in Figure 8-26). Also, you can even see if a kernel version solves a particular security issues or has some regressions (Figure 8-27), and if a particular kernel version is recommended. I think this is a better way to manage things for beginners.

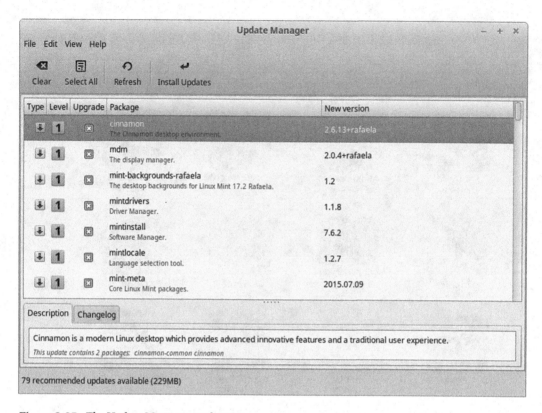

***Figure 8-25.*** *The Update Manager application*

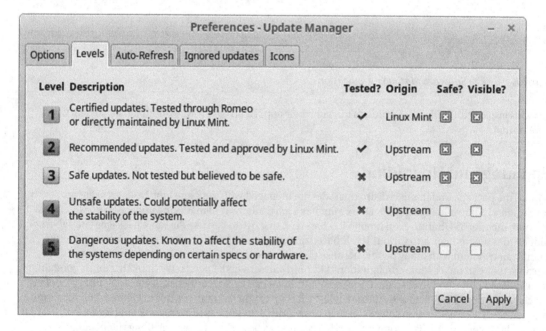

***Figure 8-26.*** *The update levels of the Update Manager*

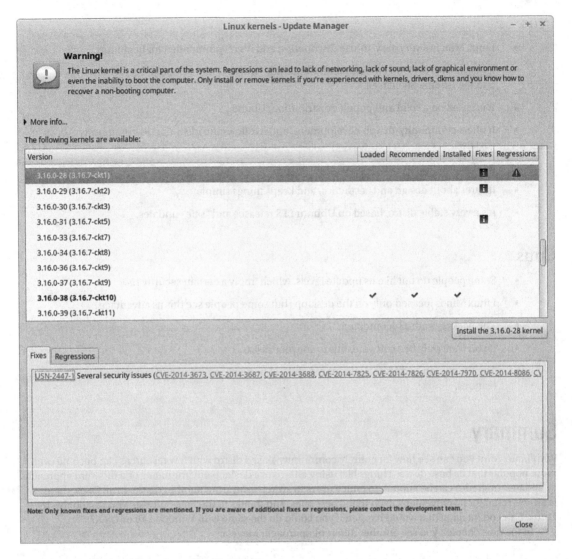

*Figure 8-27.* *The kernels section of the Update Manager*

The Update Manager can also deal with the distro upgrades; when a new release is available, you will see a new option to upgrade the distro in the Edit menu. If a beginner follows the Linux Mint way and does not update any unsafe update, it will be a safer upgrade than the Ubuntu regular one (but always remember to make a backup first!).

# Pros and Cons

The following list contains some things that I personally see as pros and cons of the Linux Mint distribution. Of course there is always room for discussion in this matter, but I have tried to be as objective as possible.

## Pros

- Linux Mint is a very easy-to-use distribution and it's recommended for beginners.

- It has its own desktop environment, Cinnamon, which is more popular than Unity and the Gnome Shell itself.

- It is based on a solid and popular distribution, Ubuntu.

- It offers community-driven development, and it follows the ideas that its community suggests.

- It offers multimedia support out of the box.

- It cares about design and aesthetics, and keeps things simple.

- It's a very stable distro, based on Ubuntu LTS releases and "safe" updates.

## Cons

- Some people do not like its update levels, which imply a certain security risk.

- Linux Min is focused only on the desktop (but some people see this as advantage).

- The packages are a bit outdated.

- If you want only free software, this is not your distro.

- The Cinnamon and Mate desktops are still not perfectly polished and lack some features.

# Summary

With Linux Mint you can see how an entirely community-based distro with few resources can become even more popular that its base distro. Things like using alternative desktop environments or a different approach to updates/upgrades can be enough to entice users to switch away from another distro. In all OSes, there is always room for improvement, even in the best ones, and thanks to the Free Software you can do this in Linux. Can you imagine that would happen if you could do the same with Windows 10 or OS X?

In the next chapter, you see another different approach: Mageia.

# CHAPTER 9

# Mageia

Mageia is one of the newer Linux distributions that I selected to analyze in this book, and it's the third most popular European Linux distro. Mageia is a fork of an older distribution, Mandriva (formerly Mandrake), which is discontinued but is the second most famous European Linux distro of all times. Mandrake was originally a fork of Red Hat. It was also inspired by SUSE, and today you can still find echoes of that in Mageia.

## History

Mageia is the Greek term for "magic" and it is a gesture to the original Mandrake distro, which was named after the Italian-American magician Leon Mandrake. Mageia is a community distro supported by a non-profit organization, Mageia.org.

Mageia was born in the agony of Mandriva. Mageia is one of the heirs (along with PCLinuxOS and others) of a great lineage that started with Mandrake in 1998. It merged with another old Red Hat fork, Conectiva (1997), in 2005 and eventually changed its name to Mandriva (Mandrake + Conectiva). Mandriva/Mandrake was always a company-supported distro, but the company had problems staying afloat financially. Anticipating its coming demise, a bunch of developers of the company behind Mandriva and some other community members decided to fork the distro; as a result, the Mageia project was announced in September of 2010. The first version was released in June of 2011. Mandriva shipped is last release in the same year.

Mandriva/Mandrake was a French distro and it was commercialized, presented, and evolved similarly to the other great European distro, OpenSUSE/SUSE; this was no accident. You can see similarities and influences in both distros. In fact, I saw how these distros evolved, but even I can't remember who inspired who in each aspect.

## Philosophy

Well, the truth is that the main purpose of Mageia was to perpetuate the legacy of Mandriva and continue the distribution where it left off. One of the major goals of Mageia/Mandriva was to create a pleasant and easy-to-use distro for all users. For a long time, this was the distro (along with SUSE) for new users who wanted an amicable distro. Mageia defines its mission these days as building great tools for people.

© Jose Dieguez Castro 2016
J. Dieguez Castro, *Introducing Linux Distros*, DOI 10.1007/978-1-4842-1392-6_9

# Distro Selection Criteria

Now that you know some history, let's see how Mageia rates on the selection criteria from Chapter 2.

## Purpose and Environment

Mageia is a general purpose distribution that in the same manner as Mint, only it focuses on the desktop. Mageia offers a unique version for this environment.

## Support

The old Mandriva had a great support; it even published a manual as a book (shipped with the Mandriva Powerpack), as SUSE did in the past. But now Mageia is a community-based distro and the support comes from members. It is not as complete as the support a company could provide. But there are many good ways to get support from the community:

- **Documentation**: www.mageia.org/en/doc

- **Wiki**: https://wiki.mageia.org/en/

- **Forum**: https://forum.mageia.org/en/

- **Mailing lists**: https://ml.mageia.org/

- **IRC**: #mageia at freenode

## User Friendliness

Mageia (more exactly, the former Mandriva) had a reputation of being very user friendly. This prestige comes from the omnipresent Control Center (the equivalent of the OpenSUSE's YaST) from where you can configure almost all the most important parameters of your user distribution (from a user perspective). But it is important to know that this easiness is not an absolute value that you can measure objectively, because even when you can control almost anything from one place, you still have to know what you are doing. Thus, for a user used to Linux, Mageia or OpenSUSE can seem very easy to use and friendly, but to a newcomer it seems difficult. A newcomer will probably prefer other distributions like Ubuntu, Mint, or elementary OS. The reality is that that glory came from years ago, when installing Linux was not an easy task, and Mageia was a welcomed alternative for those afraid of installing Debian or harsher ones like Slackware. But when Ubuntu arrived, it changed all that; since then, Mageia/OpenSUSE and similar ones went down a step in what a new user considers friendly (and being frank, it would be stupid to ignore the influence that Mac OS X has had in all of this).

## Stability

Mageia is a reasonable stable distribution. It follows a standard release model and tries to release a new version each nine months, followed by 18 months of support.

When this release cycle program was announced in 2011, a LTS version was considered but it never happened. The community lacks the muscle (maintainers and QA team) to achieve this big effort. This is a perfect example of a distro that was accustomed to having a company behind it but was later "diluted" by various community forks that want to keep the pace and the quality but are still working to return it to its past glory. This does not mean that Mageia is not a stable distro with a reasonable quality; it just means that maintaining a LTS version, or several different versions, is an expensive task that not too many distros can afford (specially community ones).

There is a development version called Cauldron that is always up to date. Of course, it is inherently unstable and it is aimed at Mageia packagers.

## Hardware Support

Mandriva was traditionally seen as a good distro regarding hardware support, and its successor seems to continue along this line. Mageia provides proprietary drivers and it does good work detecting hardware, so I can say it has good hardware support.

## Aesthetics

There is not too much of a focus on aesthetics in this distro, apart from the backgrounds, colors, and logos. All of the rest is the default DE aesthetic.

## Desktop Environment

Mageia supports various desktop environments, eight of them officially from the DVD ISO image of the distro: KDE, Gnome, XCFE, Mate, Cinnamon, LXDE, LxQT, and Enlightenment. The traditional DE of Mageia/Mandriva is KDE.

## Init System

Mageia uses systemd as its init system. In fact, it was one the early adopters, in 2011.

## Package Management System

As part of the legacy inherited long ago from Red Hat, the package management system used in Mageia is RPM. There is a graphic tool to manage the packages (rpmdrake) and several command line tools (urpmi, urpme, urpmq, urmpf) instead of a unique terminal tool to do all the operations.

## Architecture

It only supports two major architectures, the AMD/Intel 32- and 64-bit architectures.

## Security/Anonymity

The security in Mageia is very similar to other general purpose distros. A firewall is enabled by default and a "standard" level is selected by default in the security tool (called MSEC). Of course, as with almost every Linux, you can always harden your installation, but MSEC is very helpful to manage this topic in an easy way (or with grain too). MSEC is developed by Mandriva and it supports the usual tools like Apparmor or SELinux by default.

## Principles and Ethics

The core repositories of Mageia offer only free software but you can always install proprietary software or mixed ones (e.g. that use patented and copyrighted code) from the "non-free" and "tainted" repos. Thus, the compromise about free software is addressed in a very pragmatic way, as it is in the majority of distros. On the other hand, Mageia was the first distro to make the switch to MariaDB from MySQL to avoid Oracle's copyright.

## Live CD

Mageia has Live ISO images available for download as DVD and CD. The only inconvenience is that the CD images are only available in English, and you have to choose if you want the KDE or the Gnome desktop environment.

## Professional Certification

There is no professional certification available specifically for Mageia.

# Installation

Until now, all of the distro installations shown in this book were made on a system with a traditional BIOS, but for the past few years new computers (mostly laptops) have come with the modern "replacement" of that traditional, essential firmware, the UEFI. Some UEFI firmware has a legacy BIOS-compatible mode and you can choose which of those modes you want to boot your system in. The legacy BIOS mode is useful for those people who still feel uncomfortable with UEFI because even though it is better than BIOS, it is also more complex. But it is useful for installing distros that do not support UEFI. All of the distros shown previously in this book support installation in UEFI mode, but as the installation process is also more complex, in some distributions this can be more difficult or cumbersome (for all of the previous distros, it is not very hard to do), and some users prefer to boot in BIOS mode. In Mageia, following its tradition of making things easier, it's not much harder to install the distro in UEFI mode than in BIOS mode.

First things first, go to the Mageia site (`www.mageia.org/en/downloads`) to download the ISO image (see Figure 9-1).

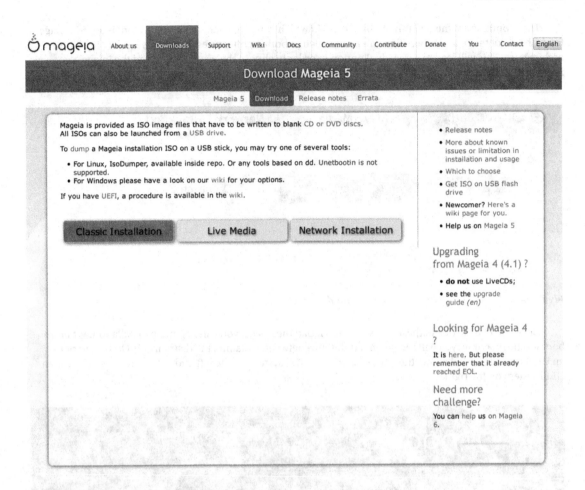

***Figure 9-1.*** *The Mageia downloads page*

As with many other distros, you must choose the type of image you need. In this case, you can choose between the standard image, the live image, or the network one. Pick the standard one (Mageia call it "Classic") and you'll get three new options to select from, as seen in Figure 9-2.

***Figure 9-2.*** *The architecture options for the ISO image*

These options are the different architectures in which you can install the image. There is an ISO image for each one of them, and others that can be installed in both architectures. In this case, select the 64-bit architecture. This will lead to a new dual option in order to choose the way to download the image, via BitTorrent or the standard HTTP link (see Figure 9-3).

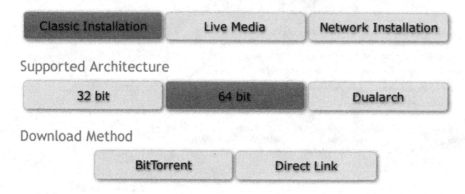

**Figure 9-3.** *The available protocols to download the ISO image*

Once you choose one of these ways and download the image, you can begin the installation. When you boot for the first time, you will see the first difference between installing the distro in a BIOS system or in an UEFI one. Figure 9-4 shows the boot screen for a BIOS system on the left and at the similar screen for an UEFI system on the right.

**Figure 9-4.** *The boot screen for both firmware types*

As you can see, the menus are different but they basically have the same options for installing Mageia. The other options are not essential for this task. One of the options available in the BIOS mode is the Hardware Detection Tool; this was not in the boot menu of any of the distros you saw previously, but it was very common in the past in many distros. It is a tool that can be very useful to troubleshoot hardware problems, and you can take a look at it in Figure 9-5.

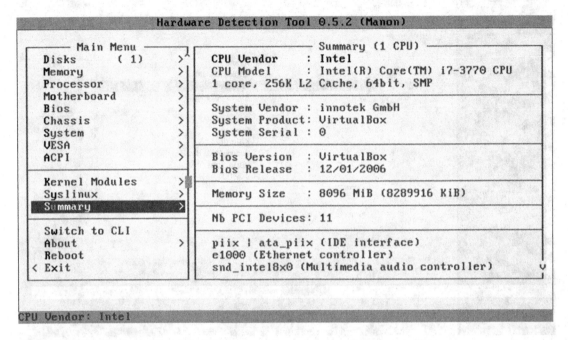

***Figure 9-5.*** *The Hardware Detection Tool*

In the menu of the UEFI mode, choose the "Start Mageia install from …" option (or wait a few seconds for it to start automatically) to go to the next step. From here, the installation is similar for both cases, so I'll show you only one screen. The first screen that appears in the Mageia installer is the one shown in Figure 9-6, the usual option to select the language to use in the installation process and/or distro. One peculiarity is that you can choose to use multiple languages from this screen (by clicking the "Multiple languages" button) and then you can then switch between them when you are using Mageia.

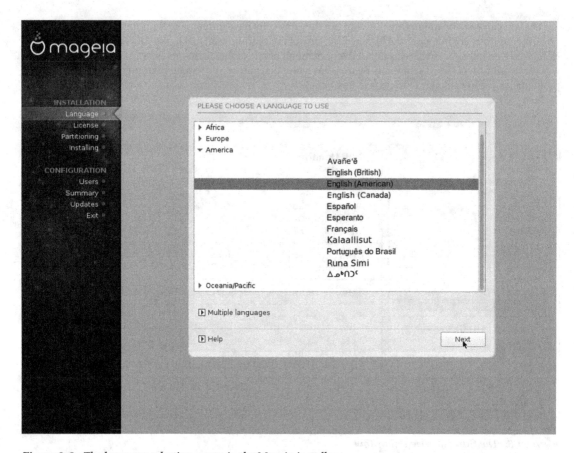

***Figure 9-6.*** *The language selection screen in the Mageia installer*

The next step (Figure 9-7) is the one where you have to accept the License Agreement in order to continue the installation process (people don't usually read this, but I recommend you do so; it's always good to know something about how this license works and then you can compare it to the EULA of other OSes).

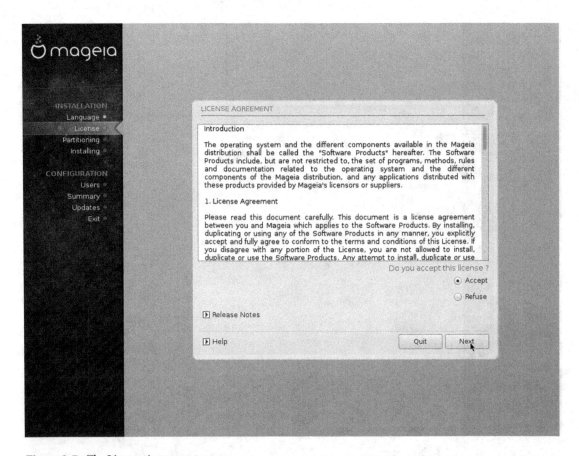

***Figure 9-7.*** *The License Agreement screen*

If you accept the license, you can continue to the next screen (Figure 9-8) where you can choose the layout of your keyboard.

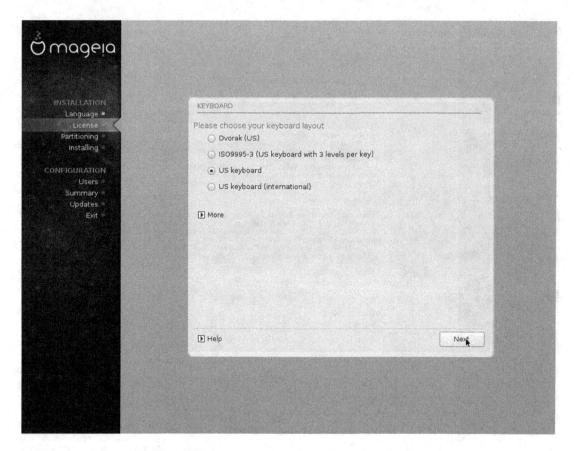

**Figure 9-8.** *Keyboard layout selection*

As in previous distros, the correct keyboard layout should be selected by default; if not, select the right one for you and press the Next button. This next step is always the most crucial one; it's where you choose how you are going to partition your disk drive. As you can see in Figure 9-9, this screen shows the current status of the disk drive selected and gives you two options to partition: an automated one using the free space on your disk or via a customized partitioning.

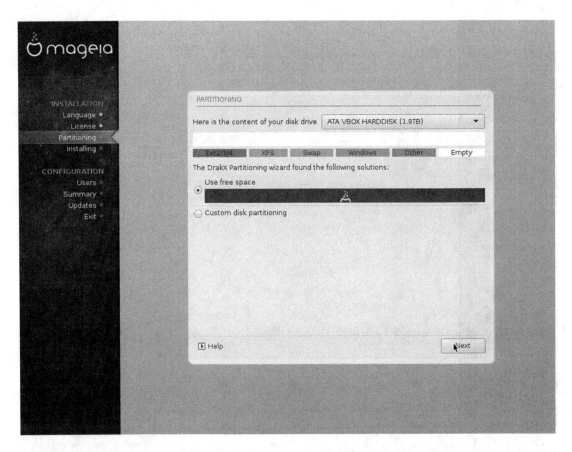

***Figure 9-9.*** *The partitioning tool*

Let's do the custom partition option. This will also show the subtle but important differences between a BIOS and a UEFI installation. So select "Custom disk partitioning" and press the Next button.

Figure 9-10 shows how this custom option works. There are two options to choose from, an automated option (the same as before but now in this part of the tool) called "Auto allocate" or to manually partition the disk through the interface (by clicking on a partition or free space). Also, you can choose between the normal and expert mode, where more information is shown and more options are available to configure. In order to show the differences between the BIOS/UEFI installations, the best way is to select the automated partition option to view how the partition scheme is created in each case. Well, first, let's change to the expert mode to show more information. Next, create the predefined partition scheme by pressing the "Auto allocate button." As you can see in Figure 9-11, a new dialog emerges, asking you which type of partition you want (this dialog only appears in the expert mode).

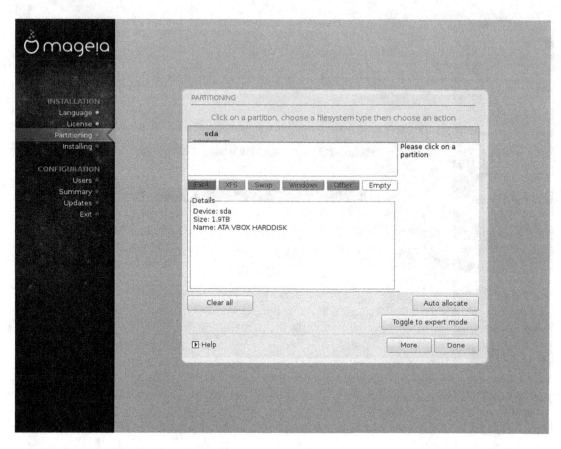

**Figure 9-10.** *The custom partitioning option*

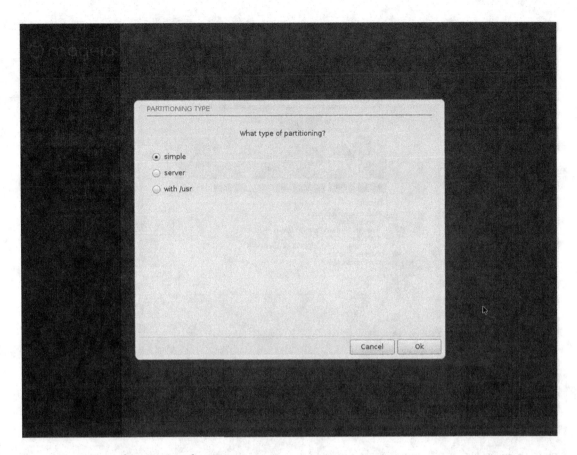

***Figure 9-11.*** *Type of partition to choose*

Choose the "simple" option and click the Ok button. A new partition scheme is created where appears for first time in the book a new partition, allocated at the beginning of the disk that is "colored" as a Windows partition (in blue) and is mounted under `` `/boot/EFI` ``. This partition stores the necessary system files to boot the system and it is a DOS partition type, which is why it appears as a Windows partition. The rest of the partitions are the usual ones (`/`, `/home` and `swap`). You can see the result in Figure 9-12 and compare it to Figure 9-13, which shows doing the same in a BIOS system.

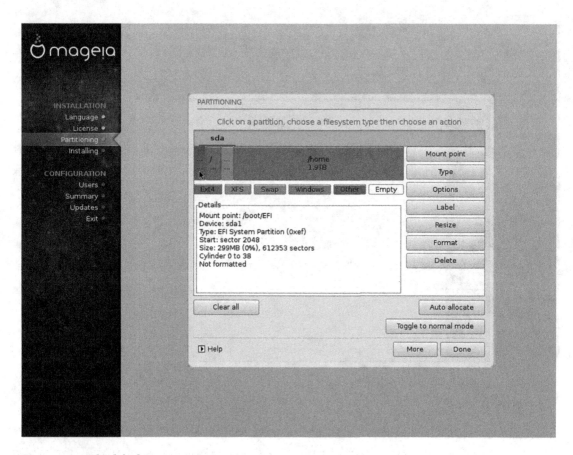

***Figure 9-12.*** *The default partitions in a UEFI system*

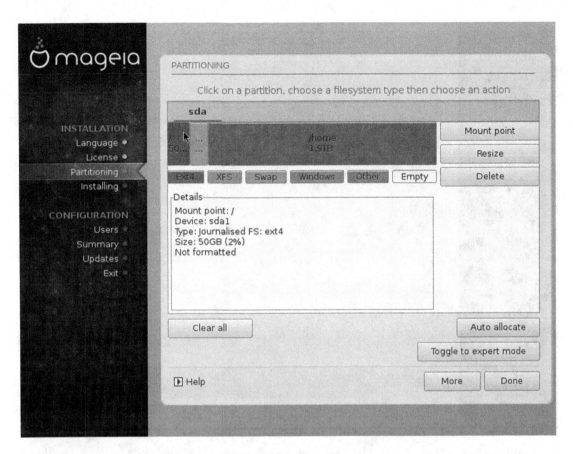

***Figure 9-13.*** *The default partitions in a BIOS system*

Now that you have created the partitions, you can press the Done button. After the usual warning about making the changes to the disk, the partition process completes and you advance to next step. This step is something you saw in other distros like OpenSUSE, where you are asked if you have another media available to use in the installation (shown in Figure 9-14).

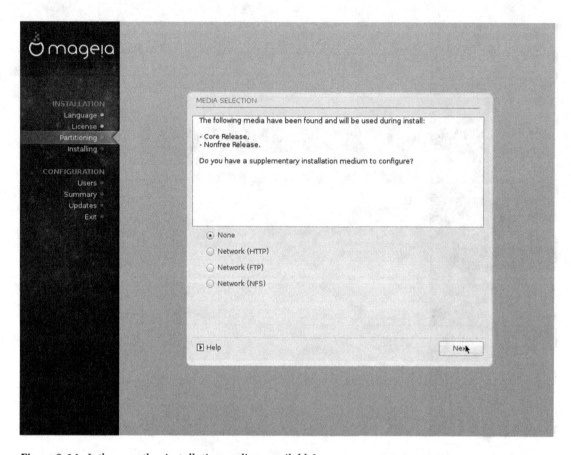

***Figure 9-14.*** *Is there another installation medium available?*

In the following screen you can pick packages you want to install (Figure 9-15). You can stick with the core packages or you can add non-free packages (e.g. private firmware) to the installation. This screen seems a little confusing to me, because some people could confuse the local repositories with the online ones and get the wrong idea.

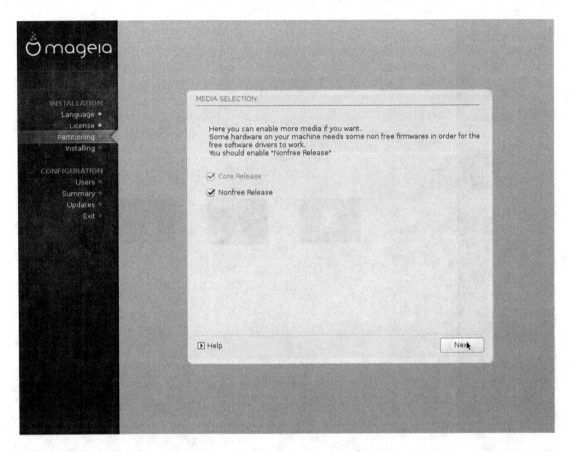

**Figure 9-15.** *Select local repositories*

Next, you get to choose which desktop environment (Figure 9-16) you want to use in your Linux installation. You can opt for one of the major ones, KDE or Gnome or another alternative (Cinnamon, LXDE, LxQT, Enlightenment, MATE, and XFCE). The default DE is KDE because it was the traditional DE of Mandriva. So let's choose it and continue the installation process. It copies the system files to the disk, as shown in Figure 9-17.

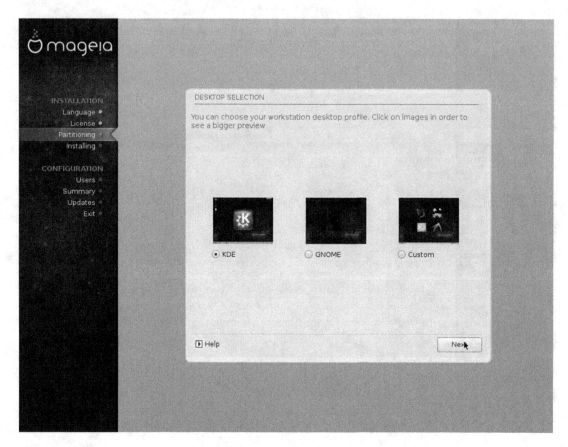

*Figure 9-16.* *Select the desktop environment*

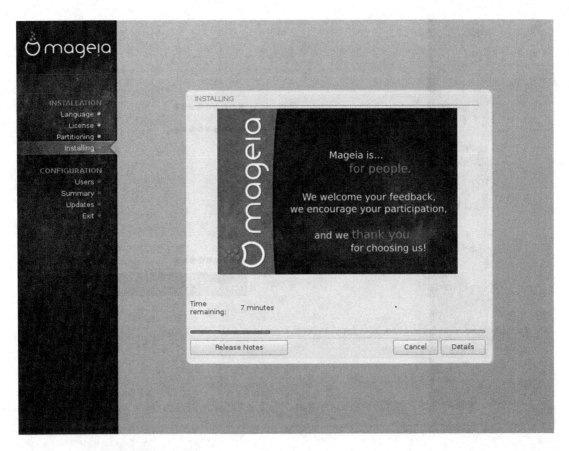

*Figure 9-17. Copy the files to the disk*

When the Mageia installer finishes the task, you must introduce the root and user information. There's nothing here that you haven't seen before. As it should be, Mageia will show you warning that the password couldn't resist a basic attack, which implies that it is not a strong password (Figure 9-18).

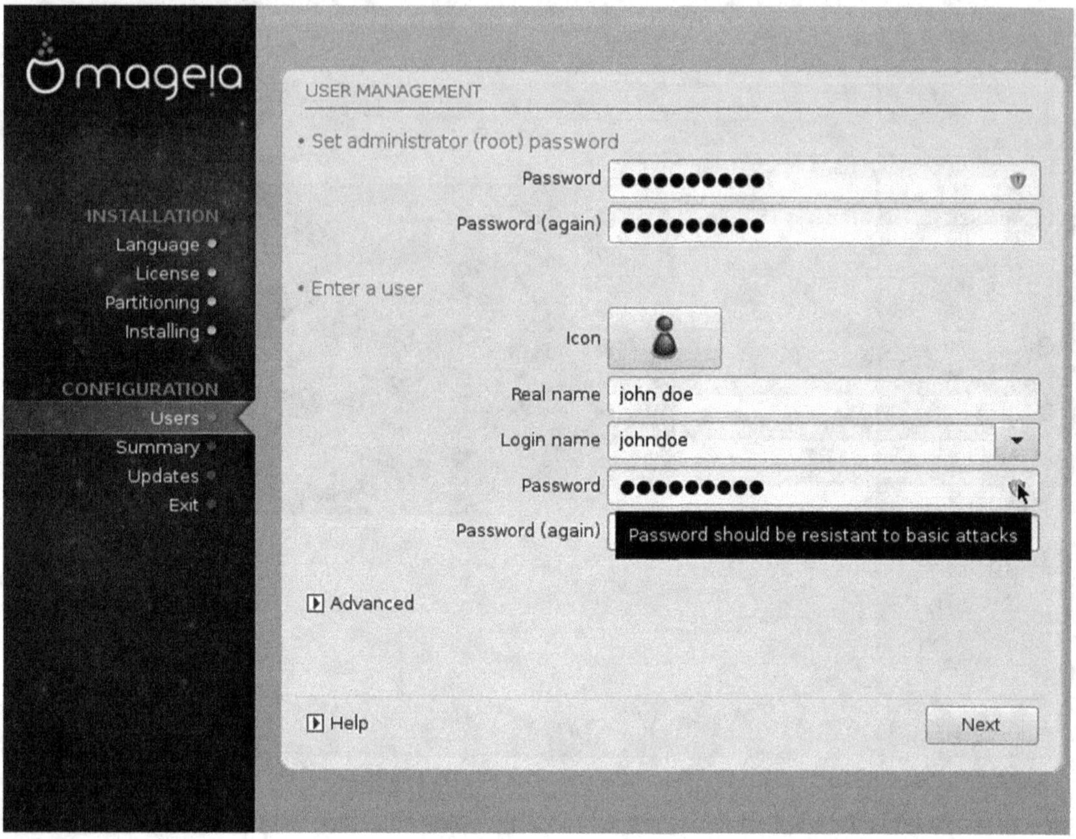

**Figure 9-18.** *The user information*

The next is an odd request: the installer tool asks you to choose a monitor from a set of options (Figure 9-19). Most distros detect this setting automatically, so it's rare to see this request these days. I suspect that it is related to the installation on a virtual machine; it is possible that installing this distro on a real system would skip this step. Either way, if you see this screen, select a plug'n play one (or a generic one) if you don't know exactly which monitor you have.

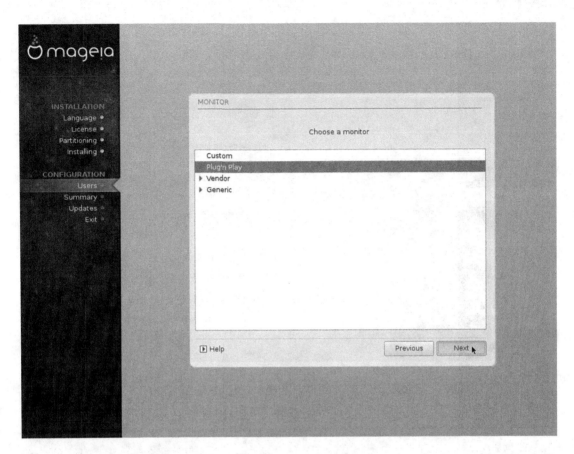

**Figure 9-19.** *Monitor selection*

After that, the installer will show you a summary of the installation, with details about the system and the settings; you can make corrections here (Figure 9-20). The summary is divided in four sections: System, Hardware, Network & Internet, and Security. There are some advanced options that only can be changed from here (of course you can always change the system configuration after the installation). If you don't know or understand each option, leave it as is.

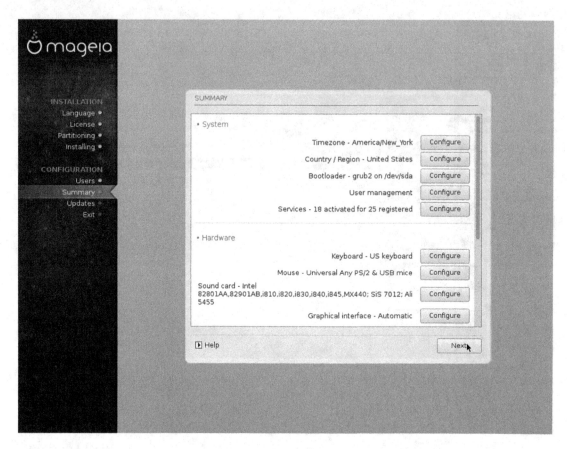

*Figure 9-20.* *The installation summary*

The following step is to decide if you want to use the online repositories to get any possible package updates that could exist there (Figure 9-21).

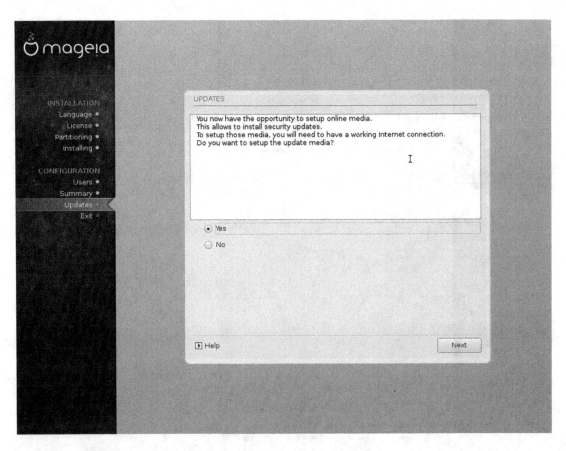

***Figure 9-21.*** *Use the online repositories to install the last security updates*

If you elected to use the online repositories, it will start downloading all of the security updates. After downloading all of the security updates, a screen asks you to confirm that you wish to download all of the updated packages (Figure 9-22).

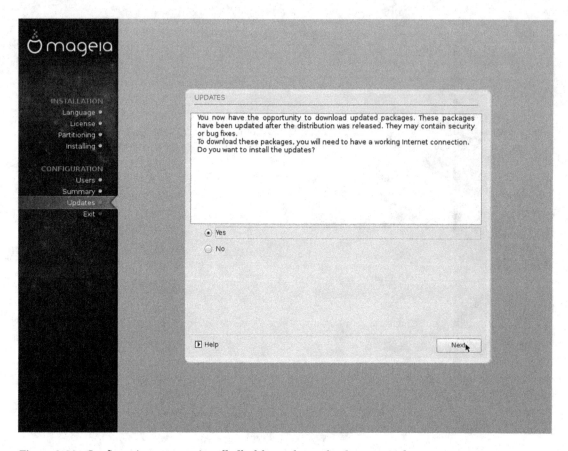

*Figure 9-22.* *Confirmation screen to install all of the packages that have an update*

Some pop-up dialogs will appear, asking for your permission to install those packages. If you give your permission, the installation ends when all of the packages are installed on the disk drive. You know that the installation is finished when you see the screen shown in Figure 9-23.

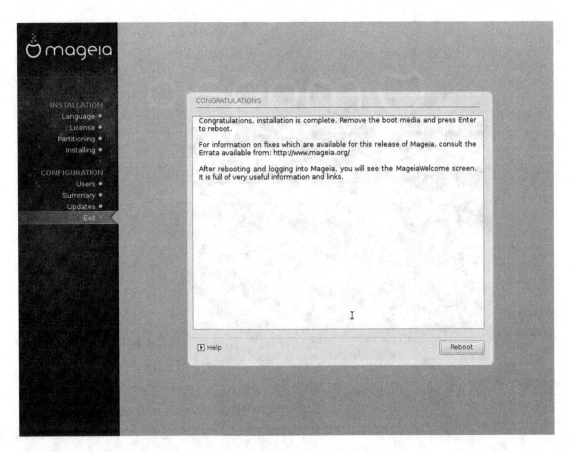

*Figure 9-23.* *It's done. You have installed Mageia*

Now is the time to restart your system and enjoy your Mageia Linux for the first time. The first screen that you see when you boot your system is the last difference that you will see between the traditional BIOS and the modern UEFI. They are very similar (both have the boot loader Grub) but there are subtle differences in how they are presented. Figure 9-24 shows the BIOS Grub and Figure 9-25 shows the UEFI Grub.

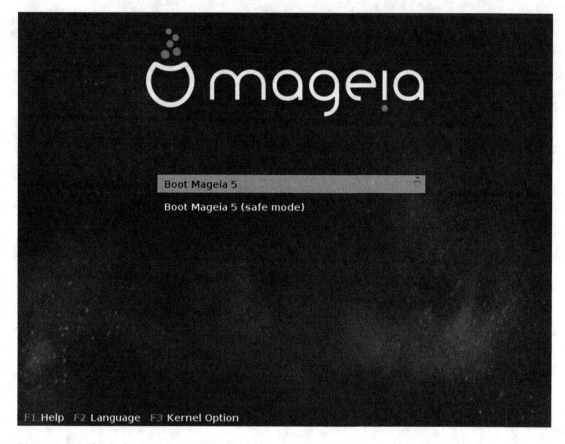

*Figure 9-24.* *The Grub screen in a BIOS system*

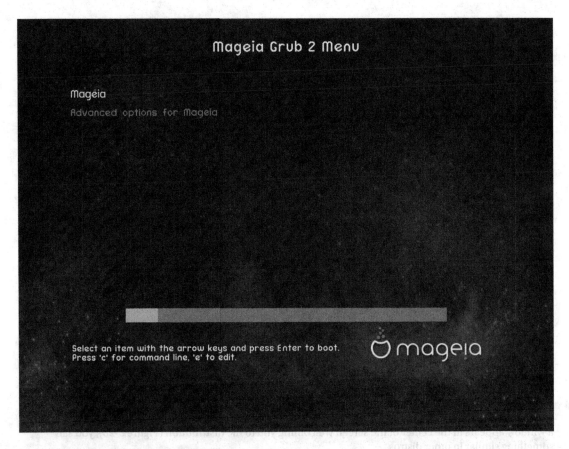

***Figure 9-25.*** *The Grub screen in an UEFI system*

The login screen is your welcome to your new Mageia distro. Enter your password and go to the desktop. This login screen has an older design (Figure 9-26) because it still uses KDE 4.

***Figure 9-26.*** *The login screen for KDE*

The desktop is typical of KDE 4 with a Mageia custom background (Figure 9-27). After a few seconds, a window appears in the center of the screen welcoming you to the distribution (Figure 9-28); you saw something similar in other distros.

***Figure 9-27.*** *The KDE Mageia desktop*

***Figure 9-28.*** *The welcome window*

217

Like OpenSUSE, a distro very similar to Mageia, it detects that is being installed inside a VirtualBox machine and shows you a warning to update the Guest Additions to the last version (Figure 9-29). This is a nice touch.

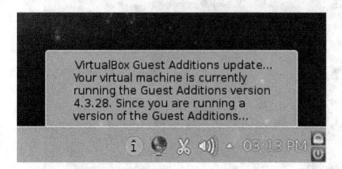

**Figure 9-29.** *Mageia detects VirtualBox*

As you can see, there are not many differences in installing the distro in a BIOS system versus a UEFI system, and this is why I chose the traditional BIOS system to install all the previous distros. In some distros, these differences are bigger, but these are usually the advanced ones.

# Maintenance

The maintenance tasks in Mageia are done in a similar way to OpenSUSE, and you can do almost all of them from GUI interfaces without needing to use the command line. The exception is the distro upgrade.

## Updating and Managing Apps

The obvious path to follow in Mageia is to go to the Control Center for essential administration tasks. This is also the ideal way to deal with upgrading and managing apps (Figure 9-30).

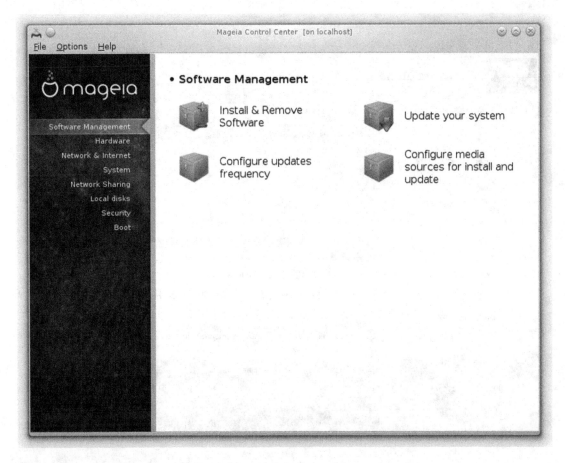

*Figure 9-30.* *The Software Management section of the Mageia Control Center*

From there you can manage your apps or update them. Both options will open a GUI program (which you can call directly if you wish), rpmdrake and drakrpm-update, respectively (Figure 9-31). These tools are only a front end to the urpmi tool, and you have the option to use it from the console instead, which many users prefer.

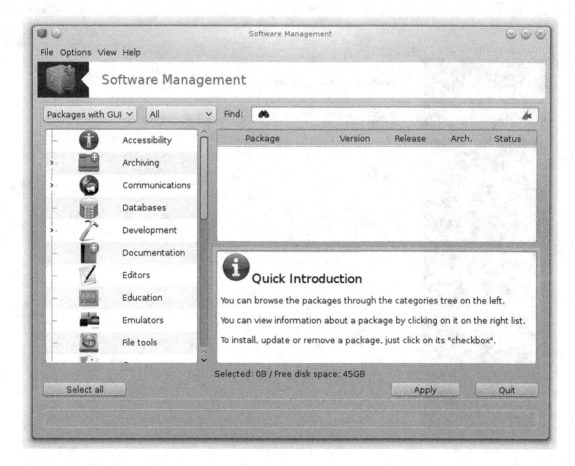

*Figure 9-31. The Software Management tool (rmpdrake)*

As with other distros, you will be warned when new updates are available and you can use the same dialog to perform the task from here.

# Upgrading

Upgrading is always one of the most sensitive tasks to perform in a distribution; some distros don't have a proper way to do it, and others have an intricate way to do it. Mageia has two options:

- Follow the instructions that will appear when a new release is available. The packages will be fetched from the Internet repositories.

- Use the ISO image of the new release and select the upgrade option from the installation program. You can use the online repositories to update all the packages not included by default in the ISO image (and this is recommended). You can take a look at the upgrade option in the installation menu in Figure 9-32.

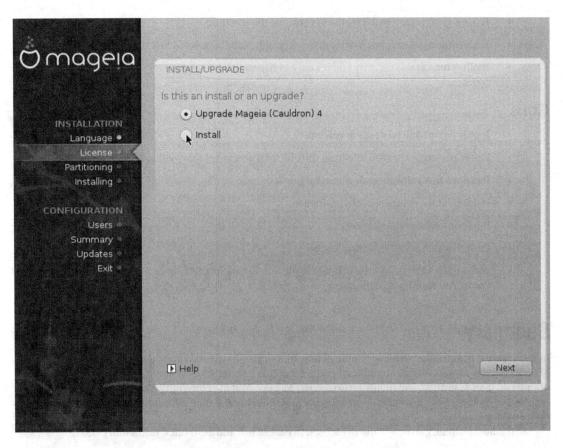

***Figure 9-32.*** *An upgrade option is available on the installation program*

The non-obvious way to do this is to use the command line and the urpmi tool to upgrade the distro. This way is best suited for advanced users, but it is also the most reliable way to upgrade the distro.

# Pros and Cons

The following is a list of some things that I personally see as pros and cons of the Mageia distribution. There's always room for discussion in this matter, but I've tried to be as objective as possible.

## Pros

- The Mageia Control Center makes it easier to tweak and admin the distro.
- Mageia uses the rpm package format.
- It has a regular release scheme.
- It's a community-driven distro.
- It's a stable distro, but it's a bit outdated.

- It has a great legacy and it seems to continue the tradition.

- It's an original distro, not a derivative (although Mandrake was a fork of Red Hat).

- It offers reasonable security and it's easy to harden it a bit more.

## Cons

- It only has an official desktop version.

- Fewer packages are available from the official repositories than with other distros.

- It is not a free software-only distro for purists.

- It doesn't take enough care of aesthetics.

- It has no commercial support.

- Only two architectures are supported.

- Although it's a very popular distro (mostly in Europe), its community is not very big compared to other great distros.

# Summary

In this chapter, you saw the perfect example of how free software is a fundamental aspect of the survival of Linux distros. Mageia was an abandoned project that was rescued by a community. It started life as Mandrake, then Mandriva, and finally resurfaced as Mageia. And the community keeps improving the distro, with an eye on the past to maintain its great legacy and the other eye on the future to improve itself and the future of Linux.

In the next chapter, I analyze a distro focused in ease of use and aesthetics, elementary OS.

# CHAPTER 10

■ ■ ■

# elementary OS

elementary OS is the newest distro that I analyze in this book. It is only five years old and has only delivered three major releases to date. It also has an unusual origin, a very small community behind, and it is an Ubuntu derivative. Despite all these odds against it, elementary OS has become a very popular distro and the best known representative of a new generation of Linux distros (together with Solus, Cub, deepin, and others) that want to establish a new level of friendliness and design in Linux, as Ubuntu did years ago.

These distros do not pretend to be one-for-all distros. On the contrary, elementary OS and the others focus on the user who has simple needs, like browsing the net and managing a few documents, videos, and photos. Minimalism, great design, and ease of use are the pillars of this new generation of Linux distros. (And yes, in case you are wondering, "elementary" always start with a lower case "e," even at the beginning of a sentence.)

## History

In the beginning, elementary OS was not a Linux distribution. In fact, it was not even a software project, but a design one. elementary OS started as a Gnome 2 icon set and then a Gnome theme that was intended to be used with Ubuntu. Daniel Foré created it in 2009, and the theme quickly become very popular. Foré even ended up working for Canonical (the corporation behind Ubuntu) as a designer for almost two years, thanks to this notoriety. Before leaving Ubuntu, he began a new project that could fulfil his vision of what a Linux distro (actually an OS) should be: the elementary project.

The elementary project started first as a mock-up/concept of an ideal desktop environment. Then some developers developed a few things, like a modified Nautilus (the Gnome 2 file manager), and Dexter and Postler (a contact manager and e-mail client, respectively). Then they built its own desktop environment, Pantheon, and finally its own distribution, elementary OS.

The first release of elementary OS, based on Ubuntu 10.10, was Jupiter in March of 2011. Luna was released in August of 2013 and Freya was released in April of 2015. Jupiter was released with a customized Gnome desktop; Luna was the first release to have Pantheon as its desktop environment.

## Philosophy

The elementary OS philosophy is contained in its own name. Simple, easy, minimalistic, beautiful, basic, and uncomplicated are the words that define the goals and vision of this project. The developers say that they want to be the beautiful and intuitive alternative to MS Windows and OS X. A more realistic description is that they are an alternative to Chrome OS or the different projects that are going to bring Android to the PC (like Remix OS). In a few words, if you ever thought that a tablet could cover all of you needs and you want to ditch your laptop/desktop in favor of one, this is a good clue about what you can expect from elementary OS (I'm not saying that elementary OS works on tablet, because it doesn't; I'm talking about the kind of

© Jose Dieguez Castro 2016
J. Dieguez Castro, *Introducing Linux Distros*, DOI 10.1007/978-1-4842-1392-6_10

tasks that you would expect to perform on a tablet). Being a Linux distro you can always go beyond that basic functionality, of course, but at the cost of breaking the simplicity/design consistency across all of the applications.

In order to do maintain design consistent, the developers use Ubuntu as a basis and then add their own desktop environment plus a few minimalistic apps to cover the simple needs of a big group of users. The out-of-the-box apps include a mail client, a calendar, multimedia management (photos, music, and videos), a text editor, a way to browse the Internet, and some system management apps (files, terminal, and settings). Basically, they replace the usual DE and apps with a very simple and friendly alternative. Again, a similar alternative is Chrome OS, which uses the cloud and the simpler Google apps to do tasks; however, elementary OS uses a traditional local storage and local apps approach.

I think that elementary OS may offer very interesting things in the future, even if it just works as an inspiration for other projects. But, at the same time, it has some obstacles to address. As I see it, it only can grow in one direction, that of adding more built-in apps, because by its own definition, if it adds more features to the current ones, it will break its own principles.

# Distro Selection Criteria

Let's see how this particular distro fares on those decision-making points from Chapter 2.

## Purpose and Environment

elementary OS focuses only and exclusively on the desktop; it only has a desktop version.

## Support

The community behind elementary OS is very small. There are currently about 30 regular developers. So you cannot expect the same level of support as with a big corporate or community distro. However, elementary OS has a reasonably good level of support from various sources:

- **Documentation**: https://elementary.io/docs/

- **Q&A**: https://elementaryos.stackexchange.com/

- **Forum**: https://elementaryforums.com/index.php

- **IRC**: #elementary on irc.freenode.net

## User Friendliness

The intentions of the elementary OS project are very clear on this topic.

> *Our primary motivation for developing elementary OS has always been to build the absolutely best computing experience we possibly can.*
>
> —Daniel Fore, in an interview for LME Linux, January 2014

Have they succeeded? Well, many people feel that elementary OS is the best Linux distro available; others feel that it is on its way to achieving greatness; still others feel it's merely a bad copy of OS X; and still others think there are more important things than design and simplicity. I classify computer users into two big groups: content creators and content consumers. For the first group, clearly elementary OS has little to offer, even if some of them like the design and vision a lot. The majority of elementary OS fans are in the second group, where many of them will have all they need with only the built-in applications and others will only have to install a few more.

It is precisely in that last point where the major weakness of elementary OS appears. If you only need to use the built-in apps, then you have an install-ready OS that is easy to use and comes with what you need. It's very basic and amicable. But once you install more apps, you may maintain the Pantheon theme, but other than that, the consistency is gone. You may even experience some basic problems due to poor integration with the desktop environment. In fact, I saw that with an app like Blender and another KDE app.

But is elementary OS a very friendly Linux distro? Sure, if you use it as intended and you do not need something more from it. The reality is that it is very hard in a small project like this to get consistency because of the nature of open and free software and the lack of universal guidelines for design, GUI development, and user experience. It's difficult even for the large Linux distros In fact, even Apple, with its closed ecosystem, has problems with third party apps that do not always respect their guidelines. Likewise, Android has the same problem with the small adoption of Material Design by app designers.

Having said that, it is quite remarkable how a small group of people achieved such a level of ease-of-use and excellence with so few resources. Imagine what they could do with the resources of a corporation like Canonical.

## Stability

After the second release, Luna, elementary OS switched to being based on the LTS releases of Ubuntu. Thus, it follows a regular release scheme, but it is not a rigid schedule; the new releases appear when they are ready. The release number scheme began with a 0.1, and each major release will add another 0.1 to that number, like so:

- **0.1 Jupiter**, based on Ubuntu 10.10
- **0.2 Luna**, based on Ubuntu 12.04 LTS
- **0.3 Freya**, based on Ubuntu 14.04 LTS

0.4 Loki (based on Ubuntu 16.04 LTS) is expected to be the next elementary OS release. Two minor releases of Freya, 3.1 and 3.2, fixed some errors and introduced new features and updates.

So, because it's based on the LTS versions of Ubuntu, elementary OS should be a little outdated but rock solid, right? Actually, there are always minor errors and glitches, due to the small team behind elementary OS, and this makes the distribution a little unstable sometimes, and even a bit annoying occasionally.

## Hardware Support

The hardware support is essentially the same as the underlying Ubuntu version that it is using at the moment, so it is good support.

## Aesthetics

Since the goal of this project is minimalistic and beautiful design, the aesthetic of every little thing is very well polished. The use of their own built-in apps helps to ensure consistency of design across the environment (but not if you install third party applications). As soon as you boot up the distro, you notice the clean design.

Some detractors say that elementary OS is merely a copy of the OS X design, and the inspiration is undeniable. The color palette, the look of the icons, and the dock all reference OS X (Figure 10-1). But this is not anything new; there are and were a lot of themes, icons, and distros that wanted to replicate the look and feel of other OSes like OS X or Windows. In fact, you can tweak the desktop environment of almost any distro until you get close to looking like one of those OSes. Regardless, you cannot deny the effort put into the distro to get a professional-level design and the further steps of developing new apps to get a cohesive design.

***Figure 10-1.*** *The elementary OS dock (Plank)*

Is the elementary OS design the best and the most beautiful? Well, I don't want to introduce an opinion here. I want to show you how the design of an essential tool, a file manager, can vary between distributions. You can judge for yourself how important design is to you and which distros offer the most eye-candy. To do this, look at three distros that handle aesthetics (Figures 10-2, 10-3, and 10-4) and another distro that doesn't (Figure 10-5). You can see how some of them cast shadows and others don't; that's a desktop environment feature, but it's also a design decision. It's obvious that the first three offer better designs, taste aside, than the last one. But between the first three, which one is the best? It's quite subjective.

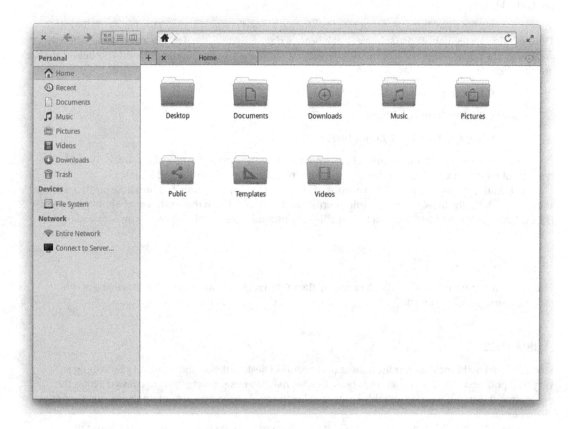

***Figure 10-2.*** *The elementary OS file manager on a Pantheon DE*

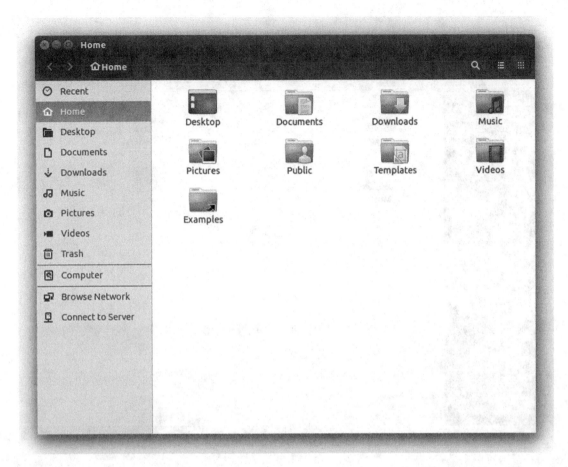

*Figure 10-3. The Ubuntu file manager on a Unity DE*

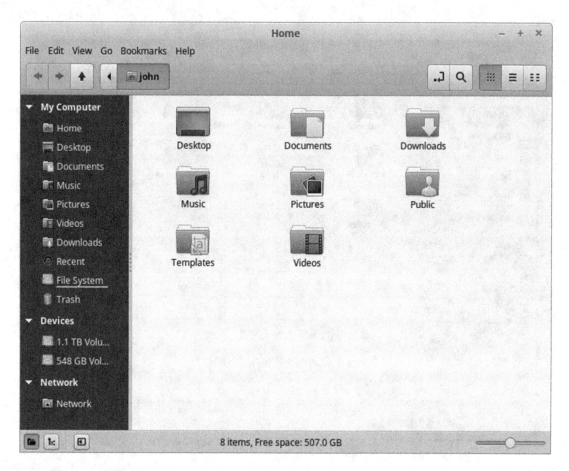

***Figure 10-4.*** *The Linux Mint file manager on a Cinnamon DE*

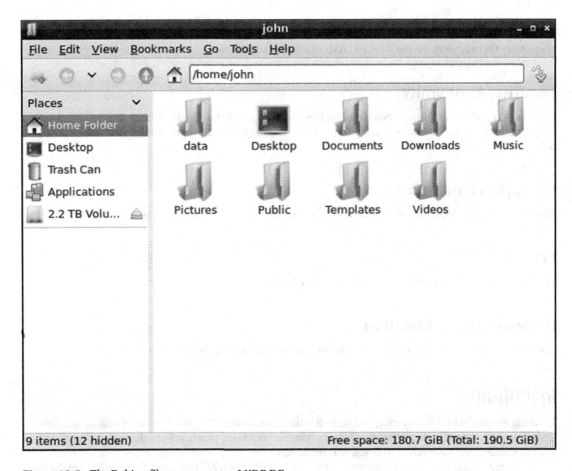

*Figure 10-5.* *The Debian file manager on a LXDE DE*

## Desktop Environment

elementary OS uses its own desktop environment, Pantheon. It uses the GTK 3 toolkit (originally from Gnome) and is programmed in Vala and C. Although this DE was developed by the elementary OS team, you can install it unofficially on other distros, like Arch Linux or Ubuntu.

## Init System

Since elementary OS is based on Ubuntu, it uses the same init system, but because the current Freya release is based on an old Ubuntu version, 14.04, it is still using the sysv init system. This will change after the next release, Loki, which will be based on Ubuntu 16.04 LTS and thus will use systemd.

## Package Management System

Because it's based on Ubuntu, elementary OS uses not only the same package management system, but also the Ubuntu repositories and software management apps. In fact, elementary OS's software is obtained and updated through PPAs (Personal Package Archives) hosted in Launchpad (from Canonical).

229

## Architecture

elementary OS only supports the Intel and AMD 32/64-bit architectures.

## Security/Anonymity

In terms of security, elementary OS is based on Ubuntu, so it should be equal to Ubuntu. As for anonymity, the elementary OS project claims that it doesn't make advertising deals or collect any sensitive personal data.

## Principles and Ethics

Also, the principals and ethics are similar to Ubuntu, since elementary OS uses Ubuntu's repositories.

## Live CD

The ISO image of elementary OS also works as a Live DVD.

## Professional Certification

Obviously, in a very small project like this, there is no professional certification available.

# Installation

Installing elementary OS is very easy, and since it is based on Ubuntu, like Mint, it uses the same installer. Since I already covered in detail the installation of Ubuntu and Mint, please refer to those chapters. Here I will just mention the main differences you will encounter.

As always, you should go to the elementary OS web site, `https://elementary.io`, to download the ISO image. In Figure 10-6, you can see that it seems like you have to pay to download it; in fact the button says "Purchase elementary OS." This is merely a way to suggest that you make a donation to sustain the project, but you can enter a $0 quantity to download it. This was a controversial step at the time, but the reality is that Ubuntu does something similar without too much noise. So select a predefined quantity or introduce a custom one and click the "Purchase elementary OS" button. The next window asks you to choose the version you want to download, 32- or 64-bit (Figure 10-7). I recommend choosing the 64-bit version.

*Figure 10-6. The elementary OS site where you can download the OS*

*Figure 10-7. Choosing the elementary OS version to download*

Then you have to install the distro, which is exactly like Ubuntu but in a grey color palette. When you first boot the system, and after you log in, you will see the desktop shown in Figure 10-8. And those are the only differences that you will experience when installing elementary OS.

*Figure 10-8.* *The elementary OS desktop*

You can learn more about the elementary OS installation at `https://elementary.io/docs/installation`.

# Maintenance

Maintaining elementary OS is similar to maintaining Ubuntu, for obvious reasons.

## Updating and Managing Apps

Currently elementary OS uses the same application as Ubuntu, the Software Center, to perform updating tasks. A new application for this same purpose, AppCenter, is being developed, and it will be the default probably in the next release, 0.4 Loki.

## Upgrading

There is no predefined or easy way to upgrade elementary OS. Even the developers suggest you make a clean install.

# Pros and Cons

The following are some of the things that I personally see as pros and cons of the elementary OS distribution. There is always room for discussion in this matter, but I'll do my best to be as objective as possible.

## Pros

- It is one of the easiest to use.

- It has an exquisite, modern, and consistent design.

- Because Ubuntu is its base system, you can benefit from its advantages.

- The built-in apps are simple, intuitive, lightweight, and fast.

- It is suitable for users with few requirements or computer experience.

- It is a good start pointing for users coming from other OSes.

## Cons

- Technically, it is Ubuntu with a different desktop environment and other default apps.

- Due to the small team behind it, it is not rare to find several errors every time a new release is launched, which are usually resolved via small updates.

- The built-in apps are too simple to perform any semiprofessional tasks.

- You cannot expect the same pure design and simplicity from third party apps.

# Summary

In this chapter, you saw a new paradigm in Linux distros, a distro that could be attractive to those who choose with their eyes and those who want uncomplicated things. elementary OS is basically all about design and simplicity. You won't choose this distro for technical prowess. It covers a niche, and based on its popularity, it seems to do it pretty well.

In the next chapter, I talk about another distro that covers another niche, advanced users and tweakers who wants a very customizable system: Arch Linux.

■ ■ ■

# CHAPTER 11

# Arch Linux

Arch Linux is the first distro covered here that is targeted to advanced users and the first one that is a pure rolling release distro. It's also not user-friendly, but that hasn't stopped it from becoming very popular. Perhaps its success lies in its simplicity, because Arch only gives you a very basic foundation upon which you can build the Linux you need or want. The other key to its fame is its appeal to the type of user who always wants to have the most recent version of any software. But none of this would be possible without the support of the impressive documentation and the great community behind it.

## History

In 2001, a Canadian programmer named Judd Vinet started developing a new Linux distro inspired by the simplicity of others like CRUX and BSD Unix. He liked the inherent elegance that came with that simplicity, but he strongly disliked the lack of package management in those options, so he also developed a new package manager, pacman, based on the same principles. He released the first version of this new distro, Arch Linux 0.1 (Homer), on March 11, 2002.[1]

Judd Vinet passed the role of main developer and leader of the distro to the American programmer Aaron Griffin in late 2007, who remains at the helm to this day.

Arch Linux's reception by the community would be gradually, growing steadily over the years. Even today it still has a modest install size compared to distributions like Ubuntu or Debian.

## Philosophy

Minimalism, simplicity, and code elegance (the KISS Principle) were the core guidelines of the development of Arch Linux. The Arch Philosophy, commonly known as the Arch Way, is defined as follows:

- **Simplicity**: No unnecessary additions or modifications to the software. The packages are almost identical to their original developer's release of them; essential (and minimal) changes are made only when necessary to run the distro.

- **Modernity**: Offer the latest stable releases of software and the newest features available in Linux. Be a bleeding-edge distro.

- **Pragmatism**: Arch is a facts-and-needs–based distro, not an ideological one. This approach spans the development decisions to the license of the software; you are free to choose between free and proprietary software.

---

[1]www.archlinux.org/news/arch-linux-01-homer-released/

© Jose Dieguez Castro 2016
J. Dieguez Castro, *Introducing Linux Distros*, DOI 10.1007/978-1-4842-1392-6_11

- **User centrality**: Arch Linux does not try to be everything to everyone; it tries to satisfy the needs of its contributors and community. It promotes a DIY (do it yourself) attitude.

- **Versatility**: Arch provides a very basic command-line system. You can install and set up whatever you want for whatever tasks and needs you have in mind.

---

▪ **Note**  The KISS (Keep it simple stupid) Principle states that any system works at best if simplicity is a key goal in its design. Unnecessary complexity is to be avoided. It is a widely used principle in engineering and computer science, and it is behind great achievements like the design of the UNIX OS, and therefore Linux too.

---

# Distro Selection Criteria

Now that you know some history, let's see how Arch Linux rates on the selection criteria outlined in Chapter 2.

## Purpose and Environment

Arch Linux is a general purpose distribution. In fact, it's hard to be more general than this distro. Since nothing is predefined, you can build the system you want, even a task-oriented one (which proves that Arch Linux is a general as it can be). It offers one version as one ISO image.

## Support

As a community distro, the support is obviously less professional and extensive than in a company-backed one. Furthermore, its philosophy is one of expecting its users to solve their own problems. So you might think that the community support would be small and of poor quality. But here is the paradox, Arch Linux has one of the most open, friendly, and helpful communities of all distros, and it has perhaps the best documentation around (which is maintained by the community itself). It's a known fact that many users of other distros use the Arch Wiki to answer questions about their distros. Perhaps the reason for the quality of the documentation is because it's better to write down a topic on the wiki once than answer the same question several times in other channels. Everyone expects you to consult the docs first before asking any questions.

The channels you can use to get support from the Arch community are the following:

- **ArchWiki** (Documentation): https://wiki.archlinux.org

- **Forums**: https://bbs.archlinux.org/

- **Mailing lists**: https://lists.archlinux.org//listinfo/

- **IRC**: #archlinux at irc.freenode.net
  More at https://wiki.archlinux.org/index.php/IRC_channels

## User Friendliness

As mentioned, the Arch Linux philosophy does not emphasize user friendliness. The typical Arch Linux user is one who has advanced knowledge or is willing to do it all by themselves by reading the documentation first (tinkerers).

I do not recommend this distro for beginners. However, many people are attracted by the rolling release scheme and are tired of upgrading their user-friendly distros. Thanks to the extraordinary quality of the documentation, they were tempted to test this distro, and a good part of them are still Arch Linux users. There is also a kind of user that wants to know more about Linux itself, and using a low-level distro like this one can teach you a lot. Of course, if you hate the command line, avoid this distro.

## Stability

Arch Linux is as unstable as it can get. It follows a rolling release scheme, so you always have the latest version of the software, from the kernel to the rest of the packages. This way you never need to upgrade your distro; you install Arch Linux once and you only have to do regularly updates to keep current. Arch Linux updates its ISO image monthly, but you only need to make a fresh install if something goes terribly wrong.

You can adjust your level of stress and instability to a more reasonable level or just stay on the bleeding edge. You can do this by selecting which repositories you want to enable. If you enable the testing repositories, you will always have the latest and most unstable version; if you don't, you will have a reasonable stable system, given the context. For example, if you don't use the test repositories, you may experience a delay of a few months before you get the latest version of the kernel. Also, one of the advantages of the rolling release scheme is that if one of the releases has a bug, and that particular bug is solved in the next version, you have the solution available in your system almost at the very moment as it is released by its author. In a standard release scheme, it could take years to get the fix. If you want more stability, you can also install the linux-lts kernel, which is a more stable kernel that does not upgrade frequently.

So how reliable can an Arch Linux system be? Well, it depends. First, you should not use Arch Linux in a production server unless you really know what you are doing. Otherwise, there a good number of programmers, system administrators, and other IT professionals who use Arch Linux on their main computer without problems for years. It all depends on how you manage it and your level of knowledge. Let's use an example: me. I've used Arch Linux on several machines for years. The oldest is a desktop of four years, the same age as its Arch Linux installation. I haven't had to make a fresh install on any of them. But I use a minimal setup. I don't use a desktop environment, just a window manager (Awesome WM). I don't have a dedicated graphics card; I use the one integrated in the processor. I also disabled the testing repositories. I always update the packages on a daily basis. As a result, I've only had one or two annoying problems in those machines, and they were easily solved in a couple of hours or less. Part of the secret is that the desktop managers and hardware drivers (especially graphics ones) are the most troublesome packages in almost every Linux distribution. If you remove these parts of the equation, you will have statistically less problems.

## Hardware Support

The hardware support in this distribution relies on the kernel and the drivers available in the repositories. Also, you can use the ABS system and AUR repository to find or build additional drivers. As with other aspects of this distro, this topic depends heavily on the user and his capabilities or willingness to learn.

## Aesthetics

Obviously, in a very minimal distro like this one where you are responsible for what you build, there is no focus on aesthetics.

## Desktop Environment

There is nothing predefined in this distribution, and this includes the desktop environment. Do you want a command line-only distro? This is it. Do you want to install a traditional desktop environment? You can do so, choosing from eight officially supported ones (Gnome, KDE Plasma, Cinnamon, MATE, LXDE, LXQt, Enlightenment, and Xfce) or from about fifteen unofficial ones (including Unity, Pantheon, Deepin, etc.). Do you want to install a window manager instead? You can do so, choosing from about sixty different ones. You can even choose the windows server, either Xorg or either Wayland. Basically there are many possibilities available so you only have to choose one (or more, if you want) and use it.

## Init System

Arch Linux adopted systemd as the default init system in October of 2012.

## Package Management System

Arch Linux uses its own package management system, pacman, a name that is shared by the command line tool used to manage the packages. It is not as popular as dpkg or rpm (it is used mostly by its derivatives), but it has a great reputation of being a simple and solid package manager. The pacman packages have the .pkg.tar.xz extension.

It also has the Arch Build System (ABS), which allows any user to customize any official package or even create her own packages from third party sources. These packages are configured in the form of a package description known as PKGBUILD (a shell script) that can be compiled from the source and built into a package that can then be installed via pacman. This characteristic is exploited to create the Arch User Repository (AUR), a repository of PKGBUILDs created and maintained by the users. These packages are by default not supported officially and are insecure, but this system is broadly used and has been proven over time to be a great way to make a very big number of packages available to users. Thanks to the AUR, a lot of packages are available a few hours after the author releases them, which gives Arch Linux a great advantage over other distros, which have a wait period before you can install the same package. And there's the option of making your own PKGBUILD and submitting it to the AUR; this one of the reasons why Arch Linux is so popular with some developers.

## Architecture

Arch Linux only supports the Intel and AMD 32-/64-bit architectures. There is also an unofficial and independent port to the ARM architecture, the Arch Linux ARM.

## Security/Anonymity

As with every other aspect of this distribution, making Arch Linux secure is mostly the responsibility of the user. You can harden Arch to paranoid levels if you want (by using the grsecurity kernel or sandboxing your browser), but it is up to you. You can refer to the wiki for guidelines to help you; go to https://wiki.archlinux.org/index.php/security.

## Principles and Ethics

As stated by the Arch Way, this distro is pragmatic to a fault, and the ideological or ethical motivations are the responsibility of the final users. You can build a distro using only free software, or not; it's up to you.

## Live CD

A Live CD makes no sense in a distro like this, one that is tailor-made by each user.

## Professional Certification

There is no specific professional certification for this distribution.

# Installation

Installing Arch Linux is a completely different process from the other distros previously covered in this book. The difference is not that all of the installation is done on the command line; you can do that in Debian and in the majority of the other distros if you wish. The main difference is there is no program to assist you in the workflow. The installation process is completely manual and unassisted. In the past, there was a text-based app to help you, but now only a few derivative distros have a program to do this (some of them graphical). Keep in mind that this is a distro inspired by the KISS principle and the DIY culture; however, you are not alone. There is excellent documentation to help you. So, if you are new to this way of installing a Linux distribution, I strongly recommend you go to the Beginner's Guide at https://wiki.archlinux.org/index.php/Beginners'_guide.

Well, first things first. Go to the Arch Linux Downloads page at www.archlinux.org/download/. As you can see in Figure 11-1, it lists the release info about the current month's release and several ways to download it. In this case, get the worldwide HTTP direct download by clicking the rackspace.com link.

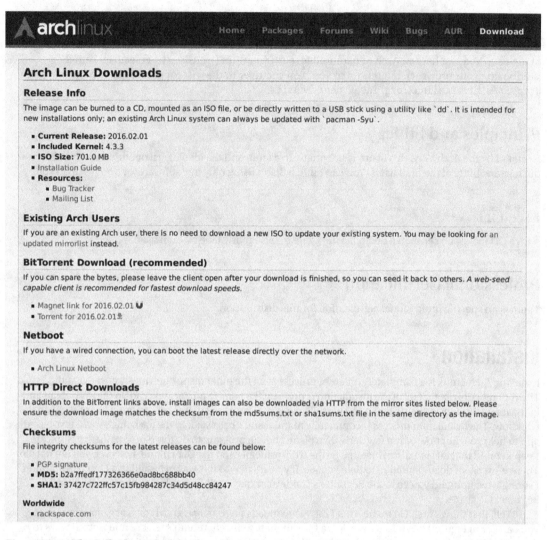

*Figure 11-1.  The Arch Linux Downloads page*

If you use an HTTP server to download the image, you will see the different files available (Figure 11-2). Click the ISO image file link and proceed to the download.

# Index of /archlinux/iso/2016.02.01

- Parent Directory
- arch/
- archlinux-2016.02.01-dual.iso
- archlinux-2016.02.01-dual.iso.sig
- archlinux-2016.02.01-dual.iso.torrent
- archlinux-bootstrap-2016.02.01-i686.tar.gz
- archlinux-bootstrap-2016.02.01-i686.tar.gz.sig
- archlinux-bootstrap-2016.02.01-x86_64.tar.gz
- archlinux-bootstrap-2016.02.01-x86_64.tar.gz.sig
- md5sums.txt
- sha1sums.txt

*Figure 11-2.* *The Arch Linux files available to download*

Once you have downloaded the ISO image and boot your system from it, the first screen you will see if you boot in a classic BIOS system (shown in Figure 11-3) is very similar to the ones you saw in the other distros. The main difference here is it is a dual architecture ISO image, so it lets you choose to boot in the corresponding one. It does not even try to detect it by itself.

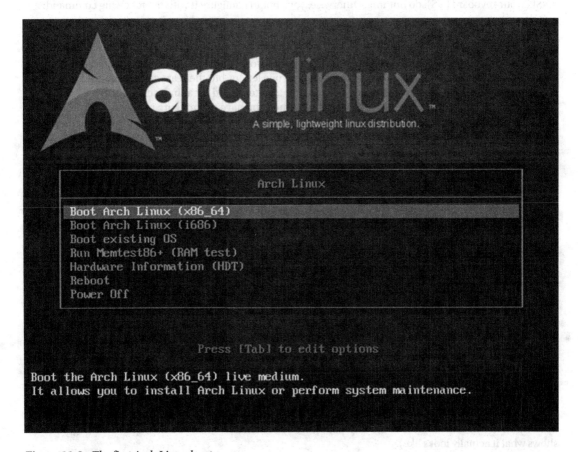

*Figure 11-3.* *The first Arch Linux boot screen*

Think of a modern UEFI system. In this case, the system boots automatically and you end up in a simple zsh shell prompt, logged in as the root user (you would get the same end result if you had booted in a BIOS system). You can see this in Figure 11-4. For beginners, this is hell on earth because they are totally lost, but there was a time when almost all of the distros were installed this way.

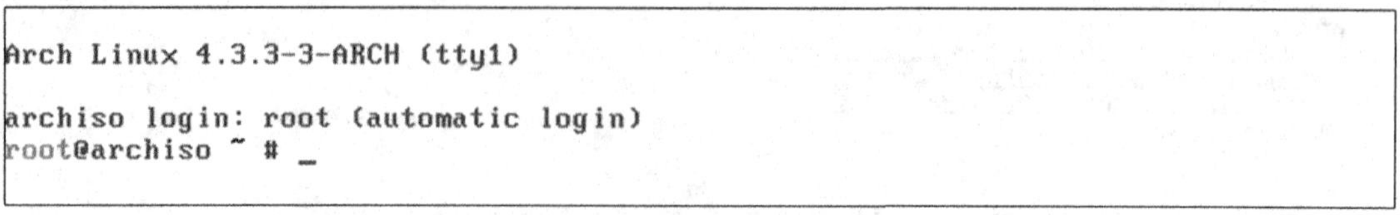

```
Arch Linux 4.3.3-3-ARCH (tty1)

archiso login: root (automatic login)
root@archiso ~ # _
```

**Figure 11-4.** *The root zsh shell where you boot for the first time*

I will guide you through a simple installation, and let you decide if it as horrible as the rumors say, or not.

Note that the kernel version is a very recent one; it's usually the latest available in the core repository at the moment of building the ISO image. The first step is to configure your keyboard layout. If you are using an ANSI layout keyboard (US), do nothing. Otherwise, you should configure it with the following command:

```
# loadkeys es
```

In this example, if you were using a Spanish ISO layout, you would now have the correct layout for your keyboard loaded. Usually the layout is a country code of two letters, but there are some variants. I'm from Spain but I use an ANSI keyboard regularly because it is a better suited for admin servers and programming, so I did nothing here. But do not take this step lightly; when you have to configure passwords, this could make the difference between being able to log in or not. (When you enter or create the password, you cannot see the characters that you are typing. If the layout is not the one that you are using on your keyboard, well, you can imagine what could go wrong.)

The next step is to configure your network. If you are using a wired network, as in my case, and you have a router with a DHCP server, you will probably already be connected to the Internet because the systemd dhcpd daemon has already started. The best way to check this is to ping to a known address like google.com or one of its DNS servers like 8.8.8.8. If your router or firewall does not block the ICMP response, you should see the server answering you.

```
# ping 8.8.8.8
PING 8.8.8.8 (8.8.8.8) 56(84) bytes of data.
64 bytes from 8.8.8.8: icmp_seq=1 ttl=63 time=46.6.ms
64 bytes from 8.8.8.8: icmp_seq=2 ttl=63 time=14.5.ms
^C
--- 8.8.8.8 ping statistics ---
2 packets transmitted, 2 received, 0% packet loss, time 1002ms
rtt min/avg/max/mdev/ = 14.505/30.585/46.666/16.081 ms
```

Another way is to use the already installed elinks text web browser to open a known URL (you can exit later by pressing "q" and then "yes"). This can be a very helpful resource to assist you in installing the distro: you can switch to another terminal (via CTRL+ALT+F2), log in with root (without a password), and then open the ArchWiki and navigate to the installation section to check it when you have questions (Figure 11-5 shows what it actually looks like).

```
# elinks wiki.archlinux.org
```

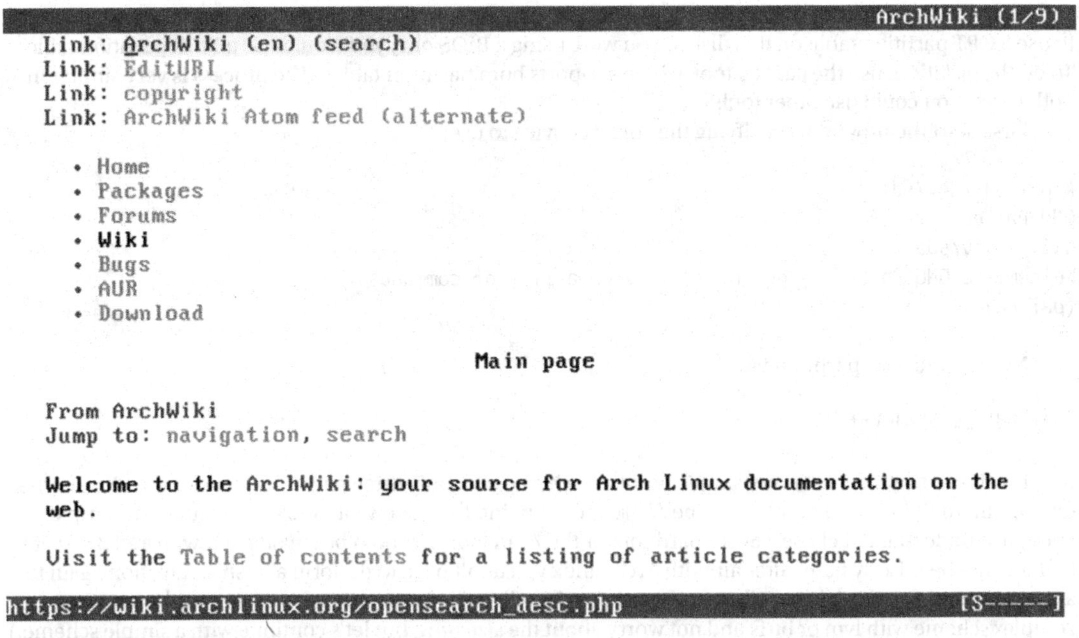

```
ArchWiki (1/9)
Link: ArchWiki (en) (search)
Link: EditURI
Link: copyright
Link: ArchWiki Atom feed (alternate)

     • Home
     • Packages
     • Forums
     • Wiki
     • Bugs
     • AUR
     • Download

                    Main page

From ArchWiki
Jump to: navigation, search

Welcome to the ArchWiki: your source for Arch Linux documentation on the
web.

Visit the Table of contents for a listing of article categories.
https://wiki.archlinux.org/opensearch_desc.php                    [S-----]
```

*Figure 11-5.* The ArchWiki in a elinks browser in a terminal

I'm going to suppose here that everything is ok and you are actually connected to the Internet. If not, consult the ArchWiki to help you set up the network (there are several situations you could have here, and I can't cover all of them in this book).

Now you must sync your system clock to ensure that the time is accurate. This could seem like a superfluous step, but if your system time is not correct, you could have problems installing packages later because it might be hard to import the needed pgp keys. To do so, use the following command:

```
# timedatectl set-ntp true
```

Next, check the status with

```
# timedatectl status
```

The critical step in all distro installations is the disk partitioning, and that's your next step. First of all, you need to identify your current disks and partitions to operate on them. In this example, I am using an empty 2TB hard disk. So execute the following tool, lsblk, to list the block devices in your system like hard drives, CD-ROM readers, DVD readers, and so on:

```
# lsblk --paths
NAME          MAJ:MIN RM   SIZE RO TYPE MOUNTPOINT
/dev/sda          8:0  0     2T  0 disk
/dev/sr0         11:0  1   701M  0 rom  /run/archiso/bootmnt
/dev/loop0        7:0  0 307.8M  1 loop /run/archiso/sfs/airports
```

What we have here is a hard disk of 2TB called sda in the path /dev/sda. The Arch Linux ISO image mounted as sr0 and there's another auxiliary virtual device used only in the installation. It's not showing any partition on the sda device.

Now you must do the partition. In this case, I am installing Arch Linux in a UEFI system, so I am going to use a GPT partition table on this disk. If you were using a BIOS one, you would use a MBR partition table. To do the partition, use the parted tool, which supports both partition tables. The process is very similar in both cases (you could use other tools).

First, start the program, specifying the correct device to use:

```
# parted /dev/sda
GNU Parted 3.2
Using /dev/sda
Welcome to GNU Parted! Type 'help' to view a list of commands.
(parted)
```

Next, create your partition table:

```
(parted) mklabel gpt
```

In this case, let's create a very simple partition scheme with only three partitions, one for the EFI, another for the / mount point, and another for the /home mount point. I will show all the steps, but they are simple enough to understand. I chose a 50GB partition for the / directory; it could be smaller, but with a 2TB disk it's better to not be miserly here. After all, with Arch Linux you don't have to perform a fresh installation again for a long time and you don't know what you're going to install in the future. (Of course you could have a more complex scheme with lvm or btrfs and not worry about the size now, but let's continue with a simple scheme.)

```
(parted) mkpart ESP fat32 1MiB 513MiB
(parted) set 1 boot on

(parted) mkpart primary ext4 513MiB 50.5GiB
(parted) mkpart primary ext4 50.5GiB 100%
```

The final scheme is like the one you can see in Figure 11-6, after executing the following commands inside parted:

```
(parted) unit GiB
(parted) print
```

```
(parted) unit GiB
(parted) print
Model: ATA VBOX HARDDISK (scsi)
Disk /dev/sda: 2048GiB
Sector size (logical/physical): 512B/512B
Partition Table: gpt
Disk Flags:

Number  Start     End       Size      File system  Name  Flags
1       0.00GiB   0.50GiB   0.50GiB   fat32              boot, esp
2       0.50GiB   50.5GiB   50.0GiB   ext4
3       50.5GiB   2048GiB   1997GiB   ext4

(parted)
```

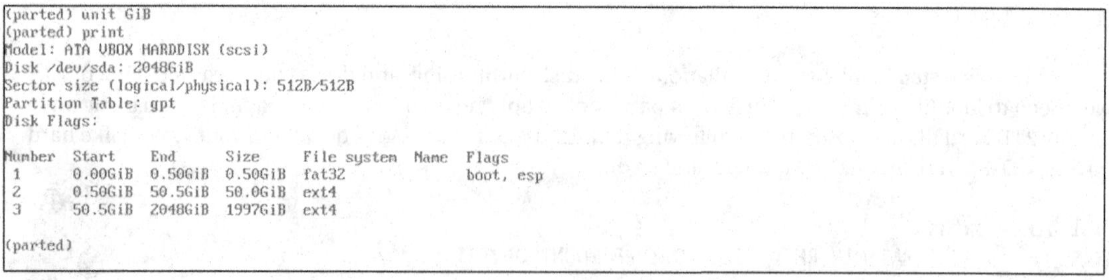

*Figure 11-6.* *The partition scheme*

Finally, exit the parted tool with the `quit` command, and get the status of your block devices:

```
(parted) quit
# lsblk --paths
NAME            MAJ:MIN RM   SIZE RO TYPE MOUNTPOINT
/dev/sda          8:0    0    2T   0 disk
 ├─/dev/sda1      8:1    0  512M   0 part
 ├─/dev/sda2      8:2    0   50G   0 part
 └─/dev/sda3      8:3    0    2T   0 part
/dev/sr0         11:0    1  701M   0 rom  /run/archiso/bootmnt
/dev/loop0        7:0    0 307.8M  1 loop /run/archiso/sfs/airports
```

Now it's time to format the partitions and mount them. The EFI (sda1) partition needs to be a FAT32 one, and for the rest, choose a safe bet, like ext4. Let's format them:

```
# mkfs.fat -F32 /dev/sda1
# mkfs.ext4 /dev/sda2
# mkfs.ext4 /dev/sda3
```

You must mount them in the live system to perform the installation; those are not the definitive mount points:

```
# mount /dev/sda2 /mnt
# mkdir -p /mnt/boot
# mount /dev/sda1 /mnt/boot
# mkdir -p /mnt/home
# mount /dev/sda3 /mnt/home
```

You can see the current status of the partitions in Figure 11-7.

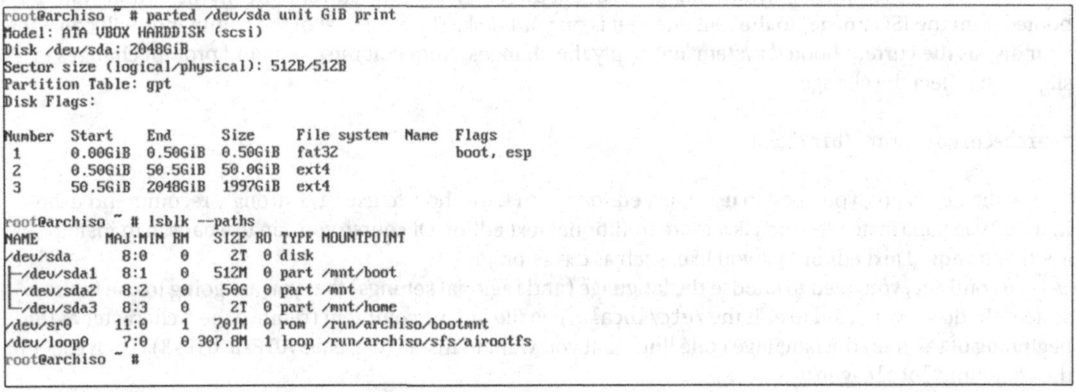

*Figure 11-7.* *The disk is ready to perform the installation and the partitions have been made*

After preparing the disk, continue the installation by installing the base system first. You do this with the `pacstrap` script (the base-devel is to build packages with ABS or from the AUR). Install this package in the / `mnt` directory that is going to be your future / root directory:

```
# pacstrap -i /mnt base base-devel
```

The script will show you the packages that will be installed and it will ask for your confirmation, as you can see in Figure 11-8. There are around 150 packages in this release and although they will take up 750 MiB on the disk, pacman uses a very good compression algorithm (lzma2) so you will download only about 230 MiB of data.

```
root@archiso ~ # pacstrap -i /mnt base base-devel
==> Creating install root at /mnt
==> Installing packages to /mnt
:: Synchronizing package databases...
 core                          122.5 KiB  1263K/s 00:00 [#############################################] 100%
 extra                        1776.7 KiB  1754K/s 00:01 [#############################################] 100%
 community                       3.3 MiB  2.51M/s 00:01 [#############################################] 100%
:: There are 50 members in group base:
:: Repository core
   1) bash  2) bzip2  3) coreutils  4) cryptsetup  5) device-mapper  6) dhcpcd  7) diffutils  8) e2fsprogs  9) file
  10) filesystem  11) findutils  12) gawk  13) gcc-libs  14) gettext  15) glibc  16) grep  17) gzip  18) inetutils
  19) iproute2  20) iputils  21) jfsutils  22) less  23) licenses  24) linux  25) logrotate  26) lvm2  27) man-db
  28) man-pages  29) mdadm  30) nano  31) netctl  32) pacman  33) pciutils  34) pcmciautils  35) perl  36) procps-ng
  37) psmisc  38) reiserfsprogs  39) s-nail  40) sed  41) shadow  42) sysfsutils  43) systemd-sysvcompat  44) tar  45) texinfo
  46) usbutils  47) util-linux  48) vi  49) which  50) xfsprogs

Enter a selection (default=all):
:: There are 25 members in group base-devel:
:: Repository core
   1) autoconf  2) automake  3) binutils  4) bison  5) fakeroot  6) file  7) findutils  8) flex  9) gawk  10) gcc  11) gettext
  12) grep  13) groff  14) gzip  15) libtool  16) m4  17) make  18) pacman  19) patch  20) pkg-config  21) sed  22) sudo
  23) texinfo  24) util-linux  25) which

Enter a selection (default=all): _
```

**Figure 11-8.** *The base system installation script*

After all of the base packages are installed, you will create the fstab file that manages how the partitions are going to be mounted on your system with the right mount points (which are identical to the current ones without the preceding /mnt directory) and parameters.

```
# genfstab -U /mnt >> /mnt/etc/fstab
```

Next, create a chroot jail, which changes the root directory from the current one (in the virtual system booted from the ISO image) to the real one that is on your disk. Thus, the rest of the commands will consider your disk as the current booted system and apply the changes. Note that the command prompt changes slightly to reflect the change:

```
# arch-chroot /mnt /bin/bash
```

In the next steps, you need to use a text editor. If you know how to use vi, I strongly recommend using it; if not, use nano instead, which is a more traditional text editor. Of course you can use pacman to install another terminal text editor that you like, such as emacs or joe.

To continue, you need to choose the language (and regional settings) that you are going to use in the system. To do so, you need to edit the /etc/locale.gen file and uncomment (remove the # character at the beginning of the line) the language code lines that you want to install (e.g. enUS.UTF-8 UTF-8). Then execute the command locale-gen:

```
# vi /etc/locale.gen
# locale-gen
```

Now you need to create the /etc/locale.conf file where you specify the language that you are going to use as default, such as LANG=enUS.UTF-8. If you also set a different keyboard layout than ANSI US, you need to edit the /etc/vconsole.conf file too; check the ArchWiki if you need help.

```
# vi /etc/locale.conf
# cat /etc/locale.conf
LANG=en_US.UTF-8
```

The time zone is the next step. First, get the code for the time zone with the tool tzselect, which saves you from the tedious work of having to look up your time zone in the /usr/share/zoneinfo directory. When you invoke this tool, it shows several options to choose from and narrows the search until you have your local time zone. At the end, it shows you the path of the appropriate file. So run tzselect, and after following the instructions, use that time zone code (for example, America/New_York) to make the changes permanent via a symbolic link to its path in the global /etc/localtime configuration file. Finally, adjust the time and set the time standard to UTC (this is strongly recommended).

```
# tzselect
# ln -s /usr/share/zoneinfo/America/New_York /etc/localtime
# hwclock --systohc --utc
```

Next, you need to install a boot loader. There are several options (I use rEFInd) but let's use the one that comes with systemd, systemd-boot. Next, configure a default boot entry on the /boot/loader/loader.conf file. Finally, add that entry to the boot loader, using a helper command to get the PARTUUID of the root partition.

```
# bootctl install
# vi /boot/loader/loader.conf
# cat /boot/loader/loader.conf
default  arch
timeout  3
editor   0
# blkid -s PARTUUID -o value /dev/sda2
58507240-c577-41c0-b228-e5fee0dfaee3
# vi /boot/loader/entries/arch.conf
# cat /boot/loader/entries/arch.conf
title       Arch Linux
linux       /vmlinuz-linux
initrd      /initramfs-linux.img
options     root=PARTUUID=58507240-c577-41c0-b228-e5fee0dfaee3 rw
```

Next, configure the network. In my case, this was very simple and only required two steps: setting the name of the system and enabling the systemd-dhcpcd service.

```
# echo myarch /etc/hostname
# cat /etc/hostname
Myarch
# ip link
1: lo: <LOOPBACK,UP,LOWER_UP> mtu 65536 qdisc noqueue state UNKNOWN mode DEFAULT group default
    link/loopback 00:00:00:00:00:00 brd 00:00:00:00:00:00
2: enp0s3: <BROADCAST,MULTICAST,UP,LOWER_UP> mtu 1500 qdisc fq_codel state UP mode DEFAULT
group default qlen 1000
    link/ether 08:00:2a:3b:64:15 brd ff:ff:ff:ff:ff:ff
# systemctl enable dhcpcd@enp0s3.service
```

The last step is to get a basic Arch Linux system installed. First, set the root password, then unmount the partitions and reboot. Remember to set a very strong password for your root user.

```
# passwd
# exit
# umount -R /mnt
# reboot
```

And that's it! You have now a very basic Arch Linux distro installed on your system. When you boot your new Linux distro for the first time, if you press Enter over the Arch Linux entry or wait 4 seconds, you will end up again in a Linux terminal session (see Figure 11-9). And that's because all you have installed is the distribution, nothing more; it's the basic core. As mentioned, now you build into the installation what you really want; nothing is predefined. Thus, contrary to other Linux distros, when you boot up the system for the first time, your real job begins; friendly distros are ready to use immediately. At this time, you only have a root user and no graphical environment of any kind. But this is a DIY distribution, so this is what you get.

```
Arch Linux 4.4.1-2-ARCH (tty1)

myarch login: root
Password:
Last login: Fri Feb 19 05:18:33 on tty1
[root@myarch ~]#
```

*Figure 11-9.* *An Arch Linux base system before any customization*

From here, it's hard to say what a "standard" path is. I will show you a few very basics steps to help you get an idea of where to go. Don't follow them as a guide, because I do not cover security, multimedia, repositories, and so on. To completely customize an Arch Linux installation can take several hours, depending on what you want to do and your knowledge. But remember, you install this once and then you don't have to reinstall it for years, and you always have an up-to-date system.

The first thing to do is add a user to use the root user only for admin tasks. Also, let's install sudo to escalate the privileges of your user to do admin tasks like updating the distro.

```
# useradd -m -G users,wheel johndoe
# passwd johndoe
# pacman -S sudo
```

Now let's give your user the authorization to use sudo, by giving those privileges to the wheel users group to which you previously added for user. The first command is necessary only if you don't want to use the vi editor and use nano instead. With the command visudo you have to edit the /etc/sudoers file and uncomment the line # %wheel ALL=(ALL) ALL The last command installs the package bash-completion to make it easier to write commands in the terminal with auto-completion.

```
# EDITOR=nano visudo
# visudo
# sudo -lU johndoe
User johndoe may run the following commands on myarch:
    (ALL) ALL
# pacman -S bash-completion
```

The last step that I will show you is to install a graphic environment and a very simple window manager, (instead of installing a classic desktop environment, which you can do if you wish). Start by installing the Xorg server and the video drivers. It will present some choices; if you don't have an Nvidia graphics card, the defaults are fine. The second command is to identify your video card, and the third lists all of the video drivers available. I'll pick an Intel driver.

```
# pacman -S xorg-server xorg-server-utils xorg-apps
# lspci | grep -e VGA -e 3D
00:02.0 VGA compatible controller: Intel Corporation Xeon E3-1200 v2/3rd Gen Core processor
Graphics Controller
# pacman -Ss xf86-video
# pacman -S xf86-video-intel
```

Now it's time to install the window manager. First, you need to install a display manager to be able to log in and select the window manager/desktop environment that you want to use. You could start the window manager directly or boot in the terminal and start the window manager manually, but I think it is friendlier (and equivalent to what you saw in other distros) to do it in this way. I used to do this with Slim, but it is currently discontinued. Now I prefer to use LightDM, which works with multiple DMs and WMs and is very light. There are many options and you can use the one you prefer.

```
# pacman -S lightdm lightdm-gtk-greeter
# systemctl enable lightdm.service
```

There are also several choices of window manager. Let's choose a tiling window manager. (I personally use Awesome WM, and I also like i3 or dwm.) Select i3 because it is one of the easiest to learn. Also, let's install some auxiliary programs; when you are asked about what to install after this command, choose all by default. Finally, let's install a graphical web browser and a terminal tool to show you how they look in i3. Then you need to restart your system to see how it boots directly to the display manager.

```
# pacman -S i3 dmenu termite
# pacman -S chromium htop ttf-dejavu
# systemctl reboot
```

After the system restarts, you can see that you end up in LightDM and not the terminal (Figure 11-10). Introduce your password and then go to the i3 window manager. If it asks you about the configuration, simple press ESC to go with the default one. What you will see is a black screen with a minimal text status bar below; it's as minimal as you can get. If you open a pair of programs like a terminal with htop and the Chromium browser, you will see something similar to Figure 11-11. One of the advantages of a minimal system like this is that, as you can see in the htop output, only a few programs started and the resource use is minimal. To put this into context, I tested a similar scenario in Ubuntu 15.10 and I got 715MB of memory and 120 tasks versus the 212MB and 34 tasks (I only show you the ones initiated with the current user) that you can see here. And in a system configured like mine, the difference with this example is not too much and even very far from the Ubuntu example (that could be Fedora, openSUSE ...).

**Figure 11-10.** *The LightDM screen to log into your i3 session*

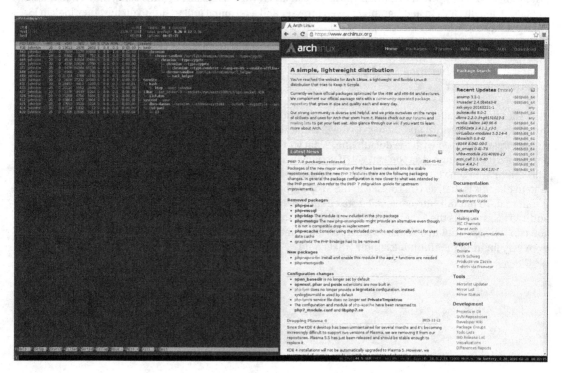

**Figure 11-11.** *The window manager i3 with a pair of windows opened*

To be fair, with a distro like this, where the job of installing is much more complex than with a traditional distro, you must consider the level of customization and lightness that you can achieve. For example, in a case like mine, where I prefer to work with a window manager instead a desktop environment, if I installed an Ubuntu distribution I would have two options after installing and setting up the window manager:

- Use the window manager and keep the default DE (Unity, in this case) with the accompanying waste of space and resources. Also, I'd need to update the large number of packages that usually come with a DE.

- Use the window manager and uninstall the default DE. This is not an easy task. In a distribution like Ubuntu, because of the dependences, it could be impossible to perform a clean uninstall; it might even break the system if you are not careful.

So, in a case like mine, it's usually a better choice to build up a system from a minimal base than to try to make a traditional distro lighter or under-use it. Of course, you have to accept several compromises and give up some conveniences.

# Maintenance

In Arch Linux, you only have to managing apps and perform updates; it's a rolling release distro so there's no need to upgrade it.

## Managing Apps and Updating

The tasks of managing apps and upgrading them are performed in Arch Linux from the command line. There are some tools that work as graphical front ends, but no one uses them and they not are officially supported. You use the same app for both tasks, pacman. To install an app, use this command:

```
# pacman -S firefox
```

To remove it, use this command:

```
# pacman -R firefox
```

And for making regular updates, the command should be like this one:

```
# pacman -Syu
```

With those simple commands a majority of people can survive for a long time without major problems. Of course, there are some necessary long-term tasks, like refreshing the keyring, but this distro expects that you feel comfortable in a DIY culture and can take care of yourself. In a distro like this, it is strongly recommended that you perform updates frequently, even daily, because if there are changes that require manual intervention or ones that introduce changes in the setup of the distro or the way it works, it could stop working properly if these updates are postponed for too long. The current package releases expect these tasks to be performed immediately. In brief, updating regularly saves you from some unnecessary headaches.

As for packages installed from the AUR, there are several tools that can help you do that automatically, like pacaur or yaourt, or semi-automatically, like cower. All of them are unofficial apps. Some people prefer to do this by hand in order to have more control in the process.

---

**■ Note** I'm using the term "updating" in all of the chapters in this book for consistency, but Arch Linux people prefer to use "upgrade" because they say that what you are really doing is upgrading the full system regularly and not simple updating it. And that's true since it doesn't support partial upgrades; you must update all of the packages available. (You still can block package updates, and do partial upgrades, but it is not recommended.) So technically you can say that you are fully upgrading the system each time. However, to compare distros, I think it is easier to understand it as "updating."

---

# Pros and Cons

The following points are things that I personally see as pros and cons of the Arch Linux distribution. I tried to be as objective as possible.

## Pros

- It is a rolling release distro, so it is always on the bleeding edge.
- It offers great documentation.
- It has a very welcoming community.
- It comes with a great package manager, and ABS and AUR.
- Arch Linux is what you make of it; it's fully customizable.
- You can use free and proprietary software, and if none is available officially you can probably make your own package.
- It is an original distro, not a derivative.

## Cons

- It is oriented to users willing to do it all by themselves, so it's not a friendly distro.
- It has the instability inherent to being a rolling release distro.
- You have to be comfortable with the command line to even install it.
- No aesthetics at all; the look is up to you.
- It has no commercial support.

# Summary

Arch Linux was the first Linux distro I covered that is suited for advanced users; it's also the first genuine rolling release distro I covered. You can see the huge differences between this kind of distro and the traditional ones. This kind of distro not only requires you to do it all by yourself, but it also requires that you know what you want to build because there are no predefined setups for you.

In the next chapter, you will see another distro of this kind, but Gentoo goes a step further.

# CHAPTER 12

■ ■ ■

# Gentoo Linux

Gentoo Linux is the quintessential custom Linux distro. In fact, it's so adaptable that the Gentoo people prefer to call it a metadistribution. As with Arch Linux, Gentoo can be whatever you need it to be. It's also a rolling release distro, but it goes a step further; you can build every package from source code to optimize them for your system and needs. Its popularity has taken the opposite trajectory of Arch Linux's: it was once a very popular distribution but this has decreased over the past few years. However, it still has a strong and loyal community behind it.

## History

In April of 1999, Daniel Robbins, an American programmer, started writing the Enoch Linux distro. The idea was to create a Linux distro that was as fast as possible by compiling each package tuned to specific hardware instead of using generic precompiled binaries. You only had to install the packages you really needed/wanted, so it was also a light and versatile distribution.

In May of 1999, after buying a new machine (a dual Celeron), Robbins found out that the Linux kernel would not boot on it, so while other programmers continued to maintain the Enoch distro, he switched to FreeBSD until the bugs were fixed. After several months of using FreeBSD, he returned to developing Enoch, and he started with two important moves:

- He changed the name of the distribution to Gentoo Linux (this name was a suggestion from another contributor).

- He incorporated some ideas from FreeBSD to create Portage, a modern ports system.

The first release of Gentoo Linux (there was a previous one as Enoch) was released on March 31, 2002.

Two years after that release, Daniel Robbins left the Gentoo project as Chief Architect and transferred all Gentoo intellectual property to the non-profit Gentoo Foundation, which he created. The Gentoo Linux project still is under the umbrella of the Gentoo Foundation today, so it is a community-based distribution. Daniel Robbins now works at Zenoss and simultaneously collaborates on the Funtoo project, a Gentoo derivative he created in 2007.

One proof of the power of the customization and versatility of Gentoo, and also of the type of user/use that it has, is that Google used Gentoo in July of 2009 as the base for its own web-based OS, Chrome OS, to work with its cloud.

© Jose Dieguez Castro 2016
J. Dieguez Castro, *Introducing Linux Distros*, DOI 10.1007/978-1-4842-1392-6_12

---

■ **Note** The Gentoo name was an idea from Bob Mutch, and it is related to the Linux mascot. As mentioned in Chapter 1, the Linux mascot is a penguin. Gentoo is a species of penguins; they are considered the fastest underwater swimming penguins, reaching speeds of 22 mph (36 km/h). The idea was to transmit the association between the fastest penguins and the fastest Linux distro.

---

# Philosophy

The philosophy of Gentoo shares some points with that of Arch Linux, but Gentoo takes a more radical approach. Everything can be customized and optimized to suit the user. You can compile the kernel and practically all of the packages from the source code, customizing at very basic levels like what compiler options use or which dependencies (if any) you want to install for each and every package. Thus, if in Arch you get to build your system as you want it, in Gentoo you have almost full control about every tiny aspect of your distribution. And on top of that, Gentoo also follows a rolling release model, so the most recently updated packages are available.

The goal is to have a full customized Linux installation that is much more finely tuned, optimized to your hardware and needs. But this comes at a huge cost in terms of time invested in the installation (and updating it). If installing an Arch Linux system takes several hours for a hugely customized installation, Gentoo can take more than a day just to compile the packages you want to install. As a result, Gentoo users are very particular ones who prefer full control and are prepared to take the time to make it happen; this includes system administrators, developers, enthusiasts, and in general very advanced users. If I had to define the Gentoo philosophy in only one word, it would be "choice."

The strong constraints that both distros impose generate a similar outcome in two critical aspects of any distro: a very welcoming and helping community and documentation of extraordinary quality.

# Distro Selection Criteria

Now that you know a little history, let's see how Gentoo Linux fares on the selection criteria from Chapter 2.

## Purpose and Environment

Obviously Gentoo is practically the definition of a general purpose distro. Because you can built whatever Linux you want with Gentoo for whatever purpose, it can be used to create a task-oriented installation too. Therefore, there is only one version of this distro. Actually there is another version available for the two main architectures (amd64/x86) called Hardened Gentoo, but it's essentially a same version that has been predefined with security measures to obtain a very hardened Linux system. So I hardly consider it as a different version.

## Support

Gentoo gets support from its community, which is of a modest size, but they are technically well-versed and helpful. The community maintains a detailed and quality documentation. Perhaps it doesn't covers as many themes as the Arch Linux one, but it covers some topics in at more technical and deeper level. The channels for support are the following:

- **Documentation**: www.gentoo.org/support/documentation/
- **Wiki**: https://wiki.gentoo.org/wiki/Main_Page
- **Forums**: https://forums.gentoo.org/

- **Mailing lists**: www.gentoo.org/get-involved/mailing-lists/

- **IRC**: #gentoo at irc.freenode.org
  More at www.gentoo.org/get-involved/irc-channels/

## User Friendliness

This is not a user-friendly distro, not only because you need to do it all on your own, without a tool to assist you, but also because you need to compile the packages, which requires more knowledge. Happily, there is excellent documentation to guide you. Another unfriendly aspect is the time it takes to compile just one big package (e.g. OpenOffice, Mozilla Firefox, or a desktop environment); this is probably the main cause of the decrease in popularity of the distro.

A few inexperienced users are still attracted to this distro because is one of the best for learning about Linux at a low level; also the documentation has very good coverage on Linux fundamentals. Aside from that, I would not recommend this distribution to beginners, especially newcomers, because the compilation process is one of the main points used to criticize Linux (which is unfair because it's something you rarely do in more conventional distros nowadays). But if you want to really learn how an OS works at a low level, Gentoo is one of my recommendations for sure.

## Stability

As with Arch Linux, Gentoo is inherently unstable because it is a rolling release distribution. As with Arch, you can choose your level of recklessness; you can choose the stability of your packages from three levels:

- **Stable**: Stable packages with no issues, security or otherwise.

- **Keyword masked**: Packages are still insufficiently tested.

- **Hard masked**: It has broken or very insecure packages.

The stable packages can be a bit outdated (but still fresher than classical distros) but the system is reasonable stable. If you follow a strategy similar as the one outlined in Chapter 11, you can end up with a more-than-reasonably stable system, for a rolling release distro. Also, contrary to Arch Linux, you can be very selective about the packages that you want to update without risking the stability of the distribution (in Arch, doing this is not recommended). Moreover, you can select the stability for individual packages, such as setting stable packages for the core system and testing ones for developer tools. By adhering to this practice very rigorously and meticulously you can achieve a very robust system, one that can be as stable as Debian stable. After all, Gentoo is whatever you want it to be.

## Hardware Support

Gentoo's hardware support relies on the kernel, firmware, and the drivers available on the Portage tree and overlays. As with other aspects of this distro, this topic depends heavily on the user and her capabilities or willingness to learn.

## Aesthetics

Gentoo follows the philosophy of building a unique installation suited for you. It doesn't impose any particular aesthetic at all. Only a few branding patches are applied here and there, but they're mostly incidental (and you have to compile the packages with that option).

# Desktop Environment

There is almost nothing predefined in this distro, and this extends to the desktop environment. You get to decide what you want to install. There is a wide variety of desktop environments you can install (Gnome, KDE, Unity, Mate, Cinnamon, Pantheon, LXDE, LXQt, Budgie, and Xfce). In a similar way, if you prefer a window manager instead, you can also choose from a variety (Awesome, Xmonad, Dwm, i3, Openbox, Sawfish, Fluxbox, Enlightenment, Ratpoison, FVWM, and Wm2). As with Arch Linux, you can even decide if you want to use the traditional X.org window server or the new Wayland, or none at all if you want just a command line.

# Init System

Gentoo is one of the few distros that still does not implement systemd as its init system, and there is no intention to do so in the future. Gentoo uses OpenRC, a BSD-based init system. But you can optionally install and use systemd, if you want to use Gnome 3, for example, but again, it's your call.

# Package Management System

Gentoo uses its own package management system, Portage. Portage is based on the experience that Robbins had with FreeBSD; it's based on its ports system and written in Python. Portage is the soul of Gentoo and it defines the distribution. Portage manages the packages in a different manner than the traditional Linux package managers. It doesn't get binaries from repositories; it compiles the packages from the source code. Even when you can also compile packages in the other distributions, or some others like Arch Linux have its own ports based system like ABS, in Portage the norm is to compile all the packages.

Portage has a collection (usually known as Portage tree) of ebuilds (shell scripts), which are recipes that define how each package is going to be build. To manage this, there's another tool called emerge that works as an interface to Portage. There's also a local ebuilds collection, which you can think of as a sort of local repository that can be synced with the main repository, the Portage tree, and emerge is the tool to manage this local repository. Take this with a grain of salt; I won't get into detail here. I just want you to get a rough idea of how it works.

There are some GUI interfaces for Portage that can be used instead of emerge, like Porthole and Himerge, but usually the people that choose Gentoo as their distribution are more inclined to use command line tools.

Portage/emerge is a very powerful tool, and it allows you total control over the packages and your system. You can configure global settings to compile all the packages via the profile and "CFLAGS and USE flags." You can also set individual settings by package or temporary ones.

Compiling the packages instead of using precompiled binaries has some inconveniences, such as the following:

- **It's a very slow process**: A simple package like Chromium took me about three hours to compile when using the setting MAKEOPTS="-j2" (two simultaneous jobs, one core), and about one hour with MAKEOPTS="-j5" (five jobs, four cores) with an Intel i7 processor. So, imagine building a complete system like the default installation of Fedora or Ubuntu. Of course, you can use some precompiled packages (you can find them using # eix *-bin; currently there are 94 packages), and this will help a little, but it will still take a long time. However, this factor is getting less and less annoying as computers get faster over time and package sizes grow at a much slower pace.

- **A package build can fail**: And sometimes there is no easy to fix, even after changing compilation options. On rare occasions it's even impossible, and only upstream changes can fix it.

But it has some advantages too, like the following (among others):

- **You can choose the dependencies/components**: You can choose, for example, to remove the support for the desktop environment KDE/Qt and only have support for Gnome/GTK in packages that support both. Or you can remove the graphical interfaces for the tools that support it and the command line in servers.

- **You can compile packages for your hardware**: For example, this can allow you to build an updated Linux system in obsolete architectures that are merely supported for other distros or not at all (e.g. PowerPC). It's also great for taking advantage of computing/multimedia packages.

- **You can choose versions and maintain various versions**: You can manually choose the version of a package from the available ones and even have various ones installed in the same system with the slots functionality. This used to be a great advantage for developers before the arrival of virtual machines and containers.

- **You can update an unmaintained system**: You can easily resuscitate a Gentoo system that has not been updated for a long time. As always, it is not immediate; it takes time and effort, but you can't do this in the majority of distros (even in Debian unstable or Arch Linux this can be very painful, something I know firsthand), and it would probably be impossible without a fresh install.

Aside from the Portage main repository, Gentoo also supports overlays, which are a way to create additional repositories of ebuilds, something roughly equivalent to Arch's AUR (or Ubuntu's PPAs). There are official and unofficial overlays; the latter ones are supported and maintained by the community. There are some tools to manage overlays like layman, eix, and emaint. Currently Gentoo only keeps about 19,000 packages in the Portage tree, and the rest of the packages are usually obtained from these overlays.

Years ago, the gain in performance was a strong point in favor of compiling all the packages suited to your hardware, but nowadays the difference in performance against binary package distros is not that big and it doesn't make up for the time spent on the compilation. Only when you need an extremely tuned system for specific tasks can you justify to choosing Gentoo over other distros in terms of performance. In a few words, performance is not the reason why users choose Gentoo as their distro anymore, even if they say it is.

## Architecture

Gentoo supports a wide spectrum of hardware architectures. It covers the usual Intel/AMD 32- and 64-bit options plus Alpha, ARM, Sparc, PowerPC, Itanium, and PA-RISC. Three more are supported only as experimental ones: MIPS, S390, and Super H.

## Security/Anonymity

In a distro like this one, it all depends how you manage security and anonymity. However, Gentoo is well known for taking this topic seriously. From the very beginning, packages compiled with Portage/emerge are optionally built and installed in a sandbox (isolated) environment before they are merged into the actual system. Also, the stable packages are free of known security flaws, and Gentoo includes tools for checking for insecure packages in your system.

Also, the fact that binaries or the kernel can be heavily customized for your hardware and taste makes it less likely that a specific package vulnerability can affect you in the same way it would in other distros.

There is an entire project to help you to harden your Gentoo system: the Hardened Gentoo project. It has a great reputation in the security world. You can use it to harden your Gentoo system and get a very secure one, up to paranoia levels. You can see it at https://wiki.gentoo.org/wiki/Hardened_Gentoo and https://wiki.gentoo.org/wiki/Project:Hardened.

## Principles and Ethics

Gentoo is a very pragmatic distro in terms of principals and ethics. It does not impose any particular vision; you choose your way to address these issues. But you can easily set up the system to only install free software by change an option in Portage to `ACCEPT_LICENSE="@FREE"`.

## Live CD

Gentoo offers a LiveDVD that it calls Hybrid ISO (more about this in the Installation section). Obviously, in this case (unlike in other distros), it is only a proof of concept of what you could build, not what you would have at the end of the installation process (no two Gentoo installs are alike). Also, this DVD is released sporadically; the last one available is from August 2014.

---

■ **Note**    Gentoo calls also their minimal ISO image a Live media. It is true; it's a live Linux system, but not in the sense that I'm using in this book.

---

## Professional Certification

There is no professional certification for this distribution.

# Installation

The Gentoo philosophy, summarized by choice, is something that you can perceive from the very first moment you try to install Gentoo. Unlike the norm in other distros, you can start the installation of Gentoo from its minimal installation ISO or from its LiveDVD, as well as from another LiveCD/DVD, a netboot image, another distro already installed, etc. Basically you can install Gentoo from almost any basic minimal Linux environment. You can do something similar with other distros like Slackware, but Gentoo does not impose anything from the beginning.

It's impossible for me to cover all of the possible scenarios here, especially with a distro like this one, so I strongly recommend taking a look at the Gentoo Handbook at `https://wiki.gentoo.org/wiki/Handbook:Main_Page`. Also, I'm not going to spend too much time on topics I covered in Chapter 11 about Arch Linux because I want to focus on topics specific to the Gentoo installation.

I'm going to use the minimal installation CD that Gentoo provides on its web site because I think this is the choice of the majority of users, although a lot of them prefer to use a LiveCD that gets them a live desktop environment like the Ubuntu one to prepare the installation with graphical tools like Gparted to do the partitions.

As always, first go to the Downloads page of the Gentoo web site at `www.gentoo.org/downloads/`. You can see how it currently looks in Figure 12-1. Note how the images are organized by architecture; in each architecture you have "Boot Media" (the ISO images) and "Stage Archives" (more about this later). At the bottom of the page (not shown in the picture) you can also select other architectures or advanced choices for the architectures already shown at the top. Some of these choices include a "Hardened Stage 3" (only for amd64 and x86), which you can use to obtain a previously secured environment to get a very secure Gentoo system. In this case, download the Minimal Installation CD for the amd64 architecture. These minimal installation ISOs are released every week, so they are always updated.

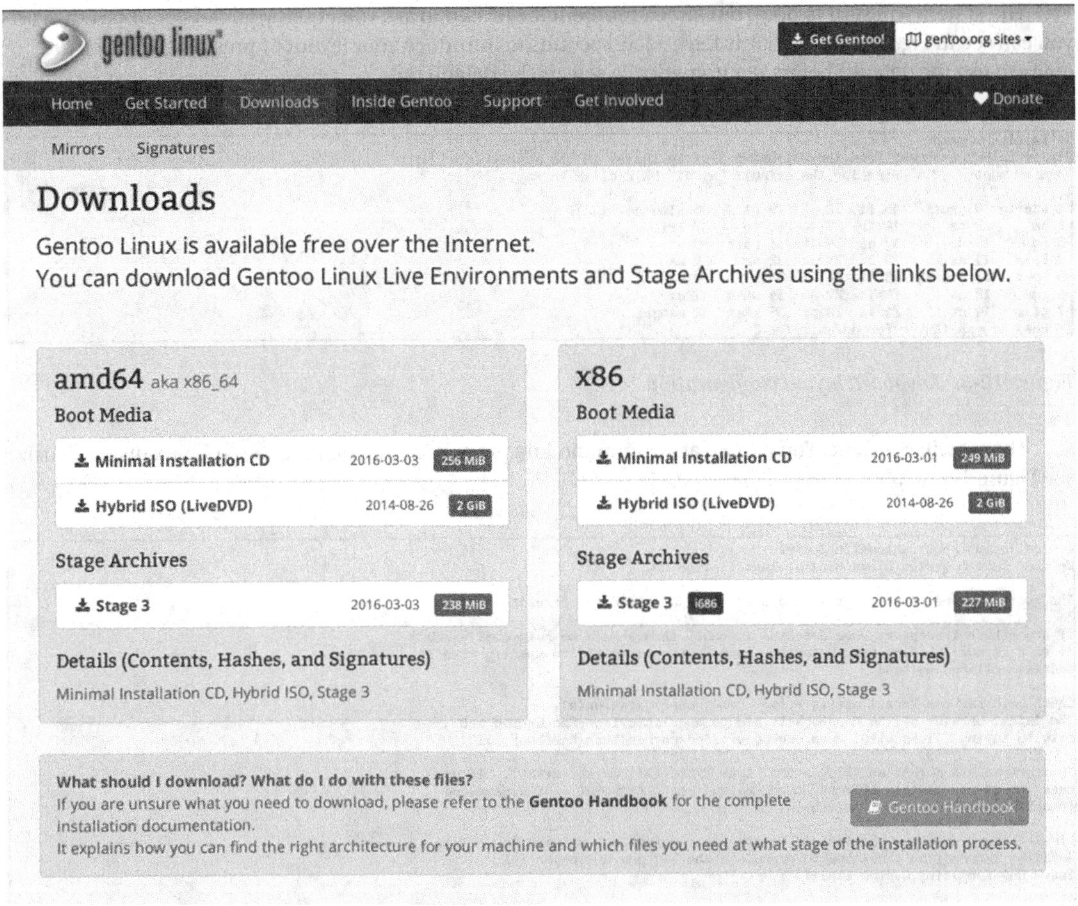

**Figure 12-1.** *The Gentoo Linux downloads page*

Once the download is finished, you must boot your system from the ISO. The first screen that you get (like the one in Figure 12-2) is harsher that what you've seen in the other distros earlier in this book. And if you don't press any key in 15 seconds, it will try to boot from your hard disk. So if you want to continue, press Enter or, as in other distros, you can opt to change the defaults with the F1 (kernels) and F2 (options) keys. So press Enter to continue.

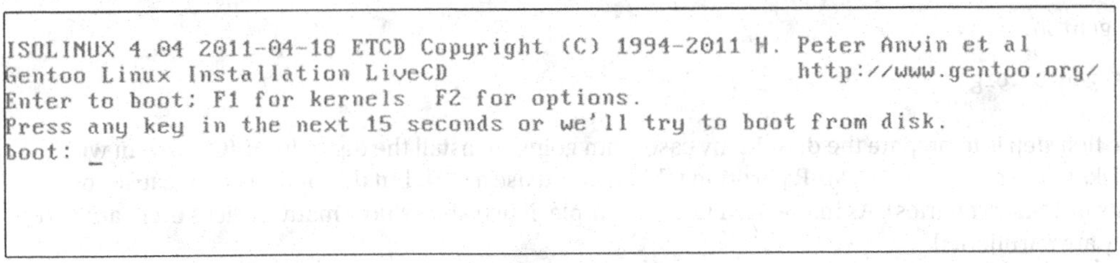

```
ISOLINUX 4.04 2011-04-18 ETCD Copyright (C) 1994-2011 H. Peter Anvin et al
Gentoo Linux Installation LiveCD                          http://www.gentoo.org/
Enter to boot; F1 for kernels  F2 for options.
Press any key in the next 15 seconds or we'll try to boot from disk.
boot: _
```

**Figure 12-2.** *The ISOLINUX boot loader of Gentoo's Minimal Installation CD*

The system will start to boot, but after a moment it will stop to ask you about your keyboard layout, as you can see in Figure 12-3. You only have a few seconds to introduce your layout or press Enter (if you are going to use the default) before it automatically selects the default one.

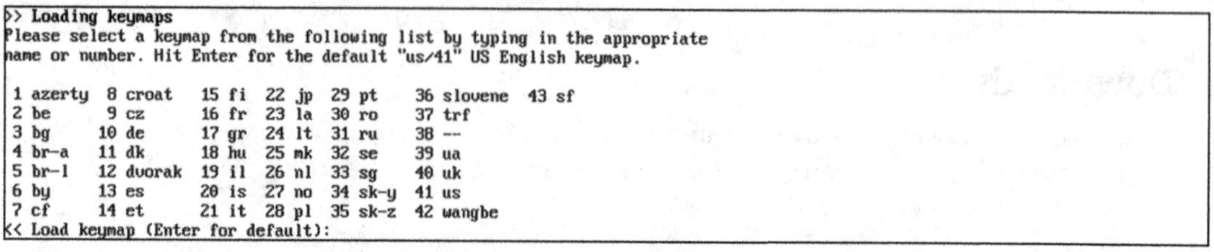

```
>> Loading keymaps
Please select a keymap from the following list by typing in the appropriate
name or number. Hit Enter for the default "us/41" US English keymap.

 1 azerty   8 croat    15 fi   22 jp   29 pt    36 slovene  43 sf
 2 be       9 cz       16 fr   23 la   30 ro    37 trf
 3 bg      10 de       17 gr   24 lt   31 ru    38 --
 4 br-a    11 dk       18 hu   25 mk   32 se     39 ua
 5 br-1    12 dvorak   19 il   26 nl   33 sg    40 uk
 6 by      13 es       20 is   27 no   34 sk-y  41 us
 7 cf      14 et       21 it   28 pl   35 sk-z  42 wangbe
<< Load keymap (Enter for default):
```

*Figure 12-3.* *Keyboard layout configuration*

Then it will continue. You end up at a command line prompt (as you do in the Arch Linux installation); see Figure 12-4.

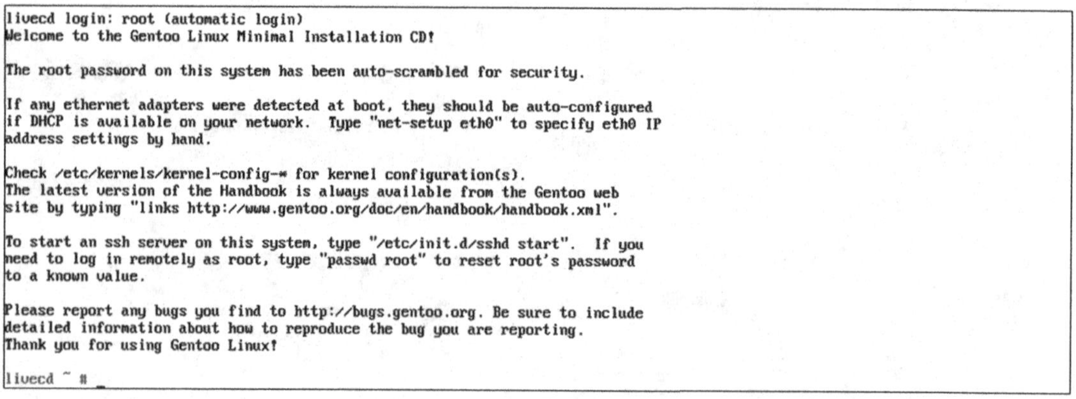

```
livecd login: root (automatic login)
Welcome to the Gentoo Linux Minimal Installation CD!

The root password on this system has been auto-scrambled for security.

If any ethernet adapters were detected at boot, they should be auto-configured
if DHCP is available on your network.  Type "net-setup eth0" to specify eth0 IP
address settings by hand.

Check /etc/kernels/kernel-config-* for kernel configuration(s).
The latest version of the Handbook is always available from the Gentoo web
site by typing "links http://www.gentoo.org/doc/en/handbook/handbook.xml".

To start an ssh server on this system, type "/etc/init.d/sshd start".  If you
need to log in remotely as root, type "passwd root" to reset root's password
to a known value.

Please report any bugs you find to http://bugs.gentoo.org. Be sure to include
detailed information about how to reproduce the bug you are reporting.
Thank you for using Gentoo Linux!

livecd ~ #
```

*Figure 12-4.* *The prompt of Gentoo's Minimal Installation CD*

This is where all the work starts. By default, it should have set your Ethernet connection already if your Internet card was detected and you have a DHCP server. If not, follow the instructions or take a look at the Gentoo Handbook. Open the Handbook via the text browser links (better yet, do it in another console). You can check the connection with a ping to gentoo.org or open the site with links (remember to exit with the "q" key).

```
# ping gentoo.org
```

```
# links gentoo.org
```

The first step is to prepare the disk. In my case, I am going to install the distro in a BIOS system with a 2TB disk, so I'm going to use a MBR partition table (I could use a GPT, but this option could cause some problems in some scenarios). As in the Arch Linux example, it first shows how many devices there are and how they are partitioned.

```
# lsblk --paths
NAME            MAJ:MIN RM   SIZE RO TYPE MOUNTPOINT
/dev/sda          8:0   0     2T  0 disk
/dev/sr0         11:0   1   256M  0 rom  /mnt/cdrom
/dev/loop0        7:0   0 224.5M  1 loop /mnt/livecd
# parted /dev/sda
GNU Parted 3.2
Using /dev/sda
Welcome to GNU Parted! Type 'help' to view a list of commands.
(parted) u GiB
(parted) p
Error: /dev/sda: unrecognised disk label
Model: ATA QEMU HARDISK (scsi)
Disk /dev/sda: 2048GiB
Sector size (logical/physical): 512B/512B
Partition Table: Unknow
Disk Flags:
```

What it shows is a disk without any partition or partition table yet. Let's create the partitions in the disk using parted. Use a very simple partition scheme with only the root partition and the /home partition, both ext4.

```
# parted /dev/sda
GNU Parted 3.2
Using /dev/sda
Welcome to GNU Parted! Type 'help' to view a list of commands.
(parted) u GiB
(parted) mklabel msdos
(parted) mkpart primary ext4 1MiB 50.5GiB
(parted) set 1 boot on
(parted) mkpart primary ext4 50.5GiB 100%
(parted) q
# lsblk --paths
NAME            MAJ:MIN RM   SIZE RO TYPE MOUNTPOINT
/dev/sda          8:0   0     2T  0 disk
├─/dev/sda1       8:2   0    50G  0 part
└─/dev/sda2       8:3   0     2T  0 part
/dev/sr0         11:0   1   256M  0 rom  /mnt/cdrom
/dev/loop0        7:0   0 224.5M  1 loop /mnt/livecd
```

Now format the partitions and mount them.

```
# mkfs.ext4 /dev/sda1
# mkfs.ext4 /dev/sda2
# mount /dev/sda1 /mnt/gentoo
# mkdir -p /mnt/gentoo/home
# mount /dev/sda2 /mnt/gentoo/home
```

---

■ **Note**  Take into account that with the Minimal Installation CD you only have the tools to make ext2, ext3, and ext4 filesystems. You should use another medium to install it if you want to use another filesystem, such as btrfs.

---

Finally you have a hard disk partitioning scheme, as shown in Figure 12-5.

```
livecd ~ # parted /dev/sda u GiB p
Model: ATA QEMU HARDDISK (scsi)
Disk /dev/sda: 2048GiB
Sector size (logical/physical): 512B/512B
Partition Table: msdos
Disk Flags:

Number  Start     End       Size      Type     File system  Flags
 1      0.00GiB   50.0GiB   50.0GiB   primary  ext4         boot
 2      50.0GiB   2048GiB   1998GiB   primary  ext4

livecd ~ # lsblk --paths
NAME           MAJ:MIN RM   SIZE RO TYPE MOUNTPOINT
/dev/sda        8:0     0     2T  0 disk
|-/dev/sda1     8:1     0    50G  0 part /mnt/gentoo
`-/dev/sda2     8:2     0     2T  0 part /mnt/gentoo/home
/dev/sr0       11:0     1   256M  0 rom  /mnt/cdrom
/dev/loop0      7:0     0 224.5M  1 loop /mnt/livecd
livecd ~ # _
```

*Figure 12-5.* *The disk partitioning scheme*

Next, check the date, and correct it if necessary. Note that the syntax is very particular: *MMDDhhmmYYYY*. This stands for month, day, hour, minute, and year.

```
# date
```

The next step is the first one that is properly exclusive of Gentoo. You will download and install the Stage 3 tarball that you see on the Gentoo downloads page. A stage3 is an archive containing a minimal Gentoo environment to continue with the installation. The result of this process is something almost similar to the `pacstrap` script execution in the Arch Linux installation. The best way to download the stage 3 file is to use the links browser to go to the download mirror, choose the one nearest to you, and download the file. You could use another tool like `wget` or `curl`, but you should know the complete URL (and write it). Getting accustomed to this way will make easier to adapt to future changes in the Gentoo web site. Once you choose one mirror and open it, you should look for the `releases/amd64/autobuilds/` directory. Once there, look for the current stage 3 file for amd64 (or your architecture) and download it by pressing "d". It should be a compressed tarball file (with extension `.tar.bz2`) like the one shown in Figure 12-6. There are other stage 3 files there, but you don't care about them. Later, if you grow fond of Gentoo, you'll learn about them for sure.

```
# cd /mnt/gentoo
# links https://www.gentoo.org/downloads/mirrors/
```

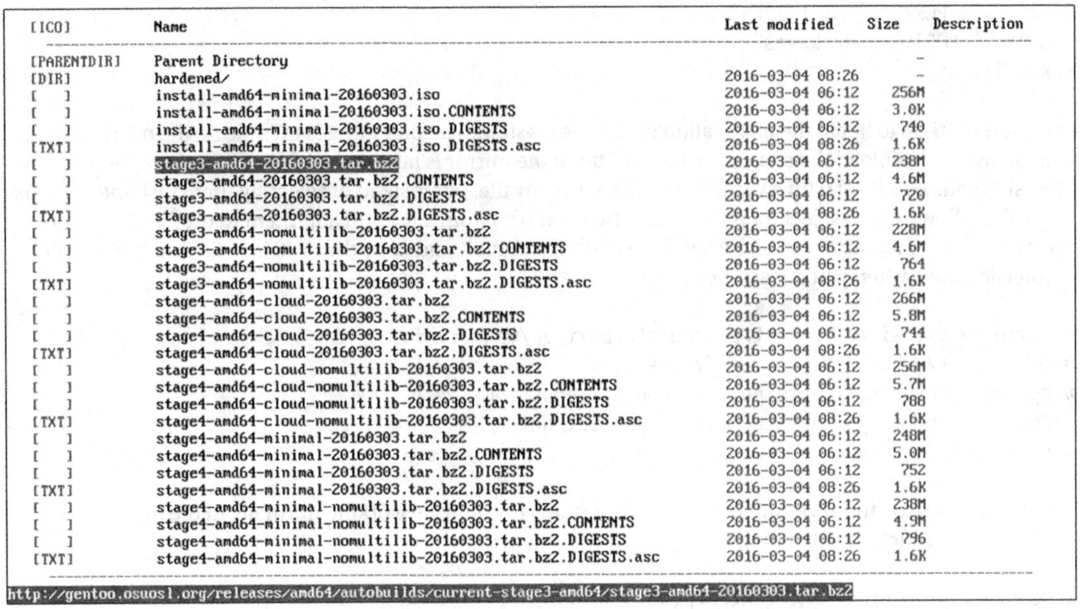

| [ICO] | Name | Last modified | Size | Description |
|---|---|---|---|---|
| [PARENTDIR] | Parent Directory | | – | |
| [DIR] | hardened/ | 2016-03-04 08:26 | – | |
| [   ] | install-amd64-minimal-20160303.iso | 2016-03-04 06:12 | 256M | |
| [   ] | install-amd64-minimal-20160303.iso.CONTENTS | 2016-03-04 06:12 | 3.0K | |
| [   ] | install-amd64-minimal-20160303.iso.DIGESTS | 2016-03-04 06:12 | 740 | |
| [TXT] | install-amd64-minimal-20160303.iso.DIGESTS.asc | 2016-03-04 08:26 | 1.6K | |
| [   ] | stage3-amd64-20160303.tar.bz2 | 2016-03-04 06:12 | 238M | |
| [   ] | stage3-amd64-20160303.tar.bz2.CONTENTS | 2016-03-04 06:12 | 4.6M | |
| [   ] | stage3-amd64-20160303.tar.bz2.DIGESTS | 2016-03-04 06:12 | 720 | |
| [TXT] | stage3-amd64-20160303.tar.bz2.DIGESTS.asc | 2016-03-04 08:26 | 1.6K | |
| [   ] | stage3-amd64-nomultilib-20160303.tar.bz2 | 2016-03-04 06:12 | 228M | |
| [   ] | stage3-amd64-nomultilib-20160303.tar.bz2.CONTENTS | 2016-03-04 06:12 | 4.6M | |
| [   ] | stage3-amd64-nomultilib-20160303.tar.bz2.DIGESTS | 2016-03-04 06:12 | 764 | |
| [TXT] | stage3-amd64-nomultilib-20160303.tar.bz2.DIGESTS.asc | 2016-03-04 08:26 | 1.6K | |
| [   ] | stage4-amd64-cloud-20160303.tar.bz2 | 2016-03-04 06:12 | 266M | |
| [   ] | stage4-amd64-cloud-20160303.tar.bz2.CONTENTS | 2016-03-04 06:12 | 5.8M | |
| [   ] | stage4-amd64-cloud-20160303.tar.bz2.DIGESTS | 2016-03-04 06:12 | 744 | |
| [TXT] | stage4-amd64-cloud-20160303.tar.bz2.DIGESTS.asc | 2016-03-04 08:26 | 1.6K | |
| [   ] | stage4-amd64-cloud-nomultilib-20160303.tar.bz2 | 2016-03-04 06:12 | 256M | |
| [   ] | stage4-amd64-cloud-nomultilib-20160303.tar.bz2.CONTENTS | 2016-03-04 06:12 | 5.7M | |
| [   ] | stage4-amd64-cloud-nomultilib-20160303.tar.bz2.DIGESTS | 2016-03-04 06:12 | 788 | |
| [TXT] | stage4-amd64-cloud-nomultilib-20160303.tar.bz2.DIGESTS.asc | 2016-03-04 08:26 | 1.6K | |
| [   ] | stage4-amd64-minimal-20160303.tar.bz2 | 2016-03-04 06:12 | 248M | |
| [   ] | stage4-amd64-minimal-20160303.tar.bz2.CONTENTS | 2016-03-04 06:12 | 5.0M | |
| [   ] | stage4-amd64-minimal-20160303.tar.bz2.DIGESTS | 2016-03-04 06:12 | 752 | |
| [TXT] | stage4-amd64-minimal-20160303.tar.bz2.DIGESTS.asc | 2016-03-04 08:26 | 1.6K | |
| [   ] | stage4-amd64-minimal-nomultilib-20160303.tar.bz2 | 2016-03-04 06:12 | 238M | |
| [   ] | stage4-amd64-minimal-nomultilib-20160303.tar.bz2.CONTENTS | 2016-03-04 06:12 | 4.9M | |
| [   ] | stage4-amd64-minimal-nomultilib-20160303.tar.bz2.DIGESTS | 2016-03-04 06:12 | 796 | |
| [TXT] | stage4-amd64-minimal-nomultilib-20160303.tar.bz2.DIGESTS.asc | 2016-03-04 08:26 | 1.6K | |

http://gentoo.osuosl.org/releases/amd64/autobuilds/current-stage3-amd64/stage3-amd64-20160303.tar.bz2

*Figure 12-6.* *The directory for the stage 3 tarball file in a Gentoo mirror*

After you download the file, you need to extract and decompress it in the hard disk (remember that now you are in the /mnt/gentoo directory that is actually /dev/sda1, your future root partition).

```
# tar xvjpf stage3-*.tar.bz2 --xattrs
```

This is going to take a little while, about a minute in my machine. Next, you need to change a few things in the compilation options configuration file that is at /etc/portage/make.conf. You can change several things here to optimize the compilation, but let's only change two things: the CFLAGS line and a new one for the variable MAKEOPTS (see the following code). I have chosen a value of 7 for this last variable because I created a virtual machine with six cores and I want to use them all to speed up the compilation. If I left the default of 2, I would spend a lot of time waiting. To do this, you can use one of these text editors: nano, vi, and Emacs.

```
# vi /mnt/gentoo/etc/portage/make.conf
# cat /mnt/gentoo/etc/portage/make.conf
# These settings were set by the catalyst build script that automatically
# built this stage.
# Please consult /usr/share/portage/config/make.conf.example for a more
# detailed example.
CFLAGS="-march=native -O2 -pipe"
CXXFLAGS="${CFLAGS}"
# WARNING: Changing your CHOST is not something that should be done lightly.
# Please consult http://www.gentoo.org/doc/en/change-chost.xml before changing.
CHOST="x86_64-pc-linux-gnu"
# These are the USE flags that were used in addition to what is provided by the
# profile used for building.
USE="bindist mmx sse sse2"
PORTDIR="/usr/portage"
```

```
DISTDIR="${PORTDIR}/distfiles"
PKGDIR="${PORTDIR}/packages"
MAKEOPTS="-j7"
```

Now it's time to begin the installation of the base system. The first thing is to indicate the mirrors you want to use to download the source code. It's better if the mirror is fast, and usually that means the one closest to you. This is set with a variable in the make.conf file, but instead of selecting them by hand, there is a tool that allows you to select them (I suggest two or more) from a list and add them to the file. Next, copy the main Gentoo repository configuration file to its destination and copy the DNS info to keep the Internet connection alive when you restart the system.

```
# mirrorselect -i -o >> /mnt/gentoo/etc/portage/make.conf
# mkdir /mnt/gentoo/etc/portage/repos.conf
# cp /mnt/gentoo/usr/share/portage/config/repos.conf
  /mnt/gentoo/etc/portage/repos.conf/gentoo.conf
# cp -L /etc/resolv.conf /mnt/gentoo/etc/
```

You must also mount certain necessary filesystems to continue working normally in the new environment (which you are going to jail root in a moment).

```
# mount -t proc proc /mnt/gentoo/proc
# mount --rbind /sys /mnt/gentoo/sys
# mount --make-rslave /mnt/gentoo/sys
# mount --rbind /dev /mnt/gentoo/dev
# mount --make-rslave /mnt/gentoo/dev
```

Let's get into the new environment with a jail root (chroot). Then all the commands will apply to that environment that is set with your hard disk as the base, and not in the live one. The last line works as a good hint to remind you that you are in a chroot environment.

```
# chroot /mnt/gentoo /bin/bash
# source /etc/profile
# export PS1="(chroot) $PS1"
```

Next, configure Portage. First, get a snapshot of the current Portage tree and then sync the latest updated version with your new local tree. Ignore the errors about the /usr/portage location and the warnings about the news (this is a very nice feature and I recommend you look at it in the documentation).

```
# emerge-webrsync
# emerge --sync --quiet
```

You should have to select a profile now that, without diving into it now, should define the global settings for compilation of the future packages and more. Since I want to show you something similar to the Arch Linux installation, the right choice in this case is to select the "desktop" profile.

```
# eselect profile list
Available profile symlink targets:
  [1]    default/linux/amd64/13.0 *
  [2]    default/linux/amd64/13.0/selinux
  [3]    default/linux/amd64/13.0/desktop
  [4]    default/linux/amd64/13.0/desktop/gnome
  [5]    default/linux/amd64/13.0/desktop/gnome/systemd
```

```
    [6]    default/linux/amd64/13.0/desktop/kde
    [7]    default/linux/amd64/13.0/desktop/kde/systemd
    [8]    default/linux/amd64/13.0/desktop/plasma
    [9]    default/linux/amd64/13.0/desktop/plasma/systemd
    [10]   default/linux/amd64/13.0/developer
    [11]   default/linux/amd64/13.0/no-multilib
    [12]   default/linux/amd64/13.0/systemd
    [13]   default/linux/amd64/13.0/X32
...
# eselect profile set 3
```

Next, you could/should configure the USE variable to set the global options to compile the packages. It's an important step, but in this case you are going with the defaults. I suggest you get comfortable with Gentoo and read the docs carefully before dealing with this.

Let's take another step, a traditional one in all distros: setting the time zone and the language and local values. The first command will show you the directory tree where the files for the time zones are stored; then you must set one and update the date automatically. Next, edit the locale.gen file (in this environment you only have nano to edit the files) and uncomment the language(s) that you want to use (in this case, enUS.UTF-8 UTF-8). Finally, use eselect again to select the system-wide language and reload the environment.

```
# ls /usr/share/zoneinfo
# echo "America/New_York" > /etc/timezone
# emerge --config sys-libs/timezone-data
# nano -w /etc/locale.gen
# locale-gen
# eselect locale list
Available targets for the LANG variable:
  [1] C
  [2] POSIX
  [3] en_US.utf8
  [ ] (free form)
# eselect locale set 3
# env-update
# source /etc/profile
# export PS1="(chroot) $PS1"
```

It's time for the most daunting task among Linux newcomers, the stuff of many rumors and myths: installing and configuring a Linux kernel. Sorry, but you must do it, so let's do it in the least painful way possible: automatically. I assure you, it is not that scary or terrible, but I understand that you may need some experience to gain confidence. First, you need to install it.

```
# emerge --ask sys-kernel/gentoo-sources
```

This will take a while, about three minutes on my system. To configure the kernel, you are going to use a tool named genkernel to do it automatically. First, you need to install the tool.

```
# emerge --ask sys-kernel/genkernel
```

Now you need to edit the /etc/fstab file and comment the /boot and swap lines since you didn't create those partitions; you also need to create a new line for the /home partition.

```
# nano -w /etc/fstab
# cat /etc/fstab
# /etc/fstab: static file system information.
#
# noatime turns off atimes for increased performance (atimes normally aren't
# needed); notail increases performance of ReiserFS (at the expense of storage
# efficiency). It's safe to drop the noatime options if you want and to
# switch between notail / tail freely.
#
# The root filesystem should have a pass number of either 0 or 1.
# All other filesystems should have a pass number of 0 or greater than 1.
#
# See the manpage fstab(5) for more information.
#

# <fs>            <mountpoint>   <type>      <opts>       <dump/pass>

# NOTE: If your BOOT partition is ReiserFS, add the notail option to opts.
#/dev/BOOT       /boot       ext2        noauto,noatime  1 2
/dev/sda1        /           ext4        noatime      0 1
/dev/sda2        /home       ext4        noatime      0 2
#/dev/SWAP       none        swap        sw      0 0
/dev/cdrom       /mnt/cdrom  auto        noauto,ro   0 0
#/dev/fd0        /mnt/floppy auto        noauto      0 0
```

Next, configure the kernel automatically with genkernel.

```
# genkernel all
```

This will take a while, about seventeen minutes on my system. This first not-fast compilation shows you what it will take to compile almost everything. Next, configure the modules that you need to start automatically via /etc/conf.d/modules. In this case, let's assume that you don't need any additional modules. But I suggest that you install the firmware because you never know, and some drivers require it (especially in laptops).

```
# emerge --ask sys-kernel/linux-firmware
```

Continue configuring the system. Let's set up the network now. The first step is to change the default hostname of "hostname" to the one you want. After that, configure the Internet to use DHCP, and make it the network that starts at boot.

```
# nano -w /etc/conf.d/hostname
# cat /etc/conf.d/hostname
# Set the hostname variable to the selected host name
hostname="does_pc"
# emerge --ask --noreplace net-misc/netifrc
# nano -w /etc/conf.d/net
# cat /etc/conf.d/net
config_eth0="dhcp"
```

```
# cd /etc/init.d
# ln -s net.lo net.eth0
# rc-update add net.eth0 default
```

You must set a password for the root user. Remember to use a strong password, especially for this user.

```
# passwd
```

If you have a keyboard layout different from the default ANSI US, and you selected "other" when you booted from the minimal installation image, you should now configure the keyboard layout to avoid problems (like not being able to recreate the password later depending on the characters you used) when you reboot the system. To do so, you must edit the /etc/conf.d/keymaps file.

```
# nano -w /etc/conf.d/keymaps
```

Let's install some tools necessary for the system. Let's start with the logging tool to log what happens in your system, then a cron tool, a file indexing tool, some file system tools, and a DHCP client. Here you're using the classic or easiest tools for each task, not necessarily the best ones.

```
# emerge --ask app-admin/syslogd
# emerge --ask app-admin/logrotate
# rc-update add sysklogd default
# emerge --ask sys-process/cronie
# rc-update add cronie default
# emerge --ask sys-apps/mlocate
# emerge --ask sys-fs/e2fsprogs
# emerge --ask net-misc/dhcpcd
```

You are getting close to the moment of booting up your new Gentoo system for the first time. First, you need to install and configure a bootloader, Grub2 in your case. Prepare to wait again; this will take a while to compile (about 10 minutes on my system).

```
# emerge --ask sys-boot/grub:2
# grub2-install /dev/sda
# grub2-mkconfig -o /boot/grub/grub.cfg
```

Finally, exit and reboot the system. Cross your fingers!

```
# exit
# cd
# umount -l /mnt/gentoo/dev{/shm,/pts,}
# umount /mnt/gentoo{/boot,/sys,/proc,}
# reboot
```

And voila! You have started your brand new Gentoo Linux system for the first time! After it completes the boot up, you should find a screen like the one in Figure 12-7.

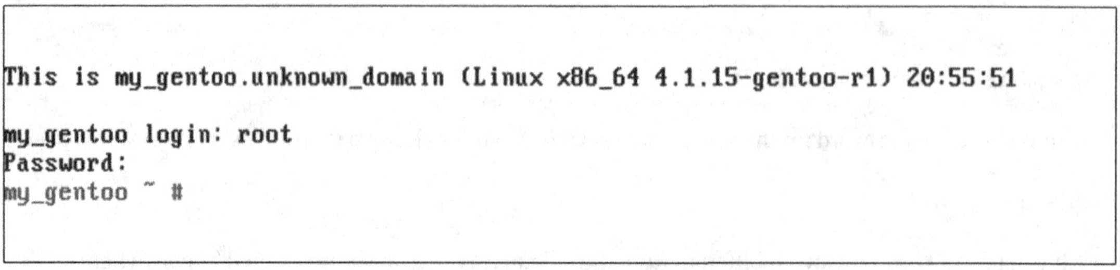

```
This is my_gentoo.unknown_domain (Linux x86_64 4.1.15-gentoo-r1) 20:55:51

my_gentoo login: root
Password:
my_gentoo ~ #
```

***Figure 12-7.*** *The first boot up of your brand new Gentoo system*

All that work and you end up at a simple command prompt again! Well, from here it is up to you; you can build what you want. The profile you selected previously and the dependencies of each package are going to "spend your time." I'll give you an example: in my new system, I didn't have the tools installed that I had in the minimal installation environment, like emacs, vi, or links. I want to have links to be able to access the documentation from the terminal in case something goes wrong. Well, this package has as a dependency on certain components of the X windows server. It took 20 minutes to install a text mode browser. Do the math: how long would it take to install Gnome or KDE from source? On the other hand, you only have to install those dependencies once.

But first you must create a new user. To do that, you need to log in with the root account and then add it. Add the user to the group wheel (to use su and sudo) and audio.

```
# useradd -m -G users, wheel,audio -s /bin/bash johndoe
# passwd johndoe
```

You can now safely remove the stage3 tarball file from your system.

```
# rm /stage3-*.tar.bz2*
```

From here, things get a little more complicated and they depend heavily on your specific hardware. If you want a similar scenario as the one we set up in Arch Linux, the first step is to install a video driver for X.org. But here is where the things get messy, because depending on your graphics card, emerge is going to tell you that you need to add some options to the USE variable, and these options are not always the same. So, you should add those variables in the /etc/portage/make.conf file and also add a new pair of variables to define the input devices and the video card. In this case, let's suppose that you have an Intel card: INPUT_DEVICES="evdev synaptics" and VIDEO_CARDS="intel". And it gets better; after this you probably need to recompile your kernel and (wait for it) update your whole system because of the changes in the USE variable (and it could take a while!). And finally, install the X.org server. As a rough resume,

```
# emerge --ask x11-drivers/xf86-video-intel
# genkernel all
# emerge --ask x11-base/xorg-server
```

Next, let's install a display manager. In this case, even though it's obsolete, I've chosen Slim because it's light and takes less time to compile. Next, let's install a tiling window manager, Awesome WM. But don't forget that you have to also configure them; look at the documentation to do so. You should then init your display manager to get a login screen (Figure 12-8) and finally log in to get the window manager (Figure 12-9).

```
# emerge --ask x11-misc/slim
# vi /etc/conf.d/xdm
# cat /etc/conf.d/xdm
DISPLAYMANAGER="slim"
# rc-update add xdm default
# emerge --ask x11-wm/awesome
$ mkdir -p ~/.config/awesome/
$ cp /etc/xdg/awesome/rc.lua ~/.config/awesome/rc.lua
# emerge --ask xterm
# emerge --ask feh
# /etc/init.d/xdm start
```

*Figure 12-8.* *The Gentoo Slim login manager*

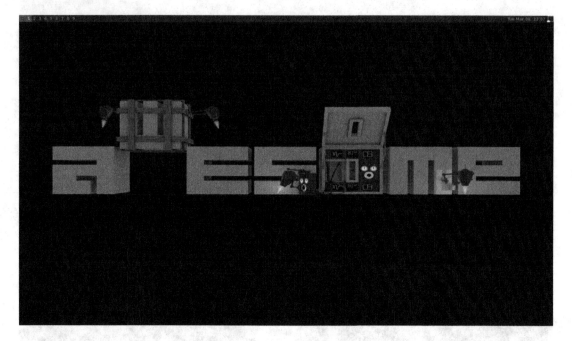

*Figure 12-9. The Awesome WM window manager in Gentoo*

There are still a lot of things to do to get a reasonable system, so be prepared to work with it on a daily basis. At this pace, I would need at least another chapter to cover all of that here.

Don't worry if you fail the first time and don't get a working Gentoo system; it's normal. There are a lot of things to take into account; something as simple as a typo could keep the system from booting. This is essentially the way Linux was installed in almost every distro years ago, and the origin of so many rumors and myths about the harshness of Linux. If you read the previous chapters, you already know that there is a huge difference between installing Linux in this way and installing a user friendly distro like Ubuntu. But I'm sure you've already realized too that the level of control and customization that you can get with an advanced distro like Gentoo or Arch is miles away from what you can get with a distro like elementary OS.

# Maintenance

In Gentoo, all of the essential maintenance is done with the Portage/emerge tool. Being a rolling release, you can keep it permanently updated. Basically you don't need to upgrade it in the traditional way.

## Updating and Managing Apps

Although I'm going to show you an easy way to perform these tasks, note that Portage is a very powerful tool. It lets you completely control how you compile and install every package. There are other ways of doing this, with slightly different commands. If you want to use this distro, you need to get familiar with this tool through Gentoo's docs. As you know already, to manage Portage you use the emerge tool and a lot of patience.

Installing an app using emerge can be as simple as this:

```
# emerge firefox
```

But usually it is better to first search for the app and then install it in this way:

```
# emerge --search firefox
# emerge --ask www-client/firefox-bin
```

If you want to remove a package:

```
# emerge --unmerge firefox
```

To update your system, it's also very simple. First, sync the Portage tree. Then, launch the automate update.

```
# emerge --sync
# emerge --uD world
```

I mentioned that you can do all of this with graphical tools like Porthole, but usually the people that are willing to go through the effort of installing this distro from the command line are the least inclined to later use a graphical tool to maintain it. The users that choose Gentoo are usually pursuing total control and fine-grain settings. Porthole is a very good tool, but it can't compete with emerge.

## Upgrading

As with Arch Linux, upgrading Gentoo has totally different meaning from that for traditional distros. Even though the packages are always updated, sooner or later there will be changes in the core of the distro. Arch has a special way to do this: when a change is made, it is announced and you are given instructions about the changes that you must make (usually by hand). This modality has great inconveniences, because if you leave a system unattended for a long time, reconstructing these changes could be very painful or even impossible without doing a fresh install. In other words, Arch Linux waits for no one. If you want it updated, you have to keep the pace.

But Gentoo is very good at this. It solved this problem in a smart way that allows you to make "upgrades" smoothly and at your pace. The instrument to do this is the "profile," which if you remember from the "Installation" section is also used to determine the type of systems that you want to build in a certain manner. Also, remember that the new Gentoo releases are done weekly, and some of these releases bring a new profile. When a new release comes with a new profile, you can choose to migrate to the new profile or perform only the package updates. But don't get me wrong; these migrations can be easy or a titanic job. You can safely ignore one profile migration and after it becomes deprecated, do the task. It is not a perfect solution, but at least it is a solution. You can leave a system unattended a long time, and then with patience, time, dedication, and care, you can end up with an updated system without having to make a fresh install. I suggest you look at the documentation to get a complete understanding of this (this is a little lie; you never really understand these things until you do them yourself) at the Gentoo Wiki at https://wiki.gentoo.org/wiki/Upgrading_Gentoo.

## Pros and Cons

The following list is some things that I personally see as the pros and cons of the Gentoo Linux distribution. There's always room for discussion in this matter, but I've been as objective as possible.

## Pros

- It is a rolling release distro, so it's always on the bleeding edge.
- It has great documentation.
- It has a good and helpful community of advanced users.
- You can compile the packages optimized to your hardware and needs.
- It's fully customizable, offering amazing flexibility and total control.
- It has an astounding package manager, Portage.
- It has a big focus on security. Although it's up to you, you have the tools and docs.
- It is an original distribution, not a derivative.
- It supports multiple architectures, even obsolete ones.
- If you stick with this distro, you'll learn a lot about Linux.

## Cons

- To compile almost all the packages could be a waste of time.
- Thanks to modern hardware, the performance gain is negligible (with exceptions).
- It's not user friendly. It's one of the most demanding of all distros.
- Maintaining it costs time and dedication.
- It has no commercial support.
- It does not focus on aesthetics.
- It's unstable by nature (unless your learn enough and have a lot of free time).

# Summary

Here you saw a distro that allows the maximum level of customization possible. To go further you could only take one more step: build your own distribution. Gentoo is a distribution for advanced, patient, and very meticulous users. It's an example of the freedom and power that Linux can provide to the user at the cost of the necessary knowledge.

In the next chapter, you are going to see an historical and ancient distribution that has not changed much through time: Slackware. It's known for being harsh and unpractical, but it shares some points with Gentoo.

# CHAPTER 13

# Slackware

Slackware is the most ancient distribution alive. It was born a few months before Debian, which seems hard to believe, seeing the evolution of both. A lot of people think Debian is much too conservative; these same people would call Slackware a dinosaur. Yes, Slackware has not changed too much over the years, but far from being ashamed, the Slackware community is proud of this. Slackware claims to be the most "Unix-like" Linux distribution.

## History

Slackware and Debian don't just share a long history as Linux distros; they also share a common origin: the SLS (Softlanding Linux System) distro. While Debian was created as a better alternative to SLS, Slackware was created as an evolution of it.

Patrick Volkerding was a student at the Minnesota State University Moorhead (MSUM) in 1993 when his AI professor asked him to install SLS in the computer lab to get the benefit of its better LISP interpreter. Volkerding did so, and then he improved the distro itself by fixing bugs and making modifications for future installations at the lab. Later, seeing that the SLS distro didn't have any more releases, that the bugs remained unfixed, and that there was great demand on the Internet for a good product, he asked if anyone was interested in his work. After many positive responses, and encouraged by his friends at the university, he uploaded to one of the university's anonymous FTP servers the first Slackware 1.00 release on July 17, 1993.

Today, Volkerding is still the main developer of Slackware; he is known as "The Man" or Slackware's BDFL (Benevolent Dictator for Life). And Slackware continues to be a small but popular distribution.

---

■ **Note**   The origin of the Slackware name comes from an internal joke related to the slack term as homage to J.R. "Bob" Dobbs, the figurehead of the Church of SubGenius (a parody religion which was very popular in Internet subculture in those days). It was never intended to be the definitive name of the distro; he kept the name when he first released the distro with the intention that nobody would take it too seriously.

---

## Philosophy

The philosophy of Slackware is difficult to understand without much knowledge of the history of UNIX and Linux itself. While the distro claims to be conservative in terms of simplicity, stability, and power (and yet user friendly), a new user coming from a friendly OS/distro would probably have a very different opinion about that. First of all, most people would not considerate Slackware a friendly distro; in fact, quite the opposite. And they would find it hard to consider it simple and powerful since it lacks tracking package dependencies. But if you see it from the perspective of Slackware's author and the community, it seems easier to understand. They didn't want to stray too far from the original UNIX design, like the current BSDs do, for a simple and powerful reason. An experienced UNIX user would feel almost at home with Slackware, and it would be very easy for her jump in and use it. Regardless of whether you share this opinion, you must recognize that time supports their decision; other friendly distros disappeared a long time ago.

Thus, Slackware tries to follow the KISS principle (explained in Chapter 11), being conservative in its core design and not introducing changes in its packages. Broadly speaking, Slackware is a BSD with a Linux kernel. In that search for simplicity and purity, each package is configured independently; there is no global configuration. The majority of the configuration is made through simple text files. Nothing is predefined by default; you are supposed to know what you are doing and what you want.

Don't get me wrong; being conservative about its core design does not mean it lacks innovations or necessary changes (like support for 64-bit architecture). Slackware tries to be in sync with the times and supports "recent" innovations like UEFI or the Btrfs file system, and the packages are very recent when a new release appears. But generally Slackware follows the motto of "If it's not broken, don't fix it."

# Distro Selection Criteria

Now that you know a little of Slackware's history, let's see how this particular distribution fares on the selection criteria from Chapter 2.

## Purpose and Environment

Slackware is a general purpose distro with a unique version for all purposes and environments. Still, there are two different branches of flavors that you can install: the stable one and the "current" one, which works as the development tree of the distro.

## Support

Although Slackware (and Volkerding himself) are supported by the sales from the store, and it once had a commercial distribution (for a brief period of time), it is not a purely commercial distro (you still can get it free), and it does not have commercial support at all. Support only comes from its developers and its small, but loyal, community. The ways to get support from the community are the following:

- **The Slackware Book Project**: www.slackbook.org

- **Wiki**: http://docs.slackware.com/

- **FAQ**: http://docs.slackware.com/slackware:faq

- **Slackware forum at Linux Questions**: www.linuxquestions.org/questions/forumdisplay.php?forumid=14

- **Mailing lists**: www.slackware.com/lists/

- **IRC**: #slackware at irc.freenode.net

## User Friendliness

Slackware is not for beginners. Although it's easier than Arch or Gentoo, it is not a user-friendly distro. You still need to know a lot of things about the command line and Linux itself, and you should be comfortable with how Slackware manages its packages. Traditionally the Slackware user was stereotyped as a typical "neck beard" system administrator and alike. While it is true that Slackware users are usually technically well-versed, it is not true that it is as hard as portrayed. A lot of users sweat more with Gentoo, for example.

## Stability

Slackware, due to its inherent simplicity, proven design, and the frequency of its releases, is a very stable distro. It follows a standard release model and there is no fixed schedule; a new release appears when is ready, well tested and stable enough (it's very well known for this). As a result, the current release, the 14.1, is from 2013 and the packages are outdated. A beta version of the future 14.2 release is currently in progress, and it will have fresh packages. Some people prefer to use the "current" development version as their daily system because of this. And for the support part, there is no official policy; from time to time, support is suddenly dropped from older releases.

## Hardware Support

As with Arch and Gentoo, you must be willing to learn how to support hardware not included on the kernel or official packages/drivers, and depend heavily on third party maintained builds/binaries.

## Aesthetics

There is no focus on aesthetics, aside from the DVD packaging and merchandising of the Slackware store.

## Desktop Environment

The de facto official desktop of Slackware is KDE but it also gives you the option to install Xfce and several window managers (Fluxbox, Blackbox, WindowMaker, FVM2, and TWM).

## Init System

The init system Slackware uses is a BSD-style one based on rc files, which is also compatible with traditional System V (sysv) scripts. There is no plan in the future to make a migration to systemd; a great part of the community is against a future systemd implementation in the distro.

## Package Management System

Slackware has a very particular way of managing packages. These packages are simple tarballs (compressed or not), in which files are usually simply extracted in their respective paths followed by the execution of several doinst.sh scripts. There is no management of dependencies at all; you are supposed to take care of it. There are two official tools for managing packages in Slackware: pkgtools and slackpkg. The latter is the most recent one and it can manage network packages, not just local packages like pkgtools.

There are several unofficial package repositories for Slackware; SlackBuilds.org at http://slackbuilds.org is probably the most popular. There are also several unofficial tools to manage packages, like swaret or slapt-get, which both have dependency resolution. The packages from these repositories can be built from source; compiling them, and also allows you to create your own packages. In fact, these packages come with a recipe (similar to Gentoo's ebuilds or Arch's pkgbuild) to build them, and the SlackBuilds repository is based on this.

## Architecture

Slackware officially supports the Intel/AMD architectures in 32/64 bits, but there are also ports to the ARM and S/390 architectures.

## Security/Anonymity

As with Arch or Gentoo, security depends more on the user than in other distros (although the user is always the weakest link in any OS), but the small official package base, and the stability and age of the packages helps a little to control vulnerabilities. Also, the packages are always updated to fix a security vulnerability; they are announced through the security mailing list. And a big part of the Slackware community is technically adept so they can handle these issues better than most.

## Principles and Ethics

There is nothing written down about principles and ethics; you are expected to manage them for yourself as you wish. There are non-free binary blobs in the kernel, some non-free software, and nothing to stop you from installing third party packages in your distro.

## Live CD

There is no official Live CD image for this distro, but Eric Hameelers (also known as AlienBOB, and one of the greatest contributors to Slackware) is currently working on a project to have a Slackware Live CD Edition. It will probably be released with the Slackware 14.2 release, which is currently in beta status.

## Professional Certification

There is no specific professional certification available for Slackware.

# Installation

Installing Slackware is a bit awkward. It's not like Debian or a friendly distro like Ubuntu, and it's not like Arch or Gentoo. It's in a sort of middle ground between the two experiences. It uses a setup tool that helps to make great part of the installation process easy, but it requires the use of the command line in the beginning and at the end. It reminds me a little of the Arch installation when it uses an ncurses tool (a text-based graphical environment) to install it. And of course it reminds me of back when almost all of the Linux distros had a very similar way of installation. In other words, Slackware is easier to install than Gentoo or Arch, but it is still a vintage experience and one that is harsh for the beginner.

Start by obtaining the ISO image file to install the distro. Go to the Slackware web site's "Get Slack" section at www.slackware.com/getslack/ (see Figure 13-1). Here you must choose between going to the store and purchasing a physical DVD/CD to install the distro or downloading an ISO image via BitTorrent or a Slackware mirror. I usually choose to go to the most popular path, which is to download an ISO image from a mirror. So do that and click the mirrors link to get redirected to the Mirrors page (shown in Figure 13-2).

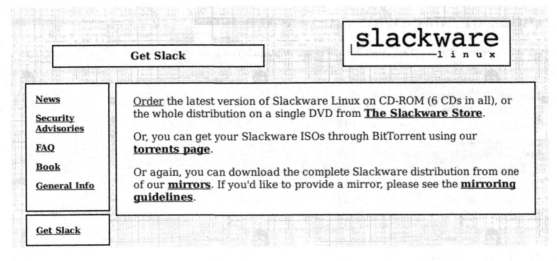

***Figure 13-1.*** *The section of the Slackware web site where you can obtain the ISO image*

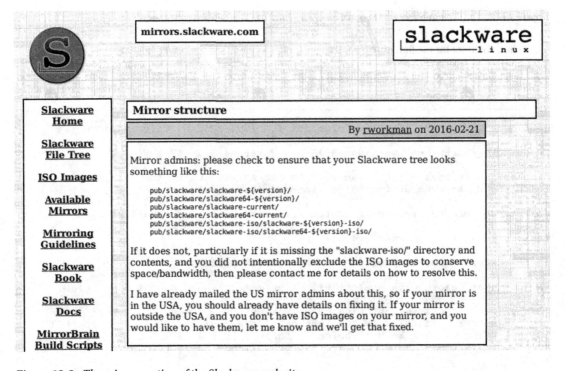

***Figure 13-2.*** *The mirrors section of the Slackware web site*

Here you can select a mirror from "Available Mirrors" or get an ISO image directly from "ISO Images." Both of these links are shown in the side menu. If you follow the latter link, you end up in the directory tree of the main mirror, as you can see in Figure 13-3. The last version is currently z4.1 from November 2013 and there are 32- and 64-bit versions. Go to the last folder where the 64-bit version is and download the DVD ISO image file that is inside.

# Index of /slackware/slackware-iso

| Name | Last modified | Size | Description | Metadata |
|------|---------------|------|-------------|----------|
| Parent Directory | | - | | |
| slackware-12.0-iso/ | 02-Jul-2007 05:10 | - | | |
| slackware-12.1-iso/ | 01-May-2008 23:50 | - | | |
| slackware-12.2-iso/ | 09-Dec-2008 11:13 | - | | |
| slackware-13.0-iso/ | 27-Aug-2009 19:37 | - | | |
| slackware-13.1-iso/ | 19-May-2010 18:43 | - | | |
| slackware-13.37-iso/ | 26-Apr-2011 22:05 | - | | |
| slackware-14.0-iso/ | 29-Sep-2012 00:12 | - | | |
| slackware-14.1-iso/ | 06-Nov-2013 08:22 | - | | |
| slackware64-13.0-iso/ | 27-Sep-2012 20:50 | - | | |
| slackware64-13.1-iso/ | 19-May-2010 19:05 | - | | |
| slackware64-13.37-iso/ | 26-Apr-2011 22:05 | - | | |
| slackware64-14.0-iso/ | 28-Sep-2012 01:55 | - | | |
| slackware64-14.1-iso/ | 11-Nov-2013 20:32 | - | | |

*Figure 13-3.* *The directory tree in the main Slackware mirror*

When you boot for the first time from the ISO image, you will see the screen shown in Figure 13-4. It's a simple text screen with instructions on how to boot the system. If you do not want to use any option, you must press Enter and wait two minutes to boot.

```
ISOLINUX 4.06 0x513e7151 ETCD Copyright (C) 1994-2012 H. Peter Anvin et al

Welcome to Slackware64 version 14.1 (Linux kernel 3.10.17)!

If you need to pass extra parameters to the kernel, enter them at the prompt
below after the name of the kernel to boot (huge.s etc).

In a pinch, you can boot your system from here with a command like:

boot: huge.s root=/dev/sda1 rdinit= ro

In the example above, /dev/sda1 is the / Linux partition.

To test your memory with memtest86+, enter memtest on the boot line below.

This prompt is just for entering extra parameters.  If you don't need to enter
any parameters, hit ENTER to boot the default kernel "huge.s" or press [F2]
for a listing of more kernel choices.  Default kernel will boot in 2 minutes.

boot: _
```

*Figure 13-4.* *The first screen after the boot from the Slackware ISO image*

After a few seconds, it will ask you for the keyboard layout (shown in Figure 13-5). If you use a layout different from US ANSI, press 1 and follow the instructions (it will show you a menu where you can select a layout from various options). Just press Enter and continue.

```
<OPTION TO LOAD SUPPORT FOR NON-US KEYBOARD>

If you are not using a US keyboard, you may now load a different
keyboard map.  To select a different keyboard map, please enter 1
now.  To continue using the US map, just hit enter.

Enter 1 to select a keyboard map: _
```

***Figure 13-5.*** *The option to select a different keyboard layout*

After this you go directly to a terminal session where you have to log in as root without a password (shown in Figure 13-6). During this process, before login and after, you are provided with basic instructions and the steps you should follow. The first thing to do is prepare the disk before launching the setup tool. The instructions suggest using classic tools like fdisk or gdisk, but I'm going to use parted. I like to use this tool because is probably the most versatile one since it supports both MBR and GPT partitions. Again, I'm using a 2TB disk and making a simple partition scheme (/ and /home) with a MBR partition table. Note that the kernel version is too old (3.10.17) and also the same happens with some tools like lsblk where you cannot use the option--paths.

```
Welcome to the Slackware Linux installation disk! (version 14.1)

######  IMPORTANT!  READ THE INFORMATION BELOW CAREFULLY.  ######

- You will need one or more partitions of type 'Linux' prepared.  It is also
  recommended that you create a swap partition (type 'Linux swap') prior
  to installation.  For more information, run 'setup' and read the help file.

- If you're having problems that you think might be related to low memory, you
  can try activating a swap partition before you run setup.  After making a
  swap partition (type 82) with cfdisk or fdisk, activate it like this:
    mkswap /dev/<partition> ; swapon /dev/<partition>

- Once you have prepared the disk partitions for Linux, type 'setup' to begin
  the installation process.

- If you do not have a color monitor, type:   TERM=vt100
  before you start 'setup'.

You may now login as 'root'.

slackware login: _
```

***Figure 13-6.*** *The terminal login prompt where you end up after boot up*

```
# parted /dev/sda
(parted) mklabel msdos
(parted) mkpart pri ext4 1MB 50GB
(parted) mkpart pri ext4 50GB 100%
(parted) set 1 boot on
```

```
(parted) u GiB
Model: ATA VBOX HARDDISK (scsi)
Disk /dev/sda: 2199GB
Sector size (logical/physical): 512B/512B
Partition table: msdos
Disk Flags:

Number  Start    End     Size    Type     File system  Flags
 1      1049kB   50.0GB  50.0GB  primary  ext4         boot
 2      50.0GB   2199GB  2149GB  primary  ext4
(parted) q
# lsblk
NAME        MAJ:MIN RM   SIZE RO TYPE MOUNTPOINT
sda          8:0    0     2T  0 disk
!—sda1       8:1    0    50G  0 part
`sda2        8:2    0     2T  0 part
sr0         11:0    1   2.3G  0 rom
```

After you finish partitioning the disk, you can run the setup program that will help you to almost complete the rest of the installation. A text-based interface (using the ncurses library) will appear, as you can see in Figure 13-7.

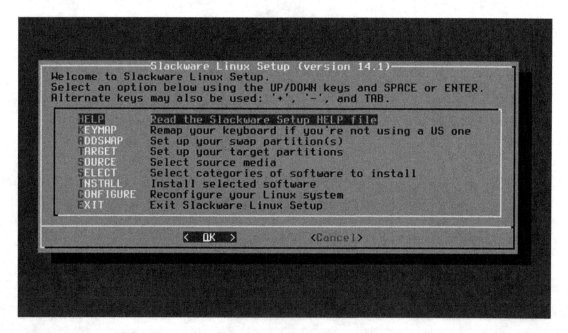

*Figure 13-7.* The setup tool to help you with the installation

It's a menu with multiple options, the Help entry being the first one. This help gives you instructions mostly about the first part of the installation (preparing the disk), which you just did. You can safely ignore the next two options if you already set your keyboard layout and if you are not using a swap partition, as in this case. So go directly to the Target entry and press Enter. Here you can see the available partitions (shown in Figure 13-8). Select each one of them and the tool will ask you to format it (Figure 13-9) and then select one of the available file systems (Figure 13-10). Choose the quick format and the ext4 file systems for both partitions. For the first partition, the tool is going to assume that it is the / partition, and for the last one you must enter the mount point (in this case, /home). At the end, it shows a resume of how the disk partitions are formatted and mounted, which is shown in Figure 13-11.

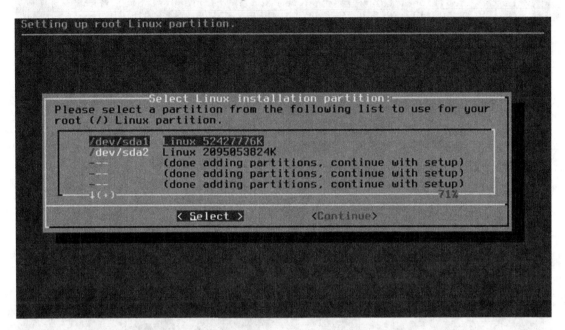

***Figure 13-8.*** *The current partition on the disk*

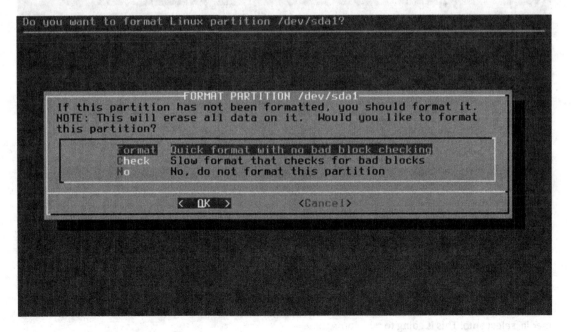

***Figure 13-9.*** *Choose the type of formatting*

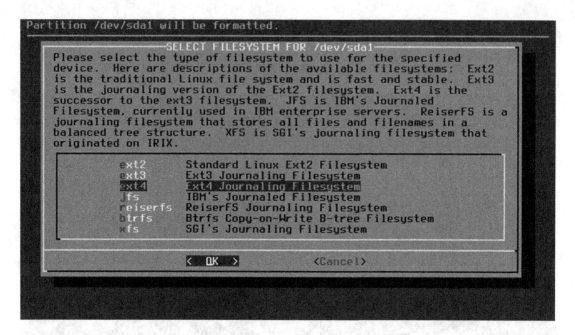

**Figure 13-10.** *Select the file system of the partition*

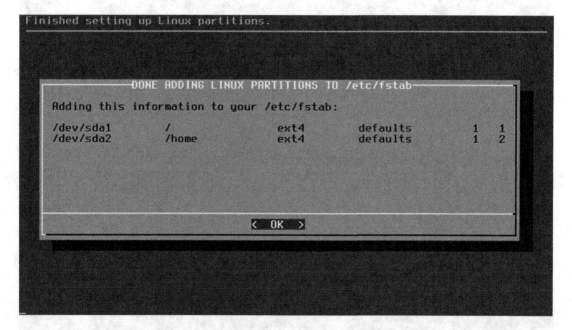

**Figure 13-11.** *The summary of the current status of the disk partitions*

In the next step, the tool will ask you what media you are using to install Slackware (Figure 13-12). In this case, select the first option. Once selected, it asks you to perform an auto or manual scanning of the media; select auto. This is going to take some time.

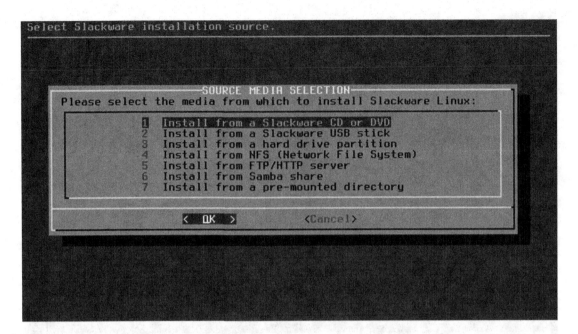

**Figure 13-12.** *Select the installation media*

Once it has scanned the media and knows the packages that you have available to install, you will be asked to select which ones you want to install. If you have doubts, it is better to use the ones selected by default or select all of them. In any case, the partition is big enough that you don't need to worry too much about this. You can see this in Figure 13-13. Press OK.

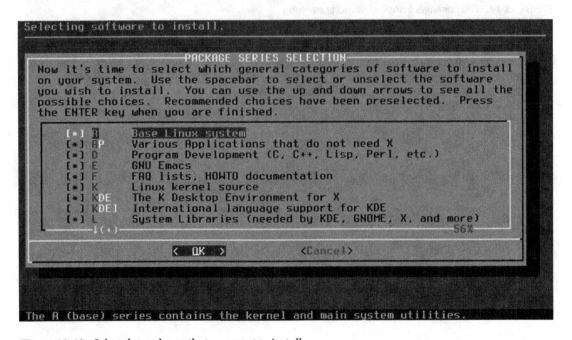

**Figure 13-13.** *Select the packages that you want to install*

The next screen asks you to choose how you want to install the packages (Figure 13-14). The first two entries are totally automatic and do not require your intervention; the rest are for choosing which packages you want to install. If you are not sure which packages install, I suggest you choose the first option, which is also the fastest one. Then press OK. The installation of the packages is going to take several minutes (about 9 minutes in my system).

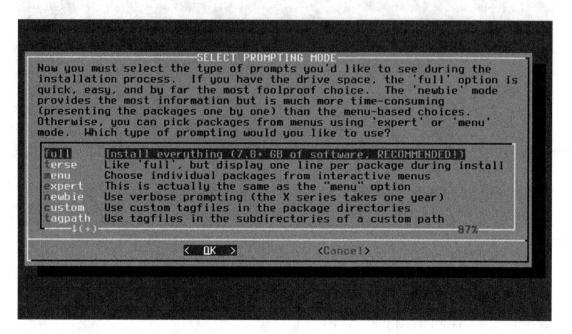

***Figure 13-14.*** *The packages installation mode selection*

After all packages are installed, it will suggest that you create a USB stick to boot the system from (if your system is capable of that). See Figure 13-15. This could be very useful if the process to write the boot loader to the disk fails or simply if you do not want to install a boot loader on your disk and want to boot from the USB stick. It's your choice; in my case, I skipped this step.

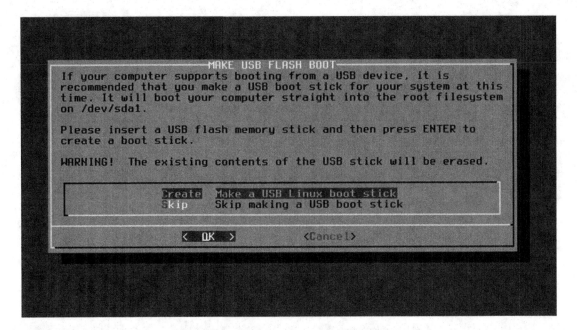

*Figure 13-15.* Create an optional USB stick to boot the system

The next step is to install the boot loader on your hard disk (Figure 13-16). The tool to install is LILO, a traditional and old boot loader that today is discontinued; almost no other distro continues to use it. (But we have to take into account that Slackware 14.1 is from 2013, and LILO was discontinued in December 2015, so given the conservative nature of Slackware it's understandable.) Anyway, LILO does its job without any trouble, so let's install it on the hard disk. I choose the automatic method because it works well most of the time. Next, you can choose between several screen resolutions (Figure 13-17); in almost all modern systems, the last one, 1024x768x256, should work well. It will ask you one more thing about LILO, which is if you want to add any optional parameters to be passed to the kernel at boot time, but leave that blank and continue.

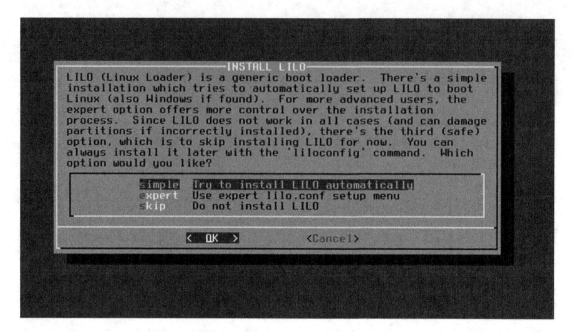

***Figure 13-16.*** *The LILO boot loader installation step*

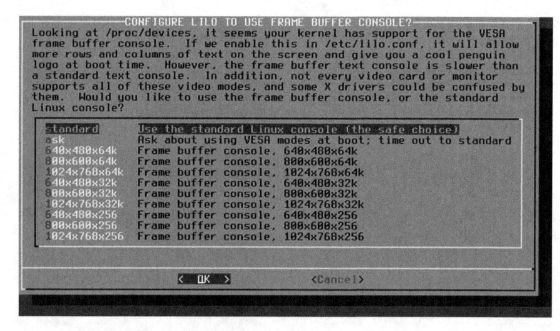

***Figure 13-17.*** *Choose a screen resolution to use with LILO*

Next, it will ask if you want to use the UTF-8 mode in the text consoles (the command line), and it will warn you about possible conflicts. Choose no if you are not sure, but I tested this with UTF-8 and I didn't find any problems so far. So select Yes and continue (Figure 13-18).

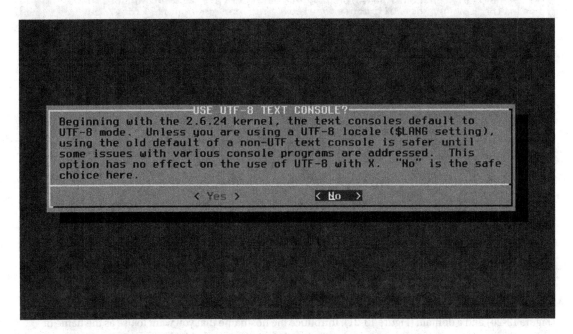

**Figure 13-18.** *Choose if you want to use UTF-8 in the text console*

Finally, it will ask you where to install LILO. Choose MBR to install it in the Master Boot Record of your hard drive and continue. The next screen sets up the mouse that you are going to use. Most people have an USB mouse, so this is a safe choice; if you are still using a PS/2 mouse and yours is not on the list (which is likely), the "ps2" entry is a safe option here. I selected "usb" (see Figure 13-19) and pressed OK. Now it will ask you if you want to install the gpm program to be able to copy and paste in the console with a mouse; choose Yes and continue.

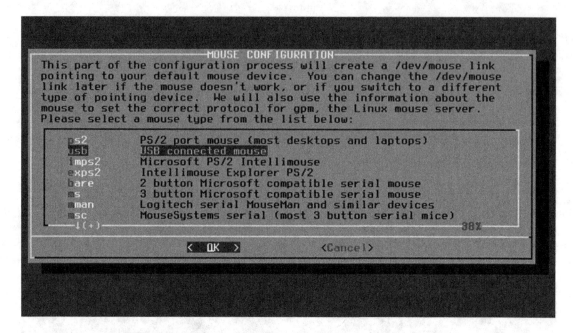

**Figure 13-19.** *Select which mouse type you want to use*

Then it will ask if you want to configure your network. Choose Yes, and it will ask you to set a hostname (Figure 13-20) and a domain (Figure 13-21). Introduce the hostname that you want to use as the name of your system, and a space if you do not want to setup a domain (you probably don't).

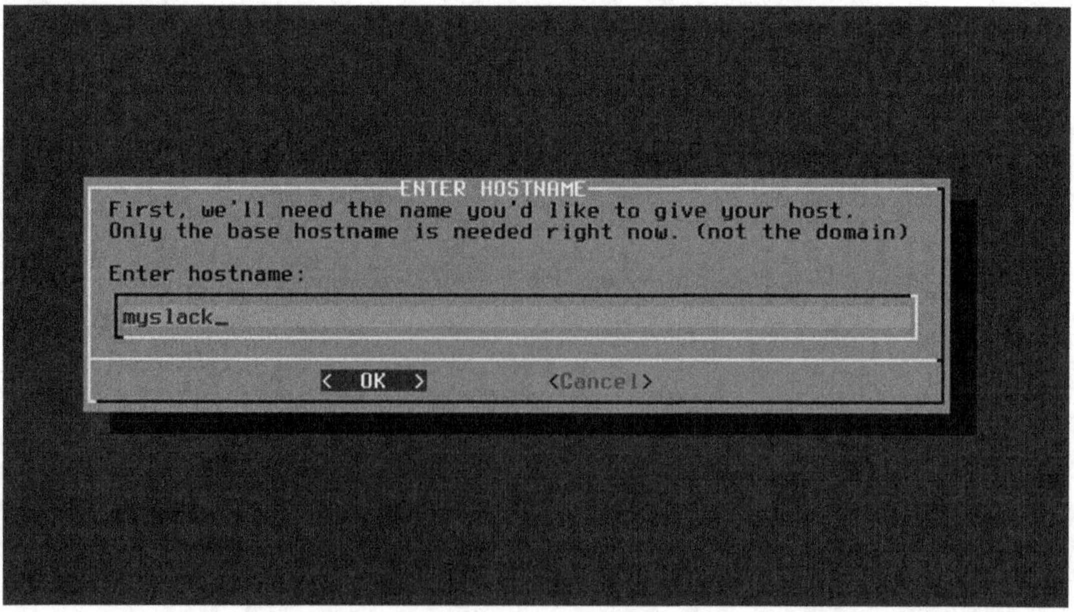

**Figure 13-20.** *Set the hostname of your system*

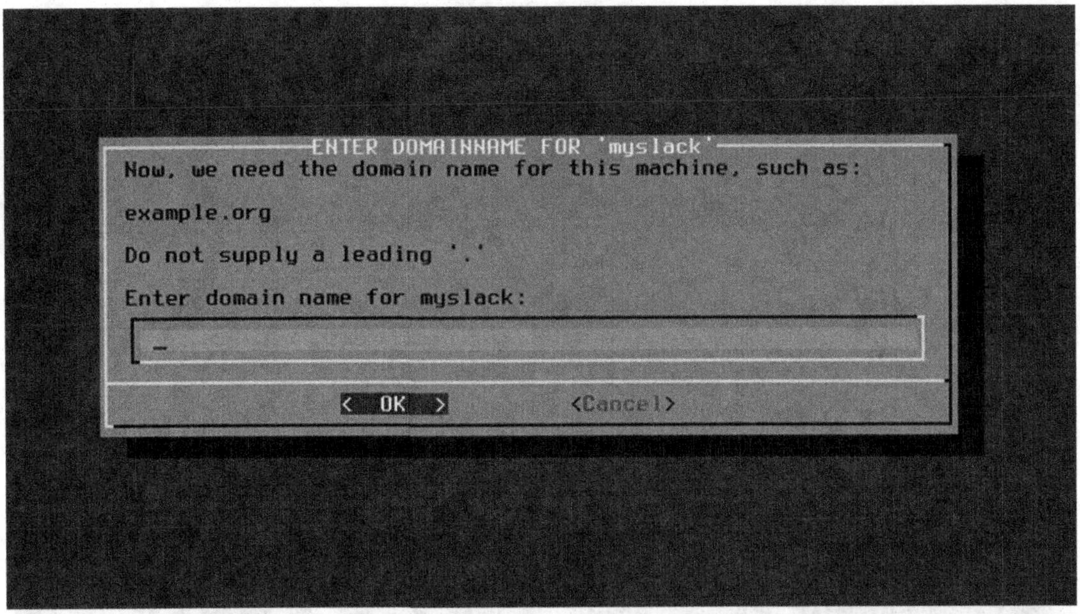

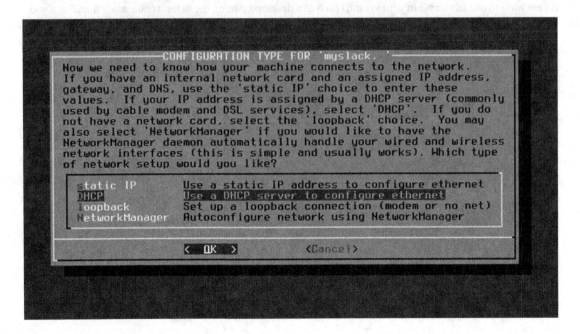

**Figure 13-21.** *Set the domain of your system*

Now it is time to set the IP address of your system on the network (see Figure 13-22). If you want a fixed IP address, use the first option. If you have a DHCP server, use the second one (the default). Finally if you have a wireless adapter, use the last one. I choose the default. Then it will ask you for a DHCP hostname; you usually don't need this, so leave it blank and continue.

**Figure 13-22.** *Configure the IP address of your system*

At the end it shows a summary of your network configuration (see Figure 13-23). If everything is OK, go to the next step.

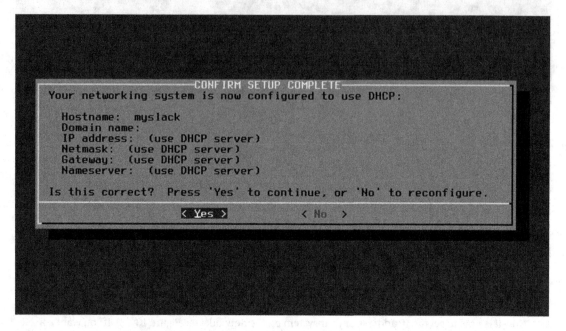

**Figure 13-23.** *The network configuration summary*

Now you must select what services you want to be started at boot time (see Figure 13-24). Usually, if you do not want to use any server in your system (such as a desktop system), the default choices are fine. But if you want to start bind to have a local DNS server as a local cache to navigate faster or a CUPS server for printers, etc., make your choice here. If you are not sure, go with the defaults; you can always set this later. To the question asking if you want to set up a console font configuration, choose No and continue.

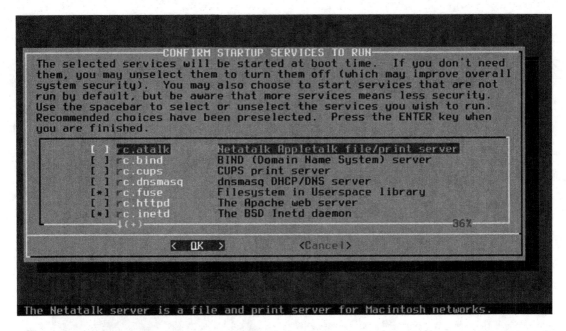

*Figure 13-24.* Select what services to start at boot time

Now you have to configure the clock (Figure 13-25) and the time zone settings (Figure 13-26). I'm going to give you one piece of advice here, but first you have to know that you have two clocks in your system: the hardware clock and the software clock. These were the same thing a long, long time ago, but nowadays they are separate. The first is set in the BIOS/UEFI (which can also be set from the OS) and the second one is in your OS. The hardware clock is the reference that the OS takes when the system is booted, then the OS uses the time zone information to present you the right local time. If your OS is properly configured, it will also synchronize the time periodically with the time on Internet servers (via the NTP, network time protocol). Thus you can set your hardware clock either to your local time or the UTC (Coordinated Universal Time). My advice is that you always set your hardware clock to UTC time, and then set your OS time function to be the time zone where you live. Doing it this way is going to save you some headaches in the future (like forgetting to change the clock for Daylight Saving Time events twice a year) or if you use more than one non-Window OS or distribution on the same machine. Windows is very particular about this topic, and it follows a different approach from almost all other OSes; Windows always assumes that your BIOS is set as your local time. If this is the case, that you have Windows and Linux at the same time in your PC, I suggest you use your local time for the hardware clock.

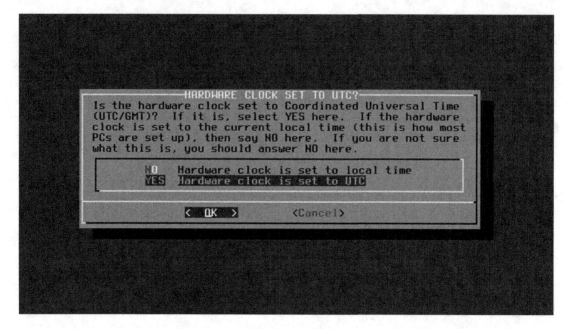

*Figure 13-25.* *The clock setting (use UTC)*

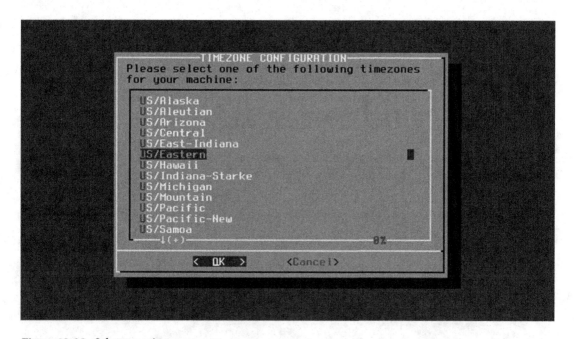

*Figure 13-26.* *Select your time zone*

The next step is to choose a desktop environment or a window manager as you default graphic environment (Figure 13-27). You probably want to select the KDE desktop environment, but I will select Fluxbox to show you a window manager that is different from the others you've already seen in this book.

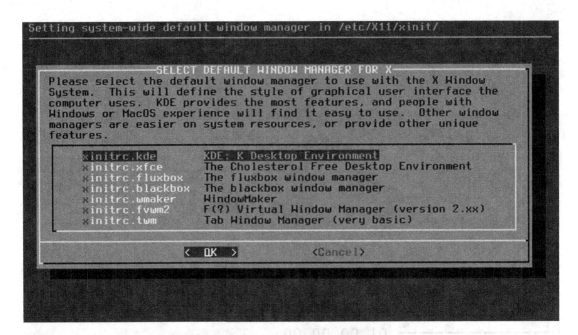

*Figure 13-27.* *Select a default DE or WM as your graphic environment*

You have to set a root password now. Remember to always create a very strong password with this account. This is shown in Figure 13-28.

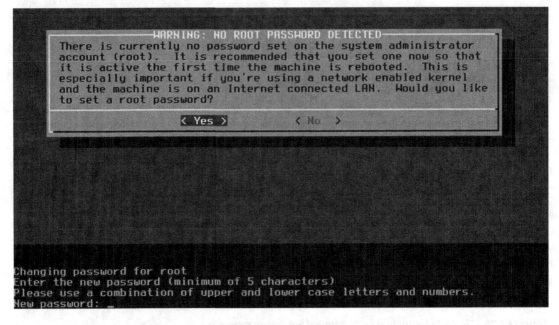

*Figure 13-28.* *Set a strong password for the root account*

That's it! You finished your job with the setup tool. The tool will show you a message telling you this. Press OK and it will take you to the main menu of the tool (shown back in Figure 13-7). Select Exit, press OK, and then enter the proper command in the console to reboot your system:

```
# reboot
```

This first time you start your new Slackware system, you will get the screen shown in Figure 13-29.

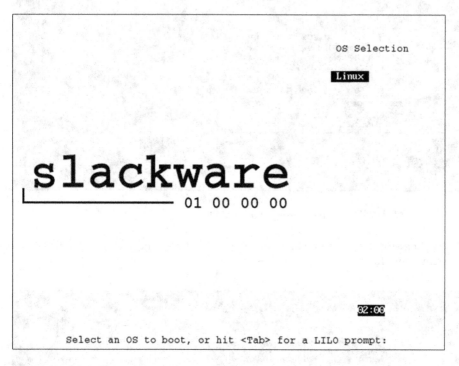

*Figure 13-29.* *The LILO boot loader of your new Slackware system*

You can wait two minutes to boot automatically or you can press Enter to start to boot your system. Either way you are going to end up in a terminal session where you have to log in as root. After showing you a cookie fortune message (a package that used to be installed in many Linux distros by default a long time ago), you will get a root prompt (Figure 13-30).

```
Welcome to Linux 3.10.17 (tty1)

my_slack login: root
Password:
Linux 3.10.17.
Last login: Mon Mar 14 15:17:54 -0400 2016 on /dev/tty1.
You have mail.

Don't speak about Time, until you have spoken to him.

root@my_slack:~#
```

*Figure 13-30.* *The first prompt in a fresh installed Slackware system*

Notice that you do not start in your windows environment by default; you could do it now with the command startx, but you should do something else first. Maybe you noticed that you were never asked to create a user account. You should create a user account now so that you don't have to use the root account by default (never, never do that). Use the adduser script to do this:

```
# adduser
Login name for new user []: johndoe
User ID ('UID') [defaults to next available]:
Initial group [users]:
Additional UNIX groups:
...
Press ENTER to continue without adding any additional groups
Or press the UP arrow to add/select/edit additional groups
: audio cdrom plugdev video power
Home directory [ /home/johndoe]:
Shell [/bin/bash]:
Expiry date (YYYY-MM-DD) []:
...
Creating new account:
...
Full Name []: John Doe
Room Number []:
Work Phone []:
Home Phone []:
Other []:
...
New password:
Re-enter new password:
...
Account setup complete
# exit
myslack login: johndoe
password:
$
```

Finally, after you log in with your new user account, you can start the window manager with the command $ startx. Fluxbox is a very simple window manager, but it's usable with modern apps like Firefox or older ones like Emacs (see Figure 13-31). You can, of course, configure it to make it more elegant.

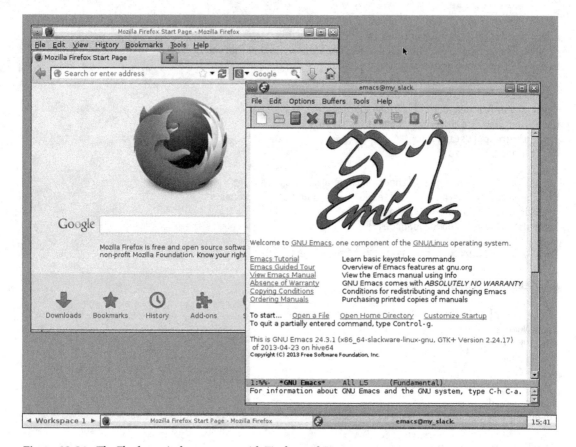

***Figure 13-31.*** *The Fluxbox window manger with Firefox and Emacs*

This is a very basic system and you may still have to install some packages and do some configuration to have a reasonable system to work with every day.

# Maintenance

The maintenance tasks in a distro like Slackware are made via the command line. Basically you use the same tools to perform all the operations: pkgtools or slackpkg.

## Managing Apps and Updating

Three are two official tools to manage the packages. I'll show you how do it with slackpkg. The traditional tool, pkgtool, can also be used through an interactive menu (see Figure 13-32) or via commands.

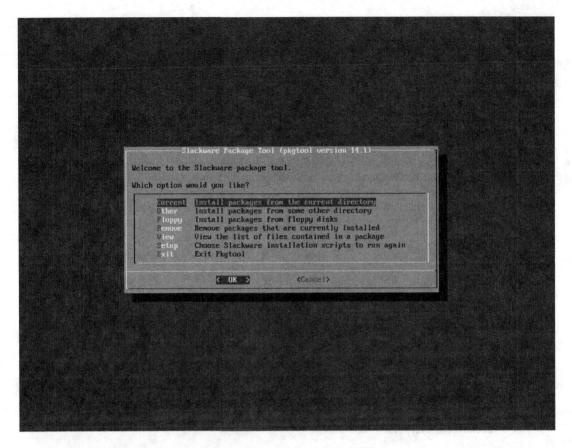

***Figure 13-32.*** *The pkgtool interactive menu*

To install a package, use this code (don't forget to select a mirror by uncommenting it in /etc/slackpkg/mirrors):

```
# slackpkg update
# slackpkg search firefox
# slackpkg install mozilla-firefox-24.1.0esr-x86_64_1
```

To remove it:

```
# slackpkg remove mozilla-firefox-24.1.0esr-x86_64_1
```

And to update a package:

```
# slackpkg upgrade mozilla-firefox-24.1.0esr-x86_64_1
```

Don't forget that this tool does not manage dependencies, and it's up to you to ensure that they are installed before using an installed package.

# Upgrading

Slackware needs to be upgraded each time a new release is launched (use the current branch or opt for a fresh install) because it does not follow a rolling release scheme. You can do this operation with slackpkg:

```
# slackpkg update
# slackpkg install-new
# slackpkg upgrade-all
# slackpkg clean-system
```

Upgrade Slackware can vary from release to release, so the best way to perform this operation is to follow the instructions that are shipped in every DVD/CD in the file UPGRADE.TXT in the root directory. Here are a series of commands that can help you to do this easily. I suggest you do it in another console. Press CTRL+ALT+F2 to be able to watch while you perform the steps in the first console.

```
# mkdir /mnt/cdrom
# mnt /dev/sr0 /mnt/cdrom
# cd /mnt/cdrom
# less UPGRADE.txt
```

# Pros and Cons

Here is a list of things that I personally see as pros and cons of the Slackware distro. There is always room for discussion in this matter, but I've tried to be objective as possible.

## Pros

- Slackware is a very stable distribution.
- It offers a very simple UNIX-like design.
- It is an original distribution.
- It's highly configurable.
- It offers very simple configuration trough scripts and text files.
- The packages are almost pure upstream ones, without modifications.

## Cons

- The package managers do not resolve dependencies.
- It is not a user-friendly distro.
- There's a long time between releases, so it has outdated packages.
- If you want additional packages, you have to use third party repositories.
- It has no commercial support and a very small community.
- It has poor documentation and it's outdated.
- No Gnome support.
- There is only the outdated LILO as boot loader.

# Summary

Slackware is the last of the distros suited to advanced users, at least in a traditional way. Slackware is a veteran distro: conservative, a little harsh, and yet after all this time, against all odds, still surviving and attracting new users while keeping a number of very enthusiast and loyal ones.

In the next chapter, you will see a distro that ushers in a new paradigm. It may be the future of Linux distros. NixOS offers some interesting new ideas of how a distro could be, and it's an example of the bleeding edge design of Linux distros.

# CHAPTER 14

# NixOS

NixOS is a very different Linux distro from those you've seen up to now. In fact, it is a state of the art distribution, ahead of everything. It's still not mature, it's continuing to evolve, it has still its quirks, and nobody can say if its bleeding edge technology is going to be adopted as the future of Linux. There are a few other proposals (like GuixSD, GoboLinux, and Qubes) that are also trying to make a difference and exploring new horizons. I include NixOS because it has very interesting concepts. It has already been adopted by about 5,000 professionals as their daily working distro; however, give it a wide when comparing it to others.

## History

In 2003, Eelco Dolstra was a Dutch student at the Utrecht University, collaborating on the TraCE (Transparent Configuration Environments) project as part of his PhD research. He started to develop the Nix package manager, which later would become the core of his PhD thesis[1] and the core of the NixOS distro itself. Under the umbrella of the same TraCE project, another collaborator and student named Armijn Hemel would later develop the first prototype of NixOS, the Linux distro based on the Nix package manager, as part of his Master's thesis[2].

Thus Nix was created as part of academic research and NixOS was created as a proof of concept that Nix could be used to manage a whole Linux distro. Dolstra also would develop other tools like Hydra, which is a Nix-based continuous integration tool, and NixOps, which is a tool for provisioning and deploying NixOS machines.

In 2015, as a strategy to support the development of NixOS, the cost of the infrastructure (Hydra hardware, AWS costs), and another related projects, the NixOS Foundation was created. This foundation is supported mainly by individual donations.

Today a few developers, researchers, users, and professionals are part of the still-little community of the NixOS distribution, but it is growing steadily. Perhaps the most receptive users are the Haskell (a purely functional programming language) developers; they also like the idea of a functional-driven Linux distro.

---

[1]https://nixos.org/~eelco/pubs/phd-thesis.pdf
[2]https://nixos.org/docs/SCR-2005-091.pdf

© Jose Dieguez Castro 2016
J. Dieguez Castro, *Introducing Linux Distros*, DOI 10.1007/978-1-4842-1392-6_14

# Philosophy

NixOS is a distribution built around its package manager, Nix, which is a proof of concept of how to achieve a model of software deployment that is purely functional. What does that mean? The best way to explain it is to use the authors' own words:

> *Existing package and system configuration management tools suffer from an imperative model, where system administration actions such as package upgrades or changes to system configuration files are stateful: they destructively update the state of the system. This leads to many problems, such as the inability to roll back changes easily, to deploy multiple versions of a package side-by-side, to reproduce a configuration deterministically on another machine, or to reliably upgrade a system. In this article we show that we can overcome these problems by moving to a purely functional system configuration model. This means that all static parts of a system (such as software packages, configuration files and system startup scripts) are built by pure functions and are immutable, stored in a way analogous to a heap in a purely functional language. We have implemented this model in NixOS, a non-trivial Linux distribution that uses the Nix package manager to build the entire system configuration from a modular, purely functional specification.*

> —Eelco Dolstra, Andres Loh, and Nicolas Pierron,
> "NixOS: A Purely Functional Linux Distribution," Cambridge University Press, 2010

Thus, the philosophy of NixOS is to prove that this goal can be achieved, to be a live laboratory of the Nix development and concepts. Nix brings a series of advantages that also defines this distribution and makes it unique; this is explained further in the "Package Management System" section.

# Distro Selection Criteria

Now that you know a little history, let's see how NixOS fares on the selection criteria listed in Chapter 2.

## Purpose and Environment

NixOS is a general purpose distribution with a general version for all environments. There are two branches of this version, the "stable" and the "unstable," the latter of which is used for development. There also ISO images for virtualization/cloud environments, specifically for VirtualBox and Amazon EC2.

## Support

Although NixOS has a very small community, you can get support for it through diverse channels:

- **NixOS documentation**: http://nixos.org/nixos/manual
- **Nix documentation**: http://nixos.org/nix/manual
- **Wiki**: https://nixos.org/wiki
- **Mailing list**: http://lists.science.uu.nl/mailman/listinfo/nix-dev
- **IRC**: #nixos at irc.freenode.net

One thing about the NixOS distro is the proportion of advanced Linux users and professional developers is much higher than in other distro communities, mostly because these folks are usually the early adopters of new advances, like the ones offered in this distro. Due of the immaturity of the distro, the best help should come from the mailing lists and IRC; not everything is covered in the documentation and wiki, and not everything is updated.

## User Friendliness

NixOS is not a user-friendly distro; you must know how to deal with the command line and the peculiarities of its package manager, and you must learn how to write the declarative configuration file to even install it. In fact, a lot of new users start using this distribution by copying and modifying another configuration file from another user. I'll go a step further: I don't think it's even a friendly distro for advanced Linux users because they have to change the way they think about Linux and learn how to follow the NixOS guidelines.

## Stability

Is NixOS stable or not? Well, that's a tricky question to answer. On one hand, it's an immature, still-evolving distro with some bugs and a small community far from reaching the necessary critical mass, which implies that the main developers are overloaded with too much work. On the other hand, it's a distro that allows multiple configurations, multiple package versions, and the ability to make rollbacks, so if something goes wrong with an update or setting, you always can come back to a more safe and stable previous configuration. Also, you can update or install packages only in your user environment without affect the global one (managed by root). Thus, you have a tremendous flexibility to achieve a very stable system, aside from the inevitable bugs and little inconvenience. And finally you can even opt between the stable and unstable branches.

NixOS follows a standard release model, and the new releases usually appear when they are tested and stable enough, without a fixed schedule. However, the goal is now to follow a release model more similar to the one for Ubuntu: a new release every six months. At this time, NixOS has released five stable releases, which follow a numbering scheme similar to Ubuntu's: year.month codename. The last release was 16.03 Emu.

## Hardware Support

NixOS offers hardware detection. It supports the hardware that the kernel supports, it supports some wireless cards, and you can use CUPS for printers, but other things may not be supported. NixOS is relatively new, it's in development, and it has a small community (and a small install base), so users will need to fend for themselves when it comes to certain hardware support.

## Aesthetics

Given the size of the community around this distribution and its blank-slate nature, it is understandable that there is not any effort to focus on the aesthetics of the distro, apart from the usual logos and backgrounds in Grub, desktop managers, and desktop environments.

## Desktop Environment

Like Arch or Gentoo, you have plenty of options when it comes to desktop environments. You can choose a traditional desktop environments like KDE, Gnome, or Xfce or window managers like Awesome, Xmonad, i3, IceWM, etc. The default "official" one is KDE, because like Nix it is cross-platform.

## Init System

NixOS has used systemd as its init system since December of 2014. Previously, it used System V.

## Package Management System

In a distribution like this, which was built only to be the testing ground of a package manager, everything begins and ends in Nix. And Nix is a very special package manager and a very unique concept. There is nothing out there similar to it (the closest one, GNU Guix, is actually based on Nix). The new paradigm that Nix introduces has multiple advantages but some drawbacks, so you must change the way you think about some things or you are going to hit the wall so many times that you will end up frustrated.

First of all, in NixOS, everything is managed by Nix: the kernel, system packages, user packages, system-wide configuration files, and so on. Nix uses a lazy pure functional language designed especially for it, which is used in a declarative mode based on a configuration file(s) that defines how the system has to be built. No matter how many times you build up a system using the same configuration, you always get the same system state.

NixOS stores every package isolated from others in the Nix store (`/nix/store/`) using a cryptographic hash (obtained from the input used to build it) as a unique identifier used in the store path and for internal references. Every change in the Nix expression used to build the package generates another hash and therefore is stored in another different path; this allows different releases and customized versions of the same package to coexist. The same happens with the configuration files of packages/services, and as result you can keep several system configurations or states simultaneously on the same machine.

Nix repositories are called channels, and they contain the recipes to build the packages, called nix expressions (usually a .nix file, some scripts, and some auxiliary files) and also the binaries (however, some packages are built from source). Nixpkgs, which is essentially a git repository, contains all of the nix expressions to build all of the official packages. The prebuilt packages in the channels are generated by Hydra, a Nix-based continuous build system, which when a new release of a package is available, builds it, tests it, and if it passes, releases it. (Actually, it's not quite like that because all of the new packages have to pass the test to release a new channel version). There is a farm of machines to host this service. Official channels are usually a tag or branch of the Nixpkgs git repository. The stable channel is called nixos (few weeks behind Nixpkgs HEAD) and the unstable is called nixos-unstable (a delay of few days). You can subscribe to the channel that you want to use.

Thanks to this package/system management model, Nix provide a series of advantages to NixOS over the ordinary Linux distros:

- **Reliable upgrades**: While the configuration remains the same, you can upgrade your system safely to always obtain the same result, as if it were a new, fresh installation.

- **Atomic upgrades**: Changes in a configuration are made in a transactional way, thus they are atomic, and changes are only applied when the transaction is finished. For instance, if an upgrade is interrupted or fails, the previous state continues to work. If you keep on your system one configuration that works (such as the initial one), your system will always boot up.

- **Rollbacks**: You can always go back (rollback) to a previous state, make a global configuration change or a local user one, install/remove a package, etc. This is possible because a new configuration never overwrites a previous one. In fact, you can choose the configuration you want to use from the Grub menu when booting the system (you can do the same without boot, of course). Because the configurations are kept simultaneously on the disk, this works almost instantaneously, without have to restore anything from disk or overwrite anything. A rough comparison would be to say that they work as snapshots instead of backups (in reality, they work with symbolic links).

- **Test changes safely**: Thanks to the rollback capabilities and simultaneous configurations, NixOS allows you to test (as an option) a configuration, and if doesn't work, it doesn't make it the default one. Even better, NixOS has an option that allows you to test this configuration on a virtual machine that works as a sandbox and contains your previous system state and the new changes that you want to test. This process is very efficient (it uses QEMU but does not clone your current system in a disk image). The only drawback is that your data, your home partition, is not present in this VM. This also helps you to avoid populating your Grub entries with a lot of minor changes.

- **Reproducible system configurations**: You can copy a configuration from a machine in a similar machine and get the same system (except user data, obviously, and "mutable state" like /var contents). This is ideal for making changes on test machines before applying changes on production machines or for deployments (in fact, there is a dedicated tool, NixOps, to do that with NixOS).

- **Mixed model with source and binaries**: Nix builds packages from source by default, but since compiling is a slow process, there are prebuilt binaries available to download from a cache server (the URL for which is included the channels) when they are available. In the stable branch, this lets you build only a few packages, so upgrading or installing a system is fast enough. But in the current branch, the packages are more recent ones and frequently you must build too many packages.

- **Consistency**: When a package or configuration changes, all the necessary packages or dependencies are rebuilt too. The same happens with the kernel and the modules (this is not something new; you can have this in other distros with DKMS). Also, when a library is updated, all the packages that use it are linked to the new version.

- **Multi-user package management**: In NixOS, the packages installed with the root user are available for all the users, but each user can also install their own packages in their profile. The packages are still stored and managed in the Nix store, and different users can have different versions of the same package. Still, if two users install the same version of the same package, only one copy is stored and shared among them. Also, there are security measures to avoid potential vulnerabilities, like not allowing setuid binaries.

But the Nix model also imposes some drawbacks and disadvantages. Some of them relate to the willingness of the user to adapt to NixOS, which is a significant issue.

- **The Unix FHS (Filesystem Hierarchy Standard) is broken**. Directories like /bin, /sbin, /lib, /usr, or /opt either do not exist or simply contain links to some point of the /nix/store directory (a read-only one). This makes some administrative tasks and problem solving more complex; you must rely on Nix. Also, because it breaks compatibility with standard FHS, it's impossible to install any package directly compiled from source (e.g. with $ make install); you have to "nixify" it first. Usually it's not that hard, but it's a little inconvenient.

- **The broken FHS has annoying side effects**. Apps expect to find their dependencies in the usual places. Those that depend on path variables that define environments or that have package managers of their own, such as programming languages like Python, Ruby, etc. have problems with this. There a lot of tricks and workarounds made by package maintainers that are available in the wiki, but increases the room for errors. You can also use **nix-shell**, a tool used to build sandbox environments. As the distro base grows, this will happen more often, and it's a crucial challenge to address in order for this distro to be adopted by more people. You can avoid some of these problems via isolated VMs or containers per project or dealing with different NixOS configurations, but at the end you are going to have to fight this in other situations, too. For instance, I tried to use my Emacs config. Most of it worked, but it needed some extensions to be compiled in order to work, which was not a fun experience.

- **Hashes make readability difficult**. Using the hash at the beginning of every package/file name in the /nix directory hierarchy makes it harder to find/sort your searches. For instance, you can have a Firefox package stored in the nix store at /nix/store/5rnfzla9kcx4mj5zdc7nlnv8na1navg-firefox-3.5.4/. Fortunately, you can still use the whereis, which, and locate commands to find many things. But you only need to run a printenv command to view the environment variables to get a headache again.

- **Potential heavy disk usage**. The disadvantage of having many different versions of a package and many different configurations is the cost of the disk space used, which can be considerable, especially if there are multiple users on the system with very different profiles. And thanks to the rollback functionality, removed or obsolete packages are not removed physically from the disk. You still can perform Nix's garbage collector by hand or periodically trough a systemd service to remove old, unreferenced packages. And you can also opt to use the Nix optimization that uses hard links for identical files; this saves a lot of space.

- **Changed packages can suffer big delays before they are available**. The Hydra farm that built the packages only updates a channel when the rebuild is entirely done (all the packages that needed to be rebuilt). When a change affects many packages (such as a security one or an important library like gcc), this rebuild can take few days. And this matter will get worse as the package base grows over time. Of course, if you have the resources, there's nothing to stop you from making your own Hydra setup to build packages for you.

- **The package base is still behind another distros**. Nixpkgs has around 30,000 packages available currently, whereas other distros have around 50,000 packages in their repositories. This means that if you want to use some of those packages, you have to make a Nix recipe for them. The good news is that you can commit that recipe to the Nixpkgs GitHub repository and make it available to the rest of the community very easily and thereby help maintain the distro.

In summary, if you are capable of adopting the Nix way of doing things for everything, you can avoid many of the aforementioned problems and use it safely for some tasks. I still have serious doubts about NixOS as a multi-purpose desktop or even a server distro. It might make a good way to build a minimal server with a reliable configuration, but once problems appear, it would be unpleasant to debug that machine. Regardless, I have to say that I want to see this distro mature in order to see what it will achieve. Ultimately, I would like to see all packages adapt to the way in which NixOS works, and to that end, administrating a machine would end up like programming the state of it. In an ideal world, a NixOS paradigm (or something similar with the same benefits), would be the perfect solution for so many current problems, which usually are poorly solved with many workarounds.

## Architecture

Currently NixOS only supports the Intel/AMD 32-/64-bit architectures. There also unofficial ports to ARM.

## Security/Anonymity

Due to the particular nature of this distro, as with Arch or Gentoo security and anonymity depended heavily on the user. There are some options to help harden NixOS, like using the grsecurity kernel or AppArmor, but they are currently very unstable or depend too much on how the user configures them. For example, I use the grsecurity kernel by default in my Arch installations, and you can do the same with Gentoo without trouble, but if you try that now with NixOS, many packages won't work, e.g. some browsers.

## Principles and Ethics

There is nothing explicitly said about principles and ethics. The distro has some proprietary software included, like binary blobs and drivers, and nothing stops you from creating ("nixifying") your own package from a proprietary software as binary. Otherwise, you must explicitly set that you want to use "unfree" packages in your configuration to be able to use the available ones (e.g. Nvidia drivers, Adobe Flash).

## Live CD

NixOS has a KDE-based Live CD, which gives you a general idea about NixOS. You can also use it to install the distribution.

## Professional Certification

Obviously, no professional certification covers this distribution.

# Installation

Installing this distribution is a unique experience, as is maintaining it. To those people introduced to the DevOps tools, it would be like to use a tool like Ansible, Puppet, Salt or Vagrant to instead of define the final state from a previous VM/Docker Linux image, define the final state without an image. Thus, you no longer need to depend on a previous image to create what you want; you create the system that you want directly from the beginning and it stays like that even after upgrades. This operation is more natural because you do not have to rely on immutable images (in DevOps, if you change your base image, you usually have to change the operations), because you are creating the image itself in its desirable final state. Now imagine the possibilities of this combined with a DevOps tool like NixOS. Take this with a grain of salt; it's an oversimplification and a gross approximation.

The first step is to go to the NixOS web site and get the ISO image at http://nixos.org/nixos/ download.html. You can see this web page in Figure 14-1. The ISO images to download are in two formats: minimal and graphical. You also have images for VirtualBox and Amazon EC2. The obvious choice for most users is the graphical Live CD (notice that is only available for 64-bit architecture). The major difference between the two is that in the graphical image you can use graphic tools to do the installation like a partition tool or a text editor, while in the minimal one you must use the command line tools. But I think that given the nature of this distro and the operations to perform, you need to use the terminal anyway; and if you feel comfortable with that, you should prefer the minimal installation CD (you still can choose the graphical one and simply not start the windows session). So click the graphical live CD option to download it.

# Getting NixOS 16.03

The latest stable release series is **16.03**. Below are links to CD/DVD images and VirtualBox appliances containing the latest release in this series.

Next Step: Manual →

## Installation CDs/DVDs

You can install NixOS on physical hardware by burning one of the CD images onto a blank CD/DVD disk, or by copying it onto a USB stick. For **installation instructions**, please see the manual.

Please note that NixOS at the moment lacks a nice, user-friendly graphical installer. Therefore this form of installation may not be suitable for novice Linux users.

The **graphical installation CD** contains the NixOS installer as well as X11, KDE 4 and several applications. It's a *live CD*, so it allows you to get an impression of NixOS (and the Nix package manager) before installing it.

- Graphical live CD, 64-bit Intel/AMD (SHA-256) **Recommended for most users**

The **minimal installation CD** does not contain X11, and is therefore a lot smaller. You have to run the installer from the console. It contains a number of rescue tools.

- Minimal installation CD, 64-bit Intel/AMD (SHA-256)
- Minimal installation CD, 32-bit Intel/AMD (SHA-256)

## VirtualBox appliances

This is a demo appliance for VirtualBox (in OVA format) that has X11 and KDE enabled, as well as the VirtualBox guest additions. To use it, download the OVA file, open VirtualBox, run "File → Import Appliance" from the menu, select the OVA file, and click "Import". You can then start the virtual machine. When the KDE login screen appears, you can log in as user demo, password demo. To obtain a root shell, run sudo -i in the KDE terminal (konsole).

- VirtualBox appliance, 64-bit Intel/AMD (SHA-256)

## Amazon EC2 AMIs

If you are an EC2 user, you can fire up a NixOS instance instantly by using one of the AMIs listed below.

***Figure 14-1.*** *The downloads section of the NixOS web site*

Note that I'm using a traditional BIOS system with a 2TB hard disk. I use the ISO image to boot the system and so the first screen is the typical one shown in Figure 14-2. Usually the first option should work in the majority of systems; if you have trouble with your graphics card, choose the second one instead. After finishing the boot up, you end in a terminal root prompt, like the one in Figure 14-3.

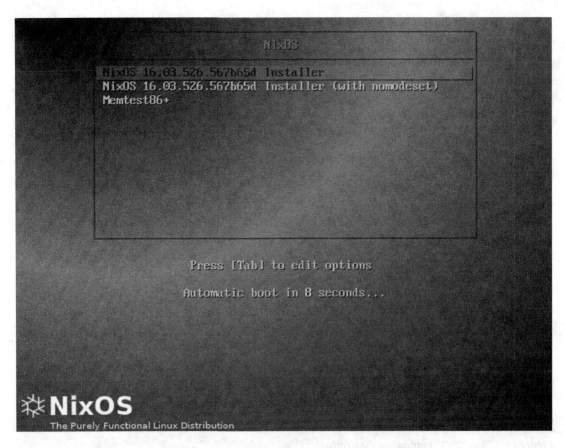

*Figure 14-2.* *The first screen after booting up from the NixOS ISO image*

```
<<< Welcome to NixOS 16.03.526.567b65d (x86_64) - tty1 >>>

The "root" account has an empty password.  Type `start display-manager' to
start the graphical user interface.


Press <Alt-F8> for the NixOS manual.

nixos login: root (automatic login)

[root@nixos:~]# _
```

*Figure 14-3.* *The NixOS root console that you get at the end of the boot up*

In order to start the graphical session, you must enter a command, but as I said previously, if you are OK with working in the command line, you can continue the installation from here and use terminal tools. Help is always available in the eighth console, as you can see in Figure 14-4, and it uses the same HTML manual on the Web via the w3m text browser. I would usually install it in this way, but let's try it the other way: start the graphical session by typing the # start display-manager command.

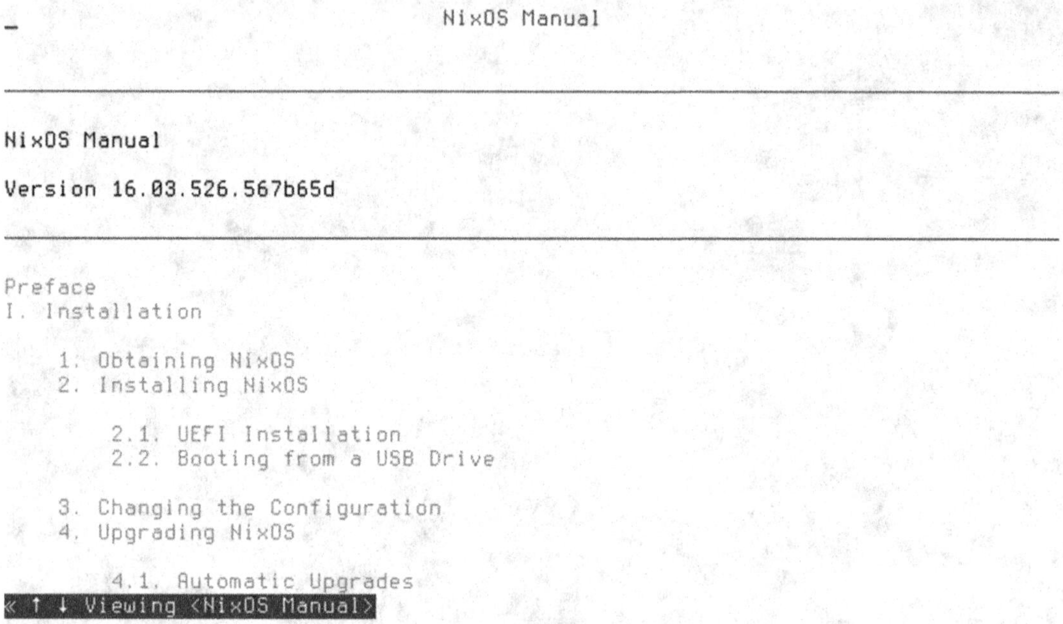

```
_                            NixOS Manual

──────────────────────────────────────────────────────────────────────

NixOS Manual

Version 16.03.526.567b65d

──────────────────────────────────────────────────────────────────────

Preface
I. Installation

   1. Obtaining NixOS
   2. Installing NixOS

       2.1. UEFI Installation
       2.2. Booting from a USB Drive

   3. Changing the Configuration
   4. Upgrading NixOS

       4.1. Automatic Upgrades
« ↑ ↓ Viewing <NixOS Manual>
```

***Figure 14-4.*** *The NixOS manual on the terminal*

A KDE session is opened; in a folder on the desktop are the three essentials tools that you are going to need to install the distro: a partition tool (GParted), a terminal (Konsole), and the NixOS manual (see Figure 14-5).

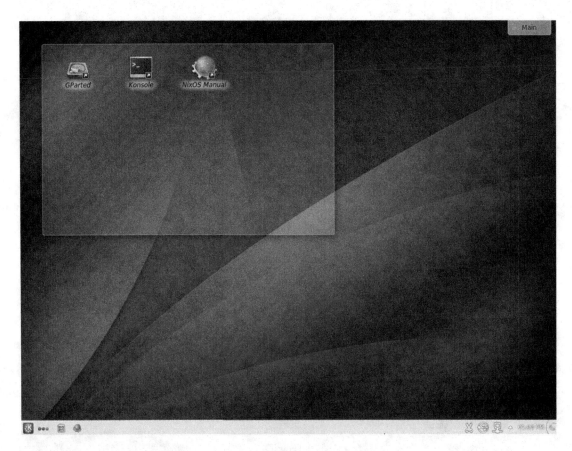

***Figure 14-5.*** *The default KDE session of the NixOS Live CD*

Let's assume that the network was well detected and is working perfectly. The first thing you need to do is partition the disk, and for that, use the GParted tool (shown in Figure 14-6) and a very simple partition scheme, with only the / and /home partitions. You start creating the partition table by selecting the Device ➤ Create Partition Table menu entry. By default an msdos type should be selected and if not, select it as shown in Figure 14-7 and click Apply (ignore the warning; in my case, the disk is empty).

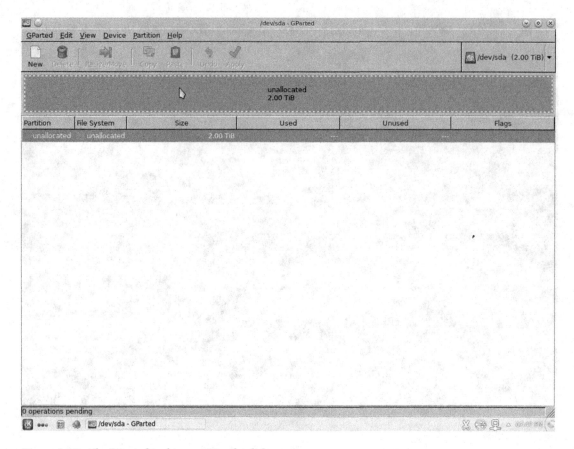

***Figure 14-6.*** *The GParted tool to partition the disk*

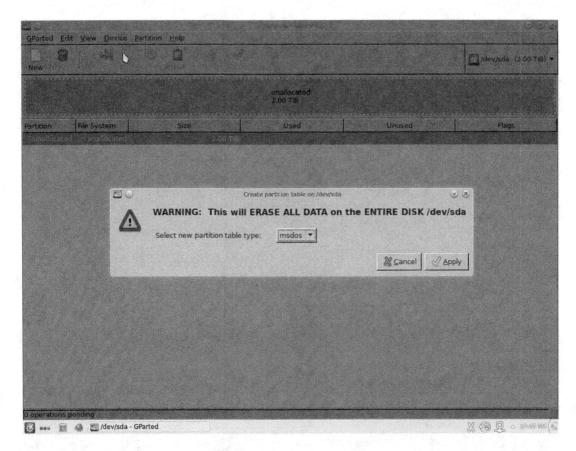

**Figure 14-7.** *Creating the partition table on the disk*

Create your first partition by clicking the New icon. Create an ext4 100GiB partition with a label of nixos (as in Figure 14-8). This may seem like a very big partition for just the system files, but in NixOS you can store several configurations and several versions of the same packages, and depending on the packages, this can take up a lot of disk space. The idea of putting labels on your partitions is very helpful in a distro like this, where if the device changes, the configuration can be reapplied via the labels. You can also use the UUIDs, but this way is easier (in the hardware configuration file, the UUID is added to the partition through the name when the configuration files are generated automatically for the first time). Next, create another ext4 partition with the rest of the disk in the same way, but with home as the label. Finally, click Apply. You should have something similar to the partition scheme shown in Figure 14-9.

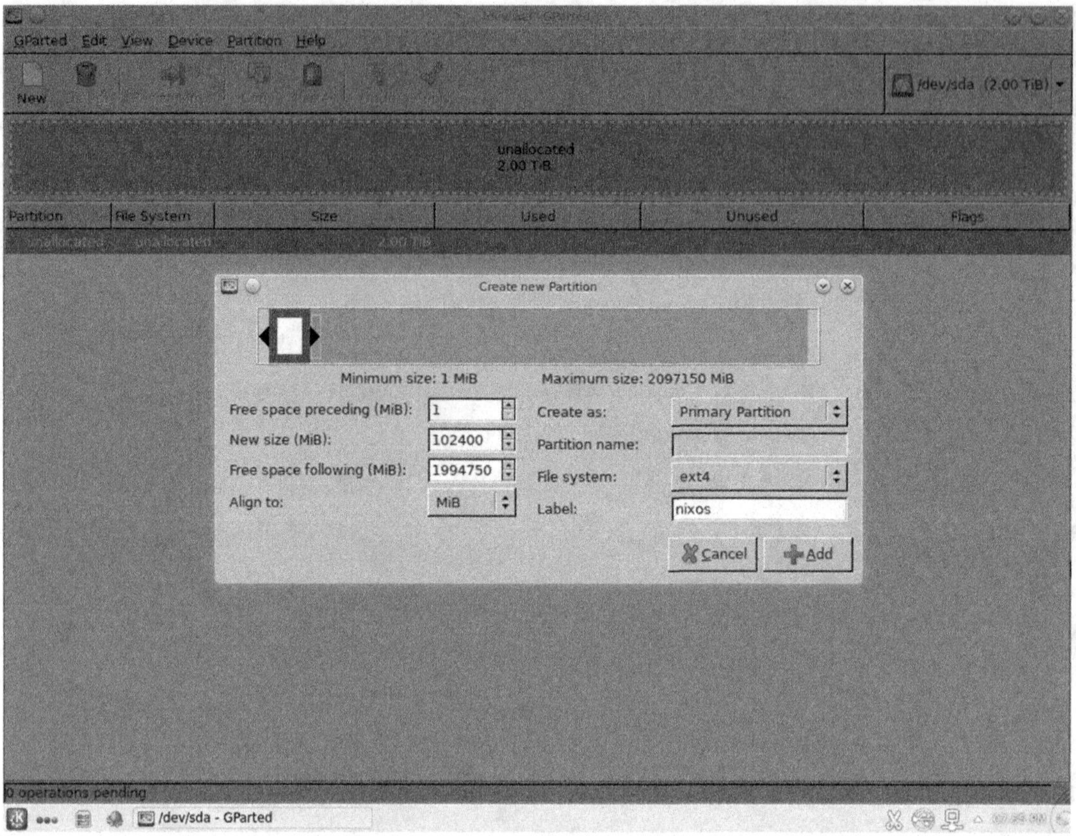

*Figure 14-8. Creation of the first partition*

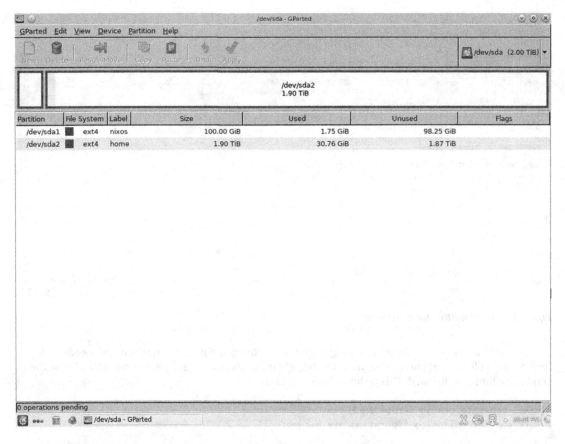

***Figure 14-9.*** *The final partition scheme*

The next step is to mount the partitions. To do so, open the Konsole terminal and enter the following commands. In Figure 14-10, notice the partition labels and the UUIDs.

```
# lsblk -pf
# mount /dev/disk/by-label/nixos /mnt
# mkdir /mnt/home
# mount /dev/disk/by-label/home /mnt/home
```

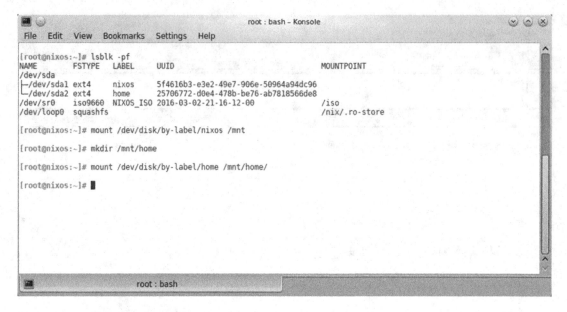

*Figure 14-10. Mounting the partitions*

Now you must generate the initial configuration file of NixOS and then edit it to suit your needs. The configuration file will be generated in the path /mnt/etc/nixos/configurations.nix and you will use the graphical editor Kate to edit it. This is shown in Figure 14-11.

```
# nixos-generate-config --root /mnt
# kate /mnt/etc/nixos/configuration.nix &>/dev/null
```

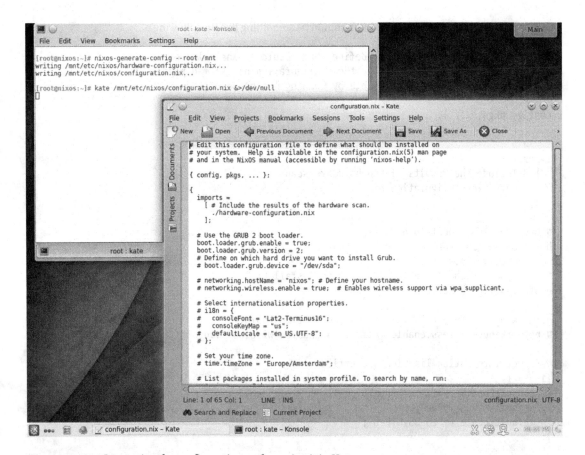

***Figure 14-11.*** *Generating the configuration and opening it in Kate*

Let's take a moment for a sidebar. I'm going to tell you the easiest way to install NixOS and get a very minimal system going, quite similar to the one you get when installing Arch, Gentoo, or Slackware, for example. The only thing you need to do is very simple: first, edit the configuration file to uncomment the line that contains the option `boot.loader.grub.device` and execute the command `# nixos-install`. The system will be installed automatically. At the end, it will ask you for the root's password, and you only have to reboot the system to get a minimally functional NixOS system. This process will take a while because certain packages must be downloaded and compiled (if you choose the unstable version, then a lot of packages will be compiled from source). However, doing it this way means that you need to create a user, and configure the time zone, network settings, etc. after the installation is done. And worse, you have to install the packages you want after that, as with other distros. This is a waste of the advantages of this distribution. Remember, for example, you can install packages in a global way so they are available for all users, and/or packages for each user individually. Some packages, like a desktop environment or a window manager, should be easy if you install them directly and automatically from the configuration.

I strongly recommend that you read the manual (accessed via the desktop icon, which points to a local version of the web manual at `http://nixos.org/nixos/manual/index.html`) to have a more general impression of what you can do and how. Also, I strongly recommend that you check out the different options available for the configuration at `http://nixos.org/nixos/options.html`.

Let's start to edit the initial file to get a minimal configuration:

```
# kate /mnt/etc/nixos/configuration.nix &> /dev/null
```

The contents of the file after the editing should be something like the following :

```
# Edit this configuration file to define what should be installed on
# your system. Help is available in the configuration.nix(5) man page
# and in the NixOS manual (accessible by running 'nixos-help').

{ config, pkgs, ... }:

{
  imports =
    [ # Include the results of the hardware scan.
      ./hardware-configuration.nix
    ];

  # Use the GRUB 2 boot loader.
  boot.loader.grub.enable = true;
  boot.loader.grub.version = 2;
  # Define on which hard drive you want to install Grub.
  boot.loader.grub.device = "/dev/sda";

  networking.hostName = "nixos"; # Define your hostname.
  # networking.wireless.enable = true;  # Enables wireless support via wpa_supplicant.

  # Select internationalisation properties.
  i18n = {
      consoleFont = "Lat2-Terminus16";
      consoleKeyMap = "us";
      defaultLocale = "en_US.UTF-8";
  };

  # Set your time zone.
  time.timeZone = "America/New_York";

  # List packages installed in system profile. To search by name, run:
  # $ nix-env -qaP | grep wget
  environment.systemPackages = with pkgs; [
    wget
    firefox
    htop
  ];

  # List services that you want to enable:

  # Enable the OpenSSH daemon.
  # services.openssh.enable = true;

  # Enable CUPS to print documents.
  services.printing.enable = true;
```

```
# Enable the X11 windowing system.
services.xserver.enable = true;
services.xserver.layout = "us";
# services.xserver.xkbOptions = "eurosign:e";

# Enable the KDE Desktop Environment.
#services.xserver.displayManager.kdm.enable = true;
services.xserver.desktopManager.kde4.enable = true;

# Define a user account. Don't forget to set a password with 'passwd'.
users.extraUsers.johndoe = {
  isNormalUser = true;
  uid = 1000;
  description = "John Doe";
  extraGroups = ["wheel" "audio"];
};

# The NixOS release to be compatible with for stateful data such as databases.
system.stateVersion = "16.03";

}
```

When you have the configuration ready, introduce the following command in the console to automatically install the system:

```
# nixos-install
```

After installing all of the packages, the installation program will ask you to introduce the root password, so introduce a strong one. The program exits and the installation is done. Reboot the system and set a password for the user that you specified in the configuration, in this case johndoe. To do that, the nixos-install program allows you to jail root in the newly installed environment (because obviously the new user does not exist in the Live CD environment). Now you can reboot the system again.

```
# nixos-install --chroot
# passwd johndoe
# exit
# reboot
```

When the machine restarts, the first screen that you will see is the Grub menu (Figure 14-12). Notice that the second entry says "NixOS - All configurations." Here you should see the configurations stored automatically (the ones that you did not add manually to the boot menu).

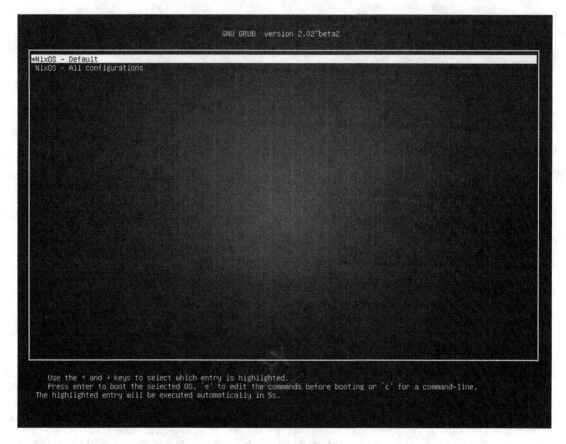

*Figure 14-12.* *The Grub menu of a fresh installation of NixOS*

Select the first entry to boot NixOS for the first time. After a few seconds, you will see the Slim desktop manager, which is the default one used in NixOS (see Figure 14-13). Enter your user and password.

*Figure 14-13.* *The desktop manager, Slim, is the default one for the NixOS*

Again you land up in a KDE environment like the Live CD I show you here, with the apps that I told you to specifically install (Figure 14-14). I'm afraid that the capture is too small to see clearly, but if you could, you would see that the binaries paths in the htop tool are awkward because all of them are in the /nix/store directory. Anyway, you can see how the KDE desktop manager and the htop and Firefox packages were installed as established in the configuration file. This is a powerful way to configure and install a system once you know how to do it, but the first time is a little awkward. If you want to make something more elaborate, you will have to navigate through the nix manual, and maybe even the mailing list and IRC too. This is not unusual with other advanced distributions, but even advanced user must learn a lot of things with NixOS if they want to use it continuously. That's it! You have a NixOS installed in your system.

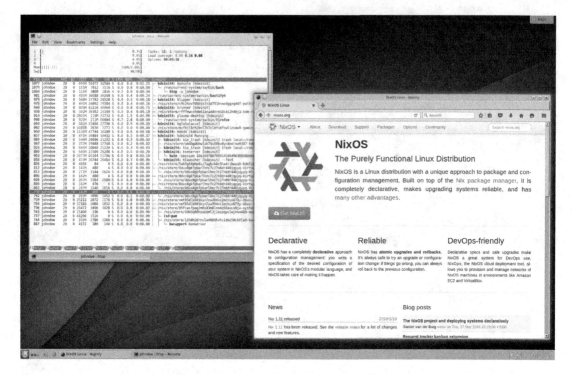

***Figure 14-14.*** *The NixOS KDE with Firefox and htop (inside Konsole) running in the desktop*

Now I'll show you how easy it is to change your configuration and the default desktop manager. You must again edit the configuration file that is now at /etc/nixos/configuration.nix and uncomment the line (remove the preceding #) #services.xserver.displayManager.kdm.enable = true; and then execute this command into the Konsole terminal:

```
$ sudo nixos-rebuild test
```

If all goes well, you can log out from KDE and you will now have now KDM as your new desktop manager, as you can see in Figure 14-15. Log in. You can make this configuration the default one by running this command:

```
$ sudo nixos-rebuild switch
```

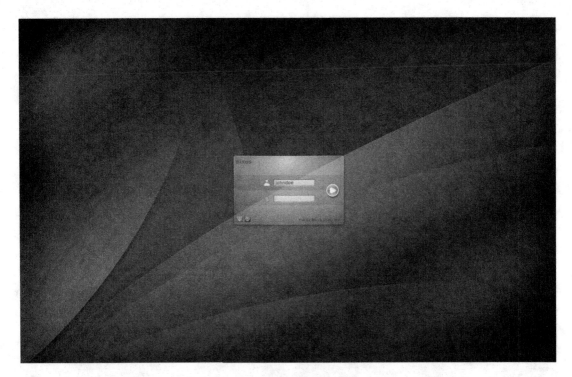

*Figure 14-15. You succesfully changed Slim for KDM by changing a line in the configuration*

But you make bigger changes, like using GDM and Gnome 3 instead of KDM and KDE, with only a few changes in the file; with other distros, this can be a big headache. You only have to change the following section of the configuration file:

```
# Enable the KDE Desktop Environment.
# services.xserver.displayManager.kdm.enable = true;
services.xserver.displayManager.gdm.enable = true;
# services.xserver.desktopManager.kde4.enable = true;
services.xserver.desktopManager.gnome3.enable = true;
```

Perform the same operations as before. If you restart the system, you will now have GDM as your login manager and a completely functional Gnome 3 as your desktop manager (see Figure 14-16).

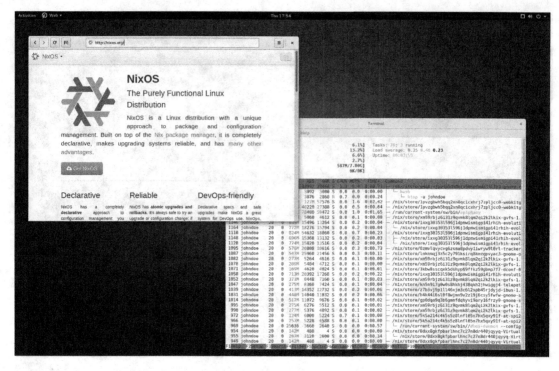

***Figure 14-16.*** *A Gnome Shell session from changing two lines*

I think you can see how amazing this distro can be. All of the "mutable state" is kept between changes, of course; you can see that all of the operations you already performed in the terminal are present in the history.

And finally, when you restart the system, if you choose the second menu option, you will see something similar to Figure 14-17, which shows all of the configurations that you made. There's nothing to stop you from booting in the previous configuration, returning to KDE, and with $ sudo nixos-rebuild switch, making it your default configuration again. And if you want to switch frequently between configurations, you even can give them a name and add them as a new menu entry in the main Grub menu.

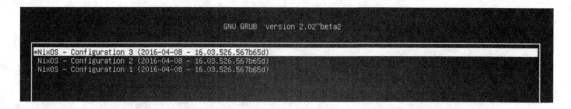

***Figure 14-17.*** *In the Grub menu, you can choose between all of your previous configurations*

Many Linux users would really like to have something like this in their current distributions, myself included. I look forward to seeing how NixOS evolves.

# Maintenance

All the maintenance in this distro is Nix related, and you should use Nix tools to perform the tasks to make sure they go as smoothly as possible.

## Managing Apps

There are two different ways to install/remove applications in NixOS, either in a declarative way through the configuration file(s) or in an imperative way, as with traditional package managers. If I were managing a multi-user system I would use the declarative way to install all of the global packages available for all users, and I would let the users install their own packages in an imperative way. In the case of a one-person machine, I would install all the base packages from the configuration and I would only use the command line to install a few packages, such as those I only needed temporarily.

Installing packages in NixOS is very easy. Use this simple command:

```
$ nix-env -i firefox
```

To remove it, there are two options: make a rollback (I would only use this option if there are no other operations later that would change the state, like modifying the configuration or installing/removing/updating packages) or remove it. Use this code:

```
# This would remove the package (remember, not phisically from disk)
$ nix-env -e firefox

# This would perform a rollback
$ nix-env rollback
```

## Updating

Again, there are two ways of updating packages in NixOS. You can update them using the imperative way with Nix or using the declarative way by rebuilding the entire system. With the first way, you can even upgrade packages individually.

To update something in an imperative way, first you must update the channel information (using the nixos channel):

```
$ nix-channel --update nixos
```

Now it's time to update a package or all of the available updates. First, here's how to update an individual package:

```
$ nix-env -u firefox
```

To update all of the packages that have a new version available, use the following code:

```
$ nix-env -u '*'
```

And for updating all of the packages in the declarative way, you only have to rebuild your configuration, and it will perform all the needed updates:

```
$ nixos-rebuild switch
```

# Upgrading

One of the advantages of NixOS is precisely this, to do reliable distro upgrades. These upgrades are made via the NixOS official channels (a sort of repository). When you install NixOS from a current release (16.03 in this case), you are usually subscribed to this channel, and the system updates are made through this channel. When a new release appears, you only have to subscribe to that release channel and do an upgrade via `nixos-rebuild` to upgrade your entire system. If you installed from the unstable branch or you subscribed your system to the unstable channel, then the distribution would follow the rolling release model and would always be updated.

Let's see how to do this. First of all, you need to know that official channels are available:

```
$ nix-channel --list | grep nixos
```

When a new release appears, you switch to the new channel release. Say that a new release appears this year in September (as scheduled):

```
$ nix-channel --list | grep nixos
nixos https://nixos.org/channels/nixos-16.09
$ nix-channel --add https://nixos.org/channels/nixos-16.09 nixos
```

Finally, you upgrade the entire system:

```
$ nixos-rebuild switch --upgrade
```

Once this process is finished, you end up with a final state that is the same as if you made a fresh install with your current configuration.

# Pros and Cons

The following is a list of some of the things that I personally see as pros and cons of the NixOS distribution. There is always room for discussion in this matter, but I tried to be as objective as possible.

## Pros

- You can build your system automatically from configuration file(s) that can be version controlled with a reliable final state.

- NixOS offers bleeding-edge technology that has so many advantages: reliability, consistency, rollbacks, atomicity, reproducibility, etc.

- NixOS offers a state-of-the-art package manager that can be used apart from this distro; it's also multiplatform.

- Together with NixOps and Disnix, it makes a very promising tool for DevOps.

- It's an original distro and package manager, not a fork.

## Cons

- It's not a user-friendly distro. Even advanced Linux users must learn the NixOS way of doing things.

- The documentation is incomplete, sometimes outdated, and you must rely on other support channels when you try to do something non-trivial.

- It's still in development and has some challenges to solve in order to become a real alternative.

- For non-trivial things, like building your own packages, you must learn the Nix functional language.

- There are serious drawbacks and bugs if you try to do something outside the Nix way. You have to follow the Nix way for everything, even for your dotfiles if you want a nice experience.

- It has small community, and a far way to go to reach the critical mass necessary to be a real alternative and evolve faster.

- It has a small install base.

- The Nix interface could be improved (for things like searching packages).

# Summary

In this chapter, you got a glimpse of a possible and promising future Linux scenario. Although it still has a long way to go, NixOS is the most advanced, and with a better theoretical foundation, of all the existing experimental Linux distros at the present. There are already a considerable number of people (about 5,000) who are using this distro as their daily Linux OS. Together with systemd, this distro could trace the path to follow in the future.

In the following chapter I cover more alternative distros (like Qubes). Unfortunately, I only have room to give you a brief summary of each of them, but I hope it helps you get a broader vision of the Linux distros panorama.

■ ■ ■

# CHAPTER 15

# Other Alternatives

In this chapter, I show you some general purpose distros that I want to analyze in detail, because they either offer a good alternative or have peculiarity that is remarkable enough to draw your attention. There are notable absences like Red Hat, SUSE or CentOS, but the type of user who is going to choose to install and manage those corporate-oriented distros mostly likely won't need to read a book like this to make that decision. Also, because of that, I focused this book on desktop distros and skipped environments like the cloud or servers, and other interesting and promising desktop distros like Papyros and Apricity OS are not covered here.

There are flavors of popular distros that differ only in the desktop environment. For example, in the case of Ubuntu you can find Kubuntu, Xubuntu, Lubuntu, Ubuntu Gnome, Ubuntu MATE, Ubuntu Kylin, Mythbuntu, and Edubuntu (and those are only the official ones). I won't cover these flavors, but maybe one of them will suite your needs. If you want to explore the wide variety of Linux distros available, go to http://distrowatch.com. This web site makes a big effort to keep up with the highly volatile distro scene and offers the best compilation available.

## Zorin OS

The Irish Zorin OS (first released in 2009) is another distribution based on Ubuntu (as are Linux Mint and elementary OS). Zorin OS provides the closest experience to the Microsoft Windows OS. To do so, it provides a similar look for several Windows versions (or OS X), and it installs Wine by default. Wine is a tool that allows you to execute native Windows applications in Linux. But not all Windows applications can be executed with Wine, so you may often experience apps that hang or have some functionality disabled.

Zorin OS is a good option for long-time Windows users reluctant to use Linux because of the unfamiliarity of the interface. It's also a good option in a mixed corporate environment where you need to run Linux but still need to run some Windows apps. You can also install Wine in other distributions (some even have it installed by default or its alternative, PlayOnLinux), but Zorin is a ready solution out of the box with this kind of user in mind. It's currently a popular distro but with a smallish install size.

It offers free and commercial versions. The latter come with a very low price for additional looks, additional software, and more support directly from the developers. The support for the commercial versions is basically to help in the installation of the distro, but I have serious doubts about the need for this kind of help in an Ubuntu-based distro. The distro has a default Windows 7-based theme, which can be changed for Windows XP or Gnome. The commercial versions have additional themes to look like Windows 2000, OS X, and Unity.

The distro selection criteria for Zorin OS are summarized in Table 15-1. You can learn more about Zorin OS at http://zorinos.com.

© Jose Dieguez Castro 2016

J. Dieguez Castro, *Introducing Linux Distros*, DOI 10.1007/978-1-4842-1392-6_15

***Table 15-1.*** *Distro Selection Criteria for Zorin OS*

| | |
|---|---|
| **Purpose and Environment** | Two free versions: Core and Lite. Two commercial versions: Business and Ultimate. |
| **Support** | Commercial and community |
| **User Friendliness** | A user-friendly distro, especially for former Windows and OS X users. |
| **Stability** | Stable as Ubuntu at first. Same release scheme as Ubuntu with an added delay. |
| **Hardware Support** | Same as Ubuntu. |
| **Aesthetics** | Windows 7, Windows XP, and Gnome. Commercial: Windows 2000, OS X, and Unity. |
| **Desktop Environment** | Gnome or LXDE. The commercial version adds Unity. |
| **Init System** | systemd for the current version, Upstart in older ones. |
| **Package Management System** | dpkg |
| **Architecture** | Intel/AMD 32-/64-bits |
| **Security/Anonymity** | Same as Ubuntu. |
| **Principles and Ethics** | Nothing in particular. |
| **Live CD** | Yes |
| **Professional Certification** | No |

# Trisquel

Released in 2007, Trisquel is another distro that uses Ubuntu as its base. In this case, this Spanish distro is notable for being one of the few distros that the Free Software Foundation recognizes and endorses as a Free GNU/Linux distribution. Of these recognized distros, Trisquel is the most popular and active. It uses the Linux-libre kernel and removes all the proprietary software that Ubuntu originally supports, as well as any kernel firmware binary blobs and proprietary drivers.

It is a community distro supported only by donations and by a small community. As a result, even though is it a friendly distro, due to the restriction of only offering free products, there is limited support for hardware. You will probably have problems with graphic cards, wireless devices and so on, so I recommend researching your hardware options before choose this distribution.

It has a special version called Sugar TOAST, which is aimed at learning environments that use the Sugar desktop interface designed for teachers and children. This desktop environment was originally developed for the OLPC (One Laptop per Children) project.

Trisquel is the Spanish word for triskelion, a motif consisting of three interlocked spirals; it's from the Celtic culture, which one flourished in Galicia (where Trisquel and I were born). The distro's logo is a triskelion, a tribute to the Debian distro.

The distro selection criteria for Trisquel are summarized in Table 15-2. You can learn more Trisquel at https://trisquel.info.

**Table 15-2.** *Distro Selection Criteria for Trisquel*

| Purpose and Environment | A main version, a "mini" one (only English/Spanish), and a Sugar TOAST version |
|---|---|
| Support | Community |
| User Friendliness | A user-friendly distro, but with hardware restrictions. |
| Stability | Based on Ubuntu LTS releases, therefore it's very stable. |
| Hardware Support | Less than regular distros, because it only supports free software. |
| Aesthetics | Aside from custom logos and themes, nothing more. |
| Desktop Environment | Gnome or LXDE. Sugar desktop for Sugar TOAST version. |
| Init System | Currently Upstart because it's based on Ubuntu 14.04. In the future, it will be systemd. |
| Package Management System | dpkg |
| Architecture | Intel/AMD 32-/64-bits |
| Security/Anonymity | Same as Ubuntu, but provides tools/docs to preserve anonymity/privacy. |
| Principles and Ethics | Only Free Software. Endorsed by the Free Software Foundation. |
| Live CD | Yes |
| Professional Certification | No |

# PCLinuxOS

The American distro PCLinuxOS is another descendant of Mandrake (later Mandriva), like Mageia. However, while Mageia tries maintain the legacy of Mandriva, PCLinuxOS started down its own path a long time ago. PCLinuxOS was forked from Mandrake in 2003, and that in part explains the divergence with Mageia, because it was created 8 years prior. One of the peculiarities of this distro is the Full Monty edition, which comes with a plethora of preinstalled applications to suit several needs, each with its own predefined KDE virtual desktop.

One of the big differences with Mageia is that PCLinuxOS is a rolling release distribution, with major releases from time to time. Even as a rolling releases distro, the packages are not always the latest versions but are instead stable packages that are merged into their repositories. Another big difference is that it is one of the few distros that still uses System V as its init system, since its community strongly opposed the change to systemd.

Another remarkable difference is the package management system, APT-RPM, which is a customization of the original Debian app tool; APT-RPM works with rpm packages instead of dpkg ones. PCLinuxOS also uses a traditional dpkg graphical tool, Synaptic, as its default graphical package management tool. Only a few distros currently use this package system.

PCLinuxOS is the perfect choice for users who like the Mageia/Mandriva style and rpm, need a friendly distro, do not like systemd, and prefer a rolling release scheme.

The distro selection criteria for PCLinuxOS are summarized in Table 15-3. You can learn more about PCLinuxOS at www.pclinuxos.com.

*Table 15-3. Distro Selection Criteria for PCLinuxOS*

| | |
|---|---|
| **Purpose and Environment** | Unique version with an ISO image for each flavor: KDE, MATE, and Full Monty. |
| **Support** | Community |
| **User Friendliness** | A user-friendly distro |
| **Stability** | Rolling release scheme, but packages are only released if they are stable enough. |
| **Hardware Support** | Same as Mageia: very good. |
| **Aesthetics** | Its own layout, customization, and design in the Full Monty edition. |
| **Desktop Environment** | KDE and MATE. The Full Monty edition has a customized KDE. |
| **Init System** | System V (sysv), by community decision to not switch to systemd. |
| **Package Management System** | APT-RPM |
| **Architecture** | Intel/AMD 32-/64-bits |
| **Security/Anonymity** | Reasonable security out of the box. |
| **Principles and Ethics** | Pragmatic approach: leaves these decisions to the user. |
| **Live CD** | Yes |
| **Professional Certification** | No |

# Manjaro

Manjaro is an Austrian/German/French distribution that was first released in 2011. It's an Arch Linux-based, friendly alternative for users who want to have the advantages of Arch but want to avoid the non-friendly process of installing it. Since it is based on Arch Linux, Manjaro can use its repositories and its package manager, but Manjaro provides a friendly installer and tools to manage the packages, repositories, and the basic system settings.

By default, Manjaro has its own repositories and documentation, but you can use the Arch counterparts, which is an additional advantage. One known disadvantage, and a source of frequent criticism, is that it is still a slightly immature distro, with some fiascos (some of them serious security ones) in the past. In spite of being a controversial distro with many detractors, it is still a very popular distro, probably because there are many people who love the goods of Arch but not its problems, and Manjaro is like a breath of fresh air for them.

The official desktop managers are KDE and Xfce, but the community also maintain versions like Cinnamon, Gnome, MATE, Enlightenment, LXDE, LXQT, Fluxbox, Openbox, Netbook, and PekWM.

The Manjaro installer tool, Calamares (an independent Linux installer used by several distros), is very similar to the one used in Ubuntu. There were several attempts in the past to develop a friendly Arch Linux distro, and Manjaro seems to be the first that did it well. These days it is more popular than Arch itself.

The distro selection criteria for Manjaro are summarized in Table 15-4. You can learn more about Manjaro at https://manjaro.github.io.

***Table 15-4.*** *Distro Selection Criteria for Manjaro*

| | |
|---|---|
| **Purpose and Environment** | One version with two flavors: KDE and Xfce. A net edition is available. |
| **Support** | Community support. Documentation is not as good as the original from Arch. |
| **User Friendliness** | A user-friendly distro |
| **Stability** | Rolling release scheme, and still a bit unreliable. |
| **Hardware Support** | Better than Arch, with hardware automatic detection. |
| **Aesthetics** | Customized themes, installer, and general look. |
| **Desktop Environment** | KDE and Xfce. Several others supported by the community: Gnome, MATE, etc. |
| **Init System** | systemd |
| **Package Management System** | Pacman with its own repositories, plus the ability to use the Arch ones. |
| **Architecture** | Intel/AMD 32-/64-bits |
| **Security/Anonymity** | Regular out-of-the-box offerings. It should take these topics more seriously. |
| **Principles and Ethics** | Same as Arch: the user has the last word. |
| **Live CD** | Yes |
| **Professional Certification** | No |

# Antergos

The Spanish Antergos distro (originally named Cinnarch because Cinnamon was the original desktop environment of the distro) is one of the latest Arch Linux derivatives (circa 2012) oriented to be user friendly, like Manjaro. It basically adds a graphical installer tool, Cnchi (originally developed from scratch and inspired by the Ubuntu one) to the Arch Linux base, keeping almost all the other stuff intact. It also offers a graphical package manager, pamac, that was developed on Manjaro, and it uses the original Arch Linux repositories plus its own one. In a few words, Antergos is Arch Linux made easy.

During the installation process you must select which desktop environment you want to use, from a selection of the most common ones. You can choose a browser or an office suite, but any choice will still install some common applications, in a similar way to other user-friendly distros like Ubuntu.

Antergos has become quite popular lately because it's a vanilla Arch Linux-based distro with a friendly graphical installer. Some Arch users choose it to install a new "pseudo" Arch Linux system without needing to do it manually.

Several companies support the maintaining of the distribution, but it is still a community-developed one. Antergos is a Galician word (the original and main developer is from Galicia, Spain) that means ancestors; picking this word suggests homage to its ancestor, Arch.

The distro selection criteria for Antergos are summarized in Table 15-5. You can learn more about Antergos at `https://antergos.com`.

*Table 15-5.* *Distro Selection Criteria for Antergos*

| | |
|---|---|
| **Purpose and Environment** | One main version available as Live or minimal ISO. |
| **Support** | Community support, plus the possibility to use Arch Linux docs. |
| **User Friendliness** | A user-friendly distro |
| **Stability** | Rolling release scheme, as stable as Arch Linux. |
| **Hardware Support** | Better than Arch Linux, with automatic hardware detection. |
| **Aesthetics** | Theme and icons made in collaboration with the Numix project. |
| **Desktop Environment** | Gnome, Cinnamon, MATE, KDE, Xfce, and OpenBox |
| **Init System** | systemd |
| **Package Management System** | Pacman using the Arch Linux repositories. |
| **Architecture** | Intel/AMD 32-/64-bits |
| **Security/Anonymity** | The same as Arch Linux. |
| **Principles and Ethics** | Pragmatism: the user gets the last word. |
| **Live CD** | Yes |
| **Professional Certification** | No |

# Sabayon

The Italian Sabayon (circa 2005, formerly RR4 Linux) works as an amicable alternative to Gentoo, upon which it is based. It's a user-friendly distro that follows the Gentoo philosophy but with a few differences that allow novice users to use it, like a graphical package manager that manages binaries instead of source. Advanced users can have an almost similar experience to Gentoo. It uses the same graphical installer as Manjaro, Calamares, and supports several desktop environments by default by selecting the corresponding ISO image. It can be a good distro for users who want to start with Gentoo but do not want to do so in one big step, instead preferring to learn at their own pace while still being able to enjoy the advantages.

The main differences from Gentoo are the package management and the init system. Sabayon uses systemd instead of Gentoo's OpenRC as its init system. More interesting yet is that Sabayon manages packages in a very particular way. It has two package managers: Entropy and Portage. The first one was developed by Sabayon and works with binary packages from its own repositories; it's aimed at novices and it has a graphical interface, Rigo, to be friendlier. Advanced users still can use Gentoo's Portage to build packages from source. The binary packages are usually more outdated and stable than the source code, from where you can build your packages with Portage.

The name Sabayon comes from the French word for a traditional Italian dessert, Zabaglione or Zabaione. The distro selection criteria for Sabayon are summarized in Table 15-6. You can learn more about Sabayon at `https://sabayon.org`.

***Table 15-6.*** *Distro Selection Criteria for Sabayon*

| | |
|---|---|
| **Purpose and Environment** | Versions for Desktop, Server, ARM, Docker, and Vagrant. |
| **Support** | Community |
| **User Friendliness** | User friendly, but suitable for advanced users. |
| **Stability** | Rolling release scheme. |
| **Hardware Support** | Better than Gentoo because it supports hardware auto-detection. |
| **Aesthetics** | The default ones of each desktop environment. |
| **Desktop Environment** | KDE, Gnome, MATE, Xfce, and Enlightenment |
| **Init System** | systemd |
| **Package Management System** | Entropy and Portage |
| **Architecture** | Intel/AMD 32-/64-bits. Also ARM (currently only Raspberry Pi 2). |
| **Security/Anonymity** | Normal. Less focused that Gentoo. |
| **Principles and Ethics** | Nothing in particular. |
| **Live CD** | Yes |
| **Professional Certification** | No |

# GoboLinux

Like NixOS, the Brazilian GoboLinux distro tries to innovate the way a Linux distro works. Started in 2003, GoboLinux has a different approach than NixOS; its focus is not on the package management, it is on the file system. GoboLinux does not use the Filesystem Hierarchy Standard (FHS); it uses its own directory hierarchy, storing all the programs under the same root directory (/Programs), classified by categories and using symbolic links to another directory that works as an index (/System/Index). The rest of the root directories are /Users, /Files, /Mount, and /Depot. To maintain compatibility with standard Linux programs, it uses several hidden (by default) symbolic links that recreate the standard FHS. This has some advantages, like the possibility of have more than one version of the same package available at the same time.

The packages are compiled from source with the Compile tool using recipes (scripts that defines how a package has to be build and installed), and it uses its original filesystem hierarchy as a sort of a native database of packages (thanks to the index). A graphical tool is also available to manage the packages. GoboLinux also uses its own simplistic init system based on a few simple scripts. For a long time, the root user was named Gobo, another peculiarity of this distro.

It's a small distro with a very small community and it has not get received much recognition. Also, the different root directory structure is controversial. The distro selection criteria for GoboLinux are summarized in Table 15-7. You can learn more about GoboLinux at www.gobolinux.org.

*Table 15-7.* *Distro Selection Criteria for GoboLinux*

| | |
|---|---|
| **Purpose and Environment** | Unique version available as a Live ISO image. |
| **Support** | Community |
| **User Friendliness** | Reasonably easily to install and maintain, but still not user friendly. |
| **Stability** | Rolling release alike, based on recipes. |
| **Hardware Support** | Reasonable, with hardware auto-detection. |
| **Aesthetics** | Basically the default of Enlightenment. |
| **Desktop Environment** | Enlightenment |
| **Init System** | Its own simple system based on a few scripts. |
| **Package Management System** | Compile, but it also uses the filesystem hierarchy to manage the packages. |
| **Architecture** | Intel/AMD 32-bit newer than Pentium IV (i686) |
| **Security/Anonymity** | Reasonable, plus the different file hierarchy. |
| **Principles and Ethics** | Nothing in particular. |
| **Live CD** | Yes |
| **Professional Certification** | No |

# Qubes OS

Like Android, there is some controversy over whether Qubes OS is a Linux distribution or not. Qubes OS defines itself as an OS instead of a Linux distro, and in fact it is not a Linux distro in a strict sense. Its co-creator, Joanna Rutkowska (a well-known computer security researcher), defines it not as Linux distro or as a hypervisor, but as a hypervisor user. I cover it here because a lot of people refer to it as a Linux distribution. Qubes OS is an American OS released in 2012, and it tries to be the most secure desktop OS possible using "security by isolation." To achieve this, it uses several virtual machines hypervisor, in which processes are completely isolated from the others.

Qubes OS runs a Xen hypervisor under the hood, which uses a customized Fedora as its "dom0" domain (the most privileged domain that manages the hypervisor). The user domains (also known as Qubes) usually are a Fedora, Debian, or Whonix Linux distro, but can also be a Windows OS. There are system and user domains; the system domains are separated into Secure GUI & Administration (dom0), Network, and Storage. The user domains, also known as AppVMs (they are actually lightweight virtual machines), are usually separated by tasks or security level: personal, work, untrusted, shopping, banking, etc. There are templates that can be used as a base for those user domains with a common base software but separate memory, storage, and networks. There is a mechanism to securely share files and copy-and-paste between those domains.

In order to use all the capabilities of the OS, it is necessary that the hardware supports certain constraints, like VT-x and VT-d CPU virtualization capabilities, TPM secure platform, UEFI, and preferably a SSD and an Intel GPU. The company provides a hardware compatibility list and even a Qubes-certified laptop provided by Purism.

Qubes is developed by a company called Invisible Things Lab, but is released as open source and free software. The support comes from the company and the community; in other words, ITL supports the official templates for Fedora and Debian, but the community also supports Whonix, Ubuntu, and Arch Linux.

The distro selection criteria for Qubes OS are summarized in Table 15-8. You can learn more about Qubes OS at www.qubes-os.org.

***Table 15-8.*** *Distro Selection Criteria for Qubes OS*

| | |
|---|---|
| **Purpose and Environment** | Unique version available as an ISO image and a Live USB image. |
| **Support** | Community and ITL |
| **User Friendliness** | Once you understand how it works, it's a reasonably user-friendly OS. |
| **Stability** | Standard release scheme. It's still a little immature. |
| **Hardware Support** | Limited if you want to use all of the OS features |
| **Aesthetics** | The desktop environment defaults |
| **Desktop Environment** | KDE and Xfce |
| **Init System** | systemd in the Fedora domain. Actually, it boots the Xen hypervisor. |
| **Package Management System** | RPM |
| **Architecture** | Intel/AMD 64-bits. Preferably with VT-x, VT-d, and TPM technologies |
| **Security/Anonymity** | Bleeding-edge technology; it's very secure and offers integrated anonymity features. |
| **Principles and Ethics** | Allows you run proprietary OSes like Windows. A pragmatic approach: the user decides. |
| **Live CD** | Yes, a Live USB |
| **Professional Certification** | No |

# Solus

An Irish distribution that originated at 2013 as a Chrome OS alternative, Solus was discontinued, later renamed twice, and finally completely retooled and released in the current form as Solus in 2015. It's an original distro that focuses on being user-friendly Linux. It has gained popularity lately for its original desktop environment called Budgie, which is not only elegant, functional, and light, but also intuitive and fresh.

Solus also has its own package manager, eopkg, a fork of PiSi (the former package manager from the Pardus distro). It has a small package base, and although its internal design is very simple, it is not precisely user friendly (it lacks a GUI). It's still an immature distro in the early stages so it has room to improve.

The distro selection criteria for Solus are summarized in Table 15-9. You can learn more about Solus at https://solus-project.com.

*Table 15-9.* *Distro Selection Criteria for Solus*

| | |
|---|---|
| **Purpose and Environment** | Unique version oriented to the desktop. |
| **Support** | Community |
| **User Friendliness** | For installation and normal use, yes. For maintenance, no. |
| **Stability** | Standard release scheme. One major release a year, two years of support. |
| **Hardware Support** | Regular, with hardware auto-detection. |
| **Aesthetics** | As one of the core values of the distro, it's pleasant to the eye. |
| **Desktop Environment** | Budgie |
| **Init System** | systemd |
| **Package Management System** | eopkg and ypkg |
| **Architecture** | Intel/AMD 64-bits |
| **Security/Anonymity** | Regular |
| **Principles and Ethics** | Pragmatic approach: the user has the last word. |
| **Live CD** | Yes |
| **Professional Certification** | No |

# Void Linux

Another independent distro that originated in Spain in 2008, Void Linux was influenced by NetBSD (where the original developer was a maintainer). In fact, the most remarkable feature of this distro, the package manager, was originally designed for BSD and later ported to Linux. As in the case of NixOS, Void was created as a testing platform for the XBPS (X Binary Package System) package manager. There is also Xpbx-src to build binary packages from source inside containers without using the root.

Another unique feature is the init system, runit, which is a very simple system based on a directory tree. Another feature inherited from BSD is the replacement of the OpenSSL library for LibreSSL by default, and more secure and reliable alternative ported from OpenBSD.

The distro selection criteria for Void Linux are summarized in Table 15-10. You can learn more about Void Linux at http://voidlinux.eu.

*Table 15-10.* *Distro Selection Criteria for Void Linux*

| Purpose and Environment | A unique version with several flavors for each desktop environment and ARM. |
|---|---|
| Support | Community |
| User Friendliness | Not a user-friendly distro |
| Stability | Rolling release scheme |
| Hardware Support | Regular |
| Aesthetics | The default of each desktop environment |
| Desktop Environment | Enlightenment, Cinnamon, LXDE, MATE, Xfce |
| Init System | Runit |
| Package Management System | XBPS |
| Architecture | Intel/AMD 32-/64-bits and ARM |
| Security/Anonymity | Reasonable security plus the use of LibreSSL |
| Principles and Ethics | By default, only free software, aside from kernel binary blobs |
| Live CD | Yes |
| Professional Certification | No |

# Alpine

An original Norwegian distribution that proclaims itself as a general purpose distribution, but almost nobody use it in that way, Alpine is a security-centered and very lightweight distro that is usually employed to build firewalls, routers, VPN, VoIP, servers, and set-top boxes. Lately, it has gained increasing popularity as a minimal Docker image (only 5MB).

It's built around musl (a C library alternative to glibc) and BusyBox (an alternative to the several Linux core utilities in one executable), both very lightweight alternatives. The security features include a Linux kernel with PaX and grsecurity patches and stack-smashing protection (SSP) in all of the packages. Also, Alpine can be loaded and run from memory RAM, one of the reasons why it is used in embedded devices.

Alpine use its own package manager, APK, with a considerable package base given its lightweight nature.

The distro selection criteria for Alpine are summarized in Table 15-11. You can learn more about Alpine at www.alpinelinux.org.

339

*Table 15-11.* *Distro Selection Criteria for Alpine*

| | |
|---|---|
| **Purpose and Environment** | Several versions and additional images for Xen and ARM platforms. |
| **Support** | Community |
| **User Friendliness** | Not user-friendly |
| **Stability** | Stable version with standard release scheme, but unstable as a rolling release. |
| **Hardware Support** | Regular |
| **Aesthetics** | The default of each desktop environment |
| **Desktop Environment** | Gnome, Xfce, MATE |
| **Init System** | OpenRC |
| **Package Management System** | APK |
| **Architecture** | Intel/AMD 32-/64-bits and ARM |
| **Security/Anonymity** | Solid security |
| **Principles and Ethics** | Nothing in particular. |
| **Live CD** | No |
| **Professional Certification** | No |

# Stali

Stali is a German distribution that was released for first time in 2016. It brings another radical approach to the Linux world. The distribution was developed by the suckless.org community, a well-known group of programmers, and creators of some popular tools like the window manager DWM, the surf browser, and dmenu. This community tries to develop quality software with a focus on simplicity, clarity, and frugality. This group has strong principles; their name is a clear statement of such.

This minimalism is apparent in all aspects of the distribution, from its size (an ISO of only 34MB) to the packages available (only a handful of carefully selected ones). Also there is no package manager available; the distro itself is a git repository and you only need to make a `# git pull` to do an upgrade. This also allows you to downgrade to a specific release with a `# git checkout 0.2`.

As recognized systemd haters, they do not implement this init system in Stali. They developed their own init system, sinit (stands for suckless init). Another notorious difference is that they not follow the FHS (File Hierarchy Standard); they use a simpler filesystem structure instead.

But the main characteristic of this distro, and the one that gave it the name (Stali stands for Static Linux), is that all the binaries are static linked, so there are no dynamic libraries at all. The C library used is musl, and as a result, Kernel modules are not supported.

The distro selection criteria for Stali are summarized in Table 15-12. You can learn more about Stali at `http://sta.li`.

*Table 15-12.* *Distro Selection Criteria for Stali*

| | |
|---|---|
| **Purpose and Environment** | Unique version available as ISO image |
| **Support** | Community |
| **User Friendliness** | Not user-friendly |
| **Stability** | Still in the early stages |
| **Hardware Support** | Poor |
| **Aesthetics** | The default of each desktop environment |
| **Desktop Environment** | DWM (window manager) |
| **Init System** | Sinit |
| **Package Management System** | None. Upgrades and installation using Git. |
| **Architecture** | Intel/AMD 64-bits |
| **Security/Anonymity** | Good. Its unique nature probably makes it less prone to common vulnerabilities. |
| **Principles and Ethics** | Nothing in particular. |
| **Live CD** | No |
| **Professional Certification** | No |

# LFS

Although it is not very popular, I think that this distro is the inspiration for many little distros over the past 15 years, because many Linux developers learned from this Canadian project, which started in 1999. The Linux From Scratch (LFS) project is not a traditional Linux distro (but it is a Linux distro); it consists of a book and a collection of source code packages to build your own Linux system from scratch. Obviously the book is the soul of the distribution, which intends to be a learning tool about how Linux works internally and the process of building a minimal but functional Linux system. There are several servers where you can download the collection of packages for each release of the book, which is continuously updated.

If you follow the instructions of the book, it is a tedious and long process to achieve what you can do in five minutes with any old, minimal distro. But at the end you will have a deeper knowledge about Linux that you could ever achieve using a friendly Linux distro like Ubuntu for 10 years. As a learning tool, LFS is priceless, but you need to have real interest in how Linux works to use this distribution.

The relative success of this project inspired other projects with the same philosophy, such as Beyond Linux From Scratch (BLFS) for building a more complete Linux system, Cross Linux From Scratch for alternative hardware architectures, Automated Linux From Scratch (ALFS) to automate the process, and Hardened Linux From Scratch to build a more secure Linux system. For example, you can use CLFS (or even LFS) to build a very minimal Linux system (under 10MB) or install it in embedded systems or obsolete platforms.

The distro selection criteria for LFS are summarized in Table 15-13. You can download the book and learn more about LFS at `www.linuxfromscratch.org`.

*Table 15-13.* *Distro Selection Criteria for LFS*

| | |
|---|---|
| **Purpose and Environment** | Unique version available as a book and source code packages collection |
| **Support** | Community |
| **User Friendliness** | Obviously not, but at the same time it's a learning experience. |
| **Stability** | Standard release scheme with stable releases and betas |
| **Hardware Support** | Very limited and basic |
| **Aesthetics** | It's a minimal, compact, command line-based Linux system. |
| **Desktop Environment** | No. KDE, Gnome, Xfce, LXDE, and LXQt in BLFS. |
| **Init System** | System V or systemd |
| **Package Management System** | None. All packages are built from source. |
| **Architecture** | Intel/AMD 32-/64-bits. Other architectures covered with CLFS. |
| **Security/Anonymity** | Nothing in particular. The HLFS project covers this topic. |
| **Principles and Ethics** | All of the packages are free software. |
| **Live CD** | No, but there are several editions of older LFS releases. |
| **Professional Certification** | No |

# Summary

In this chapter, you saw a few distros that offer a more complete vision of what a Linux distro can be. Some of them are very new, and most likely nearly half of them will never achieve great popularity. However, they are still an example of the dynamic and active nature of the Linux community. Some of the more esoteric innovations of these distros may never be part of the mainstream, and some of them will probably not exist in the near future, but all of them are a testimony to the power of free software for developing new ideas.

In the next chapter, you are going to see a compilation of task-oriented distros, which were built to focus on one specific task or area for specialized work environments.

**PART 3**

# Task-Oriented Distros

This is a short section consisting of one brief chapter. This is because covering the task-oriented Linux distros in the same way and at the same level of detail as the general purpose distros would require another book—not because there are as many task-oriented distros as general purpose ones, but because with task-oriented Linux distros there are so many different tasks to cover. So how could I select one task and one distro and not cover others? And how could I possibly know which areas would interest you?

The best solution is to present related tasks grouped by category and then provide a list and description of the relevant Linux distributions.

# CHAPTER 16

■ ■ ■

# Task-Oriented Distros

The same reasons behind the development of so many general purpose Linux distributions are behind the proliferation of task-oriented distros. The flexibility of Linux and the advantages of Free Software make it reasonably easy to make a Linux distribution that can fulfil a unique purpose. These distributions can be customized, but all of them were made with only one type of task in mind, as specific as building a firewall to protect a network from security breaches or as ambiguous as scientific research.

In this chapter, I list of several niche distros and briefly describe them. The list isn't comprehensive, but it is accurate. It only includes actively developed distros. (Why talk about distros that have been abandoned or are in an uncertain state?)

## Mobility and IoT (Internet of Things)

These distros are to be installed on mobile devices, like smartphones and tablets, or on the Internet of Things (which refers to the interconnection through the Internet of all kinds of things outside the traditional concept of computing, like home electrical appliances, vehicles, etc.). In both cases, these distros have adapted to these new environments both in functionality and interface.

### Android

The omnipresent Android system is the most extended mobile OS in the world. It currently has more than 50% of the market share on mobile devices. It was developed by Google, and it follows an open source model with some proprietary components (mostly drivers and firmware). There is some controversy over whether Android is really a Linux distro, but Chris DiBona (Google's open source chief), the Linux Foundation, and some popular journalists consider it one. www.android.com

### Ubuntu Phone/Tablet/IoT

These Ubuntu alternatives, based on the Ubuntu distro for desktops, can be used on mobile phones and tablets. The ultimate goal of Ubuntu is to be a Linux system that allows you to use your phone/tablet as a PC. Ubuntu Core (also known as Snappy) is suited for the IoT. www.ubuntu.com/phone, www.ubuntu.com/tablet, and www.ubuntu.com/internet-of-things

### Sailfish OS

Developed by Jolla, Sailfish OS evolved from the former MeeGo OS (by Nokia and Intel) that was derived from Maemo. It continues to be developed but its presence in the market is almost minimal (e.g. Fairphone 2). It's compatible with Android applications and hardware. http://sailfishos.org

© Jose Dieguez Castro 2016
J. Dieguez Castro, *Introducing Linux Distros*, DOI 10.1007/978-1-4842-1392-6_16

## Firefox OS

Firefox OS is going to be discontinued soon, at least for smartphones, but it may continue to be developed for IoT (it's currently available for smart TVs). It basically consists of a Firefox browser over a Linux kernel with HTML5 applications. Like Android, there is room for discussion about whether it's a real Linux distro. http://mozilla.org/firefox/os

# Cloud-Centered Operating Systems

These distros try to make real the Sun Microsystems motto from the 1990s that "The network is the computer," coined by John Gage in 1984. Nowadays, with the cloud available everywhere, we only have to bring this power to the desktop to close the cycle. And for that, these distros aim to replace local applications with web ones and store data on a cloud drive instead of on a local hard drive.

## Chrome OS/Chromium OS

Chrome OS and Chromium OS are based in the Google cloud (and are made by Google), where all of the apps and storage reside (recently added support for Android Apps). They use the Linux kernel plus the Chrome browser, and they were originally based on the Gentoo distro plus the Ubuntu's Upstart init system. Chromium OS is the open source version. Chrome OS is only available as an OEM OS in laptops usually called Chromebooks or mini desktop PCs called Chromeboxes, which are made by several manufactures, Google included. http://google.com/chromebook

## Cub Linux

Formerly Chromixium OS, Cub Linux is an Ubuntu-based distro that mimics the Chrome OS functionality and look. https://cublinux.com

# Router Distros

Router distros are installed in network appliances, routers, or PCs to work as a network router. They can replace a previous manufacturer's firmware, or they can be used to build a router with a simple PC and several network cards. They usually provide several network services beyond the router functionality, like an included firewall.

## OpenWrt

OpenWrt is a Linux distro for embedded devices focused on router network traffic. It is a popular and powerful alternative to the OEM firmware of many SoHo routers, but it can also be used on any Linux-compatible hardware. http://openwrt.org

## Zeroshell

Zeroshell is suited for servers and embedded systems to provide network routing services. It is available as a Live CD or Compact Flash image and is managed from a web interface (hence its name). www.zeroshell.org

## RouterOS

RouterOS is a router operating system based on Linux and developed by the computer networking manufacturer MikroTik to be used in its devices. It can also be installed in regular Intel/AMD computers. It's well known for being a solid, powerful, and secure OS. http://mikrotik.com/software

# Embedded Systems and CNC

I include here two well-known Linux distros that can be installed in embedded devices (spanning a wide range) or in CNC (computer numerical control) industrial machines. While it is common to find Linux in embedded devices, Windows is the most common OS in CNC machines. In fact, I worked for several years in industries from different fields that had different kinds of CNC machines and I never saw Linux installed on any of them.

## KaeilOS

KaeilOS is oriented to embedded devices (industrial devices, automation, medical equipment, automotive, etc.). Currently it is part of the Yocto project, a project by the Linux Foundation to produce distros suited for embedded devices. www.kaeilos.com, www.yoctoproject.org

## LinuxCNC

LinuxCNC is a distro for controlling CNC machines like milling machines, lathes, 3D printers, plasma cutters, laser cutters, robot arms, etc. It can be installed as a normal package in Debian/Ubuntu or from a Live CD with a Debian distro included. www.linuxcnc.org

# Storage / NAS

This type of Linux distro is suited for creating a NAS (network-attached storage) usually with several disks working in a RAID (redundant array of independent disks) setup. The most famous free software for this kind of task is FreeNAS, a BSD-based software that benefits from the adoption of the very reliable and powerful ZFS as its filesystem. Due to license conflicts, ZFS is not yet fully available in Linux; these distros instead work with BTRFS or other file systems to provide decent solutions.

## Rockstor

Rockstor is an advanced NAS and cloud storage solution based on CentOS and BTRFS. Basically it is a friendly alternative to FreeNAS but it is based on Linux instead of BSD. http://rockstor.com

## OpenMediaVault

OpenMediaVault is another FreeNAS alternative based on Debian and focused on the SoHo environment for building a NAS solution. It can easily be extended by plug-ins. www.openmediavault.org

# Enterprise Server and Thin Client

Some of these distributions try to replace the functionality of a Windows server with Active Directory, Outlook, and the rest of the usual suspects in a mixed corporate environment. The thin client distro is a good software alternative to the usual hardware ones.

## ClearOS

ClearOS is a web-managed commercial server platform that consolidates a lot of different services into one system (network, gateway, server, cloud, security, backup, mail, etc.). It is based on Red Hat. www.clearos.com

## Zentyal Server

Formerly eBox, Zentyal Server is a commercial replacement of a Windows Server system, with compatibility with Outlook and Active Directory. It's based on Ubuntu. www.zentyal.com

## Univention Corporate Server

Based on Debian, Univention Corporate Server works as a server for distributed heterogeneous and virtualized environments, working with Windows, OS X, and Linux systems. www.univention.com

## NethServer

NethServer is a CentOS-based Linux server for small organizations that works as a central system with a model built on pre-configured modules. http://nethserver.org

## Thinstation

Thinstation is a Linux-based thin client that can connect to Citrix, NoMachine, 2X ThinClient, MS Windows terminal services, VMWare, Cendio, Tarantella, X window systems, telnet, VMS, tn5250, and SSH. It can be booted from a network (Etherboot/PXE) or from a CD/USB/HD. http://thinstation.github.io/thinstation

# Telephony

A hardware PBX (private branch exchange), also known as a business telephone system, can be very expensive, especially if it has complex functionalities like VoIP, an answering machine, call accounting, etc. A software PBX can use basic and cheaper hardware to achieve the same functions and is more flexible and easy to manage. Asterisk is a well-recognized software PBX, and these two distros are a good way to build a complete Asterisk system to suit your needs.

## AsteriskNOW

AsteriskNOW is a CentOS-based distro that can be used to build an Asterisk system, which is a software-based PBX for managing voice calls, voice mail, VoIP, automatic call distribution, and more. www.asterisk.org/downloads/asterisknow

## Elastix

A CentOS-based distro that can unify all enterprise communications in one solution, Elastix uses Asterisk to provide a PBX with fax, instant messaging, e-mail, VoIP, and video capabilities. www.elastix.org

# System Troubleshooting

In an effort to make the lives of system administrators and computer technicians easier, a handful of distros focus on deployments, recoveries, and repairs of computers. Often running a distro off a Live CDs works, but if not, these distros can be very helpful. They're also a great choice if the software you need is not installed and there is no network connection available, or if you just like to have a set of lifesaving tools handy. In fact, several of these tools have saved my day more than once.

## GParted Live

GParted Live is a Live CD distro focused on managing disk drives, using the popular graphical tool GParted and other related tools. http://gparted.sourceforge.net

## SystemRescueCD

SystemRescueCD is a compilation of tools over a Gentoo distro oriented to rescue a failed system (Linux or not). It's shipped as a Live ISO image. www.system-rescue-cd.org

## Grml

Of interest to system administrators, Grml is a Debian-based live CD distro that offers many tools (2GB compressed into less than 500MB) for rescue systems and deployment. It can also be installed as any Linux distro. http://grml.org

## Rescatux

Rescatux is a Debian-based distro with a graphical interface that guides you through menus to easily resolve many common problems and rescue a system. www.supergrubdisk.org/rescatux

## Clonezilla Live

Clonezilla is another Debian-based Live CD that is an imaging/cloning/partition tool similar to True Image or Norton Ghost. It's useful for deployment, backups, and recovery. www.clonezilla.org

## Redo Backup and Recovery

Similar to Clonezilla but with a graphical interface that makes it user friendly, Redo Backup and Recovery is based on Ubuntu. http://redobackup.org

# Security and Anonymity

Security is a vast field in computing, covering almost every specialty you can imagine. Wherever there is hardware, software, or a network, security matters, and it is becoming even more important as time goes on. You can approach security from different points of view: penetration testing to discover weaknesses of a system, forensics to collect evidence and analyze it, blocking and analyzing attacks from outside your system, securing your identity and communications from potential eavesdropping, analyzing malware to understand how it works, and so on. These distros cover one or more of these computer security approaches.

## Kali Linux

Formerly known as Backtrack, Kali Linux is a Debian-based distribution that offers several penetration testing and digital forensics tools. It is the most recognized distro of this kind. www.kali.org

## BackBox Linux

Based on Ubuntu, BackBox Linux is focused on penetration testing, network analysis, and computer forensics. It also offers ethical hacking tools. https://backbox.org

## Fedora Security Lab

A Fedora Labs project, Fedora Security Lab offers security auditing, system rescue, and forensics, plus a safe environment in which to teach security testing. https://labs.fedoraproject.org/en/security

## BlackArch

Another alternative to Kali and BackBox, Black Arch is based on Arch Linux. It offers 1,400 tools for penetration testing and security research. http://blackarch.org

## Parrot Security OS

Parrot Security OS is a suite of tools that provide penetration testing, computer forensics, cryptography, and anonymity. It's based on Debian and is ready for cloud environments. https://parrotsec.org

## Wifislax

A Slackware-based distro, Wifislax is oriented to network security. It's a very lightweight distro with a big focus on wireless networks, and it supports a great number of wireless adapters. http://wifislax.com

## Tails

Tails stands for The Amnesic Incognito Live System and it is a Debian-based Live CD that is focused on providing complete Internet anonymity. It provides tools to navigate through Tor or I2P by default plus communication cryptographic tools. https://tails.boum.org

## Whonix

A Debian-based distro focused on privacy, security, and anonymity on the Internet, Whonix uses the Tor network by default and uses two virtual machines to separate the desktop from the network. www.whonix.org

## CAINE

CAINE (Computer Aided Investigative Environment) is an Ubuntu-based distro that offers a complete suite of tools for professional digital forensics analysis. www.caine-live.net

## DEFT

A Debian-based Live CD distribution for computer forensics and incident response, DEFT stands for Digital Evidence & Forensics Tool. http://deftlinux.net

## IPFire

An original and lightweight distribution to build firewalls to secure network traffic, IPFire is based on a modular design. It can also work as a proxy server, IDS, virus scanner, or a VPN gateway. It has an easy-to-use web interface. www.ipfire.org

## Untangle NG Firewall

Untangle NG Firewall is a network gateway distribution based on Debian. It has a modular design that can work as a firewall, IDS, VPN, web filter, etc. It also has a very friendly web interface. www.untangle.com/untangle-ng-firewall

## Endian Firewall

Endian Firewall is a firewall distribution based on RHEL (Red Hat Enterprise Linux). It can work as a firewall and offers IPS, antivirus, web, and e-mail security inspection. www.endian.com/community/overview

## SELKS

Built upon Debian, SELKS is a specialized Live CD distro for running a suite of tools based on Suricata, which is a tool that provides a network IDS, IPS, and NSM engine. The other tools are Kibana for analyzing alerts and Scirius to configure the Suricata rules. https://stamus-networks.com/open-source/#selks

## REMnux

REMnux is a very specialized Ubuntu-based distro that performs reverse engineering of Windows and Linux malware. It also provides tools to analyze Flash programs, obfuscated JavaScript, PDF files, and memory. https://remnux.org

# Old Computers

People with few resources like those in developing countries often can't keep up with the pace of the computer technology race, and so they usually have outdated (and frequently second-hand) hardware. The following distros are good options to pair with older hardware.

## Puppy Linux

Puppy Linux is a very popular Live CD distro that works well on old computers with little memory and CPU resources. It is an original distro and it is very, very lightweight; it loads into RAM (it needs 256MB at maximum, but it can work with only 48MB) to provide a fast but full-featured desktop. `http://puppylinux.org`

## Tiny Core Linux

Tiny Core Linux is a minimal distro that is about 16MB but only needs 46MB of RAM. It has a very minimalistic desktop that is not installed by default, but you can easily install it. `http://tinycorelinux.net`

## LXLE

LXLE is based on Ubuntu LTS (another lightweight distro) and it uses the lightweight LXDE desktop manager. It can work with only 512MB of RAM and 8GB of hard drive space. `www.lxle.net`

# Science

Science is unthinkable without computing anymore. Sometimes you need tools suited for your field, and sometimes you need computing power to run complex algorithms that are very resource-hungry. The following distros were built by scientists for scientific needs.

## Scientific Linux

A Red Hat-based distro originally co-developed by the Fermilab and CERN (now switched to CentOS), Scientific Linux address scientific computer needs with infrastructures and research tools. `www.scientificlinux.org`

## Bio-Linux

Bio-Linux is based on Ubuntu and offers a full-featured bioinformatics workstation with a plethora of tools focused on that environment. `http://environmentalomics.org/bio-linux`

## Fedora Scientific

Fedora Scientific is a Fedora Labs project that offers a collection of the most used open source scientific and numerical tools preinstalled by default. `http://labs.fedoraproject.org/en/scientific`

# Education

These education distributions were built to be an alternative to the proprietary OSes and software so widespread in schools and colleges around the world. These options range from being a cheaper way to build a computer lab to supporting all of the aspect of an educational institution.

## Edubuntu

Edubuntu is a special flavor of Ubuntu dedicated to education, and it was created to be used in the classroom. The main focus is to help teachers with limited computer skills create a computer lab. www.edubuntu.org

## UberStudent

UberStudent is another distro based on Ubuntu for educational purposes but it is focused on students, teachers, and schools of secondary and higher education. http://uberstudent.org

## DebianEdu

DebianEdu, also known as Skolelinux, is a Debian-based distro focused on providing a free software alternative to proprietary educational software. https://wiki.debian.org/DebianEdu

# Home Theater and Audiophile Systems

If you want to build a home theater system for your living room or you want to enjoy your music at an audiophile level, these distributions can do that for you. They can help you achieve a cheaper but yet very powerful alternative to the usual commercial ones. You can create an audiophile system with a simple Raspberry Pi, a DAC, an amplifier, and a pair of speakers. As for home theaters, the following distros make these systems more flexible than any commercial alternative.

## Mythbuntu

Mythbuntu is a derivative of Ubuntu with MythTV preinstalled, which is media center software for building a home theater PC. It can work as standalone system, as a server for several clients in the home, or in a mixed configuration. www.mythbuntu.org

## OpenELEC

OpenELEC lets you make a media center out of an embedded device or single-board computer (like the Raspberry Pi family). It uses the popular and powerful Kodi Entertainment Center software as an HTPC inside a minimal Linux system. Several manufacturers use it as an OEM OS in set-top boxes, hardware media players, and media center systems. http://openelec.tv

## OSMC

OSMC, formerly Raspbmc, is another media center for Raspberry Pi and Apple TV, a distribution that also uses the Kodi Entertainment Center software with a minimal Debian distro underneath. http://osmc.tv

## Rune Audio

Rune Audio is the distro installed in Raspberry Pi and similar devices, which you can convert to a HiFi digital audio player (usually connected to a DAC). It is based on Arch Linux and can be controlled remotely from various clients (Android, iOS Web, Windows, and Linux). www.runeaudio.com

## Volumio

Volumio is a Debian-based distro for audiophiles, and it can be installed on embedded devices like Raspberry Pi and similar. It can play music from several sources like Mp3, MPD, Spotify, SoundCloud, Last. FM, etc. It can be remote controlled from a web interface. https://volumio.org

# Gaming

The following distros can make your computer a gaming system, something traditionally reserved for Windows machines and game consoles. Linux is not at the same level as those systems, but these distros will convince you that it's possible to enjoy games in Linux.

## SteamOS

SteamOS is a Debian-based distro that works as the gaming platform for the Steam Machine video games. It was initially intended to be the OEM OS for the Stem Machines, but you can also build your own system and install Steam OS. http://store.steampowered.com/steamos

## Fedora Games Spin

A flavor (Spin) of Fedora that works as a showcase for the Fedora distribution as a gaming platform, Fedora Games Spin includes several preinstalled games. https://labs.fedoraproject.org/en/games

# Multimedia and Arts

Artists and creators are the intended audiences for these distros, which offer tools suited for their needs. OS X and Windows may have better tools in several of these fields, but they are also usually expensive, while Linux distros are cheaper or free and still let you achieve professional results. Some tools, like Blender, are very powerful and industrial grade.

## Ubuntu Studio

Ubuntu Studio is a based on Ubuntu, obviously, but it adds creative tools for audio, video, graphics, photography, and publishing tasks. http://ubuntustudio.org

## Fedora Design Suite

Fedora Design Suite provides several multimedia production and publishing tools by default.
https://labs.fedoraproject.org/en/design-suite

# Summary

This chapter covered a wide range of tasks and distros for each of them. This compilation could be more extensive, both in tasks and in distros, but I think that this is enough for you to get an idea of what you can expect. Note, however, that these distros are usually more ephemeral than the traditional ones, and they are usually abandoned or replaced by others in a matter of a few years. If you are interested in a task-oriented distro, you should search beyond the distros and tasks mentioned in this chapter.

A bonus chapter awaits you online! In it I show you several operating systems that are not Linux but have enough in common with Linux to deserve your attention. If you are willing to learn more about them, go to

# Index

© Jose Dieguez Castro 2016
J. Dieguez Castro, *Introducing Linux Distros*, DOI 10.1007/978-1-4842-1392-6

## ■ M

# Get the eBook for only $5!

Why limit yourself?

Now you can take the weightless companion with you wherever you go and access your content on your PC, phone, tablet, or reader.

Since you've purchased this print book, we're happy to offer you the eBook in all 3 formats for just $5.

Convenient and fully searchable, the PDF version enables you to easily find and copy code—or perform examples by quickly toggling between instructions and applications. The MOBI format is ideal for your Kindle, while the ePUB can be utilized on a variety of mobile devices.

To learn more, go to www.apress.com/companion or contact support@apress.com.

Printed in the United States
By Bookmasters